IN
BUSINESS

Q&A® 4
In Business

Q&A® 4
In Business

David B. Adams

SAMS

A Division of Macmillan, Inc.

11711 North College, Suite 141, Carmel, IN 46032 USA

To my Higher Power

Publisher
Richard K. Swadley

Publishing Manager
Marie Butler-Knight

Managing Editor
Marjorie Hopper

Acquisitions/Development Editor
Stephen R. Poland

Technical Editors
Don Roche, Jr., and Catherine M. Kenny

Manuscript Editor
Diana Francoeur

Editorial Coordinator
Linda Hawkins

Editorial Assistant
Tracy Kaufman

Cover Designer
Dan Armstrong

Designer
Scott Cook

Indexer
Jeanne Clark

Production Assistance
*Jeff Baker, Claudia Bell, Sandy Grieshop, Bob LaRoche,
Howard Peirce, Tad Ringo, Louise Shinault, Bruce Steed*

CONTENTS

CONTENTS by FEATURE

C O N T E N T S by F E A T U R E

This Introduction will provide a complete overview of the book and how to receive the most value from it.

How to Use This Book

To receive the maximum benefit from this book, you should read the entire Introduction and Chapters 1 and 2 before you begin modifying and developing applications. (However, if you are already familiar with Q&A, you can skip Chapter 2.) After you have read these chapters, you can skip to any application you prefer. Once you have completed an application, you can use the "Contents by Feature" (found just before the Introduction) to locate specific features of the program.

Overview

The goal of this book is to improve your personal and organizational productivity. To accomplish this goal, I have written a book that is different from the majority of computer software books on the market. Most software books seek to clarify or expand on the manufacturer's reference manuals. Others, using a tutorial approach, try to teach you the software's features by using examples that are not always applicable to your organization. This book, using predeveloped applications, will explain how you can modify and use each database to suit your own needs while you learn how to use Q&A features.

When you finish each chapter, you actually have a usable application designed for your business's needs. In addition, you have learned some specific feaures of Q&A. This strategy is ideally suited to the busy person who needs to combine learning and development efforts.

What You Will Learn

The features of Q&A are divided into logical groups. These groups are database development, menu/macro development, report preparation, data manipulation, word processing, the Intelligent Assistant, and utilities. Each of these features will be divided among the chapters and taught in the appropriate order. In this way, while reading each chapter you will learn some of the features from each group. Figure I.1 shows the relation of each of these groups.

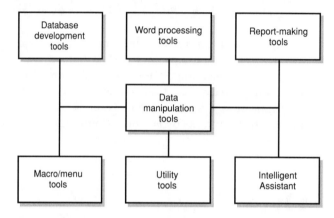

Figure I.1   Q&A features by group.

As you read each chapter, you can expect to learn how to

- Develop and modify Q&A databases.
- Manipulate your data.
- Develop reports.
- Use the word processor.
- Use the Intelligent Assistant to ask plain English questions of your database.
- Record macros.
- Create custom menus.

This book is not intended to replace the Q&A manuals or to be a features reference book. Although at the beginning of each chapter there will be a features summary, this book is best used in conjunction with the Q&A manuals.

To follow the exercises in this book, you must have a copy of Q&A Version 4.0. This is the latest release of the product. It replaces Version 3.0 and is far superior to Version 3.0. To see a list of the improvements, refer to Appendix B. If you do not have the current version of the program, you can call Symantec at (408) 253-9600 for an update or call your local dealer.

Skills Required

This book is written for the beginner who has a basic understanding of computers and has operated some type of computer program before, such as a word processor, database, or spreadsheet. It assumes that you have an understanding of your job function or organization and how it operates.

Terminology Used

I have kept the amount of technical jargon to a minimum, but some cannot be avoided. Since different interpretations of the same words are possible, I will define how I have used some common terms. The terms *database* and *database form* are used interchangeably and refer to the actual data entry screen and underlying structure.

The term *application* refers to all the affiliated databases, menus, reports, and macros associated with one key process. For example, the Inventory/Invoicing application (see Chapter 6) includes the Names database, Invoice database, Inventory database, several reports, many macros, and a few menus. Taken together, these items form the Inventory/Invoicing application.

Organization of the Book

This book begins with three helpful features. The **Contents** presents a detailed listing of all the first- and second-level headings in the book. It will guide you to the appropriate section of the desired chapter. Following the Contents is a special listing called **Contents by Feature**. It is organized by product feature so that you can reference a specific feature of Q&A without wading through the entire chapter. The ***Introduction***, which you are reading now, is the third feature. It will give you an overview of the entire book and explain how to get the most out of it.

Chapter 1, "How to Begin," helps you decide which aspects of your organization you want to automate and how to design your own programs and reports. It will guide you through the entire process of modifying and/or developing useful applications for your organization. ***Chapter 2, "Q&A Basics,"*** is a primer on using the essential Q&A features. Reading this chapter and practicing the examples will greatly improve your success with the application chapters.

The remaining chapters, ***3 through 10***, are the ***application chapters***. They explain how to modify and use eight different applications. These applications are conveniently listed on the inside of the front cover.

There are two appendixes. ***Appendix A, "Installation,"*** shows you how to install Q&A to meet your particular requirements. This includes customizing the menu, installing printers, and assigning user names if you are operating on a local area network. ***Appendix B, "What's New in 4.0,"*** gives you an overview of the main improvements over Version 3.0

At the end of this book, you will find two special features. The ***Command Reference Card*** is a tear-out quick reference card. With this handy card, you can quickly look up a feature and see the keystrokes needed to carry out the feature. On the inside of the back cover, tucked into its own pocket, is a floppy disk containing all the examples covered in the book. In Chapters 1 and 2, you will find complete instructions for loading the ***Q&A In Business disk*** onto your hard drive.

Each chapter follows the same format, except in a few cases where the requirements of the subject matter make it inappropriate to do so. At the beginning of each chapter is the ***At a Glance*** section. It summarizes the steps needed to use the key features and commands explained in that particular chapter. You will find it a quick reference when you want to execute a command but can't remember how to do so. The ***Overview*** explains in more detail about the application and its practical advantages in business.

Load the Enclosed Disk explains how to load the applications from the enclosed disk. This section is found in Chapters 1 and 2 only. You need load the disk just once. You will then have access to all the applications on the disk.

Application Explained describes the application, what the application can be used for, how it might be adapted to your needs, the procedures you'll go through to modify and use the application, and the fields used in each database. *Using the Application* guides you through using the application. At the same time you will explore features of Q&A.

Suggested Modifications offers suggestions on how you can tailor the application to your specific needs, and *Guided Modifications* steps you through making several of the modifications suggested.

> ▶ **Note:** All instructions assume that you will be beginning your command execution from the Q&A Main menu. If you must start from some place other than the Main menu, the instructions will tell you.

Conventions

Throughout this book, you will see several icons (pictorial symbols). These icons highlight important tips or procedures.

The *Beginner's Tip* icon appears when a tip applies especially to beginning users of Q&A. The tip explains basic information or procedures that the beginner may not know.

The *Business Shortcut* icon appears when a tip suggests a faster or easier way to perform a task or how to apply a particular application or feature to receive maximum value. This kind of tip also provides ideas to help you increase the quality or efficiency of your work.

The *Step* icon highlights a list of steps. These steps tell you exactly how to perform a particular task.

This book uses a special typeface to distinguish user input and computer output. Anything that you are suppose to type (user input) appears in a bold monospace font. For example, the text might instruct you: "Type the filename **INVOICE**." The word **INVOICE** appears in bold monospace;

you type only that word. Computer output, such as error messages or other information displayed on the screen, also appears in monospace, but in a lighter weight. For example, if you try to add a blank record to a database, you will get this error message: Cannot add blank record to database. Please enter data or hit Esc for File menu. The error message is shown in a lighter-weight monospace font.

When you are to enter a command, the command letter appears in regular boldface type. For example, the text might instruct you: "Press **U** for Utilities." You press the letter *U* on your keyboard. You can enter the command letter in uppercase or lowercase.

Some commands involve pressing special keys on your keyboard. These are the Enter, Esc, Shift, Ctrl, and Alt keys. The last three keys (Shift, Ctrl, and Alt) are pressed in conjunction with the function keys and regular keys. When you see two keys joined by a hyphen, press both of them at the same time. For example, *Shift-F2* means to press simultaneously the Shift key and the F2 function key.

Overview of Q&A

Q&A is the best-selling File Manager and Word Processor. The *File Manager* module allows you to develop "flat-file" databases and interconnect them to create your own applications. (See Chapter 2 for an explanation of flat-file databases.) The applications you create can be as simple as a customer list or as complex as an entire inventory/invoicing program. Using the *Word Processor module*, you can create letters, reports, and other documents. Q&A also includes a module called the *Intelligent Assistant*, which allows you to ask plain English questions of your database. Figure I.2 shows the three Q&A modules.

Q&A has been rated number one by almost every PC publication, including InfoWorld, PC Week, PC Magazine, and Software Digest. These publications have been particularly impressed with the program's power and ease of use. This combination of power and ease of use lets you develop comprehensive programs without being a programmer or having a degree in computer science.

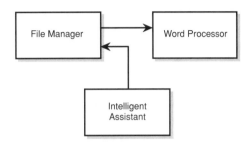

Figure I.2   Q&A modules.

This book will cover all aspects of Q&A, but it will focus particularly on Q&A's File Manager module. This is the portion of the program that you will use to develop your databases. The File Manager allows you to develop databases, or *forms*, that hold data. These forms can look identical to your current paper forms. Figure I.3 is an example of a simple name and address database form for a customer.

```
┌──────────────────── * CUSTOMER INFORMATION * ──────────────────┐
│ ENTERED: Sep 18, 1989                  UPDATED: Mar 1, 1990     │
│                                                                │
│ IDNUM: VARGA5                   FIRST: Charles      LAST: Varga │
│ COMPANY: Wilson Hardware                                       │
│ SAL 1: Mr. Varga                SAL 2: Mr. & Mrs Varga          │
│ ADDRESS: 6789 South Street      ADD A: Suite A                 │
│ CITY: Milbrae                   STATE: CA   ZIP: 94940          │
│ COUNTRY:                        HOME PHONE: 415-456-7843        │
└────────────────────────────────────────────────────────────────┘

Figure I-3: Sample Database From




C:\DBA\BOOK\FIGURE.CI                    Doc 1 Pg 3 Ln 1.38" Pos 1"
```

Figure I.3   Sample database form.

The Word Processor module allows you to write letters, proposals, and mail-merge letters. If you have a laser printer, you can add different fonts to your documents. By using fonts, you can make an ordinary proposal stand out from the crowd.

The Intelligent Assistant allows you to ask plain English questions of your database. For example: "Which customers ordered over $1000 worth of blue fabric in the first quarter of 1991?" The answer to your question can be the subject of further questioning, or it can be printed in an informative report, as shown here.

Question: Which customers ordered over $1000 worth of fabric in the first quarter of 1991?

Answer: (printed in a simple columnar report)

Client	Amount
======	======
Big Time Rag Company	$2345.89
Large Loretta's Clothes	$4567.90
Small Sam's Clothiers	$1230.00
Total	**$8143.79**
	======

All three modules are seamlessly integrated through an intuitive menu system. In addition to the three main modules, Q&A has several useful utilities that can be used for importing and exporting data from a wide range of databases and word processors. And if one of your files becomes damaged, you can repair it with the Recover utility.

The Applications in This Book

The enclosed disk contains 16 database files, 10 word processing files, and 1 macro file. One or more of these application files is the focus of each chapter and will be used to complete the respective examples for each application. The following sections briefly discuss each of the applications and how you might use them.

Master Names Application

Chapter 3, "Master Names Application," teaches you how to modify and use the "Names" database. This database is used to store all the names associated with your organization, including clients, prospects, vendors, employees, investors, etc. You will be guided through modifying the database and creating a report that lists all the names in the file. This program will become the heart of your applications and will serve as the source for retrieving information into the other files such as Sales Management and Inventory/Invoicing.

Personnel Application

Businesses must maintain specific information about their employees. Some of this information is required by federal and state governments; other information is unique to their individual operations. Almost everyone needs an easy way to calculate vacation and sick time. Chapter 4, "Personnel Application," explains how to store information on each employee and generate useful reports to manage the personnel process. The files used for this application are called: "Staff," "Health," and "Holiday."

Sales Management Application

One of the most common tasks that businesses need to automate is sales management: the tracking of leads through the sales process. In Chapter 5, "Sales Management Application," you will modify the "Sales" database and learn how to use the application to record who and when to call, what you talked about, and how to automatically generate follow-up letters.

Inventory/Invoicing Application

In Chapter 6, "Inventory/Invoicing Application," you will learn how to modify and use the product inventory and invoicing files. The Invoice database allows you to enter the customer ID number and product codes and have the program retrieve name and address information, part numbers, descriptions, and pricing information from the Names and Inventory files. As payments are received, they will be entered in the Invoice file as well. If accounts become past due, you will have the option of posting interest to all past due accounts. And when needed, you can run an accounts receivable report to help manage cash flow and improve collection efforts. This chapter uses the "Invoice" and "Invent" files.

Direct Mail Application

Direct mail is a function commonly used by most organizations. Whether you are sending three letters or three hundred letters, everyone needs an automated way of generating letters and labels. Chapter 7, "Direct Mail Application," explains how to develop the letter, the label, and the macro used to tie the process together. The letter file is called "Direct.let" and the macro is contained in the macro file "QAMACRO.ASC."

Proposal Generation Application

Most organizations need to send out proposals or estimates of some kind. Many of these require the inclusion of financial data. Chapter 8, "Proposal Generation Application," guides you through the process of generating a proposal by integrating various documents into one master document. It will also show you how to combine a Lotus 1-2-3 spreadsheet into the text. The files used are: Master, Intro, Descrip, Options, and Estimate.

Business Analysis Application

Q&A has a module called the Intelligent Assistant. The purpose of this module is to make it easy to ask questions of your databases. Chapter 9, "Business Analysis Application," explains how to analyze your data using the Intelligent Assistant and how to develop cross-tab reports, which are equally useful in analyzing your organization's data.

Menu/Macro Application

Chapter 10, "Menu/Macro Application," gives you the opportunity to tie all your applications together into an easy-to-use menu system. The menu system allows novice users to access the functions of your database programs without a lot of computer training. It also provides a way to quickly perform repetitive tasks. The menu system is stored in the macro file QAMACRO.ASC.

The Opportunity

Correctly automating your organization can have a dramatic impact on both the bottom line and the quality of life in your organization. A major goal of automation is to improve productivity. But what actually gets improved when you improve productivity?

Improving productivity comprises two parts: improving effectiveness and improving efficiency. When you improve your effectiveness, you are improving your ability to produce intended results. And when you improve efficiency, you are increasing your output: producing your results faster and with less effort. You may want to decrease the time it takes to manufacture a physical product, generate legal documents, or print invoices. No matter which areas you pinpoint to improve, your goal is twofold: improve your *effectiveness*—the ability to bring about an intended result—and improve your *efficiency*—speed up the various processes within your organization.

Another often overlooked benefit of automation is to shift the burden of repetitive tasks from people to computers. Besides the obvious benefits of improved efficiency, staff members can be freed to do more of the important and creative tasks that a computer cannot do.

Case Study

The case study that you are about to read is the process that one of our consulting clients went through to automate his business and the benefits that the business received.

George Jackson is the founder and president of The Fundraiser's Consultants, a business that he started twelve years ago. His company provides fund-raising products and services to a large number of organizations in northern California. As the president, Mr. Jackson's work is never done; you can often find him at the office on Saturday and Sunday. His staff labors equally hard.

Because of this extra effort, The Fundraiser's Consultants had become a successful company. However, the hard work was taking its toll, and the company had reached a plateau in sales.

With the advent of the microcomputer revolution, Mr. Jackson and his staff decided that a computer would help them get ahead of the game. So they bought a PC AT, a dot matrix printer, and Q&A. Since they did not have any prior computer knowledge or a model to follow, they used only the word processor portion of the product. This brought them some incremental value. They used the word processor for everything they could, including maintaining their inventory. Those of you familiar with real inventory systems know that this is not an optimum way to track inventory. Nevertheless, their productivity did improve slightly, but the new system wasn't having the impact that the advertisers had promised.

In frustration, a staff member suggested to Mr. Jackson that he hire a consulting firm to help them get the maximum value from their system. Mr. Jackson was quite reluctant at first but eventually relented and called our firm. We responded by setting up a strategy meeting in which we presented the principles that are covered in Chapter 1. Still he was less than enthusiastic. His concerns were manifold, among them: they wouldn't have time to develop the applications, they wouldn't be able to learn how to use them, and, the biggest concern, the costs would exceed the benefits. We asserted that the benefits would be realized and that they would far outweigh the costs, but that Mr. Jackson and his staff would have to devote some time to designing, developing, and implementing the applications. Mr. Jackson finally agreed to begin the project.

We began in the same way that you will begin—by looking at the entire organization and pinpointing all the processes/systems that made up the business. These processes were then ranked by how much they would improve productivity. With this done, three applications were chosen: Inventory/Invoicing/Accounts Receivable, List Management, and Sales Management. After the applications were developed, they were implemented and the appropriate staff was trained.

The results were astounding. Within twelve months, The Fundraiser's Consultants doubled their sales without adding any new staff. They now know precisely how much money is owed them at any time and have cut collection time in half. Inventory is properly managed and has been reduced to just the items they need during the appropriate season. Direct mail is a regular, cost-effective, and easy task to perform that has increased their exposure and sales. All in all, the results of the project exceeded their expectations, and they now have a model to follow for automating future processes.

I can't promise that you will have the same results. But if you follow the principles in this book, there is no reason why you can't dramatically improve your productivity.

Acknowledgments

I am quite thankful to the following people: Ted Progler, Joan McKenna, Bill Gladstone, Steve Poland, and Jeannine Howes.

Trademarks

All terms mentioned in this book that are known to be trademarks or service marks are listed below. In addition, terms suspected of being trademarks or service marks have been appropriately capitalized. SAMS cannot attest to the accuracy of this information. Use of a term in this book should not be regarded as affecting the validity of any trademark or service mark.

HP, LaserJet Series II, LaserJet III, and Hewlett-Packard are registered trademarks of Hewlett-Packard Company.

IBM is a registered trademark of International Business Machines Corporation.

Lotus and 1-2-3 are registered trademarks of Lotus Development Corporation.

Macintosh is a registered trademark of Apple Computer, Inc.

Microsoft and MS-DOS are registered trademarks of Microsoft Corporation.

MultiMate is a registered trademark of Ashton-Tate Corporation.

Novell is a registered trademark of Novell, Inc.

Q&A is a registered trademark of Symantec Corporation.

Rolodex is a registered trademark of Rolodex Corporation.

WordPerfect is a registered trademark of WordPerfect Corporation.

WordStar is a registered trademark of MicroPro International Corporation.

Research Your Needs

Do an analysis of your organization to determine which key processes you need to automate.

Create a Flowchart of the Key Processes

Draw simple flowcharts showing each key task of the processes you have chosen to automate.

Translate Processes into Databases

Using the flowchart as a guide, determine which databases you will need to develop or modify.

Formulate an Automation Plan

If warranted, summarize the automation efforts into a simple plan.

Design Database Files

Using the enclosed databases as a guide, design databases that meet your needs.

Design Reports

Based on the databases you design, draw the reports you will need.

List Macros

Make a list of the macros you want to develop.

Design Menus

Design the menus you will need. These will include menus to access your databases, reports, and macros.

Determine Access Rights

For each database, define the access rights you want each staff member to have.

Test the Applications

Make sure that the applications operate as you intended.

Document the Applications

If needed, develop a simple outline of how to use the applications.

Install the Applications

Set up the applications on the appropriate computers.

Train Users

Train each user in the use of the applications.

IN BUSINESS

How to Begin

This chapter will guide you through the procedures for automating your organization by using Q&A. It will also explain basic database principles and teach you how to design your own applications.

Beginner's Tip

An *application* is a complete program consisting of database files, reports, and macros, which automate a particular process such as order entry/invoicing. The *database* is the heart of the application, where all data is stored. *Reports* print data from the database, and *macros* speed up repetitive tasks, such as printing an invoice.

Introduction

You do not need to complete this chapter in order to benefit fully from the book. This chapter is intended to be a road map through the entire design and development process. It will present you with questions and examples that are designed to make you think comprehensively and strategically about automating your organization. By completing the step-by-step examples, you will end up with a design for each application and a simple plan to follow while making these designs a reality. Even if you do not complete the examples, you will still benefit from reading through the chapter.

Several recent studies have proven that most organizations receive only a fraction of the possible benefit from their computer systems. One of the most common reasons for this is that no one person in the company is designated to think strategically about how information systems could

3

benefit the company. Nor is a comprehensive automation plan developed, with one person given the authority to implement it. Without this master plan and one person in charge, often each department develops or buys its own system with little or no thought for its effects upon the rest of the organization. This can result in the inability to share data among the organization's computers, thereby minimizing the potential benefit.

One of the advantages of developing an automation plan is that many organizations use this time to rethink their corporate strategies and procedures and to design information systems that improve their competitive advantage. By redesigning their organization around information systems, these systems become central to their strategies and operations—they become "Strategic Systems."

In fact, a number of highly successful companies such as Federal Express and Mrs. Fields Cookies will attest to the role that such Strategic Systems have played in their success. They developed information systems that have given them a considerable advantage over their competition. At Federal Express, if you want to locate a package after you have shipped it, Federal Express can usually find it within minutes—anywhere in the world. A recent study by the Technology Group showed that properly automating complete "business processes" (Strategic Systems) *results in an average rate of return on each technology dollar of 300% and improves productivity by as much as 100%.*

As you begin this process, *keep in mind that it doesn't have to be done all at once.* The following pages will guide you through a step-by-step process that will result in a master plan for developing your applications, a flowchart of key processes, and drawings of the applications you will develop. Complete as many of these examples as you feel is appropriate for your situation.

 Note: In this chapter, you will be introduced to concepts and features of Q&A that may be foreign to you. Don't worry. They will be fully explained in later chapters.

Strategic Systems

A *Strategic System* automates the core functions of your organization. It comprises two complementary parts: process automation systems and decision support systems.

The *process automation* portion of a Strategic System automates entire processes within an organization. An example would be the order entry/invoicing process. This process consists of entering an order, removing the product from inventory, printing the invoice, and generating an accounts receivable list. By automating an entire process, there is less human intervention; thus, the work is completed faster and with fewer errors.

Contrast this with the less beneficial method of task automation. Here you might simply automate the printing of invoices and then be forced to manually write the initial order, delete the inventory, and list the outstanding receivables. Obviously, the chance for human error is increased, and the entire process takes longer to complete. Studies have shown that the cost to automate an entire process is almost as much as the cost to automate a single task.

The other half of a Strategic System is the *decision support* system. The decision support system does what its name implies: it assists you in making more informed decisions. It does this by extracting data from chosen databases and translating it into useful reports. For instance, you might request a report showing how many products each salesperson has sold during the last quarter. A report of this nature would help you analyze the performances of your sales representatives and the viability of your current product line.

This leads us to the focus of this book: creating Strategic Systems by using Q&A. The Q&A program is ideally suited to be the foundation of a small-to medium-sized organization's Strategic System. Since Q&A contains a powerful, yet easy to use, database and word processor, you can easily automate the core processes of your organization. With the Intelligent Assistant and extensive reporting features, you can easily develop decision support systems to analyze the data contained in these databases.

Overview of the Process

This section provides an overview of the application design and development process you are about to begin. The first suggestion is to assign someone to be responsible for overseeing the entire automation process. Once you have done this, choose which of your internal processes (invoicing, inventory, sales management, etc.) *can* be automated using Q&A. After you have determined which processes *can* be automated, choose the ones that *will* be automated at this time. Then develop a simple flowchart for each process. The flowchart will make it easy for you to identify the key functions of the process. After each key function is identified, it can be translated into databases. Next, you will design the databases, reports, menus, and macros that make up each application.

Together with the appropriate chapter in the book, these designs will act as a blueprint that you can follow while developing each application. If others will be using the application, you can give them the opportunity to test the application before it is implemented. If needed, you can create documentation for each application. The final steps are to install the application on the appropriate computer and train staff members on how to use it. The entire process is known as the Strategic Systems Development Model, and it is shown in Figure 1.1.

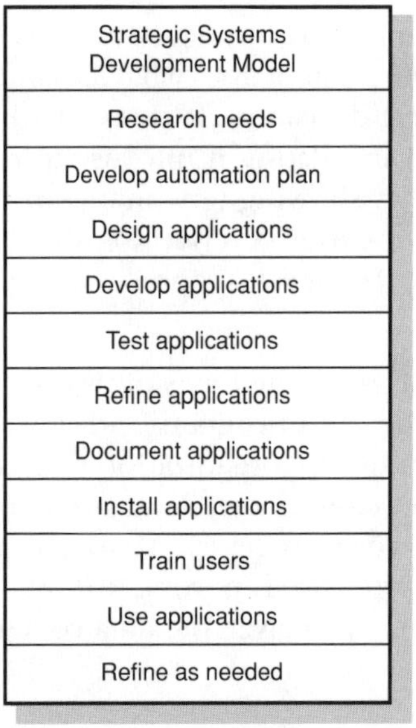

Strategic Systems Development Model
Research needs
Develop automation plan
Design applications
Develop applications
Test applications
Refine applications
Document applications
Install applications
Train users
Use applications
Refine as needed

Figure 1.1 The Strategic Systems Development Model.

Research Needs

If you are not sure which processes to automate, you may want to conduct a little research. This research should focus on identifying each of the key processes within your organization that can be automated using Q&A. To identify the key processes you want to automate, you may want to answer the questions in the next section.

Initial Research Questions

The following questions are not meant to be inclusive. Rather, they are designed to stimulate your thinking about the key processes of your organization.

- What business are you in? Remember the classic marketing axiom: many railroad companies went out of business because they thought they were in the railroad business rather than the transportation business.

- What main process is at the heart of your organization and requires the most resources (people, time, money, equipment) to complete? Is it sales, manufacturing, distribution, etc.? If you are not sure, follow the paper flow: which departments are involved; what actual forms are used; who is involved? Generally, the longest process is the main one. How long does it take to complete the entire process? How much does it cost for one cycle?

- What are the supporting processes? Which processes augment or support this main process?

- Which people are involved in these processes? What is their level of computer skill?

- Are there enough computers for the processes you want to automate?

- Does the information need to be shared among more than one person? For instance, will the sales database have several sales reps accessing the same information at the same time?

Shortcut

If you need to share information among several users, you will need a *multiuser* system. The most cost effective and common is a *local area network* (LAN). A LAN is beyond the scope of this book. However, Q&A does have a product called the Network Pack that allows you to turn your existing single-user version of Q&A into a multiuser version. Each Network Pack allows four users to access the system and can be purchased from your dealer.

- What information do you need to facilitate your decision-making process in such tasks as sales forecasting, analyzing inventory, personnel management, etc.?

- What printed output do you need from the system, for example, invoices, proposals, accounts receivable reports, inventory listings, expense reports, etc.?

Jot down these answers so you can use them in future examples.

Create a Flowchart of Processes

Using the answers to questions 2, 3, and 4, create a simple flowchart of the tasks within each process that you have decided to automate.

Creating a Simple Flowchart

1. Draw the key tasks within each process. As you can see in Figure 1.2, you do not need to follow formal flowcharting procedures. Simply draw boxes to indicate the flow of events.

> ▶ **Note:** To illustrate the rest of the examples, I am going to use a PC mail order company. This company, PC Express, sells microcomputer software. They receive orders from incoming calls in response to their advertisements and from their telemarketing efforts.

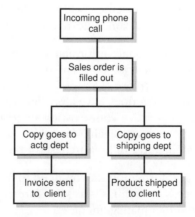

Figure 1.2 Partial flowchart of key process.

2. Indicate who is responsible for each task, as shown in Figure 1.3. For each person you have indicated, note the department that the person works in and the person's computer skill level. The computer skill level is a rating from 0 to 5. A *5* is expert, and a *0* means no previous computer experience.

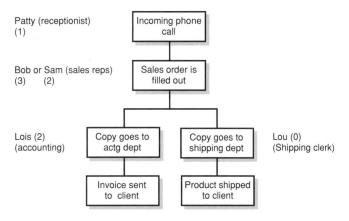

Figure 1.3 Partial flowchart with key personnel and computer skill ratings noted.

3. For each process in your flowchart, assign a priority indicating the order in which it will be automated.

Translate Processes into Databases

Using the processes you have chosen to automate, identify each key function and then translate those functions into separate databases. A *function* is a single task that generates its own unique set of information and that can be automated, such as the filling in of a sales order. Not every task on the flowchart is a function. In Figure 1.3, the incoming call is a task. It is only when the sales order is actually filled in (generating new information) that a key function has been identified.

Another way to determine which databases to develop is to identify the point in the process at which paper forms are completed. Many times these paper forms can be directly translated into a computer database. Sometimes you will combine two or more paper forms into one database.

Using the PC Express company's order entry/inventory process, you can identify the key functions and translate them into databases, as shown in Figure 1.4. When a customer places an order, the sales rep fills out a paper sales order form. Filling out this form is a key function because new information is generated. This information would be translated into both a Names database and an Invoice database. There are two databases for this function because the customer's name and address information is useful to all members of the organization, while the order information is needed to generate a permanent record of the order and to print the invoice. As the process continues, the shipping clerk is sent a packing slip and required to delete the inventory shipped from the inventory ledger cards. New information is generated; thus a new function is identified. This function would then be translated into an Inventory database. This entire process yielded three databases: Names, Invoice, and Inventory.

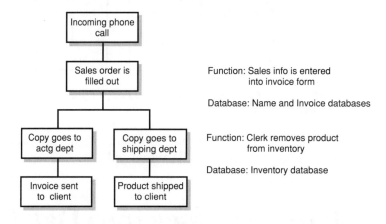

Figure 1.4 *Key functions are translated into databases.*

The Automation Plan

Depending on the scope of your work, you may or may not want to summarize your development efforts into an automation plan. If you have only one or two applications to develop and you plan to complete the examples as you read the chapter, you probably don't need to develop a plan. However, if you are developing several applications and you are not going to complete the examples at this time, or if you are assigning the development work to someone else, you will want to develop an automation plan.

Developing an automation plan is simple. As you come to sections in this chapter requiring some action that you aren't going to do now, simply note the action on the automation plan. This way, by the time you complete the chapter, you will have a complete list of things to do. A sample plan is shown in Figure 1.5.

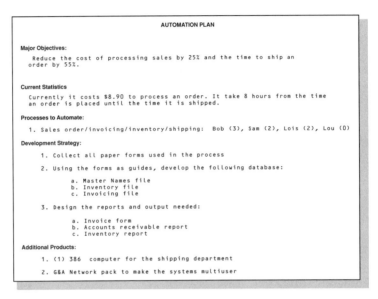

AUTOMATION PLAN

Major Objectives:

Reduce the cost of processing sales by 25% and the time to ship an order by 55%.

Current Statistics

Currently it costs $8.90 to process an order. It take 8 hours from the time an order is placed until the time it is shipped.

Processes to Automate:

1. Sales order/invoicing/inventory/shipping: Bob (3), Sam (2), Lois (2), Lou (0)

Development Strategy:

1. Collect all paper forms used in the process

2. Using the forms as guides, develop the following database:

      a. Master Names file
      b. Inventory file
      c. Invoicing file

3. Design the reports and output needed:

      a. Invoice form
      b. Accounts receivable report
      c. Inventory report

Additional Products:

1. (1) 386 computer for the shipping department

2. G&A Network pack to make the systems multiuser

Figure 1.5 Sample automation plan.

The format of the automation plan is straightforward. Just list your major objective(s) for the project. List each process that you are going to automate and, if possible, the completion time and cost. Along with each process, list the people currently involved in doing the work and note their computer skill level. Then list each database, report, macro, and menu you need to develop.

Design Applications

It is time to begin designing your applications. This section will guide you through the drawing of the necessary databases, reports, menus, and macros. The drawings you produce will be like the blueprints used by a building contractor. With these drawings in hand, you can then proceed to the appropriate chapter in the book and use the drawings as guides to making your designs a reality.

However, before you begin, you can potentially save yourself a lot of time and effort by determining how closely the existing applications meet your needs. You will fall somewhere in-between these three categories: you are able to use the enclosed applications without any modification whatsoever, you can use the enclosed applications but need to change them, or you have to develop your applications from scratch. To determine how much of the enclosed applications you can use, you should print each of the databases included with the book. If the applications are close to what you need, you will have few modifications to make.

To print the database forms, you have to load the files from the enclosed disk onto your hard drive. This process will consist of three tasks: making two subdirectories (FILE and WORD) under your QA directory, copying the files to the FILE subdirectory, and decompressing the distribution file that contains the application files. This procedure assumes that you have already loaded Q&A into the QA directory on your hard drive.

> **Caution:** Loading the files from the enclosed disk needs to be done only once. If you have completed this procedure while reading Appendix A, "Installation," or Chapter 2, "Q&A Basics," skip this procedure.

Loading Files from the Enclosed Disk

1. Insert the enclosed disk into drive A and shut the floppy drive door.

2. Change to the C drive by typing **c:** and pressing Enter.

3. Change to the QA directory by typing **cd\qa** and pressing Enter.

4. Type **md word** and press Enter to create the first subdirectory.

5. Type **md file** and press Enter to create the second subdirectory.

6. Type **md temp** and press Enter to create the third subdirectory.

7. Switch to the File subdirectory by typing **cd\qa\file** and pressing Enter.

8. Copy the file DATA.EXE to the File subdirectory by typing **copy a:data.exe** and pressing Enter.

9. Uncompress the data files by typing **data** and pressing Enter.

10. Switch to the Word subdirectory by typing **cd\qa\word** and pressing Enter.

11. Copy the file WORD.COM to the Word subdirectory by Typing **copy a:word.exe** and pressing Enter.

12. Uncompress the word processing data files by typing **word** and pressing Enter.

13. Switch to the QA subdirectory by typing **cd\qa** and pressing Enter.

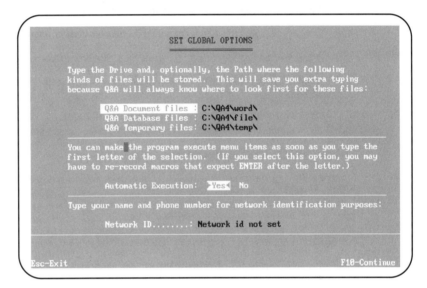

Figure 1.6   Global Options screen.

⊘ **Caution:** If you already have created macros in Q&A and stored them in the macro file QAMACRO.ASC, you will have to rename this file. To do so, go to step 13. If you have not created any macros, skip step 13 and go to step 14.

14. If you have existing macros stored in the file QAMACRO.ASC, then rename the file by typing **ren qamacro.asc qamacro.old** and pressing Enter.

15. Copy the macro file QAMACRO.ASC to the QA subdirectory by typing **copy a:qamacro.asc** and pressing Enter.

16. Start Q&A by typing **qa** and pressing Enter.

17. Now tell Q&A where your files are stored. Press **U** for Utilities and press Enter. Press **S** for Set Global Defaults and press Enter.

18. This will place you in the Global Options screen shown in Figure 1.6. Type **word** for the path of the Document files. Type **file** for the path of the Database files and **temp** for the location of the Temporary files.

19. In order to follow the examples throughout the book, you must set the Automatic Execution option to Yes in the Utilities menu. If you haven't already done so, change Automatic Execution to Yes.

20. When you are through, press F10 to save your changes.

21. Press Esc twice to return to the Q&A Main menu.

Now that you have loaded the files onto your hard disk, you are ready to print the database forms you need. Use the following list to decide which databases you want to print. Then follow the instructions for printing database forms.

Database	Description of File
Names	Basic name and address information for every organization or individual
Invoice	Invoice information
Inventory	Product inventory information
Staff	Specific personnel information
Health	Sick time information
Holiday	Vacation time information
Sales	Sales management information

Printing Database Forms

1. From the Q&A Main menu, select **F** for File and **A** for Add data.

2. Press F4 twice and Enter. This will give you a list of the available files.

3. Move to the first file you want to print and press Enter. This will place you inside the file.

4. To print the file, press F2. This will place you in the Print Options screen.

5. Press F10 to print the database form.

6. When the printing has finished, Q&A returns you to the database screen. Press Esc to exit the database.

7. Repeat the process for each database you want to print.

Design the Database

Now you are ready to put pencil to paper and design your database forms. You will want to have copies of the database forms you printed and the flowcharts you created. For each database you are going to develop, make a sketch of how the screen is to appear. If your databases are close to those enclosed with the book, just mark up the forms you printed.

If you are new to software development, here are some tips that you may want to follow while you are designing your applications:

- Draw everything on paper first; this includes database forms, reports, and menus. Show your drawings to the people who will actually be doing the data entry. Ask them if your drawing is easy to understand and contains all the necessary fields.

- If the data entry operator will fill in the database from a paper form, make sure that the database screen matches the form as much as possible. It is much easier to fill in a database if the paper form corresponds to the fields in the database.

- Place common information together. For instance, you would not want part of the insurance information on screen one and the rest of it on screen three.

- Make the screen visually appealing. Use lines to group similar information together.

- If at all possible, place the information you change most often at the top of a screen.

- *Be sure to include a common ID number field on all databases.* Q&A has a feature called *lookup*, which allows you to retrieve information from one database and place it in another one. This feature is used in the Invoice database to retrieve name and address information from the Names file. It works like this. You enter the customer's information into the Names file. Then, each time you need to generate an invoice for this customer, you type the customer's ID number in the Invoice database and press F8. Q&A looks up the name and address information from the Names file and places it in the invoice form. This saves you time because you don't have to retype the customer's name and address every time you want to generate an invoice.

Design Reports

When you feel confident that your databases are complete, you are ready to design the printed output you will need. Q&A refers to printed output as reports and gives you three options: form reports, columnar reports, and cross-tab reports. Each of these will be explained briefly here, and more thoroughly in subsequent chapters.

With your final flowcharts as guides, you can determine at what point in each process you need a report. Most manual processes already use paper forms. These forms are a good starting point in determining which reports you need the application to print.

Using the PC Express company as an example, you can see that this company needs to have an invoice for the customer, a packing slip and inventory listing for the shipping clerk, and an accounts receivable listing for the accounting department. Figure 1.7 shows an example of each kind of report.

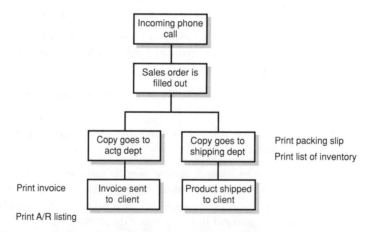

Figure 1.7 Flowchart displaying printed output.

The most common report is the *columnar report*. This report displays information in columns of information. Any one of the fields (LAST NAME is an example of a field) on your database can be a column in a report. Once you have selected the columns to appear on the report, you can perform various calculations on them. The type of calculations you can perform is defined by the data type in the column. Columns of text can be counted, and numeric and money columns can be totaled, subtotaled, averaged, etc. Also, you can sort the report by any field in the database, even one that does not appear on the report. Figure 1.8 is an example of a simple columnar report.

Oct 24, 1990			COMPLETE LIST OF NAMES				PAGE 1	
IDNUM	FIRST	LAST	ADDRESS	CITY	STATE	ZIP	HOME PHONE	SALES
101	Horatio	Alger	200 Gusher Lane	Amarillo	TX	34922	214-234-5678	$2,000
202	Bill	Smith	120 West Lane	Greenbrae	ND	12342	204-456-7855	$5,560
Count Total	2							$7,560

Figure 1.8 Simple columnar report.

The second type of report is the *cross-tab report*. This report cross-tabulates different types of information. For instance, you could cross-tabulate how many of each product type each sales representative has sold in the last quarter. This report is particularly useful for data analysis. Figure 1.9 shows a simple cross-tab report.

03/06/91 sample xtab report		DATE		
COMPANY		Jan 91	Feb 91	Mar 91
Brazilian Lumber	Avg	$3996.00	$9144.00	$3816.00
	Tot	$7992.00	$27432.00	$11448.00
	Min	$3888.00	$1944.00	$1728.00
	Max	$4104.00	$21384.00	$5184.00
Sacks: Fine Burlap Clothing	Avg	$1196.37	$2028.33	$585.00
	Tot	$3589.10	$6085.00	$1170.00
	Min	$585.00	$225.00	$135.00
	Max	$1969.10	$3385.00	$1035.00
The Blue Sky Company	Avg	$1173.29	$2342.70	$1742.70
	Tot	$5866.43	$7028.10	$5228.10
	Min	$92.70	$92.70	$542.70
	Max	$1982.70	$3917.70	$3692.70
The Good Health Hospital	Avg	$547.20	$322.43	$385.88
	Tot	$1641.61	$322.43	$771.76
	Min	$90.00	$322.43	$48.38
	Max	$1008.23	$322.43	$723.38
0 Bal & Int	Avg	$1468.40	$4086.75	$1861.79
	Tot	$19089.14	$40867.53	$18617.86
	Min	$90.00	$92.70	$48.38
	Max	$4104.00	$21384.00	$5184.00

Figure 1.9 Simple cross-tab report.

The final type of report is the *form report*. The form report allows you to place fields (of information) on the paper in two ways. The first way, known as *coordinate* printing, allows you to print information at predetermined page coordinates. For instance, a coordinate of row 3 column 7 would place the data three rows down from the top margin and seven spaces in from the left margin. Coordinate printing is particularly useful if you have to fill in preprinted forms. The second method, known as *free-form printing*, is easier to use and places the information with less precision on the paper. Figure 1.10 is an example of a form report using the coordinate method of placing fields.

```
03/06/91                          INVOICE
= = = :


BILL TO                                SHIP TO/REMARKS


The Blue Sky Company
Horatio  Alger
500 Gusher Lane
Amarillo                  Tx   34922

- - - - - - - - - - - - - - - - - - - - - - - - - - - -
REP     DATE      DUE DATE    SHIP DATE    INVOICE #    PO #
DBA     01/23/91  02/22/91                 32           22344
- - - - - - - - - - - - - - - - - - - - - - - - - - - -
ITEM #      DESCRIPTION         QTY      UNIT      EXTENDED
- - - - - - - - - - - - - - - - - - - - - - - - - - - -
BW          The Big Widget      34       $5.00     $170.00
BW          The Big Widget      34       $5.00     $170.00
BW          The Big Widget      34       $5.00     $170.00
BW          The Big Widget      34       $5.00     $170.00
BW          The Big Widget      34       $5.00     $170.00
BW          The Big Widget      34       $5.00     $170.00
BW          The Big Widget      34       $5.00     $170.00
BW          The Big Widget      34       $5.00     $170.00
BW          The Big Widget      34       $5.00     $170.00


PLEASE REMIT TO:                              $1530.00
The Famous ABC Company            TAX         $0.00
123 Glamor Avenue                 FREIGHT
Hollywood, CA 94960               CREDIT
THANK YOU FOR YOUR BUSINESS !     TOTAL       $1530.00
YOU ARE SINCERELY APPRECIATED !   PAID        $0.00
1.5% Per Mo. Will be charged on Overdue Amount   BALANCE   $1530.00
                                  INTEREST    $2.70
                                  BAL & INT.  $1532.70
```

Figure 1.10 Invoice form using coordinate printing.

List Macros

Well-designed databases and reports will greatly improve your productivity. However, accessing databases, printing reports, or performing procedures requires that you type several keystrokes to get the job done. To reduce the number of keystrokes you have to type, Q&A provides you with the ability to create macros.

When you print an invoice, you press the same keys every time. The only thing that changes is the date of the invoices you are printing. Using macros, you can record the keystrokes you press to print an invoice and save them with a macro identifier such as Alt-P. Then when you press the macro identifier, Alt-P, your recorded keystrokes are replayed.

At this stage all you have to do is list the macros you want to develop. Simply list the tasks you want the macro to perform, such as adding data to a file, printing a report, or posting interest on overdue invoices. Next to each task write the *macro identifier*, which is a keystroke combination using either the Alt or the Ctrl key and one letter, for example, Alt-P. If possible, use the first letter of the task or file, such as Alt-N for adding data to the Names file. When you are through, you should have a table that looks like Figure 1.11.

DESCRIPTION OF TASK	MACRO IDENTIFIER
Add data to Names file	Alt-N
Add data to Invoice file	Alt-I
Post interest on overdue invoices	Alt-P
Print invoices	Alt-V
Print master list of names	Alt-M

Figure 1.11 Macro table.

Beginner's Tip

I recommend that you use the Alt key for your macro identifiers. Q&A uses many of the WordStar editing commands that are assigned to the Ctrl and the *A, S, D, F, W, E, R, X, C* keys. If you will never use these key combinations, you can reassign them.

Draw Menus

If you decide to develop macros for your application, you will need a convenient method of accessing them. Q&A now offers two methods of accessing macros: the Macro menu and Custom menus. The first method, the *Macro menu*, is the easiest to develop and use. Since the Macro menu is built into Q&A, all you have to do is create a macro and Q&A automatically lists it on the menu along with the macro identifier. Figure 1.12 shows a sample Macro menu.

Custom menus have to be defined before they can be used. However, Custom menus offer several benefits. First, by displaying only essential tasks on the menu, you can isolate novice users from a potentially confusing array of options. This can speed up learning and make it easier to use the applications. Further, without a large list of options to choose from, a user's daily work tends to be accelerated. Custom menus can only invoke macros or other menus. Figure 1.13 displays a sample Main menu.

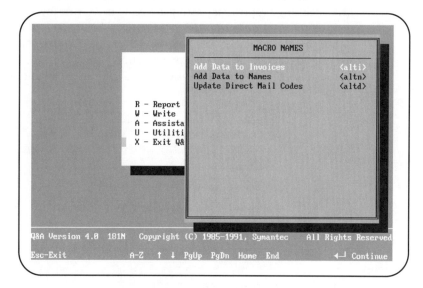

Figure 1.12 Sample Macro menu.

Figure 1.13 Sample Main menu.

Besides one *main* menu, you can also develop *submenus*. Submenus are launched from the Main menu. They are particularly useful if you have too many tasks to place on the Main menu or if want to group similar tasks. For instance, on the Main menu you might have adding data functions and on separate submenus you might have printing reports and running macros. Figure 1.14 displays a report submenu.

```
┌─────────────────────────────────┐
│          REPORTS MENU           │
├─────────────────────────────────┤
│        Print Invoice            │
│      Print Packing Slip         │
│        Print A/R List           │
│      Print Inventory List       │
└─────────────────────────────────┘
```

Figure 1.14 Submenu for reports.

As you design your menus, group similar tasks together, placing the most commonly used tasks at the top of the menu. For example, the task of adding/searching data would go at the top of the menu, since this task is used 90 percent of the time. Printing reports and running macros would be grouped together on the Main menu or placed in their own submenus. At this point, don't worry about how the menus work; just concentrate on how you want them to look.

Developing Custom menus is optional and not necessary to operate your applications.

Determine Access Rights

The last aspect of your design process is to determine security rights. Q&A offers three types of security rights: database locking, file access rights, and field security. You can give different security rights to different personnel, and the security rights can vary from locking a user completely out of the database to allowing the user complete access.

Determining access rights is optional. If your information is not sensitive or if data security is not an issue in your organization, skip this step.

Locking a file is the least troublesome method of security from a day-to-day user's point of view. To lock a file, you simply go to the Database Lock screen, shown in Figure 1.15, and assign various rights to *all* users and assign *one* password to unlock that database. (Chapter 2 explains how to move to the Database Lock screen.) There is no "scale" of rights. That is, if you limit one user's rights, you limit all users' rights. As Figure 1.15 shows, there are ten different functions you restrict users from performing. Generally, unless you have very sophisticated users, you will want to limit access to all design features. A suggested file locking scheme is to indicate Yes to the rights `Design/Redesign report`, `Edit lookup table`, and `Change palette`, and indicate No to all other rights.

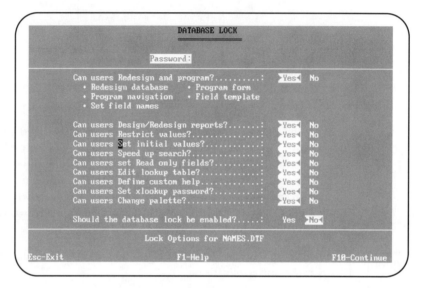

Figure 1.15 Database Lock options.

Assigning access rights is another method of limiting access to a file. With this method, you can assign passwords that allow different rights to each staff member. For example, one user could be allowed to run the Mass Update procedure but not allowed to change report designs. To define rights for everybody, make a copy of Figure 1.16. Add to it columns naming each database that you are developing. Use the copy as a form for assigning rights by placing a checkmark next to the access rights allowed under each column. Do this for each person who will be using the application, writing in the person's password where indicated on the form.

The final type of security is *field security*. This permits you to restrict access to specific fields of a database. Field security could be used on a Personnel database. For example, the company may have one person whose job it is to enter new staff members, but not enter salary and performance reviews. With this feature, you can make the SALARY and PERFORMANCE REVIEW fields invisible to one user and visible to another user, through the use of passwords.

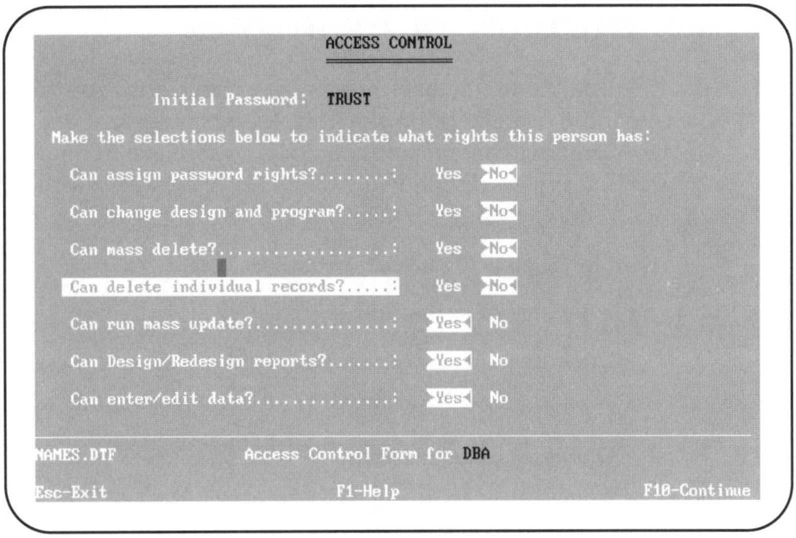

```
                        ACCESS CONTROL
                        ──────────────

         Initial Password:  TRUST

      Make the selections below to indicate what rights this person has:

         Can assign password rights?........:   Yes  ▶No◀

         Can change design and program?.....:   Yes  ▶No◀

         Can mass delete?...................:   Yes  ▶No◀

         Can delete individual records?.....:   Yes  ▶No◀

         Can run mass update?...............:  ▶Yes◀  No

         Can Design/Redesign reports?.......:  ▶Yes◀  No

         Can enter/edit data?...............:  ▶Yes◀  No

      ─────────────────────────────────────────────────────────────
      NAMES.DTF              Access Control Form for DBA

      Esc-Exit                       F1-Help                F10-Continue
```

Figure 1.16 Access Control Rights screen.

The options in field security let you define a field as: (W) Read and Write, (R) Read Only, or (N) No Access at all. The simplest way to define your fields is to make a copy of each database design for each user and then write a W, R, or N in each field. Figure 1.17 shows a field security table.

NAME	CODE	DESCRIPTION
Read and Write	W	This field can be seen and edited (default).
Read Only	R	This field can be seen but not edited.
No Access	N	This field cannot be seen; therefore it cannot be edited.

Figure 1.17 Table of field rights.

Summary of Examples

By completing this section on security rights, you have finished phase one of the overall application development process. If you have followed the examples in the previous sections, you will have completed one or more of the items in the following list. This list covers all the tasks that were presented in each section.

- Flowcharts of your key processes.

- Drawings of each database.

- Drawings of each report you need.

- List of macros to develop.

- Drawings of each menu.

- Lock options for each database.

- File security options for each database.

- Field security options for each database.

Final Procedures

At this point, you will actually begin developing your applications. Remember, as I mentioned earlier, completing the preceding examples is not essential to following along with the applications chapters. However, if you did complete the examples, the development process will go much faster and smoother, since you will eventually perform many of the tasks anyway.

The remaining sections will give you a brief overview of the next phase, developing applications. They will also list the steps you need to perform *after* you have developed the applications.

Develop Applications

At last, you can begin developing your applications. If you are already familiar with Q&A, you can skip to the chapters that cover the applications you need. If you have never used Q&A before, *I highly recommend that you complete the examples in Chapter 2, "Q&A Basics."* This chapter will acquaint you with Q&A's basic design, data entry, data retrieval, report creation, and macro building features.

> ▶ **Note:** From here on, the remaining sections deal with examples that are optional and that are performed after you finish developing your applications.

Test and Refine Applications

After you finish your applications, you will want to test them, particularly if they are going to be used by people other than yourself. Give the applications to the actual users and ask them to enter real transactions, to print reports, and to run any macros.

The testing process will likely result in suggested changes. It will also reveal any procedures that do not work correctly (bugs). When the test period is complete and all users have had an opportunity to provide you with input on how the applications run, make the suggested changes and fix the bugs. Once this is complete, you are ready to officially implement the applications.

Install Applications

The applications should now be officially installed and put into use. You will want to let your users know that this will be taking place and prepare them for the upcoming training they will need to use the applications.

Document Applications

Many organizations find it useful to develop a small user's manual. This can be as elaborate or as simple as you want, but it should contain the basic procedures for using the application. The manual should explain how to enter and retrieve data. It should also list any codes you use, display copies of each report, and explain how to run any macros you might have developed. One of the major benefits of having the applications documented is that the knowledge of how to use and update them isn't lost if the developer or key operator leaves the organization.

Train Users

The final step in the process is training the users of the program. As in developing the application, you will want to follow a logical and progressive format in training your users. If they are unfamiliar with Q&A, you will want them to gain an understanding of the features outlined in Chapter 2, "Q&A Basics." You can begin instructing them in the specifics of your application as you are training them in the add, search, and reporting features of Q&A.

Refine as Needed

Q&A makes it very easy to modify databases after they are developed. So, if changes need to be made or users suggest improvements, you can easily make them as they arise.

FILE DESIGN FEATURES

Design a File

1. Press **F** for File and **D** for Design.
2. Type the new filename and press Enter. Begin designing the file.
3. To save the design, press F10.
4. Type your Field Format specs and press F10.
5. Select your Global Format specs and press F10.

Use the Options Menu

1. Once inside the Design a File screen, press F8 and select the desired option.

WRITE

Create a Document

1. Press **W** for Write and **T** for Type/edit.
2. Enter text.

Get a Document

1. Press **W** for Write and **G** for Get.
2. Press F4 twice and press Enter.
3. Move the cursor down to the desired file and press Enter.

Define the Page

1. From within the document, press Ctrl-F6.
2. Change the margins.
3. Press F10 to save your settings.

Spell-Check a Document

1. From within the document, press Shift-F1 and follow the instructions.

Save a Document

1. From within the document, press Shift-F8.
2. Type a filename and press Enter.

Print a Document

1. From within the document, press F2.
2. Adjust the print options as needed and press F10.

INTELLIGENT ASSISTANT

Access Query Guide

1. Press **A** for Assistant and **Q** for Query Guide.
2. Type the filename and press Enter.
3. Make your requests and press Esc twice to return to the Main menu.

IN
BUSINESS

Q&A Basics

In this chapter you will learn the basic features of the File, Write, and Intelligent Assistant modules.

Overview

If you are unfamiliar with Q&A, you should complete all the examples in this chapter. This is important because the following chapters assume that you know the basic features presented in Chapter 2. On the other hand, if you have used Q&A in the past—for example, in building databases, conducting searches, developing reports, or writing letters—you probably don't need to complete all the examples in this chapter. If you are not sure how much you know, I recommend that you browse the entire chapter and then complete the examples that cover unfamiliar features.

As Chapter 1 mentioned, this book is divided into three sections: how to design your applications, how to perform Q&A's basic features, and how to change specific applications while you are learning the more advanced features. This entire process can be likened to remodeling different rooms in a house. Before you begin remodeling, you develop blueprints. Once the blueprints are done, you learn the basics of construction: sawing, hammering, etc. With the basic skills mastered, you begin remodeling the rooms.

This book works in much the same way. In Chapter 1, you should have designed your applications (developed your blueprints). In this chapter you will learn the basics of Q&A (how to saw, hammer, etc.). Lastly, each of the remaining chapters will guide you through modifying various applications (remodeling different rooms in the house) while teaching you the more advanced features of Q&A.

By following the examples in this chapter, you will end up with a simple Cardfile (Rolodex) application and a solid understanding of Q&A's basic features. This application will allow you to quickly find someone's name and number, mail letters to several people at once, and print a phone directory. Specifically, the examples will guide you through developing a database containing fields that correspond to a typical business card, creating two phone list reports, and creating a letter and macro to print the phone list. Also, you will learn how to use the Intelligent Assistant's Query Guide to ask plain English questions of your database (for example, how many organizations in California are in the insurance business?).

What Is Q&A?

Before you begin developing the application, read this section to gain an overview of Q&A and the concepts of application development. Q&A is an integrated program consisting of three modules: File, Write (word processing), and the Intelligent Assistant. Most people buy Q&A because it is easy to use and quite powerful—which are not qualities normally associated with the same program.

Q&A's *File* module is where you will probably be spending most of your time. It is through this module that you will create databases that will contain the necessary data to automate your organization. In the world of databases, there are two primary file structures: flat-file and relational. Q&A uses the flat-file structure. In a *flat-file* structure, information is stored in separate files. In a *relational* structure, information is stored in separate tables linked by a common ID number. It is much easier to develop an application with a flat-file database, and it is also easier to use a flat-file database. For most organizations, a flat-file database will fulfill all of the organization's needs. Relational databases are normally used for sophisticated and complex applications that require the added flexibility of the database's programming language.

Q&A's *Write* module is used for word processing. With Release 4.0 of Q&A, Symantec has incorporated features into the program that greatly expand its usefulness. Some of the new features that I find valuable are document previewing (the ability to preview a document before you print it), file importing and exporting to other word processors, and expanded page formatting. You can also use the word processor to perform mass mailings and generate mailing labels.

With Q&A's *Intelligent Assistant* (IA), you will be able to ask plain English questions of your databases. This feature is particularly useful if you are new to computers and want to find out some specific information. For example, you could ask

- Which company bought the most fasteners from us in 1990?
- Which ten clients generated the most fee income in the last six months?
- How many inventory items are below the minimum level?
- Which staff members are due for a raise?
- How many hourly workers have exceeded their sick time allotment?

As you can see from this list, the possibilities are endless. To use the Intelligent Assistant (IA), all you have to do is "teach" Q&A about your database. This consists of answering questions that Q&A asks about your database. Once this process is complete, you can ask questions at any time. You can even use the IA to enter data and print reports.

What Is an Application?

The word "application" has taken on a lot of meanings in the wonderful world of computer jargon. Almost everyone has a slightly different meaning for it. In this book, the term *application* means a collection of one or more related databases, reports, merge letters, and macros, tied together through a common set of menus that automate some particular business process or function. All of these items—databases, reports, macros, and menus—are the building blocks or components of an application (these terms will be fully explained soon).

The fundamental and essential component of an application is the *database*. Without it you do not have an application. However, you can have an application without the other components. Using the remodeling metaphor, a building with one room and a building with twenty rooms can both be called houses. The only difference between the two is the number and/or size of the rooms (components). The same principle applies to applications. Thus, it is the adding of the other components (reports, macros, and menus) that makes an application really useful.

The database is where information is stored. A database can also be referred to as a *database file*, or just a file. The actual screen that you see on your computer monitor is called the *database form*, or just form. When you look at a form, such as the one shown in Figure 2.1, you will notice that there are places to type information. For example, after COMPANY NAME there are blank spaces. These empty spaces are called *fields*, and the name of the field (here, COMPANY NAME) is called the *field label*.

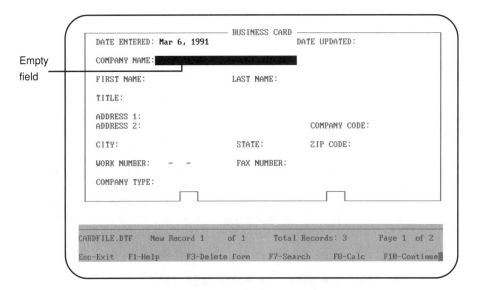

Figure 2.1   Database form with empty fields.

When the fields in a database form are filled in, the fields are collectively referred to as a *record*. Figure 2.2 shows a sample record. Some records may contain more information than others. However, as long as the form contains some information, it is considered a record—although it may be an incomplete record.

The next component of an application is a *report*. In Q&A any type of printed output, other than a letter or mailing label, is considered a report. Q&A offers three types of reports: columnar, form, and cross-tab. In this chapter you will develop and print a columnar report (Figure 2.3) and a form report (Figure 2.4), and in a later chapter you will develop and print a cross-tab report.

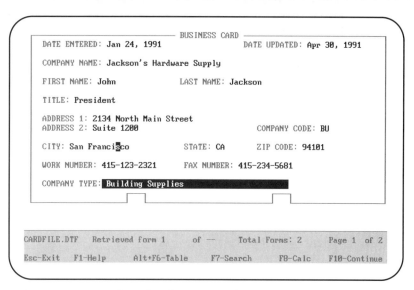

┌──────────────────────── BUSINESS CARD ────────────────────────┐
DATE ENTERED: Jan 24, 1991   DATE UPDATED: Apr 30, 1991

COMPANY NAME: Jackson's Hardware Supply

FIRST NAME: John   LAST NAME: Jackson

TITLE: President

ADDRESS 1: 2134 North Main Street
ADDRESS 2: Suite 1200   COMPANY CODE: BU

CITY: San Francisco   STATE: CA   ZIP CODE: 94101

WORK NUMBER: 415-123-2321   FAX NUMBER: 415-234-5681

COMPANY TYPE: Building Supplies

CARDFILE.DTF   Retrieved form 1   of --   Total Forms: 2   Page 1 of 2

Esc-Exit   F1-Help   Alt+F6-Table   F7-Search   F8-Calc   F10-Continue

Figure 2.2   Complete database record.

```
JAN 21, 1991                    LIST OF PROSPECTS                     PAGE 1

FIRST    LAST    COMPANY              TITLE       ADDRESS          ADD A       CITY             STATE   ZIP
-------  ------  --------------------  ---------  ---------------  ----------  ---------------  -----  -----
John     Jackson Jackson's Hardware   President  2134 North Main  Suite 1200  San Francisco    CA     94101


=====  =======  ======  ====================  ===========  ==============  =========  =========  =====  =====
Count:                                             1
```

Figure 2.3   Basic columnar report.

Macros are used to speed up repetitive tasks. Recording and running macros is easy. All you have to do is set the macro recording feature to ON, designate a macro identifier (such as Alt-S), record the desired keystrokes, and save the macro. Then when you press the macro identifier, the keystrokes are replayed. Macros are great timesavers.

```
    MAR  12, 1991              PHONE LIST              PAGE 1



    Jackson's Hardware Supply        415-123-2321
    John       Jackson               President
    2131 North Main Street           Suite 1200
    San Francisco                    CA    94101
    Wholesale building supplies
```

Figure 2.4   Basic form report.

Another component of an application is the *merge letter*. This type of letter is linked to a specific database and pulls data from the database and places the data in the letter. As you will notice in Figure 2.5, specific fields are placed in the letter. They are denoted by an asterisk on either side of the field, *FIRST NAME*. This tells Q&A where to place the variable data from the database when the merge is performed. Figure 2.6 shows you what a letter would look like after the merge. If you look back at Figure 2.2, you can see that Q&A pulled the information right from the Cardfile database.

```
            December 12, 1991



            *FIRST NAME*  *LAST NAME*
            *TITLE*
            *COMPANY NAME*
            *ADDRESS 1*
            *ADDRESS 2*
            *CITY*, *STATE* *ZIP CODE*

            Dear *FIRST NAME*:



            I am writing to explain...

  ⌊⌊⌊⌊⌊⌊⌊⌊1[s⌊⌊T⌊⌊⌊⌊2⌊⌊⌊⌊T⌊⌊⌊3⌊⌊⌊⌊T■⌊⌊4⌊⌊T⌊⌊⌊⌊5⌊⌊⌊⌊⌊⌊⌊6⌊⌊⌊⌊⌊⌊J⌊7⌊⌊⌊⌊⌊⌊
  MERGE.LET                       Ins  0 %  27  Line 16 of Page 1 of 1

  Esc-Exit  F1-Help  F2-Print  Shift+F7-Restore   F7-Search  F8-Options  ↑F8-Save
```

Figure 2.5   Merge letter.

```
December 12, 1991


John Jackson
President
Jackson's Hardware Supply
2131 North Main Street
Suite 1200
San Francisco, CA 94101

Dear John:


I am writing to explain...



Sincerely



Bill Bradshaw
```

Figure 2.6   Personalized letter after merge.

The last component of an application is a *menu*. By defining menus, you can tie all your databases, reports, and macros together into a cohesive and integrated system, making the application much easier to use. A menu is nothing more than an electronic list that contains the tasks you want to perform. To choose a menu item, move the cursor to the item you want and press Enter. These tasks can include opening a database, printing a report, or running a macro.

The guiding factors in determining which components you need in your applications are the complexity and the scope of the business process you are automating. If you are automating a simple task, such as the electronic Cardfile described in this chapter, the components are few. On the other hand, if you automate an entire order entry/inventory/invoicing process, such as the one covered in Chapter 6, the components are many. The best way to approach the issue is to let it grow organically. As you need a feature or function, add it.

Configuration

Before you can complete the examples in this and future chapters, you will have to install Q&A, load the application programs from the disk enclosed with this book, and install at least one printer. To install Q&A, refer to the section of the Q&A manual that covers installation of the program or see Appendix A, "Installation." To install the application programs and a printer, follow the instructions in the next section.

Load the Files from the Enclosed Disk

Loading the files from the disk that accompanies this book will consist of three tasks: making two subdirectories (FILE and WORD) under your QA directory, copying the files to the FILE subdirectory, and uncompressing the distribution file that contains the application files within the FILE subdirectory. This procedure assumes that you have already loaded Q&A into the subdirectory QA on your hard drive.

> ⊘ **Caution:** Loading the files from the enclosed disk needs to be done only once. If you have completed this procedure while reading Appendix A, "Installation," skip this procedure.

Loading the Files from the Enclosed Disk

1. Insert the disk accompanying this book into floppy drive A and shut the door.

2. Change to the C drive by typing **c:** and pressing Enter.

3. Change to the root directory by typing **cd\qa** and pressing Enter.

4. Type **md word** and press Enter to create the first subdirectory.

5. Type **md file** and press Enter to create the second subdirectory.

6. Type **md temp** and press Enter to create the third subdirectory.

7. Switch to the File subdirectory by typing **cd\qa\file** and pressing Enter.

8. Copy the file DATA.EXE to the File subdirectory by typing **copy a:data.exe** and pressing Enter.

9. Uncompress the data files by typing **data** and pressing Enter.

10. Switch to the WORD subdirectory by typing **cd\qa\word** and pressing Enter.

11. Copy the file WORD.COM to the WORD subdirectory by typing **copy a:word.com** and pressing Enter.

12. Uncompress the word processing data files by typing **word** and pressing Enter.

13. Switch to the QA subdirectory by typing **cd\qa** and pressing Enter.

> ⊘ **Caution:** If you already have created macros in Q&A and stored them in the macro file QAMACRO.ASC, you will have to rename this file. To do so, go to step 14. If you have not created any macros, skip step 14 and go to step 15.

14. If you have existing macros stored in the file QAMACRO.ASC, then rename the file by typing **ren qamacro.asc qamacro.old** and pressing Enter.

15. Copy the macro file QAMACRO.ASC to the QA subdirectory by typing **copy a:qamacro.asc** and pressing Enter.

16. Start Q&A by typing **qa** and pressing Enter.

17. You will now tell Q&A where your files are stored. Press **U** for Utilities and press Enter. Press **S** for Set Global Defaults and press Enter.

18. This will place you in the Global Options screen. Type **word** for the path of the Document files. Type **file** for the path of the Database files and **temp** for the location of the Temporary files.

19. In order to follow the examples throughout the book, you must set the Automatic Execution option to Yes in the Utilities menu. If you haven't already done so, change Automatic Execution to Yes.

20. When you are through, press F10 to save your changes.

21. Press Esc twice to return to the Q&A Main menu.

By setting your menus to Automatic Execution, you can easily progress through each menu simply by pressing the first key of the menu item. The Q&A Main menu is shown in Figure 2.7. To practice, press **F** for File and you will be taken to the File menu shown in Figure 2.8. Then press **D** for Design and you will be taken to the Design menu shown in Figure 2.9. Press Esc twice to return to the Main menu.

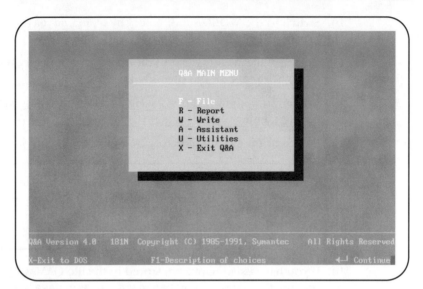

Figure 2.7   Q&A Main menu.

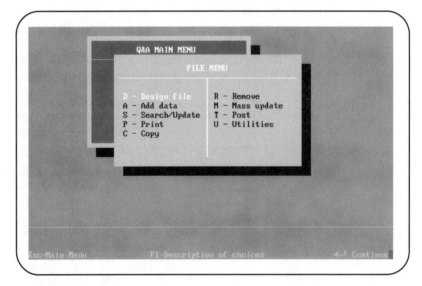

Figure 2.8   File menu.

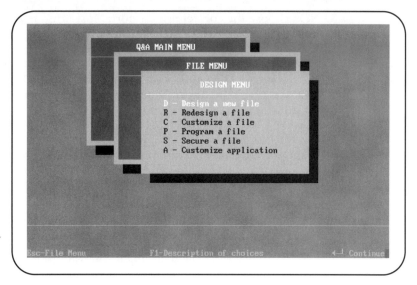

Figure 2.9   Design menu.

Installing a Printer

Before you can print reports and letters, you have to install a printer. If you have not already done so, install a printer using the following procedure.

Installing a Printer

1. From the Q&A Main menu, press **U** for Utilities and **P** for Printers. You are now at the Printer Selection menu.

Beginner's Tip

Q&A gives you the option of setting up five different printer configurations. This can be either five different printers or one or more printers configured differently. The second option is most likely. Say you have a laser printer. You can print in one of two ways: *portrait* (normal orientation) or *landscape* (sideways). Q&A will let you set up Printer A as portrait and Printer B as landscape. So if you have wide reports, simply select Printer B. This concept is similar to the way you configure dot matrix printers. You could configure Printer A as draft quality and Printer B as letter quality.

2. Choose Printer A and press Enter.

3. Next choose the correct printer port. Most printers are parallel and use LPT1. If this is the case, press Enter.

 Beginner's Tip

Printer ports are physical outlets on the back of your computer. Parallel ports are LPT1 and LPT2. Serial ports are COM1, COM2, and COM3. If you are unsure whether your printer is parallel or serial, consult the manual for your printer.

4. You should now see a list of printer manufacturers. Use the cursor to move to the manufacturer of your printer and press Enter.

5. Q&A displays a list of printer models. Use the cursor keys to move to the correct model and press Enter.

6. A menu will appear asking if you want to change the special options. You don't need to bother with this menu, so press Enter.

7. Lastly, you will see a menu asking if you want to install another printer. Select Yes if you want to add another printer and No if you are through.

8. When you are through, press Esc to return to the Main menu.

File Module

As mentioned earlier, the File module is where you will probably be doing most of your work. The next sections will teach you how to develop and manipulate a simple database that can be used to hold your business cards.

File Design Features

The basic file design features are the features you will use whenever you develop or change a database. These consist of drawing the database, designing the file and creating fields, and formatting the fields you have created.

Draw the Database

The first step in developing a new database is to *draw it on paper*. Placing the necessary fields on paper gives you the opportunity to see just what the screen will look like *before* you begin entering data. This simple task will save you time and grief later on. In the examples of this section, you will be guided through the development of a specific database rather than developing one from scratch. Thus, there is nothing to design first. However, you can personalize the Cardfile application if you wish to. To do this, make a copy of Figure 2.10. Then add any fields you need and remove any that don't apply.

You will notice in Figure 2.10 that there are numbers in each of the fields. These numbers represent how long each field should be.

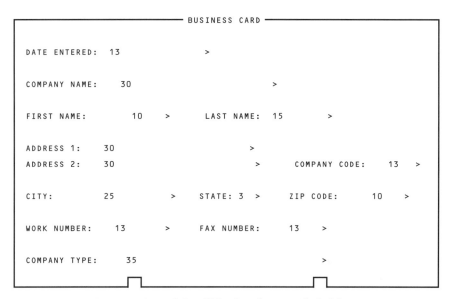

Figure 2.10   Drawing of Cardfile database with field spaces.

If you are not sure about all the fields you want on your database, don't worry. Q&A makes it very easy to go back and add fields later.

Design a File

Q&A refers to developing a database as *designing a file*. This book uses both terms interchangeably. With your paper design in hand, you are ready to begin developing the database.

> **Note:** All examples begin at the Q&A Main menu, unless otherwise noted.

Practice Designing a File

1. Press **F** for File, **D** for Design, and **D** for Design a New File.

2. Q&A will prompt you for a filename. Type **CARDFILE** and press Enter. This will leave you at a blank design screen.

> **Note:** Those of you who are familiar with Q&A or with database development in general may want to develop the application differently from what is suggested here. Feel free to do so.

3. If necessary, press Home three times to move to the top of the screen.

4. Press F8 to bring up the Options menu. Press **A** for Align Text and **C** for Center.

5. Type **BUSINESS CARD** and press Enter. This will be the title of your database.

6. Press Home twice to move to the top of the screen.

7. Press F8 to bring up the Options menu. Press **L** for Lay Out Page and **D** for Draw.

8. You are now in Draw mode, and you will draw lines from either side of the screen to the title in the center of the screen. Use the Left Arrow key ← and draw a line. Stop one space before the *B* in *BUSINESS*.

Beginner's Tip

The *Line Draw* feature, which you just used, lets you draw lines anywhere on the screen. As you found out, you can draw single lines by using the arrow keys, and the lines are drawn in the direction of the arrows. If you have a 101 keyboard, press the Num Lock key and use the arrows on the number pad to draw double lines. To erase a line, press the F8 key again and use the cursor keys to erase lines. To put the pen back into Draw mode, press F8. To move the pen to another spot on the screen without drawing lines, press F6 to pick up the pen. Move to where you want to draw lines and press F6 again to put down the pen and continue drawing.

9. Press F6 to turn the pen up and move one space past the *D* in *CARD* and press F6 again to turn the pen down.

10. Draw to the end of the screen and press F10 to exit from draw mode.

Beginner's Tip

The two features you just used, *Align Text* and *Line Draw*, were chosen from the *Options menu*. To bring up the Options menu, which is shown in Figure 2.11, press F8. This menu displays submenus, each with its own set of commands. Some of the commands can be executed only through this menu, while others can be executed by pressing the appropriate function key combinations. If an item appears faint, it is not available in this section of the program. Take time to look at each menu item and become familiar with the various options.

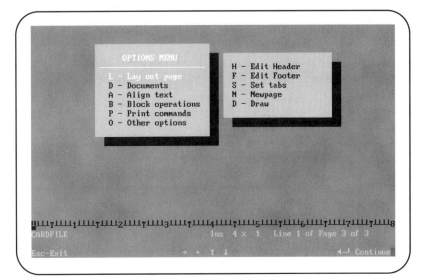

Figure 2.11   Options menu.

11. Press Home twice to move to the top of the screen.

12. Press the Down Arrow key two times, and press the Tab key to move to the first tab marker. It is here that you will begin entering fields.

Remember that a field holds a specific type of information, such
as the last name. In Q&A, *field definition* consists of placing a
: (colon) to indicate the start of the field and a > (greater-than
symbol) to indicate the end of the field. The distance between
these two symbols is the amount of space (the number of characters)
that you have for entering data.

13. Type the field name (including the colon) **COMPANY NAME:** and
    press the Spacebar 30 times. Signify the end of the field by typing >
    (greater-than).

14. Continue to type the rest of the fields as they appear in Figure 2.10.
    The number that appears in each field indicates the number of
    spaces in the field length.

15. Once you have added all the fields to the form, draw lines around
    the form as they appear in Figure 2.10. Press F8, **L** for Lay Out Page,
    and **D** for Draw. Draw the lines and press F10 when you are
    through.

16. Press PgDn to move to the second screen. Press the Tab key once to
    move to the first Tab marker and type **REMARKS**.

17. Press F8 to bring up the Options menu and press **L** for Lay Out
    Text and **D** for Draw.

18. Draw a single line from the space after the *S* in *REMARKS* to the end
    of the screen.

19. Press F6 to turn the pen up and move to the right side of the
    screen. Draw a line, stopping one space before the *R* in *REMARKS*.

20. Press F10 to exit Draw mode and press Home to move to the right
    side of the screen.

21. Press the Down Arrow key twice and type a colon (:).

22. Press the Down Arrow key 17 times and press the End key to move
    to the left side of the screen. Type a greater-than symbol (>) and
    press Enter. You have just created a one-page field. It starts at the
    colon at the top left side of the screen and ends at the greater-than
    symbol at the bottom left side of the screen. This will give you an
    entire page for Remarks.

23. With your cursor on the last line of screen 2, press F8, **L** for Lay Out Page, and **D** for Draw.

24. Draw a line the length of the page. When you are through, press F10 to exit the Line Draw mode. The second screen should look like Figure 2.12, and the first screen should look like Figure 2.10.

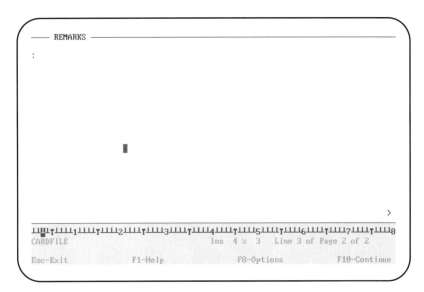

Figure 2.12   Completed REMARKS screen.

25. Press F10 to save the design. In the next section you will learn how to format your fields.

| You can have up to ten screens per database.

Format Fields

With your database completed, you are ready to format the fields. By pressing F10 in the last section, you were left with the Format Options menu on the screen. Your screen should look like Figure 2.13. Table 2.1 shows your formatting options, and Figure 2.14 shows the formatted fields.

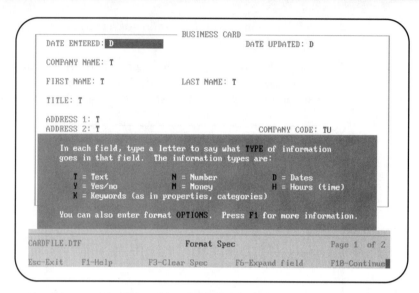

Figure 2.13   Cardfile screen with Format menu.

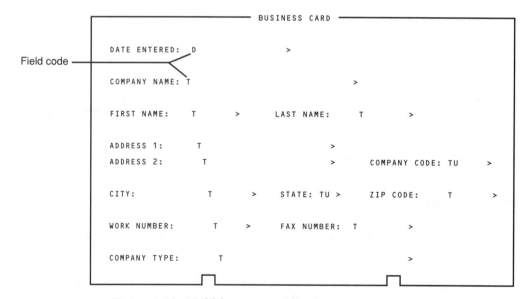

Figure 2.14   Field format specifications.

Table 2.1 Options for Format Options Menu.

Code	Type	Description
T	Text	Alphanumeric data (numbers and text)
TU	Text	Uppercase text
N	Number	Numbers only
D	Date	Dates only
M	Money	Adds dollar signs and commas to numbers
H	Hours	Time only
Y	Yes/No	Y or N; Yes or No only
K	Keyword	Alphanumeric values separated by semicolons

A *Text field* allows you to enter both text and numbers. It is also the default for all fields. So unless you specify another format, your field will be saved as a Text field. A field formatted as *Number* can contain only numbers—no text or symbols can be entered. Thus, you would format a phone number field as Text because of the dashes. The *Date field* holds only dates. You can choose from 20 different date formats in the Global Format Options screen, which is shown in Figure 2.15.

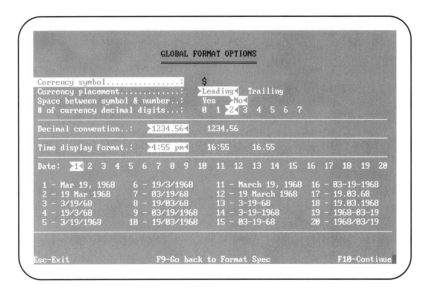

Figure 2.15 Global Format Options screen.

Formatting a field as *Money* causes any numbers placed in that field to have a dollar sign and commas added. The *Hours field* is used for formatting time fields. For a true/false field, use the *Yes/No field*. The last field type is the *Keyword field*. This field allows you to enter multiple values into one field and then search within that field for all records having one or more of the values in that particular key field. Each of the items in a Key field must be separated by semicolons, for example, `skiing;biking;sewing;`.

Beginner's Tip

Place similar items together in the same key field.

26. Place the letter that corresponds to the field type in each field. You can use Figure 2.14 as a guide.

27. When you are through formatting the fields, press F10 to bring up the Global Format Options menu. This menu is used to format the date, time, and money fields. Make your selections and press F10 to save your choices.

You have now completed the basic development and formatting of the Cardfile database. The next section will guide you through customizing the database.

Customize the File

With the basic database structure completed, you can customize it to suit your specific needs. Using the remodeling metaphor again, you have erected the basic walls but haven't yet carpeted, painted, or added the other amenities that make a room truly livable.

Figure 2.16 shows the Customize menu. This menu contains seven options for personalizing a database to your exact needs. I will cover four of the options: Format Values, Set Initial Values, Speed Up Searches, and Change Palette. The rest of the options will be covered only briefly here, but later chapters will cover them in-depth.

The *Restrict Values option* lets you restrict the values that a person can enter into a field. For instance, if you wanted specific codes entered into the COMPANY CODE field, you would enter the allowable codes through this option. Once the codes were entered, whenever a data entry operator came to that field all that he or she would have to do is press Alt-F7 and a window would pop up showing the available options.

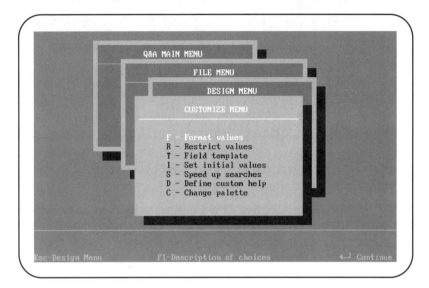

Figure 2.16   Customize menu.

To speed up data entry time, you can use the *Field Template* feature. With this option, you can format a telephone number field to automatically place the dashes in the right place or allow only numbers or text into a field.

The *Define Custom Help* feature allows you to display specific information about a particular field when the F1 key is pressed during data entry. Suppose you wanted to explain what the COMPANY CODE field is used for. You could use this option to enter your explanation. Later, if someone were unsure about which type of data to enter in the field, the person would simply press the F1 key while in this field and the explanation you typed would appear.

Format Values

The *Format Values option* lets you change the format of a field at any time without redesigning the database. It is the same option that is invoked when you are through designing a database. The details of the option were explained earlier in the section "Design a File." To change the field formats, carry out the following steps.

Practice Changing the Field Formats

1. Press **F** for File, **D** for Design, and **C** for Customize.

2. Type the name of the file you want to customize, in this case **CARDFILE**, and press Enter.

3. Press **F** for Format Values.

4. You now see the Format Spec screen superimposed on your database. Simply type the letter that corresponds to the desired field type for each field. When you are through, press F10 to save your format selections.

5. If you specified a date or time field, the Global Format Options screen will appear. It is here that you designate date, time, and money formats. Make any adjustments and press F10 to save all your format changes.

6. To return to the Main menu, press Esc three times.

Set Initial Values

The *Set Initial Values* feature allows you to automatically assign a number, the date, or the time to any field in your database. The commands for these functions are @number to assign a number, @date to assign the date, and @time to assign the time. You place these commands in the appropriate fields in the Set Initial Values section of Q&A. Then each time you add a new record, Q&A displays a number, the date, or the time in the field that contains the command. These commands work only when you are in Add mode; that is, if you later update a record, the number, date, or time in a particular field will not be changed unless you change it.

An appropriate use of the @number command would be a situation where you wanted to automatically give each invoice a unique number. You would simply navigate to the Customize menu and select Set Initial Values. Then you would proceed to the invoice number field and type **@number** into the field. Each time you entered a new invoice, Q&A would assign a new number to that invoice.

In the Cardfile database, you created a DATE ENTERED field. Using the Set Initial Values option, you will instruct Q&A to automatically enter the date for you each time you add a new record.

Practice Using the Set Initial Values Option to Automatically Enter a Date in a New Record

1. Press **F** for File, **D** for Design, and C for Customize.

2. Type the filename **CARDFILE** and press Enter.

3. Press **I** for Set Initial Values.

4. Move to the DATE ENTERED field (you should already be in it) and type **@date** and press F10 to save the Initial Values spec.

5. Press Esc three times to return to the Main menu.

Speed up Searches

If you are familiar with programming jargon, speeding up searches is the same as indexing a field. Q&A refers to indexing a field as *designating a speedy field*. When you designate a speedy field, and then look for a record using that speedy field, the record will be found four times faster than if the field weren't designated as speedy.

Once you have records in your database, you will find that you regularly locate particular records. To do this, you have to initiate a search (searches will be covered later in this chapter). When you search for a record, you move to a field, such as LAST NAME, and type the last name you are looking for. Q&A will look through all the records in the database and find the records that match your request. If you designated LAST NAME as a speedy field, the records will be found much faster than if the field were not a speedy field.

You will want to designate as a speedy field those fields that will be used most often for searches. In the Cardfile database, we will be designating FIRST NAME, LAST NAME, and COMPANY NAME as speedy fields because these are the fields you will most often use to find specific records.

Each time you designate a speedy field (index a field), Q&A places it in a special file known as an *index file*. This file works in much the same way as a book index. In a book index, the key word is listed along with the corresponding page. In a Q&A index file, the speedy field is listed along with the location of the record. This is why searches are so much faster using speedy fields.

To designate a speedy field, move to the Customize menu, choose Speed Up Searches, proceed to the field you want to designate as speedy, and type **S** or **SU** in the appropriate fields. If you type S in a field, the field is a regular speedy field. Typing SU means that each value in that field has to be unique. You would use the SU designation in an ID NUMBER field where every record must have a unique number.

Shortcut

Every time you develop a database, Q&A creates two files. The data and structure are held in the file with the .DTF extension, and the indexes are held in the file with the .IDX extension.

To designate the FIRST NAME, LAST NAME, and COMPANY NAME fields as speedy fields, use the following procedure.

Practice Designating Speedy Fields

1. Press **F** for File, **D** for Design, and **C** for Customize.

2. Type the filename **CARDFILE** and press Enter.

3. Press **S** for Speed Up Searches.

4. Move to the COMPANY NAME field and type **S**, move to the FIRST NAME field and type **S**, and move to the LAST NAME field and type **S**. Your screen should look like Figure 2.17.

5. Press F10 to save your specifications.

6. Press Esc three times to return to the Main menu.

Change Palette

Q&A lets you change the appearance of your database screens. There are seven different palettes to choose from. If you have a monochrome monitor, these options will give you various combinations of reverse video, underlined fields, and normal text. If you have a color monitor, you can choose from seven different color combinations.

Practice Changing the Palette on the Cardfile Database

1. Press **F** for File, **D** for Design, and **C** for Customize.

2. Type the filename **CARDFILE** and press Enter.

3. Press **C** for Change Palette.

4. Use F8 to toggle forward through your options and F6 to toggle back through your options, choosing a palette you like.

5. When you have found one you like, press F10 to save your selection.

6. Press Esc three times to return to the Main menu.

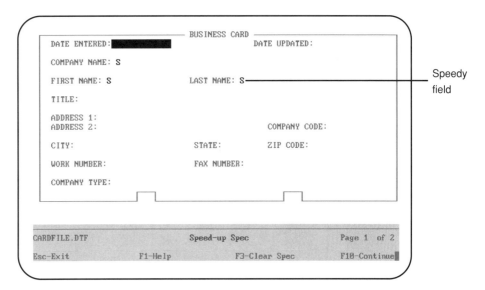

Figure 2.17   *Cardfile database with speedy fields designated.*

Redesign a File

Very few applications are designed and developed perfectly the first time. Thus, after an application has been in use for a while, it often needs to be refined. This fact leads us to one of the biggest benefits of using Q&A: the ability to quickly and easily change the database design, even if it contains records. When you need to store more data in a particular file, you can simply switch to Redesign mode and add the necessary fields.

⊘ **Caution:** There are two things you must be careful of when you redesign a file. First, make sure that you do not shorten any fields still containing data. If your address field is 30 characters long and you shorten it 5 spaces, you have just chopped off the last 5 characters of the address. Second, and this is more critical, make sure that you don't accidentally erase a field by deleting the field identifier. This will happen if you delete the two letters immediately following the colon in any field. Q&A assigns these letters to every field so that it can keep track of them. In Figure 2.18 notice that each field has two letters after the colon. These are the field identifiers.

Field identifier ———

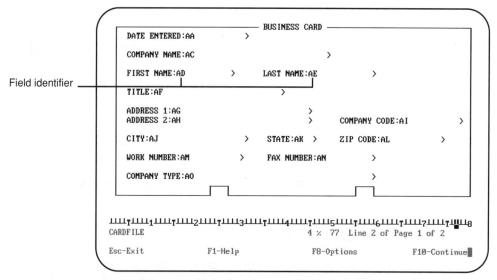

Figure 2.18   Cardfile database with field identifiers.

If you make changes that you did not intend while you are redesigning a file, simply press the Esc key and answer Yes to abandon your changes. This will allow you to start over.

Practice Redesigning a File

1. Press **F** for File, **D** for Design, and **R** for Redesign.

2. Type the filename **CARDFILE** and press Enter. You are now in Redesign mode.

3. Make sure that the Insert key is OFF.

4. Move to the same line as the field DATE ENTERED.

5. Press the Right Arrow key 48 times.

6. Type the field name **DATE UPDATED:** (don't forget the colon) and press the Spacebar 13 times. Type a greater-than symbol (>). Your screen should look like Figure 2.19.

7. Press F10 to save your design.

8. Press Enter and type a **D** in the DATE UPDATED field to format it as a date field.

9. Press F10 to save the Format spec and press F10 to exit the Global Format Options screen.

10. Press Esc to return to the Main menu.

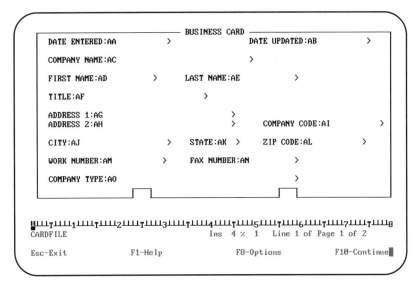

Figure 2.19   Cardfile database with DATE UPDATED field.

Program a File

Figure 2.20 shows the Programming menu. Notice that the menu contains several choices designed to relieve you of tedious tasks; that is, you can instruct Q&A to perform designated tasks so that you don't have to. In this section you'll learn about the first three menu items: Edit Lookup Table, Program Form (write simple programming statements), and Field Navigation (navigate between fields). The last two items, Read Only Fields and Set Field Names, will be described in later chapters.

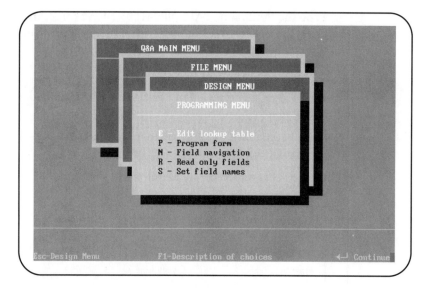

Figure 2.20   Programming menu.

Programming Statements

Often times, just being able to enter data into a database does not adequately automate a chosen task. To improve the effectiveness of the application, you may have to add programming statements to various fields in the database. This way Q&A can perform the tedious and time-consuming functions that you would otherwise have to perform manually. A *programming statement* is a group of commands, field identifiers, and numbers arranged in a specific syntax designed to produce some specific result, such as calculate year-end bonuses based on total yearly sales.

Q&A offers two different types of programming: form programming and navigation programming. With *form programming*, you instruct Q&A how to manipulate your data. For example, you might instruct Q&A how to automatically fill in a date field, calculate commissions, total an invoice, or determine the interest due on a loan; the possibilities are endless. In *navigation programming*, you tell Q&A how to move through the form. For example, you might want the cursor to move from the SALARY field to the SALARY BONUS field if the SALES field is greater than $100,000. Navigation programming lets you control which fields the cursor should move to next, based on the values in other fields.

> ► **Note:** You can combine form and navigation programming statements in the Program spec. However, if you plan to use Q&A for Macintosh and you want the data files to be compatible, you have to separate the programming statements from the navigation statements.

Before you begin writing programming statements, you need an overview of Q&A programming terminology and concepts. Writing programming statements is just like writing in another language: you must follow specific rules and syntax. After reading the information presented in this section, you should be able to immediately begin writing simple programming statements. Learning to write complex programming statements will take a little longer.

Unlike other database programs (dBASE III or Paradox), Q&A does not have a programming or procedural language. In Q&A you place the programming statements directly into the fields by using a special screen called the *Program spec*. This method can produce very powerful results and is much easier to implement than the methods used in other database programs. Since you are placing the programming statements in the actual fields, the fields that you have on your form are very important. In fact, you may even have fields on your form that do nothing more than hold programming statements.

To illustrate some of the programming concepts, I am going to use a portion of another database, rather than the Cardfile database, because it will allow me to display more complex programming statements. It is a Personnel Bonus database designed to calculate year-end bonuses. You can see this database in Figure 2.21.

```
                        * PERSONNEL BONUS RECORD *
     FIRST NAME: Bill                        LAST NAME: Smith


     TITLE: Senior Sale Rep                  HOME NUMBER: 415-478-2345


     ADDRESS 1:   245 West Covina


     CITY: Tiburon             STATE: CA    ZIP CODE:  93949



     HIRE DATE: 12/23/87       SOCIAL SECURITY: 456-90-4234


     STARTING SALARY: $18,000  CURRENT SALARY:  $28,000


     TOTAL SALES:              BONUS RATE:


     BONUS AMOUNT:
```

Figure 2.21   Personnel Bonus database.

The main purpose of this database is to calculate the year-end bonuses for the sales reps and to generate a report from which the accounting department can write the bonus checks. The way the database operates is that the user retrieves each sales rep's record and enters the rep's total sales for the year and the bonus percentage. Q&A then calculates the bonus amount.

To set up the database so that it calculates the bonuses, you must assign field numbers and enter a programming statement, as shown in Figure 2.22. In the TOTAL SALES field, enter **#1** (also known as an *expression*—more on this soon). In the BONUS RATE field, enter **#2**. In the BONUS AMOUNT field, enter the programming statement: **#3: if #1 > $99,000 then #3 = #1 * #2**. This means that if the value in the TOTAL SALES field is greater than $99,000, make the BONUS AMOUNT field equal to the value in the TOTAL SALES multiplied by the value in the BONUS RATE field. Figure 2.22 shows you the programming statement, and Figure 2.23 shows the completed record.

```
                    * PERSONNEL BONUS RECORD *
    FIRST NAME:                            LAST NAME:

    TITLE:                                 HOME NUMBER:

    ADDRESS 1:

    CITY:                    STATE:        ZIP CODE:


    HIRE DATE:               SOCIAL SECURITY:

    STARTING SALARY:         CURRENT SALARY:

    TOTAL SALES: #1          BONUS RATE: #2

    BONUS AMOUNT:  #3: if #1 > $99,000 then #3 = #1 * #2
```

Figure 2.22   Personnel database with programming statement.

```
                    * PERSONNEL BONUS RECORD *
    FIRST NAME: Bill                       LAST NAME: Smith

    TITLE: Senior Sale Rep                 HOME NUMBER: 415-478-2345

    ADDRESS 1:  245 West Covina

    CITY: Tiburon            STATE: CA     ZIP CODE:  93949


    HIRE DATE: 12/23/87      SOCIAL SECURITY: 456-90-4234

    STARTING SALARY: $18,000 CURRENT SALARY:  $28,000

    TOTAL SALES: $100,000    BONUS RATE: 10

    BONUS AMOUNT: $10,000
```

Figure 2.23   Completed Personnel record.

When you develop programming statements, it is good practice to begin by numbering all the fields that will be used in the programming statements. The reason for this is that Q&A processes programming statements in numerical field order. That is, the value in field #1 is processed before field #2, and so on, even if field #1 appears later in the form. The ramifications of this are significant. If you will be writing programming statements that rely on the values generated by other programming statements, you have to make sure that the fields are numbered so that the earlier statements are processed before the later ones.

The next issue to consider is how you want your programming statements executed. Q&A gives you three methods. The first method is to have Q&A calculate ALL the programming statements in the entire database EVERY TIME your cursor leaves a field. This method is known as *automatic calculation* and is fine if you have only one or two programming statements. But if you have several, it slows down data entry time considerably.

The second method is to press the F8 key (also known as the Calc key) after you are done entering data and have Q&A calculate all the programming statements at once. This method, known as *manual mode*, is recommended if you have many programming statements. Both of these methods are set from within Q&A's Add or Search/Update mode. Once set, they stay in effect until changed. The default mode is manual. To change it to automatic, open a database, press Shift-F8, and change to automatic.

The third calculation method, known as *individual calculation*, is designated in the programming statement itself and allows you to execute each individual programming statement as your cursor enters or exits a field. To have a programming statement execute when your cursor enters a field, precede the entire statement with a less-than symbol (<). To have a programming statement execute when your cursor exits a field, precede the entire statement with a greater-than symbol (>).

Using the bonus programming statement, if you want the statement to execute when you enter the field, write it like this: `<#3: if #1 > $99,000 then #3 = #1 * #2`. If you want it to execute when you exit the field, write it like this: `>#3: if #1 > $99,000 then #3 = #1 * #2`. When to use each one depends on the application you are writing. In the guided exercise that follows, you will be using the method that executes the statement as you enter the field. Later chapters will cover this concept in more depth.

Beginner's Tip

You can combine the manual and individual field methods of calculation in the same database.

Recall that earlier in this discussion I mentioned two programming terms, "programming statement" and "expression." Looking at the bonus amount statement, #3: if #1 > $99,000 then #3 = #1 * #2, the whole line of text is known as a *programming statement*. A programming statement is made up of expressions. An *expression* is any operation that calculates, finds, or changes a field value; the expression cannot take any other action. An expression can be a Q&A function or a mathematical term with an exact meaning. In other words, an expression is a discrete part of a statement, such as #3.

A *function* is a predefined expression that can calculate, find, or change a field value. A function is preceded by an @ symbol. In an earlier exercise, you used the @date function to display the date every time you entered the Cardfile database. Q&A divides the functions into categories: date, numbering, and financial functions, shown in Figure 2.24; math functions, shown in Figure 2.25; text functions, shown in Figure 2.26; lookup functions covered in the next section; and typecasting and miscellaneous functions, shown in Figure 2.27. Later chapters will explain how and when to use these functions.

```
              BUILT-IN DATE / NUMBERING / FINANCIAL FUNCTIONS

  @DATE        Produces today's date when executed.
  @TIME        Produces the current time when executed.
  @DOM(n)      Returns the integer which is the day of the date n.
  @MONTH(n)    Returns the integer which is the month of date n.
  @YEAR(n)     Returns the integer which is the year of date n.
  @DOW$(n)     Returns the name of the day of the date n.
  @MONTH$(n)   Returns the name of the month of the date n.

  @ADD         Executes the statement only when forms are being added.
  @UPDATE      Executes the statement only if the form is being updated.
  Note:        BOTH of the above must be used in conjunction with an IF
               statement.  For example:  #5: IF @ADD THEN #1=#2, etc.
  @NUMBER      Returns a unique integer number which is always greater by
               one than the last number it returned.  Reset with Ctrl F8.

  @CGR(p,f,l)  Compound growth rate (present value, future value, life)
  @FV(p,i,l)   Future value (present value, interest, life)
  @PMT(p,i,l)  Loan payment (principal, interest/period, life (total periods))
  @PV(p,i,l)   Present value (payment, interest, life (total periods))
  @IR(p,pa,l)  Interest rate (principal, payment amount, life (total periods))
```

Figure 2.24   Date, numbering and financial functions.

```
                    BUILT-IN MATH FUNCTIONS

Note: In the following, n can be a number, a field identifier, or an expres-
sion. x can be a text value, field id, or expression. list is a list of field
identifiers separated by commas, double dots (to express a range), or both.

@ABS(n)        Returns the absolute value of n.
@ASC(x)        Returns the ASCII decimal value of the first character of x.
@AVG(list)     Produces the average of the values of all items in the list.
@EXP(n,m)      Raises n to the mth power.
@INT(n)        Returns the integer portion of n.
@MAX(list)     Returns the maximum of all items in the list.
@MIN(list)     Returns the minimum of all items in the list.
@MOD(x,y)      Returns x modulo y.  See Pg. ?? of manual for more information.
@NUM(x)        Returns the number represented by x.
@ROUND(n,m)    Rounds off n to m decimal digits.
@SGN(x)        Returns the sign of x.
@SQRT(n)       Returns the square root of n.
@STD(list)     Calculates the standard deviation of the items in the list.
@SUM(list)     Returns the sum of the values of all the items in the list.
@VAR(list)     Returns the variance of all non-blank items in the list.
@WIDTH(n)      Returns the width of field n.
```

Figure 2.25   Math functions.

```
                    BUILT-IN TEXT FUNCTIONS

@CHR(n)          Returns the ASCII character equivalent of n.
@DEL(x,n,m)      Returns x with m characters deleted starting at position n.
@INSTR(x,y)      Returns the position of the first occurrence of y in x.
@LEFT(x,n)       Returns the leftmost n characters of x.
@LEN(x)          Returns the length of the value in field x.
@MID(x,n,m)      Returns m characters from x starting at position n.
@REPLACE(x,y,m)  Returns a modified m (Every occurrence of x is replaced by y).
@REPLFIR(x,y,m)  Returns m with the first occurrence of x replaced by y.
@REPLLAS(x,y,m)  Returns m with the last occurrence of x replaced by y.
@RIGHT(x,n)      Returns the rightmost n characters of x.
@TEXT(n,x)       Produces a text value consisting of n characters of x.

Example:         #3 = @LEFT(#2, 4)   this will put the first 4 characters
                 in field #2 into field #3.

                 #3 = @REPLACE("Hello", "Bye", #4)   this will return the
                 string from #4 with every occurrence of Hello replaced with
                 Bye.
```

Figure 2.26   Text functions.

```
                        TYPECASTING FUNCTIONS

@TONUMBER(x)   Returns x expressed as a numerical value.
@TOMONEY(x)    Returns x expressed as a monetary value.
@TODATE(x)     Returns x expressed as a date value.
@TOTIME(x)     Returns x expressed as a time value.
@TOYESNO(x)    Returns x expressed as a boolean (Yes/No) value.
@STR           Returns x expressed as a string value.


                       MISCELLANEOUS FUNCTIONS


CLEAR(list)    Clears the values in fields designated by list.
@DITTO(list)   Returns values from list of fields in previous form.
@FIELD(x)      Returns the value from field x; x is a reference to a field.
@FILENAME      Returns the name of the current file.
@GROUP         Returns the name of the current field security spec.
@HELP(n)       Displays user-defined help for field n.
@MSG(x)        Displays message x on the 24th line of screen.
@REST(x,m)     Returns true if the field referred to by x has a value that
               matches m.  m can be any valid retrieve specification
@SELECT(x,m,n,...)   If the value found in x is equal to 1, then m is
                     returned. If x is equal to 2, then n is returned, Etc.
```

Figure 2.27   Typecasting and miscellaneous functions.

Develop a Simple Programming Statement

In the upcoming exercise, you will develop a simple programming statement that will instruct Q&A to place the date in the DATE UPDATED file
every time you change one of your records. Further, you will develop
navigation statements that will move the cursor to the COMPANY NAME
field after it enters the date. To develop programming and navigation
statements, follow the procedures given here.

Practice Developing a Programming Statement

1. Press **F** for File, **D** for Design, and **P** for Program.

2. Type the filename **CARDFILE** and press Enter.

3. Type **P** for Program Form. You are now in the Program Spec
   screen. This is where you will enter your programming statements.

4. Press Enter to move to the DATE UPDATED field and press F6 to expand the field. This expanded window is known as the *Program Editor*. You can type 32,000 characters of information into each window, with a total of 64,000 characters for the entire database. Also, many of the Write features work within the Program Editor; these can be accessed by pressing F8 for the Options menu.

5. Oncc inside the Program Editor, type **#2: if @update then #2 = @date**. This statement tells Q&A to place the date in the DATE UPDATED field whenever the record is viewed or altered.

6. Press F10 to close the Program Editor.

7. Press Enter to move to the COMPANY field and type **#3**.

8. Press F10 to save your programming statement.

Now you will practice using a navigation statement. Remember that unless you plan to use your database files with the version of Q&A for Macintosh, you do not need to split your navigation and programming statements.

Practice Developing a Navigation Statement

1. While still at the Programming menu, press **N** for field Navigation. You are now ready to enter your navigation statement.

2. In the DATE ENTERED field, type **#1: GOTO #2** and press Enter.

3. In the DATE UPDATED field, type **#2: GOTO #3** and press Enter.

4. In the COMPANY field, type **#3** and press F10 to save your navigation statement.

This navigation statement tells Q&A to move your cursor through the first two fields and stop at COMPANY NAME. The navigation statement works in conjunction with the programming statement.

Beginner's Tip

If you place GOTO commands in the programming statment and in the navigation statement, the navigation statement will override the commands in the programming spec.

Lookup Table

Another function listed on the Programming menu that is quite useful is the *lookup table*. Each database has its own lookup table that can hold up to 64,000 characters—approximately 600 lines. The lookup table can store all types of information, which can be placed into any field you designate. This data can include tax codes, client terms, company codes, stock items, etc.

Through a programming statement, you tell Q&A to match the value typed into a specific field by the user with a *key value* in the lookup table. If Q&A finds a match, it places in the designated field the value you assigned to that key. Suppose you had codes that represented the industry of each of your prospects. The lookup table could store the code (key) and the full industry name: *BU for Building Supplies*. Then when a user typed the code BU, Q&A would place the description Building Supplies in the designated field.

Two components are needed to set up a lookup function. First are the codes and the descriptions, which you must type into the lookup table. Figure 2.28 is a sample lookup table showing a few codes in the KEY column, and their corresponding descriptions in column 1. The second component is the actual programming statement, which you place in the appropriate field, for example, #4: lookup (#4,1,#5). This statement says to match the key value typed in field #4 with the key value in the lookup table and place in field #5 the description found in column 1 of the lookup table.

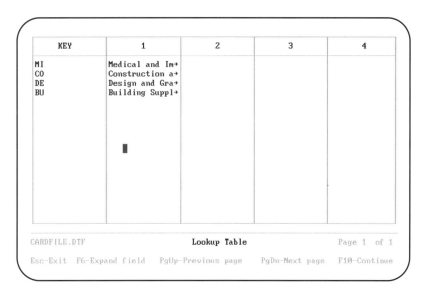

Figure 2.28   Lookup table with codes and descriptions.

Using the Cardfile database, you will place a lookup statement in the COMPANY CODE field that will instruct Q&A to place the corresponding company type in the COMPANY TYPE field. Next you will place the codes and descriptions in the lookup table. Lastly, you will test the lookup statement by adding a record to the database. To develop the lookup statement, follow the procedure given here.

Practice Developing a Lookup Statement

1. Press **F** for File, **D** for Design, and **P** for Program.

2. Type the filename **CARDFILE** and press Enter.

3. Press **P** for Program File.

4. Move to the COMPANY CODE field and type this programming statement: **#4: Lookup (#4, 1, #5)**. Press Enter. Remember to press F6 to expand the field.

5. Move to the COMPANY TYPE field and type **#5**. Press Enter. Your screen should now look like Figure 2.29.

6. Press F10 to save the programming statement.

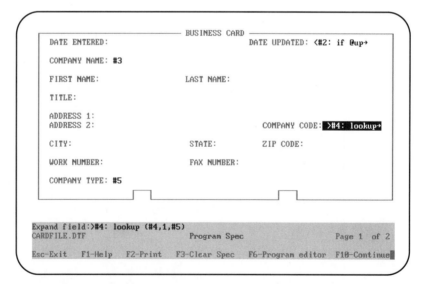

Figure 2.29   Cardfile database with lookup statement.

Practice Adding Codes and Descriptions to the Lookup Table

1. While you are still at the Programming menu, press **E** for Edit Lookup Table. You should now be at the lookup table, where you will designate your key values.

2. In the KEY column, type **MI** and press Tab. Press F6 to expand the field. Type **Medical and Imaging** and press Enter. Repeat this process with the following codes and descriptions: **CO Construction and Paving**, **DE Design and Graphics**, and **BU Building Supplies**.

3. When you are through, your screen should look like Figure 2.28, shown earlier.

4. Press F10 to save your entries.

5. Press Esc three times to return to the Main menu.

Practice Testing the Lookup Function

1. Press **F** for File and **A** for Add.

2. Type **CARDFILE** and press Enter.

3. Your cursor should be in the COMPANY NAME field. Fill in all of the fields in the record exactly as shown in Figure 2.30. Use the Enter key to move from field to field.

4. When you are through, press F10 to save the record. Press Esc to return to the Main menu.

You will now retrieve the record and add a company code to test the lookup function. As you enter the record, notice that the DATE UPDATED programming statement automatically fills in the date for the DATE UP-DATED field.

5. From the File menu, press **S** for Search and press Enter to select the Cardfile database. Press F10 to bring up a record.

6. Move to the COMPANY CODE field, type **BU**, and press Enter.

7. The COMPANY TYPE field should have been filled in with the description "Building Supplies." Your form should now look like Figure 2.31.

8. Press Shift-F10 to save the record and exit.

9. Press Esc to return to the Main menu.

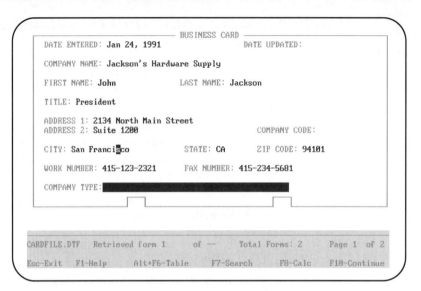

Figure 2.30 Sample business card record before lookup.

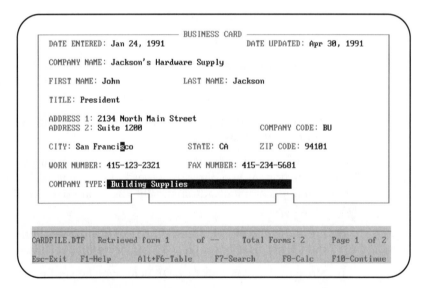

Figure 2.31 Sample business card record with lookup completed.

Secure a File

This section is optional. If you do not have sensitive data, there is no need to protect it. However, if you do need to protect your data against unauthorized access, Q&A has enhanced its security options. There are now two primary methods of security: locking a database and file/field security. The first method, *locking a database*, is easier to implement and administer, and in some cases more secure. With this method, you lock everyone out of all the functions you restricted. The other method, *file/field security*, gives you greater flexibility in assigning different access rights to different people. You can let some people delete data, while others can only view it.

Locking a database is simply a matter of looking over the list of rights and choosing which rights you want to restrict access to. Figure 2.32 gives you a suggested locking scheme to follow for most applications. If you want to access any of the restricted rights, you have to unlock the database with the password, disable the lock, and go back to use the feature.

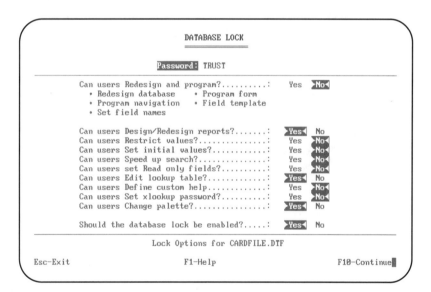

```
                        DATABASE LOCK


                   Password: TRUST

         Can users Redesign and program?.........:    Yes   ▶No◀
            • Redesign database    • Program form
            • Program navigation   • Field template
            • Set field names

         Can users Design/Redesign reports?.......:  ▶Yes◀   No
         Can users Restrict values?...............:    Yes  ▶No◀
         Can users Set initial values?...........:     Yes  ▶No◀
         Can users Speed up search?..............:     Yes  ▶No◀
         Can users set Read only fields?.........:     Yes  ▶No◀
         Can users Edit lookup table?............:   ▶Yes◀   No
         Can users Define custom help............:     Yes  ▶No◀
         Can users Set xlookup password?.........:     Yes  ▶No◀
         Can users Change palette?...............:   ▶Yes◀   No

         Should the database lock be enabled?.....:  ▶Yes◀   No

                  Lock Options for CARDFILE.DTF

   Esc-Exit                  F1-Help                   F10-Continue
```

Figure 2.32   Suggested database lock options.

Practice Locking a Database

1. Press **F** for File, **D** for Design, **A** for Customize Application, and **L** for Lock Database.

2. Type **CARDFILE** and press Enter.

3. Assign the file rights, using Figure 2.32 as a guide.

4. Move to the last item and select Yes to enable the lock.

5. Press F10 to save the lock design.

6. Now all of the features you restricted are inaccessible, even to you. To unlock a database, repeat step 1, type your password, select No to disable the lock, and press F10 to save the spec.

7. Press Esc three times to return to the Main menu.

Assigning access rights to specific files and fields gives you greater flexibility in determining who can access which data. When you assign access rights to a file, you type each user's name and password, and then you specifically select which features the person can access. When the person wants to use the database, the person has to type his or her name and password before obtaining access to a particular aspect of the file. If the person doesn't have rights to that function, Q&A returns an error message. You can also assign rights to groups of people. This is done in the same way as before, except that you designate a group name and group password.

> **Caution:** There is one serious drawback to the Assign Access Rights method of security. If someone with full rights uses the database and then doesn't reset the security level, ANYONE can come along and access the data at the same level as the previous user. To reset the security, go to the Q&A Main menu and press Shift-F6.

Practice Assigning Access Rights to a File

1. Press **F** for File, **D** for Design, and **S** for Secure.

2. Type **CARDFILE** and press Enter.

3. Type **A** for Assign Access Rights.

4. This is where you enter the user or group to whom you want to assign access rights. Type your name and press Enter.

> ⊘ **Caution:** The first person you need to give FULL rights to is
> yourself. This way you can alter the database in the future. If
> you forget your password, there is no way to find out what it is
> except by sending the database to Symantec's technical support
> staff.

5. Your screen should look like Figure 2.33. Type a password and
   press F10 to save the Security spec. By doing this, you have given
   yourself full rights to that file.

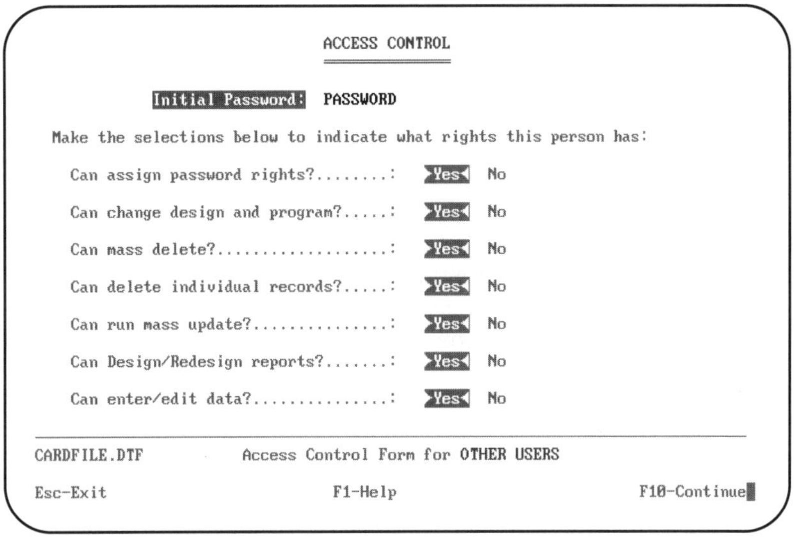

```
                          ACCESS CONTROL
                          ==============

          Initial Password:  PASSWORD

     Make the selections below to indicate what rights this person has:

         Can assign password rights?........:     >Yes<  No

         Can change design and program?.....:     >Yes<  No

         Can mass delete?...................:     >Yes<  No

         Can delete individual records?.....:     >Yes<  No

         Can run mass update?...............:     >Yes<  No

         Can Design/Redesign reports?.......:     >Yes<  No

         Can enter/edit data?...............:     >Yes<  No
     _____

     CARDFILE.DTF        Access Control Form for OTHER USERS

     Esc-Exit                  F1-Help                  F10-Continue
```

Figure 2.33   Default Access Control screen.

6. Next, assign access rights to a user. Select Yes in the dialog box to
   create another user and then type the user's name.

7. Once inside the Access Control screen, type the user's password
   and assign the appropriate rights. Figure 2.34 shows a suggested
   format.

8. Press F10 to save the user's rights.

9. Repeat this process until you are through.

10. Press Esc three times to return to the Main menu.

```
                            ACCESS CONTROL
                            ═════════════

              Initial Password:  TRUST

          Make the selections below to indicate what rights this person has:

            Can assign password rights?........:    Yes  ▶No◀

            Can change design and program?.....:    Yes  ▶No◀

            Can mass delete?...................:    Yes  ▶No◀

            Can delete individual records?.....:    ▶Yes◀  No

            Can run mass update?...............:    ▶Yes◀  No

            Can Design/Redesign reports?.......:    ▶Yes◀  No

            Can enter/edit data?...............:    ▶Yes◀  No
          ─────────────────────────────────────────────────────────
          CARDFILE.DTF        Access Control Form for OTHER USERS

          Esc-Exit                   F1-Help                   F10-Continue█
```

Figure 2.34   Suggested user security rights.

If you have more than one database that you want to restrict access to, you must repeat this procedure for each database. However, if you enter the same user name and password for each database, the user can open all databases by opening just one database.

The next level of security is *field level*. This is where you restrict access to specific fields. You can format fields in three different ways: Read and Write, Read Only, and No Access (hidden). The first format, *Read and Write*, is the default format. The next format, *Read Only*, allows a user to read the contents of the field but not alter it. The last format, *No Access,* or *hidden*, actually hides from view any field with this designation. A hidden field might be used in a personnel database to hide sensitive information, for example, salary information and other confidential data. In order to assign field-level security to a user, you must first assign file rights to the file in which you are going to assign field-level security.

Practice Assigning Field-Level Security

1. Press **F** for File, **D** for Design, and **S** for Secure.

2. Type **CARDFILE** and press Enter.

3. Press **F** for Field Level Security. You are prompted to enter your name and password.

4. Type the user's name and press Enter.

5. It is here that you designate how you want each field formatted: Read and Write, Read Only, or No Access. Make your choices and press F10 to save your spec.

6. Enter the user or group name to be assigned to this Field Security spec. Press F10.

7. Press Esc three times to return to the Main menu.

Develop a Columnar Report

Q&A offers three types of reports: form, cross-tab, and columnar. The form report will be covered in the next section, the cross-tab report will be covered in Chapter 10, and this section will focus on the columnar report. The *columnar report* prints information in columns. These columns are taken directly from the fields of the database. Figure 2.35 shows you the relationship between the columns in the report and the fields in the database. Further, each report you create stays with the database in which it is based and cannot be copied to another database. Also, there is a limit of 200 reports per database.

There are four basic steps to creating a Columnar Report spec: deciding which records you want to print, choosing which fields to include on the report and how they will be formatted, defining the print specifications, and developing headers and footers. Once you have created a Report spec, you can print that report over and over without having to go through the definition process again.

Practice Defining and Printing a Columnar Report

1. Press **R** for Report and **D** for Design.

2. Type the filename **CARDFILE** and press Enter.

3. Type the name of the report, **Master Phone List**, and press F10.

4. Select Columnar Report and press Enter.

5. You are now at the Retrieve Spec screen. This is where you tell Q&A which records you want to print. We will cover the specifics of Retrieve specs later in the chapter. For now just press F10.

6. The next screen you see is the Column/Sort Spec screen. This is where you tell Q&A which fields you want displayed, how they should be sorted, and what, if any, calculations you want to perform on the columns. Type the Column/Sort spec (the circled items) just as it appears in Figure 2.36.

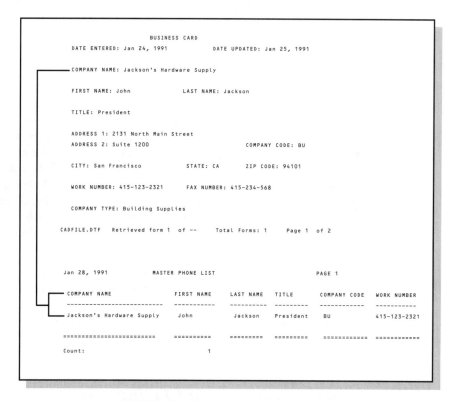

```
                              BUSINESS CARD
              DATE ENTERED: Jan 24, 1991           DATE UPDATED: Jan 25, 1991

              COMPANY NAME: Jackson's Hardware Supply

              FIRST NAME: John            LAST NAME: Jackson

              TITLE: President

              ADDRESS 1: 2131 North Main Street
              ADDRESS 2: Suite 1200                    COMPANY CODE: BU

              CITY: San Francisco         STATE: CA     ZIP CODE: 94101

              WORK NUMBER: 415-123-2321   FAX NUMBER: 415-234-568

              COMPANY TYPE: Building Supplies

              CADFILE.DTF   Retrieved form 1  of --    Total Forms: 1    Page 1  of 2



              Jan 28, 1991           MASTER PHONE LIST                 PAGE 1

              COMPANY NAME              FIRST NAME    LAST NAME  TITLE      COMPANY CODE   WORK NUMBER
              --------------------------  ----------   ----------  ---------  ------------  -----------
              Jackson's Hardware Supply  John          Jackson    President  BU            415-123-2321

              ==========================  ==========   =========  =========  ============  ============
              Count:                                   1
```

Figure 2.35   Cardfile database and columnar report.

To choose columns, all you do is place a number in each field you want to appear on the report. The number is equal to the column's order on the report. For instance, by placing the number 1 in the COMPANY NAME field it will appear first.

Shortcut

I recommend that you number your columns *2, 4, 6*, etc., rather than *1, 2, 3*. Later, if you have to add another column between 2 and 4, you won't have to renumber all your columns.

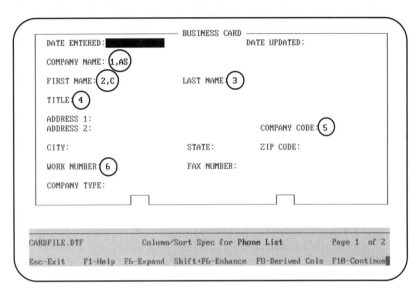

Figure 2.36 Column/Sort spec (the circled items) for the Phone List report.

The next decision is how you want the report sorted. You can have 999 sort levels in your report, although normally you will use no more than 3. To designate a Sort spec, move to the first column you want to sort and place a comma and type either **AS** for ascending order (A–Z) or **DS** for descending order (Z–A) after the field number. Look at the COMPANY NAME field in Figure 2.36 for an example of an ascending order sort. For a second-level sort, simply move to the next field and do the same thing. The fields are sorted in order of the column number.

After you designate the sort order, you may want to perform various calculations on your data. Figure 2.37 shows a list of options. In this example, the only option we are going to use is the **C** for Count option (it is in the FIRST NAME field of Figure 2.36). This option counts all the records listed on the report. Subsequent chapters will cover many of the other functions. To add other options, move to the field on which you want to perform the calculation and type a comma followed by the correct command. Keep in mind that you cannot perform calculations (total, subtotal, etc.) on any column that has a Sort spec in it (AS or DS). Always place the calculation commands one column to the right of the sorted column on which you want the calculation performed. These options work only on numeric and money fields. The Count option works on text fields.

```
AS - Ascending (low-high) Sort        T    - print column Total
DS - Descending (high-low) Sort       A    - print column Average
R  - Repeat sorted values             C    - print column Count
P  - Start new Page on break         MIN   - print MINimum value
CS - Cancel subcalculations          MAX   - print MAXimum value
DB - Break when day changes          STD   - print STandard Deviation
MB - Break when months changes       VAR   - print VARiance
YB - Break when year changes          ST   - print SubTotals
AB - Alphabetic break (on 1st letter) SA   - print SubAverages
I  - Make column Invisible            SC   - print SubCounts
K  - Make Keyword report             SMIN  - print SubMINimum value
                                     SMAX  - print SubMAXimum value
                                     SSTD  - print SubSTandard Deviat.
                                     SVAR  - print SubVARiance
```

Figure 2.37   Column Calculation options.

You may want to enhance specific columns to draw more attention to them. Suppose you print a report showing a comparison of this year's sales to last year's sales. You could enhance the better year. To do this, move to the column you want enhanced and press Shift-F6. The Text Enhancements and Fonts menu, shown in Figure 2.38, will pop up. Move to the desired enhancement or font and press Enter. Use the cursor to highlight the entire field and press F10. Now every value in the field will be enhanced according to your specifications.

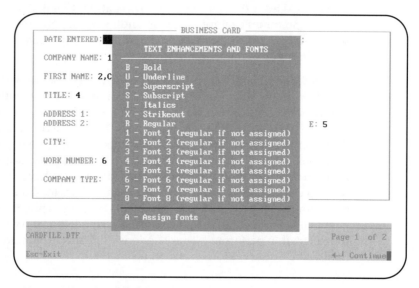

Figure 2.38   Text Enhancements screen.

Another feature that will be explored later in Chapter 5 is *derived columns*. These are special columns that are made up of other columns or fields. With a derived column, you could combine the FIRST and LAST NAME fields into one field. Derived columns are created by pressing F8 at the Column/Sort Spec screen and then entering the specifications.

7. Once you have entered the Column/Sort spec, press F10 to move to the Report Print Options screen. Here you choose which printer you want to use and you choose several other options also. Configure your Report Print Options screen like Figure 2.39. The only exception may be the printer.

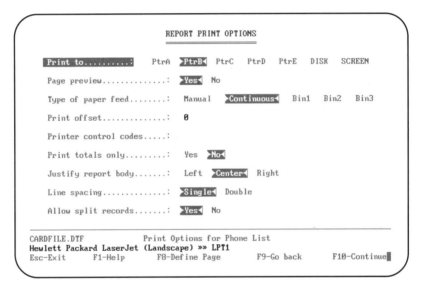

```
                        REPORT PRINT OPTIONS


   Print to..........:    PtrA  >PtrB<  PtrC   PtrD   PtrE   DISK   SCREEN

   Page preview.............:   >Yes<  No

   Type of paper feed........:   Manual  >Continuous<  Bin1   Bin2   Bin3

   Print offset..............:   0

   Printer control codes.....:

   Print totals only.........:   Yes  >No<

   Justify report body.......:   Left  >Center<  Right

   Line spacing..............:  >Single<  Double

   Allow split records.......:  >Yes<  No
─────────────────────────────────────────────────────────────────────
CARDFILE.DTF              Print Options for Phone List
Hewlett Packard LaserJet (Landscape) »» LPT1
Esc-Exit      F1-Help      F8-Define Page        F9-Go back        F10-Continue
```

Figure 2.39   Print Spec options for columnar report.

Shortcut

If you want to see exactly how your report will look prior to printing, change the Page Preview option to Yes in the Report Print Options screen. This requires a mono graphics card or a color card and monitor to work.

8. After you have selected your print options, press F8 to go to the Define Page menu. It is here that you designate page width, margins, point size, headers, and footers. Copy the example displayed in Figure 2.40.

DEFINE PAGE

Page width.: 136   Page length..: 66

Left margin: 0   Right margin.: 136

Top margin.: 3   Bottom margin: 3

Characters per inch: 10   12   15   17

---------------------------- HEADER ----------------------------
1: @date ! MASTER PHONE LIST ! PAGE #
2:
3:
---------------------------- FOOTER ----------------------------
1:
2:
3:

CARDFILE.DTF   Define page for Phone List

Esc-Exit   F1-Help   F9-Go Back to Print Options   F10-Continue

Figure 2.40   Define Page options for columnar report.

How you configure your margins, page width, and point size depends on how wide each report is. The standard $8\frac{1}{2}$-by-11-inch paper is 80 columns wide at 10 characters per inch. As you increase the number of characters per inch (CPI), you can increase the paper width. Keep in mind that as you increase paper width, you also need to increase the right margin. If a report is too narrow to fit the margins and point size, you will receive an error message asking if you want to print the report anyway or if you want to change the settings. Using a laser jet printer, with CPI set to 17, and printing in landscape mode (sideways) with a letter tray, the widest you can set your paper width and right margin is 176 columns. Using a dot-matrix printer, with a CPI of 17, printing in portrait mode on $8\frac{1}{2}$-by-11-inch paper, the widest you can set your paper width and margin is 136.

In Figure 2.40 you can see the line @date ! MASTER PHONE LIST ! PAGE # in the Header section. The @date command places the date on every page. The exclamation points tell Q&A to center the text within the exclamation marks, and the # sign places a page number on each page. These commands apply for footers as well.

9. Once you have defined your page, press F10 to save your Report spec.

10. A message will appear, telling you the report is saved and asking if you want to print it. Answer Yes.

11. Check the report. If looks like Figure 2.41, move on to the next section. If it doesn't, repeat the preceding steps to fix it.

```
Jan 28, 1991              MASTER PHONE LIST                              PAGE 1


      COMPANY NAME          FIRST NAME     LAST NAME      TITLE      COMPANY CODE    WORK NUMBER
---------------------------  -----------   ----------    ---------   -------------   ------------

Jackson's Hardware Supply    John          Jackson       President   BU              415-123-2321


===========================  ===========   =========     =========   ============    ============
Count:                            1
```

Figure 2.41   Finished columnar report.

Later in this chapter we'll cover the different ways of printing existing reports.

Develop a Form Report

In a *form report*, information is not placed in columns the way it is in a columnar report—it can be placed anywhere on the page. Examples of form reports are directory listings and invoices. Q&A offers three types of form reports: coordinate, free-form, and full-record.

The only difference between the first two types is how they are created. *Coordinate reports* allow you to place fields from the database at specific coordinates on the page. You do this by using column/row coordinates (for example, 2,6 means two rows down from the top margin and six spaces in from the right margin) or by using inches or centimeters (for example, 2",6" means two inches down from the top margin and six inches in from the right margin). Use coordinate reports for filling in preprinted forms and where accuracy is essential.

Free-form reports rely on a less precise but easier method of placing the information on the page. You will learn this method in the next exercise. Developing and printing form reports is almost identical to creating and printing columnar reports, with the exception of creating the Field spec (called Column/Sort spec in columnar reports).

79

The third type of form report is the *full-record report*. To print this way, you must be in either the Add or the Search/Update mode. Press F2, select various print options, and then press F10. With this method you have no control over which fields print and you cannot select groups of records. Your only choices are to print either the current record on the screen or all the records you have added during that session. You can specify whether you want the field labels to print.

Practice Developing and Printing a Name and Address Report

1. Press **F** for File and **P** for Print.

2. Type the filename **CARDFILE** and press Enter.

3. Press **D** for Design. Type the report name, **Name and Address List**, and press Enter.

4. The first screen you see is the Retrieve Spec screen. Here you tell Q&A which records you want to print. In the next section, you'll learn the specifics of Retrieve specs. For now, simply press F8 to proceed to the Sort spec.

   Unlike the columnar report, the Sort spec is NOT included with the Field spec. By pressing F8, you change to the Sort spec and designate how you want the report sorted. You have the option of sorting your report by any field you like, even one that will not appear on the report. Q&A offers two sorting options: ascending order (A–Z) and descending order (Z–A). To enter the command,

   • Type a number designating which sort should be performed first.

   • Type a comma.

   • Then type either AS or DS. For example, typing 1,AS in the COMPANY NAME field would sort the entire report alphabetically (A to Z) by company name.

5. Move to the COMPANY NAME field and type **1,AS**.

6. Press F10 to progress to the Field spec. The Field spec is where you tell Q&A which fields you want to print and where they should be placed on the page. Fill in the spec just as it appears in Figure 2.42.

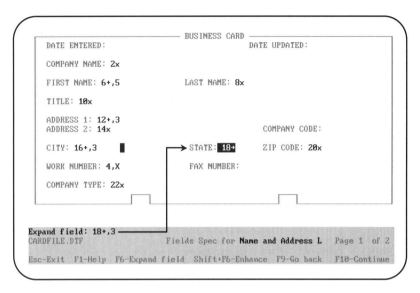

Figure 2.42   Field spec for Name and Address List.

To enter a Field spec,

- Type a number in a field. The number designates the order in which the field will appear on the form, starting from top to bottom, left to right.

- After each number, type either X (print this field and then print the next field on the following line) or + (print this field, skip one space, and print the next field).

- Optionally, type a third number to indicate the number of lines or spaces you want to skip. For example, 2X,3 means to print this field second (2), move to the beginning of the next line (X), and print three blank lines (3). Typing 4+,5 means to print this field fourth (4), do not move to the next line (+), and print five spaces following this field (5).

7. Optionally, you can enhance the fields in the report by pressing Shift-F6 to bring up the Enhancement menu.

8. Press F10 to advance to the Print Options spec. Match your File Print Options screen to the one in Figure 2.43.

```
                          FILE PRINT OPTIONS

   Print to.....:    ▸PtrA◂  PtrB   PtrC   PtrD   PtrE   DISK   SCREEN

   Page preview.................:    Yes  ▸No◂

   Type of paper feed...........:    Manual ▸Continuous◂  Bin1   Bin2   Bin3

   Print offset.................:    0

   Printer control codes.........:

   Print field labels...........:   ▸Yes◂  No

   Number of copies.............:    1

   Number of records per page....:   1

   Number of labels across.......:   ▸1◂  2  3  4  5  6  7  8

   Print expanded fields.........:   Yes  ▸No◂
   ──────────────────────────────────────────────────────────────────
   CARDFILE.DTF          Print Options for Name and Address Lis
   Hewlett Packard LaserJet (Portrait) »» LPT1
   Esc-Exit      F1-Help       F8-Define Page       F9-Go back      F10-Continue▮
```

Figure 2.43   Print spec for Name and Address List.

The File Print Options screen has two options that you should be especially aware of because the options will vary depending on the report that you are printing. The first is the number of records you want to print on each page. The default is one per page. The other option is whether you want the field labels to print.

9. Once you have the Print Options spec filled in, press F8 to move to the Define Page spec. Fill it in according to Figure 2.44.

10. Press F10 to save your Report spec.

11. A message appears, asking if you want to print. Press Yes to print the report. It should look like Figure 2.45. If it does not, go back and fix it.

Develop a Macro

Recording macros is the closest thing Q&A offers to a programming language. With Q&A's macro facility, you can record a series of keystrokes and then replay them at any time—saving you the time and effort involved in retyping those particular keystrokes. For example, if you print a list of sales calls each day, you could record that process in a macro and then simply press the macro to print the report.

```
                          DEFINE PAGE


               Page width : 80        Page length..: 66

               Left margin: 5         Right margin : 75

               Top margin : 3         Bottom margin: 3

               Characters per inch:   ►10◄  12   15   17
─────────────────────────── HEADER ────────────────────────────
1: @DATE ! NAME & ADDRESS LIST ! PAGE #
2:
3:
─────────────────────────── FOOTER ────────────────────────────
1:
2:
3:
─────────────────────────────────────────────────────────────
CARDFILE.DTF               Define page for Name and Address Lis

Esc-Exit        F1-Help          F9-Go Back to Print Options        F10-Continue▮
```

Figure 2.44   Define Page spec for Name and Address List.

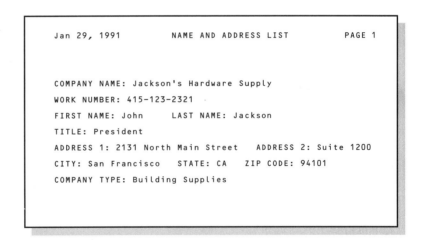

```
Jan 29, 1991          NAME AND ADDRESS LIST          PAGE 1



COMPANY NAME: Jackson's Hardware Supply
WORK NUMBER: 415-123-2321
FIRST NAME: John      LAST NAME: Jackson
TITLE: President
ADDRESS 1: 2131 North Main Street   ADDRESS 2: Suite 1200
CITY: San Francisco    STATE: CA   ZIP CODE: 94101
COMPANY TYPE: Building Supplies
```

Figure 2.45   Finished free-form Name and Address List report.

Creating macros is easy. The macro recording facility works similarly to a video camera: turn on the recorder, record the keystrokes, turn off the recorder, and then replay the macro.

Recording a Macro

1. Decide which process you want to automate.

2. Turn on the macro recording facility by pressing Shift-F2 and **D** for Define Macro.

3. Designate a macro identifier (a *macro identifier* is any keystroke combination, for example, Alt-A).

4. Perform the tasks.

5. Turn off the recording facility by pressing Shift-F2.

6. Give the macro a name and then save it by pressing F10 and Enter.

Each time you create a macro, it is saved in the default macro file QAMACRO.ASC and stored in the QA subdirectory (this file is an ASCII file and can be edited in Q&A Write or any word processor). Q&A allows you to save 3,000 characters of macros. If you create a file larger than this, you will be unable to load the macros.

To overcome the 3,000-character limitation, you must increase Q&A's macro buffer size. To do this, start Q&A with the -b switch, followed by a number slightly larger than your macro file. For example, to load a macro file having 10,000 characters, start Q&A by typing QA -b10000. Note, however, that you do not need to concern yourself with this issue until you receive an error message that Q&A has run out of memory while loading your macro file. If you should receive an error message, follow the next procedure.

Determining the Size for the -b Switch

1. From the Q&A Main menu, press **W** for Write and **G** for Get.

2. Press Shift-F4 to delete the path. Type **c:\qa** (if Q&A is not on the C drive, substitute the correct letter) and press Enter. This will give you a list of the files in the Q&A subdirectory.

3. Move to the file QAMACRO.ASC, as shown in Figure 2.46, and look under the term Size (at the bottom of the screen) to see how large it is. This is the number that you will use to determine how large to set the -b switch when you start Q&A.

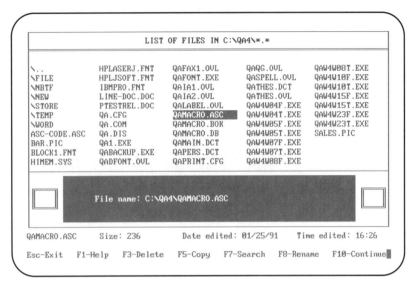

```
                    LIST OF FILES IN C:\QA4\*.*

\..              HPLASERJ.FNT    QAFAX1.OVL      QAQG.OVL        QAW4W08T.EXE
\FILE            HPLJSOFT.FNT    QAFONT.EXE      QASPELL.OVL     QAW4W10F.EXE
\NBTF            IBMPRO.FNT      QAIA1.OVL       QATHES.DCT      QAW4W10T.EXE
\NEW             LINE-DOC.DOC    QAIA2.OVL       QATHES.OVL      QAW4W15F.EXE
\STORE           PTESTREL.DOC    QALABEL.OVL     QAW4W04F.EXE    QAW4W15T.EXE
\TEMP            QA.CFG          QAMACRO.ASC     QAW4W04T.EXE    QAW4W23F.EXE
\WORD            QA.COM          QAMACRO.BOK     QAW4W05F.EXE    QAW4W23T.EXE
ASC-CODE.ASC     QA.DIS          QAMACRO.DB      QAW4W05T.EXE    SALES.PIC
BAR.PIC          QA1.EXE         QAMAIN.DCT      QAW4W07F.EXE
BLOCK1.FNT       QABACKUP.EXE    QAPERS.DCT      QAW4W07T.EXE
HIMEM.SYS        QADFONT.OVL     QAPRINT.CFG     QAW4W08F.EXE


        File name: C:\QA4\QAMACRO.ASC


QAMACRO.ASC    Size: 236        Date edited: 01/25/91    Time edited: 16:26

Esc-Exit   F1-Help   F3-Delete   F5-Copy   F7-Search   F8-Rename   F10-Continue
```

Figure 2.46   List of files with QAMACRO.ASC highlighted.

Replay a Macro

There are three ways you can replay a macro. The simplest is to type the macro identifier you assigned to the macro (for example, Alt-A). The second way is to display a list of all macros and their names by pressing Alt-F2 from anywhere in the program. The last way is to display the Macro menu by pressing Shift-F2 and choosing **R** for Run Macros. Later in this chapter, you will use the Alt-F2 method to replay the Phone List macro.

> **Caution:** Make sure that you run a macro from where you began recording it. For example, if you began recording the macro at the Q&A Main menu, you cannot replay it starting at the Program Spec menu.

Use Macro Features

All macro features are accessed through the Macro menu by pressing Shift-F2. Figure 2.47 displays the Macro menu. As you can see, there are seven options to choose from. The next two exercises will explain the first six options and give you the opportunity to use each option. The Create Menu option will be covered in Chapter 10.

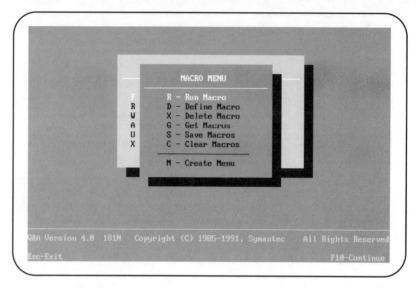

Figure 2.47   Macro menu.

The macro you will record in this exercise will automatically print the phone list created earlier.

Practice Recording the Macro for the Phone List Report

1. From the Q&A Main menu, press Shift-F2 to display the Macro menu.

2. Press **D** for Define Macro and Alt-R for the macro identifier. You are now going to record the keystrokes necessary to print the phone list report.

3. Press **R** for Report and **P** for print a report.

4. Type **CARDFILE** and press Enter. Select Master Phone List and press Enter. Type **Y** for Make Temporary Changes.

5. You are now at the Retrieve spec. This is where you tell Q&A which records you want to print. How to select records will be covered later in this chapter. For now, press Alt-F2 twice to cause the macro to pause on playback.

Beginner's
Tip

You will often want a macro to pause at some specific spot during playback so that you can enter variable text. For example, each time you print the phone list report, you won't want to print every record in the database. So that you can change this information each time, you will have to add a pause where Q&A asks you which records you want to print. Simply press Alt-F2 twice wherever you want the macro to pause. This concept applies to all macros.

6. Press F10 to progress to the Column/Sort spec. This is where you tell Q&A which fields you want to print. Press Alt-F2 twice to cause the macro to pause here on playback.

7. Press F10 to progress to the Print Options screen. Press Alt-F2 twice to cause the macro to pause to here on playback.

8. Press F10 to print the report.

9. Press Esc twice to return to the Main menu.

10. Press Shift-F2 to bring up the Macro Options screen, shown in Figure 2.48. Type **Print Phone List** and press Enter. The next option, Show Screen, gives you the option of suppressing all the unnecessary screens. For now, leave this option set to Yes. The last option will be covered in Chapter 10.

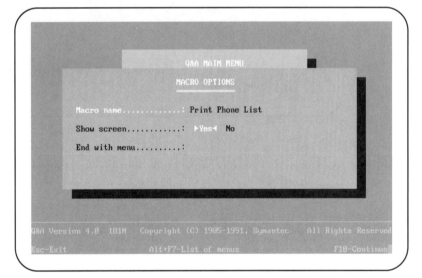

Figure 2.48   Macro Save options.

11. Press F10 and Enter to save the macro into the macro file QAMACRO.ASC.

You have successfully recorded a macro that will print a phone list any time you want. Now run the macro to make sure that it performs properly. In programming jargon, this essential step is known as *debugging*.

Practice Replaying the Phone List Macro

1. From the Q&A Main menu, press Alt-F2 to display the Macro Names menu. It should look like Figure 2.49. Press Enter to start running the macro.

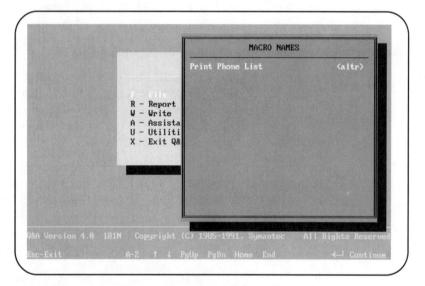

Figure 2.49   Macro Names menu.

2. The macro should pause at the Retrieve Spec screen and at the bottom of the screen should display the message:

Enter text. Press ← to resume macro playback.

This is your signal that you can enter variable text.

> ⊘ **Caution:** Do not press Enter to move between fields. If you press Enter, Q&A will restart the macro. Use the arrow and Tab keys to move between fields.

3. Since you are not going to type a Retrieve spec, press Enter to restart the macro. The macro should now pause at the Column/Sort spec and display at the bottom of the screen the same message as before. Press Enter to restart the macro.

4. The macro should pause at the Print Options screen. Press Enter to print the report.

5. If your macro did not perform correctly, re-record it. If it worked correctly, you are ready to move on.

Deleting a Recorded Macro

1. To delete a macro from the Macro file, press Shift-F2 and **X** for Delete Macro. The Macro Names menu will be displayed.

2. Move to the macro you want to delete and press Enter.

Create a Blank Macro File

Recall that Q&A stores your macros in a file called QAMACRO.ASC. However, you may wish to store some macros in a different file from QAMACRO.ASC. For example, suppose you had macros that purged old invoices or performed system utility functions that should not be made available to all users. Such actions are potentially destructive in nature. Therefore, you might want to set up a separate file for these macros. Setting up separate macro files involves two steps: initially creating an ASCII file with the correct name and then saving your macros into the new file. The next procedure explains how to create a new macro file and how to use the Clear and Get options on an existing macro file.

Practice Creating a New Macro File

1. Press **W** for Write and **T** for Type/Edit.

2. You are now at a blank Write screen. Press Ctrl-F8 to save an ASCII file.

3. Press Shift-F4 to clear the path and then type the command **c:\qa\filename.mac**, substituting for filename.mac any filename you like.

Beginner's Tip

Remember that DOS allows filenames of no more than eight characters followed by a period and an extension of no more than three characters. I suggest that you use a .MAC extension on all macro files so that you know they contain macros.

4. You now have a blank macro file in which to save macros. The next time you create a macro that you want to save into a new file, type that name at the Macro Save screen, as shown in Figure 2.50.

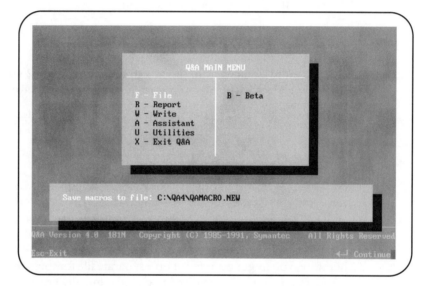

Figure 2.50   Macro Save menu.

5. To clear an existing macro file from memory, press Shift-F2 and **C** for Clear.

6. To retrieve another macro file, press Shift-F2 and **G** for Get. Type the new macro filename and press Enter.

Advanced Tip: If you are an advanced user, you can use an ASCII text editor to directly edit macro files. If you do this, make sure you save it in ASCII format.

This concludes the exercises on designing and developing files, reports, and macros. Now you are ready to actually use your databases.

File Use Features

This next section covers the basics of how to use your Cardfile database. You will learn how to add, search, sort, and print records; how to move around and between forms; and how to access on-line help.

Get Help

From most places in Q&A, you can receive on-line help that is *context-sensitive*. This means that when you press the help key, F1, a window will appear, explaining the current choice. Try this by navigating to the Q&A Main menu and pressing F1. You will see a screen that looks like Figure 2.51.

```
┌─────────────────────────────────────────────────────────────────┐
│  CHOICE      DESCRIPTION                                   VOLUME │
│ ┌───────────────────────────────────────────────────────────────┐
│ │ File        Create, fill out, and work with forms of information.  1 │
│ │                                                                   │
│ │ Report      Take information from your records, sort and arrange   1 │
│ │             it, and print results in a table or a Cross Tab.      │
│ │                                                                   │
│ │ Write       Write and print documents.                            2 │
│ │                                                                   │
│ │ Assistant   Teach your Intelligent Assistant (IA) and Query       1 │
│ │             Guide about your records then ask questions,          │
│ │             generate reports or change information in English.    │
│ │                                                                   │
│ │ Utilities   Set-up your printer, modify font files, setup         2 │
│ │             alternate programs, DOS file facilities, etc.         │
│ └───────────────────────────────────────────────────────────────┘
│ ┌───────────────────────────────────────────────────────────────┐
│ │ CAUTION:  Sudden loss or interruption of power can damage a data file. │
│ │ Never turn your machine off or reboot the system UNLESS you are at one of │
│ │ the main Q&A menus.  However, if a power loss does occur, you can probably │
│ │ recover the file (see pg. U-65).  Make frequent backups (pg. F-193). │
│ └───────────────────────────────────────────────────────────────┘
│  Esc-Exit                                                         │
└─────────────────────────────────────────────────────────────────┘
```

Figure 2.51   The Help screen for the Main menu.

Add Data

Adding data to a database is the heart of data processing; this is where it all begins. Once you have added a record to your database, you have to switch to a different mode to view it or change it. Q&A refers to these two modes as Add mode and Search/Update mode. In this next exercise you will add a record to the Cardfile database, and in a subsequent one you will search for records and update them.

Practice Adding a Record to the Cardfile Database

1. Press **F** for File and **A** for Add.

2. Type **CARDFILE** and press Enter.

3. You are now in Add mode. Because of the programming statement you entered earlier, the cursor is at the COMPANY NAME field. Fill in the form as it appears in Figure 2.52. To move to the next field, press Enter.

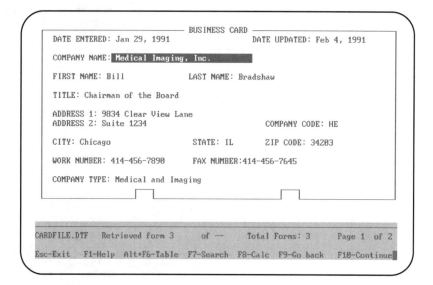

```
                        ┌──────── BUSINESS CARD ────────┐
  DATE ENTERED: Jan 29, 1991              DATE UPDATED: Feb 4, 1991

  COMPANY NAME: Medical Imaging, Inc.

  FIRST NAME: Bill            LAST NAME: Bradshaw

  TITLE: Chairman of the Board

  ADDRESS 1: 9834 Clear View Lane
  ADDRESS 2: Suite 1234                    COMPANY CODE: HE

  CITY: Chicago            STATE: IL      ZIP CODE: 34203

  WORK NUMBER: 414-456-7890    FAX NUMBER:414-456-7645

  COMPANY TYPE: Medical and Imaging


CARDFILE.DTF   Retrieved form 3      of --      Total Forms: 3      Page 1  of 2

Esc-Exit   F1-Help  Alt+F6-Table  F7-Search  F8-Calc  F9-Go back   F10-Continue
```

Figure 2.52   Sample record for Cardfile database.

4. Press F10 to save the record and resume adding.

Beginner's Tip

The other way to save a record is to press Shift-F10. This saves the record and exits Add mode.

5. At a blank screen, press Shift-F5 to copy the entire previous record and press F10 to save it. Then press Shift-F5 to copy another record and leave it on the screen.

Shortcut

To speed up data entry, Q&A offers the field-and-form Ditto feature. After you add a record and save it, a blank screen appears. It is here that you can press F5 to ditto (duplicate) the previous record's value placed in that field. Or you can press Shift-F5 to ditto the entire previous record.

6. With the duplicated record on the screen, press F3 to delete the record. You will receive a warning asking if you really want to delete the record. Answer Yes.

7. Once the record is gone, you will be left at a blank screen. Press F9 to display the previous record.

8. With the record on the screen, practice navigating around the form. (The various ways to navigate are explained in the next section.)

9. When you are through, you can press F3 to delete the duplicate record and press Esc to exit Add mode.

Navigate Around and Between Records

To move *within a field*, use the arrow keys to move one character at a time, or use Ctrl-Right Arrow to move right one word at a time or Ctrl-Left Arrow to move left one word at a time.

To move *between fields,* use the Enter, Tab, and arrow keys. Q&A's natural progression is from top to bottom and left to right, unless you have used the field navigation feature to change this order. The Enter and Tab keys move you from field to field in Q&A's natural progression. Pressing the Shift and Tab keys together moves you backward (right to left). The arrow keys move you up and down the form.

To move to the *beginning of a field*, press Home. To move to the *top of the page*, press Home twice. To move to the *top of the form*, press Home three times. The same concept applies to the End key. To move to the *end of a field*, press End. To move to the *end of a page*, press End twice. To move to the *end of the form*, press End three times. You can also use PgUp to move to the *previous page* of the form and PgDn to move to the *next page* in the form.

To move *between records,* press F9 to move to the previous record and F10 to move to the next record. To move to the *first record* in the group, press Ctrl-Home. To move to the *last record* in the group, press Ctrl-End.

Once you can move around and between forms, you will want to change and delete data. To *delete one character* at a time, press either the Backspace key or the Del key. To *delete one word* at a time, move to the word you want to delete and press F4. To *delete a line* of text, press Shift-F4. To *insert text between two words*, move between the two words, press the Ins key, and begin typing.

Search/Update Data

Once you have entered records into your database, you will need a method of finding and changing the records. The changes might be a simple address change, the addition of completely new data to an existing record, or the deletion of an entire record. All of these changes are executed by selecting the Search/Update option from the File menu. Q&A refers to this process as *searching and updating* and entering a Retrieve spec. This section explains the concepts involved in searching for information in a database. These same concepts are used to select records for a report, do a mass mailing, or print mailing labels.

When working with an existing Q&A database, you are always in either Search/Update mode or Add mode. In Add mode, you can only add records. In Search/Update mode, you can only change or delete existing records. The screen that directly precedes Update mode is Search mode. This is where you tell Q&A which records you want to retrieve. In other words, to get into Update mode so that you can change a record, you first have to select the records in Search mode.

This process can be likened to the storage of paper forms. Suppose that a manager of rental property uses rental forms to keep a record of which properties are rented and which are not. The manager stores the paper forms in a file cabinet. Inside the file cabinet is a file holder containing two manila files, one with new blank forms and another one with forms that are already filled out. Blank forms and completed forms are kept separately in their own manila folders, but both are stored in a larger file holder. The only way to get to the forms is to open the respective folders and pull out either a new form or a completed form.

This same concept applies to the way Q&A stores information in a file. Within a database file, there are both an unlimited number of new forms and forms that have already been filled in. To get to the new forms, you have to be in Add mode. To get to the completed forms, you have to be in Search/Update mode.

There are two ways to get into Search/Update mode. The first way is to press **F** for File and **S** for Search, type the filename, and press Enter. Q&A displays a blank form on the screen with the words `Retrieve Spec` at the bottom of the screen. When you see the words `Retrieve Spec` at the bottom of the screen, you are in Search mode. It directly precedes Update mode. This is Q&A's way of telling you that you can begin choosing records from the file. The other way to get into Search/Update mode is to do so from Add mode. By pressing F7 while you are in Add mode, you automatically switch to Search/Update mode. When you are viewing a record in Update mode, you can switch back to Add mode by pressing Ctrl-F6.

With Q&A in Search mode, you have to tell it which records to retrieve. This process is known as *executing a search*. When you execute a search, you fill out a Retrieve spec. Q&A then looks to see if any records match the specifications of the Retrieve spec. If any do, Q&A displays them. If they don't, Q&A asks you to make another request. Another way to think about a Retrieve spec is that it is the "restriction" placed on your database—a kind of data filter that filters out all the records except the ones you have specified.

The components of a Retrieve spec are the specifications (the values and operators) and the F10 key. For example, suppose you want to conduct a simple search to find all the companies in your database that have offices in California. To do this, move to the STATE field; then type **CA** and press F10. Q&A searches your database for all the records having CA in the STATE field. If it finds any, the records are displayed. To scroll through the records Q&A found, press F10. When you come to the last record, Q&A gives you the message `No more records. Press Esc to exit or F9 for previous form`. Then, by pressing F9, you can scroll backward through the records you just looked at.

Here is another example of a simple search. Suppose that you want to find all the people in your database having the last name of "Smith." To do this, move to the LAST NAME field; type **Smith** and press F10. Q&A retrieves the appropriate records. This type of search is known as an *exact match search*. The most basic search of all is to press F10 without entering any restrictions. Q&A will display ALL the records in the database in random order.

Practice Entering an Exact Match Search

1. Press **F** for File and **S** for Search.

2. Type the filename **CARDFILE** and press Enter. This will take you into the form.

3. Move the cursor to the STATE field. Type **CA** and press F10. Notice that the date has been automatically placed in the UPDATED field and that the cursor has moved to the COMPANY NAME field. This is due to a programming statement in the UPDATED field that places the date in the UPDATED field every time you view or change a record. By looking at the field, you will know when a record was last updated.

4. To perform another search, press F7. Press F3 to clear the last Retrieve spec you entered. You are ready for another search.

5. Practice entering several different Retrieve specs, repeating steps 3 and 4.

6. When you are through, press Shift-F10 to save the last record and exit.

Shortcut

Many of the WordStar editing commands work in Q&A, such as the key combinations of the Ctrl key and the letters *A, S, D, F, T, Y, X, W,* etc.

Sort Specs

When you add or update records, Q&A places them in the database in random order. If you want to view them in a specific order, they have to be sorted. You can sort your records on any field in the database. You can even sort them on more than one field. For example, you could sort the records by state and by zip code. In an earlier exercise, you designated certain fields as speedy fields. Because speedy fields are indexed and stored in a special file, you can sort your database four times faster by using speedy fields.

To sort records, you have to be in Sort mode. To get into Sort mode, you have to go through Search mode. That is, once you are in Search mode, simply press F8 and Q&A will indicate that it is ready for you to enter a Sort spec by displaying Sort Spec at the bottom of the screen. A *Sort spec* consists of a number between 1 and 9999 followed by either AS for ascending order, which is low to high (A–Z), or DS for descending order, which is high to low (Z–A). The number represents the sort level. You can have up to 9999 sort levels, although you will probably never use more than two or three.

Sort levels can be easily understood if you look at a school yearbook. The first sort level is the grade of each student. The second sort level is the student's last name. The sorting information displayed on the screen is the same as the sort levels you designated while developing reports.

In this next exercise, you will practice sorting data. Since you have only two records, there won't be many sort options. You may want to return to the section titled "Add Data" and add a few more records.

Practice Sorting Data

1. Press **F** for File and **S** for Search.

2. Type **CARDFILE** and press Enter.

3. You are now at the Retrieve spec. It is here that you switch to Sort mode. Press F8 to switch to Sort mode.

4. Move to the STATE field and type **1 AS**. Then move to the ZIP CODE field and type **2 AS**. You have just told Q&A to sort your records first by state and then by zip code. Press Enter.

5. The records now appear on the screen. By pressing F10, you can scroll forward through your records. By pressing F9, you can scroll backward through the records you just looked at.

6. To perform another sort, press F7 and F8.

Beginner's
Tip

You can always tell whether you are in the Retrieve spec or in the Sort spec by looking at the bottom of the screen.

7. To clear the old Sort spec, press F3. Now move to the COMPANY NAME field and type **1 DS** and press F10. This will sort your records by company name in descending order.

8. Continue practicing if you like. When you are through, press Shift-F10 to save and exit.

Print a Report

In earlier exercises you developed two reports: a form report and a columnar report. When you printed these reports, you used the Design/ Redesign a Report menu option. Use this option the first time that you develop the report. Don't use it to print the report every time. The reason is that when you go through the Design/Redesign a Report option, you are permanently changing the report. Thus, if you type a Retrieve spec or add one field to the report, your change will still be there the next time.

A better way to print your reports on a daily basis is to use the Print a Report option for a columnar report and the Print Records option for form reports. This way, any temporary changes you make aren't saved with the Report spec. The next exercise you are going to do involves a columnar report, but the procedure is the same for a form report.

Practice Printing a Columnar Report

1. Press **R** for Report and **P** for Print a Report.

2. Type **CARDFILE** and press Enter.

3. Type or select **Master Phone List** and press Enter. You are prompted: Select YES to make changes, NO to print. (If you select NO, the report is printed. That is, steps 4 and 5 do not apply.)

4. You are now at the Retrieve spec. Enter a Retrieve spec of your choice and press F10.

5. The Column/Sort spec is on the screen. Press F10.

6. You are now at the Print Options spec. Make any necessary changes and press F10.

7. Press Esc to return to the Main menu.

Write Features

Q&A's word processor is known as the Write module. Write is considered a top-of-the-line executive word processor with many of the features of dedicated word processors yet without the complexity. In fact, with the changes added to Version 4.0, Write is closing the gap between dedicated and integrated word processors. This next section will give you a brief overview of the features of the Write module and guide you through a quick exercise in creating and editing a document.

As with other word processors, you can place fonts in your document. Q&A allows you to place up to eight in one document. To do so, press Shift-F6 to bring up the Text Enhancements menu and follow the instructions.

While you are typing, you may find that a particular word doesn't properly express your thoughts. You can press Alt-F1 to bring up the thesaurus. After the document is typed, you may find that it can be used for another purpose with the exception of one or two words used throughout the document. For example, perhaps "she" needs to be replaced by "he." If this is the case, you can use the Search and Replace feature, F7, to change "she" to "he" throughout the entire document—automatically.

To select the Write module, press **W** for Write from the Q&A Main menu. This brings up the Write menu, as shown in Figure 2.53. As you will notice, the options cover the most common features of word processing: retrieving files, typing, defining the page, printing, saving files, and clearing the screen. You can also print labels and access the utilities from this menu.

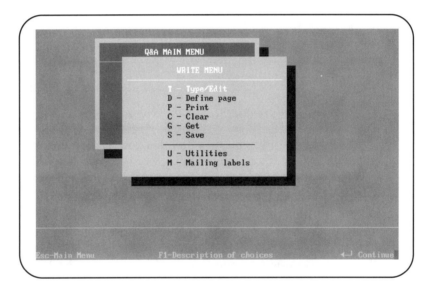

Figure 2.53   Write menu.

To begin working with your document, you need to determine how you want the page defined. *Page definition* in Q&A consists of setting the margins and determining the point size for the document. You can access page definition from the Write menu by pressing **D** (from within the document by pressing Ctrl-F6). For most documents, you may never need to change the default settings; Figure 2.54 shows the default page options.

Once you have defined your page, a blank document screen is displayed and you begin typing your document. After you press T for Type/Edit, you are also at a blank screen. This screen is known as the *working copy*. It remains the working copy until you save your file by giving it a name. Now simply type your document.

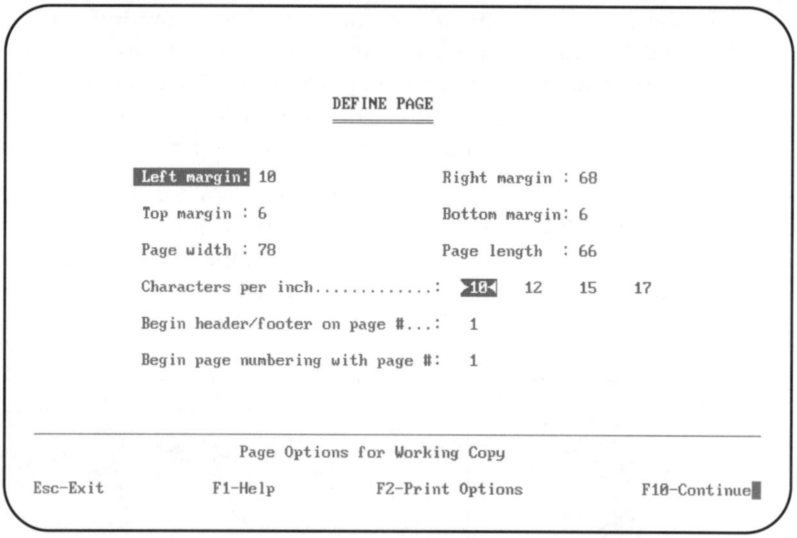

```
                          DEFINE PAGE
                          ==========


         Left margin: 10              Right margin : 68

         Top margin : 6               Bottom margin: 6

         Page width : 78              Page length  : 66

         Characters per inch............:  >10<   12   15   17

         Begin header/footer on page #...:   1

         Begin page numbering with page #:   1

         _____

                      Page Options for Working Copy

    Esc-Exit           F1-Help         F2-Print Options        F10-Continue
```

Figure 2.54   Default Define Page options.

While typing, you may find that you want to enhance your copy by boldfacing or underlining certain words. Press Shift-F6 to bring up the Enhancement menu, choose the desired options, and press Enter. Use the cursor to highlight the text and then press F10.

In addition, Q&A provides an array of tools to let you do such things as copying and moving blocks, restoring text, scrolling, using macros, and more. These tasks are executed by pressing F8 to bring up the Options menu or by using the nine function keys, F1 through F9. Figure 2.55 shows what each function key does.

After you are done typing, you can check the spelling of the document by pressing Shift-F1 and following the instructions. Just before printing, you should save your document. You can accomplish this from within the document by pressing Shift-F8 or from the Write menu by pressing Esc and **S**. Once you have saved a document, you can print it by pressing F2 from within the document or from the Write menu by pressing Esc and **P**. The next exercise takes you through the basic features of word processing.

```
┌─────┬────────────────────────────────────┬─────┬──────────────────────────────┐
│     │ Alt F1   Thesaurus                 │     │ Ctrl F2   Print text block   │
│ F1  │ Ctrl F1  Check spelling (word)     │ F2  │ Shift F2  Use macros         │
│     │ Shift F1 Check spelling (doc)      │     │      F2   Print document     │
│     │      F1  Info                      │     │                              │
│     │                                    │     │ Ctrl F4   Delete to end of line│
│ F3  │ Ctrl F3  Document statistics       │ F4  │ Shift F4  Delete line (Ctrl Y)│
│     │      F3  Delete block              │     │      F4   Delete word (Ctrl T)│
│     │                                    │     │                              │
│     │ Alt F5   Move block to file        │     │ Alt F6    Hyphenate          │
│     │ Ctrl F5  Copy block to file        │     │ Ctrl F6   Def ine Page       │
│ F5  │ Shift F5 Move block                │ F6  │ Shift F6  Enhance text       │
│     │      F5  Copy block                │     │      F6   Set temporary margins│
│     │                                    │     │                              │
│     │ Alt F7   List fields               │     │                              │
│     │ Ctrl F7  Go to page/line           │     │ Ctrl F8   Export document    │
│ F7  │ Shift F7 Restore text              │ F8  │ Shift F8  Save document      │
│     │      F7  Search & Replace          │     │      F8   Options Menu       │
│     │                                    │     │                              │
│     │ Alt F9   Calculate                 │     │                              │
│     │ Ctrl F9  Make font assignments     │     │                              │
│ F9  │ Shift F9 Scroll screen down        │ F10 │                              │
│     │      F9  Scroll screen up          │     │                              │
├─────┴────────────────────────────────────┴─────┴──────────────────────────────┤
│ Esc-Exit                    → PgDn-More ←                                     ▐ │
└────────────────────────────────────────────────────────────────────────────────┘
```

Figure 2.55   Function keys.

Practice the Basic Features of Word Processing

1. Press **W** for Write and **T** for Type/Edit a document.

2. Once at the blank screen, press Ctrl-F6 to bring up the Page Definition screen. Modify the screen as you wish and press F10.

3. Begin typing a letter to an old friend whom you haven't spoken with in some time. While you are typing, you will need to move the cursor to various parts of the screen.

4. Find a phrase that you want to enhance and place your cursor on the first letter of the phrase. Press Shift-F6 to bring up the Enhancement menu. Press **B** for Boldface and use your cursor to highlight the chosen text. Press F10 when you are done.

5. Practice moving around the document. Figure 2.56 shows you the most common cursor movement keys.

6. Practice deleting some text:

   • Press F4 to delete a word at a time.

   • Press Shift-F4 to delete one line at a time.

   • Press Ctrl-F4 to delete to the end of the line.

HOW TO MOVE AROUND THE DOCUMENT				
↑ Up one line	PgUp	Previous screen	Ctrl PgUp	Previous page
↓ Down one line	PgDn	Next screen	Ctrl PgDn	Next page
← Left one column	Ctrl←	Previous word	Ctrl Home	Top of doc
→ Right one column	Ctrl→	Next word	Ctrl End	Bottom of doc

Home(1)	Beginning of line	End(1)	End of line
Home(2)	Top of screen	End(2)	Bottom of screen
Home(3)	Top of page	End(3)	Bottom of page
Home(4)	Top of document	End(4)	Bottom of document

Figure 2.56   Cursor movement keys.

7. To restore the last text you deleted, press Shift-F7.

8. Spell-check the document by pressing Shift-F1. When Q&A finds a misspelling or a word that is not in its dictionary, it gives you several options, shown in Figure 2.57. Make the appropriate choice as you are prompted. When Q&A is finished, it returns you to your document screen.

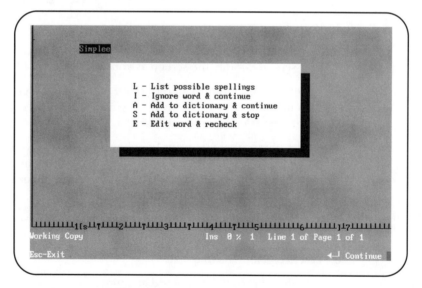

Figure 2.57   Speller options.

9. When you are through with everything, press Shift-F8 and give your document a name. This will save it and allow you to retrieve it later.

10. Print the document by pressing F2. This will take you to the Print Options screen. If all the options are set correctly, press F10 to print the document.

11. After the document is printed, press Esc to exit from the document screen.

To retrieve an existing document, press **W** for Write and **G** for Get. Press F4 twice to clear any previous filename and press Enter. Q&A will show you a list of all your word processing files. To select a file, move the cursor down to the file you want and press Enter.

Q&A has implemented the mail merge procedure better than anyone. *Mail merge* is the process of combining data from a database with a form letter to print personalized letters. This process works so well in Q&A because the database and word processor are all in one program. Mail merge is such a useful feature that most of Chapter 7 is devoted to it.

Printing labels in Q&A is equally easy because Q&A predefines Label Format specs for most of the popular label sizes. To access mailing labels, press **M** from the Write menu, select a label type, select a database, and press F2 to print the labels. All the features described in this paragraph will be fully explained in Chapter 8.

Intelligent Assistant

The *Intelligent Assistant* (IA) is a tool that allows you to ask plain English questions of your database. It is designed to make the process of accessing, extracting, analyzing, printing, and adding data easier. This is especially true with the addition of the Query Guide. In previous versions of the software, the only method you could use was the Natural Language method. You had to string together words that the IA understood. However, with Version 4.0, Symantec added the Query Guide. The Query Guide helps you build your requests with words and phrases that the IA already understands, making it quite simple to get the right information the first time. The IA can be used for many tasks, such as

- Asking various types of questions—*who, what, when, where, why,* and *how many*.

- Performing calculations on numeric and money fields.

- Running predefined reports.

- Creating new records.

- Finding/sorting/displaying various records.

- Deleting records.

The Natural Language and Query Guide methods allow you to make similar requests but through different means. The Natural Language method lets you make requests that you can't make while using the Query Guide, but the Query Guide is easier to use. You will have to experiment with each method and find the one you like better.

Before you can use the Intelligent Assistant in Natural Language mode, you have to teach it about your database. The first part of the teaching process is done for you by Q&A. But keep in mind when you begin this process that Q&A has to read through every single record in the database. So it is best to run the teaching process just after you develop the database, rather than after you have added a lot of records. The second part of the teaching process, which is optional, requires that you define fields, locations, special words, verbs, adjectives, and other items that make it easier for you to ask questions and the IA to answer them. The *lessons*, as they are called, are divided into basic and advanced.

An example of a basic lesson is to tell the IA what your database is about. For instance, if you were teaching the IA about the Cardfile database, you would say that it was about prospects, associates, clients, and friends. Then if you asked the IA to list all your friends who live in California, it would know what you are talking about. Chapter 9 explains the Natural Language method.

With the Query Guide method, you have only one teaching process to go through: telling the IA which fields you want indexed. To do this, put a Q in each field you want to have indexed. Indexing gives you more flexibility when you are requesting data. The following exercise will guide you through the basic functions of the Query Guide.

Practice Using the Query Guide

1. Press **A** for Assistant and **E** for Teach Query Guide.

2. Type **CARDFILE** and press Enter.

3. The Query Guide will ask if you want to continue with the teaching process. Press Enter.

4. This brings you to the indexing screen. Press F5 and F10 to place a Q in each field.

5. Type **Q** for Query Guide. You are now at the standard Query screen, shown in Figure 2.58. It is here that you make your requests.

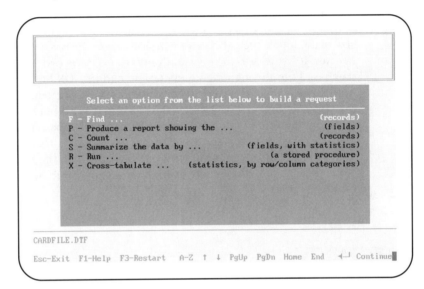

```
         Select an option from the list below to build a request

    F - Find ...                                              (records)
    P - Produce a report showing the ...                      (fields)
    C - Count ...                                             (records)
    S - Summarize the data by ...           (fields, with statistics)
    R - Run ...                                     (a stored procedure)
    X - Cross-tabulate ...     (statistics, by row/column categories)




   ─────────────────────────────────────────────────────────────────
   CARDFILE.DTF

   Esc-Exit  F1-Help  F3-Restart   A-Z  ↑ ↓  PgUp  PgDn  Home  End  ←┘ Continue
```

Figure 2.58   Query Guide.

6. Practice making three requests:

   • Press **F** for Find and **R** for Records. Type **CITY** and press Enter. Press **=** for Equals. Move the cursor down to the city Podunk and press Enter. Press **.** (period) to execute the commands. This should take you to the Good Health Hospital record. Press F10 to save the record and Esc to return.

   • Press **P** for Produce a Report. Move the cursor down to COM-PANY NAME and press Enter. Press Enter for And The. Press **W** for WORK NUMBER and press Enter. Press **F** for From and **A** for All Records; press Enter for Execute Command. Press F2 to send the report to the printer. Select a printer and press F10. When the report is through printing, press Esc.

   • Press **R** for Run a Procedure and **R** for The Report. Press Enter to select Master Phone List. Press **N** for No Changes (to print the report as is).

7. As you can see from these three examples, the Query Guide is quite versatile. Practice doing more queries if you wish. When you are through, press Esc twice to return to the Main menu.

If you plan to maintain databases of 2,000 to 3,000 records or more, you should know that the Intelligent Assistant will significantly increase the size of the index file (.IDX) and will slow down the basic data entry process because it has to add the special IA info to every record. For example, one database I ran through the Query Guide had its .IDX file increased almost nine times. Also, if you plan to copy records from one database to another, the copying time can be increased by as much as 100 percent. That is, if it takes one minute to copy 10 records from one database to another, it can take up to two minutes using the Query Guide. So if you don't think you are going to use the IA, don't put your database through the teaching process. None of this applies if you are going to maintain databases with only a few hundred records.

Summary

This concludes the basic lessons on how to use Q&A. If you tried each of the examples, you now have a good idea of how Q&A works and what you can do with it. If you didn't try the examples, you can use this chapter as a reference source should you need to learn a feature later on.

The following chapters expand on the features that you were introduced to in this chapter. You will learn how to use and modify specific applications while you are using Q&A's features. There will also be many new features that were not covered here. As you begin each chapter, check the "At A Glance" section to see which features will be highlighted. Also, you can use the Contents by Feature (located at the begining of the book) to find specific features.

USE APPLICATION

Add Data

1. Press **F** for File and **A** for Add.
2. Type the filename and press Enter.
3. Type the data and press F10 to save each record.
4. Press Shift-F10 when you are through.

Search for Data

1. Press **F** for File and **S** for Search.
2. Type the filename and press Enter.
3. Type the Retrieve spec and press F10 to retrieve the records. To enter a new spec, press F7.
4. Press F3 to clear the old Retrieve spec. Enter a new spec and press F10 to retrieve the records.

Delete a Record

1. Press **F** for File and **S** for Search.
2. Type the filename and press Enter.
3. Retrieve the record and press F3 to delete the record.

Receive Help

1. In most sections of Q&A, press F1 for help.

Print the Current Record

1. With the desired record on the screen and from within either Add or Search mode, press F2 and then F10. You can print a blank screen only from within Add mode.

DESIGN APPLICATION FEATURES

Redesign a File

1. Press **F** for File, **D** for Design, and **R** for Redesign.
2. Type the filename and press Enter.
3. Begin redesigning the file.
4. To save the design, press F10. Type your Field Format specs and press F10. Select your Global Format specs and press F10.

Draw Lines

1. Once inside the Design or Redesign a File screen, press F8, **L** for Layout Page and **D** for Draw.
2. Use the cursor keys to draw the lines. Press F8 to erase and F6 to move the pen.
3. Press F10 to exit Draw mode.

Copy, Move, or Delete a Block of Text

1. Once inside the Design or Redesign a File screen, move your cursor to the beginning of the text you want to manipulate.
2. Press F8 and **B** for Block Operations. Select Copy, Move, or Delete.
3. Move to the end of the text to select it and press F10. If you chose Delete, the text is gone. If you chose Copy or Move, move the cursor to where you want the text to appear and press F10. The text will be copied or moved.

IN
BUSINESS

Master Names Application

In this chapter you will learn about all the features listed in the "At a Glance" section. At the same time you will be learning how the Names application works and how to use it. The Names database is the heart of your applications and is designed to contain the basic name and address information for all individuals and organizations associated with your company.

Beginner's
Tip

Don't forget to load all the files from the enclosed floppy disk into the subdirectory \qa\file, located on your hard drive.

Overview

This section is an overview of the Names application. It explains what you will learn in the later sections "Using the Application" and "Guided Modifications."

If you plan to have more than one database file, and any of these other files will contain individual or company names and address information, you will want to use the Names file. The Names file is used to store all the names associated with your organization, including clients, prospects, vendors, employees, investors, etc. Each type of name in the database can be differentiated with a code. For instance, you might use the code CL to indicate client records. Then if you wanted to list all clients, you would simply type the code **CL** as the Retrieve spec. This method of using one file for all your names is the most efficient method and will save you considerable data entry time.

The Names file is generally at the heart of a group of applications and acts as the central repository for all the names in these applications. By storing all the basic name and address information in one file, you can retrieve this information into other files without retyping it. For example, suppose you are entering an invoice. Rather than retype the customer's name and address, you simply type the customer ID number and press F8. Q&A will take the name and address information from the Names file and place it in the appropriate fields of the Invoice file. Q&A refers to this retrieval process as *conducting a lookup*. The lookup feature is used in all the database applications covered in this book.

For organizations that send mail to their prospects/customers and want to keep track of what they have sent the customers, the Names file has the following mailing code fields: the date of the mailing, a code to distinguish the mailing, a line of remarks about the mailing, and a date for a response. You can instruct Q&A to fill in these fields with appropriate codes prior to each mailing. This way you can easily search for and view the records of those who received your last mailing.

Viewing information on the screen is not always enough, however. There are many times when you need a printed list of what is in the database. To facilitate this task, a report has been created that lists the names and addresses of the people in the Names database.

In the later section "Using the Application," you will learn how to do a variety of useful tasks: add and search for records; sort data; save your Retrieve and Sort specs for future use; get help; print the current record; print a list of names; import names from another file; change the record number; and run a macro.

Beginner's Tip

Remember that information is stored in a *database* or *file*. A *form* is what you actually see on the screen. An *application* is made up of files, reports, macros, and menu options, and that group of related applications is called a *system*.

The section "Guided Modifications" expands on the design concepts taught in Chapter 2 and focuses on redesigning a form. The redesign process will include adding new fields, formatting fields, simple programming, and speeding up searches, also known as field indexing. You will learn how to draw lines on the screen to enhance its visual impact and to quickly move, copy, and delete blocks of text. Finally, you will create a simple macro.

During the redesign process, you will be guided through adding a fax number field to the first page of the database form, placing a second contact section on the second page of the form, and adding six more direct mail codes.

Application Explained

Before you begin working with the application, read this detailed description of the application as it currently exists and of definitions for each field. Looking at Figure 3.1, you will notice that the top section of the Names file contains a field for the date the record was entered, one for the last time it was updated, a batch number field, and a reference ID field. These last two fields can be used for any purpose you choose. A common use for the BATCH # field is to place a number representing the batch of data you are entering. The REF ID field can be used to manually select a group of records that do not have any field values in common. For example, suppose you wanted to send a mailing to ten different customers who had no field values in common in the database. You could manually enter an asterisk in the REF ID field and then print all the records with an asterisk.

The NAME & MAILING ADDRESS section is where you enter the primary mailing address. As Figure 3.1 shows, this section has various fields for entering information.

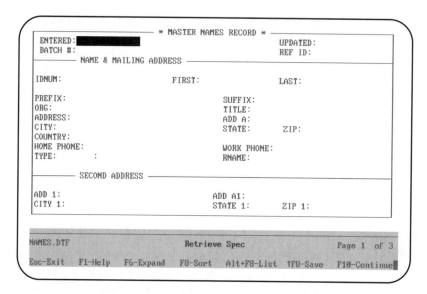

Figure 3.1   The first screen of the Names file.

Name and Address Fields in Screen 1 of the Names File

IDNUM   A unique number assigned to each entry in the database. It is used primarily as the Key field to look up information from the Names file into other files.

FIRST   The first name.

LAST   The last name.

PREFIX   Mr., Mrs., Dr., etc.

SUFFIX   J.D, M.D., Ph.D, C.P.A, etc.

ORG   The organization's name.

TITLE   The title of the person in the database.

ADDRESS   The street address of the individual or organization.

ADD A   The second address line, normally used for suite, building, mail stop, etc.

CITY   The city.

STATE   The state.

ZIP   The zip code.

COUNTRY   Any country outside of the United States.

HOME PHONE   The home phone number of the main contact.

WORK PHONE   The phone number of the organization.

TYPE   A one- to six-character alphanumeric code used to classify the name as a prospect, customer, staff member, etc. This field is programmed to place a description in the field next to the TYPE field. The description is looked up from the Codes file. The programming statement looks at the code in the field and matches it to the code in the Codes file. When it finds a match, it places the code's description in the field next to TYPE.

RNAME   The name of the company or individual. This field is used for reporting purposes. It is created based on the code in the TYPE field. A programming statement has been placed in the RNAME field that says: If the value in the TYPE field is IN for the individual, then put the individual's name in the RNAME field. If it is not IN, then put the organization's name in the RNAME field. This field is useful if you have a combination of individuals and organizations in your database and want to use only one name field on a report. It eliminates the need to place the organization's name, the first name, and the last name fields on the same report.

The SECOND ADDRESS section (Figure 3.1) is used to store another address. This could be the home address of a customer or a special billing or shipping address.

Second Address Fields in Screen 1 of the Names File

ADD 1   The second street address. This field can be used for a home address, billing address, or shipping address.

ADD A1   The second part of the street address.

CITY 1   The second city.

STATE 1   The second state.

ZIP 1   The second zip code.

The MAILING INFORMATION section, shown in Figure 3.2, holds the direct mail codes. These fields can be used to hold codes, dates, and remarks indicating the date you mailed material, what was mailed, and a line of remarks elaborating on what was mailed. By using the macro on the enclosed disk, you can automatically update these fields with the appropriate codes.

Fields in Screen 2 of the Names File

CODE   A code that represents the mailing, such as Spring92, for the mailing sent during the spring of 1992.

DATE   The date of the mailing.

RESPONSE   The date that the company or individual responded to the mailing.

REMARKS   Additional comments about the mailing.

Figure 3.3 shows the final screen on the form. This field is a full page of remarks where you can enter free-form information that does not fit neatly into one of the other fields.

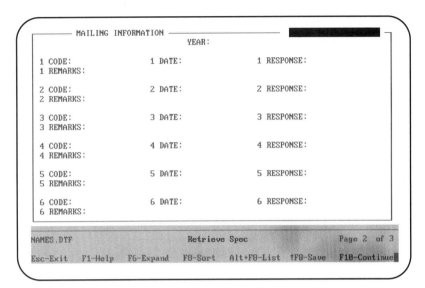

```
┌─── MAILING INFORMATION ──────────────────────┌──────────────┐─┐
│                          YEAR:                └──────────────┘ │
│ 1 CODE:            1 DATE:              1 RESPONSE:             │
│ 1 REMARKS:                                                     │
│                                                                │
│ 2 CODE:            2 DATE:              2 RESPONSE:             │
│ 2 REMARKS:                                                     │
│                                                                │
│ 3 CODE:            3 DATE:              3 RESPONSE:             │
│ 3 REMARKS:                                                     │
│                                                                │
│ 4 CODE:            4 DATE:              4 RESPONSE:             │
│ 4 REMARKS:                                                     │
│                                                                │
│ 5 CODE:            5 DATE:              5 RESPONSE:             │
│ 5 REMARKS:                                                     │
│                                                                │
│ 6 CODE:            6 DATE:              6 RESPONSE:             │
│ 6 REMARKS:                                                     │
│                                                                │
├────────────────────────────────────────────────────────────┤
│ NAMES.DTF              Retrieve Spec             Page 2 of 3   │
│ Esc-Exit  F1-Help  F6-Expand  F8-Sort  Alt+F8-List ↑F8-Save  F10-Continue│
```

Figure 3.2   Screen 2 of the Names file.

```
┌─── REMARKS ──────────────────────────────┌──────────────┐─┐
│ :                                         └──────────────┘ │
│                                                            │
│                                                            │
│                                                            │
│                                                            │
│                                                            │
│                                                            │
│                                                            │
│                                                            │
│                                                            │
│                                                            │
│                                                            │
├──────────────────────────────────────────────────────────┤
│ NAMES.DTF              Retrieve Spec             Page 3 of 3 │
│ Esc-Exit  F1-Help  F6-Expand  F8-Sort  Alt+F8-List ↑F8-Save  F10-Continue│
```

Figure 3.3   Screen 3 of the Names file.

By typing **R** for Report menu, selecting **D** for Design/Redesign a Report, and typing the filename, `Names`, you will be shown a list of reports for the Names file. Figure 3.4 shows only one report, the Master List of Names, but as you develop other reports for the Names file, they will be listed here. The Master List of Names report is a simple name and address list and can be modified as needed.

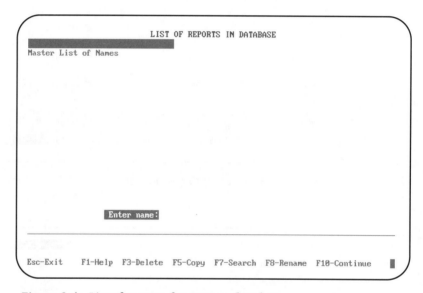

Figure 3.4   List of reports for Names database.

Using the Application

As you may recall from Chapter 2, the essential components of an application are the database file and its associated reports. The primary function of the Names application will be to store name and address information and other related data, and then print this data in a report—either columnar, form, or cross-tab. The other major function of the Names file is to store name and address information that can later be retrieved into other files, such as an Invoice or Personnel record. In this file you can store any type of name you want, including clients, prospects, staff members, patients, friends, associates, etc.

Adding Data

The first step in using any database file is to *add data*. You can accomplish this in two ways: by typing the data via the keyboard or by importing the data from an external file. The first method, typing the data, is the method you will use 99 percent of the time. The second method, importing data from an external file, is primarily used for transferring data from one system to another or to import names from an outside source such as a mailing list company.

Remember, all guided examples assume that you are starting from the Q&A Main menu. If an example is to start elsewhere, it will be thoroughly explained.

Adding data via the keyboard is very easy. All you do is select **F** for File from the Main menu and **A** for Add from the File menu. Q&A will then prompt you to enter a filename. Type the filename (**Names**) and press Enter. This places you at the first field in the database. Fill in the form with the appropriate information, and when you are finished, press F10 to *save the record*. This will clear the screen and bring up the next blank form. Repeat this process until you are through.

To review a record you just entered, press F9 to scroll back through the records. When you come to the last record, press Shift-F10 to save the last record and exit the form. This will leave you at the File menu. Figure 3.5 shows a database form completely filled in. Now try entering some data into the Names file.

Practice Entering Data into the Names File

1. Press **F** for File and **A** for Add.

2. Type **Names** and press Enter. The cursor begins at the BATCH # field. Notice that the date has been automatically placed in the ENTERED field. This is due to a programming statement in the ENTERED field. It instructs Q&A to place the date in the ENTERED field each time you add a new form.

   Also notice that the IDNUM field already contains a number. This number is placed there by the @number command in the Set Initial Values section of the Customize menu. The @number command provides a method for automatic numbering of organizations, records, invoices, etc. When a database is first developed, the

number is set at 1. To change the internal number that the
@number command starts with, press Ctrl-F8 while in Add mode,
enter a number that is one less than the number you want to start
with, and press F10. Then exit the form. When you reenter it, the
number will be reset.

3. With your cursor at the BATCH # field, press Enter three times to
   move to the FIRST name field and begin entering data.

4. When you get to the TYPE field, you need to decide how you want
   to code this particular record. If it is an individual—someone not
   associated with an organization—type **IN** in the TYPE field. If it is
   an organization, type **CO** in the TYPE field and press Enter.

   After pressing Enter, you will notice that, depending on the code
   you typed, either the word Individual or Corporation is placed
   in the field next to the TYPE field, and either the last name and first
   name or the company name is placed in the RNAME field. The
   cursor then moves to the ADD 1 field.

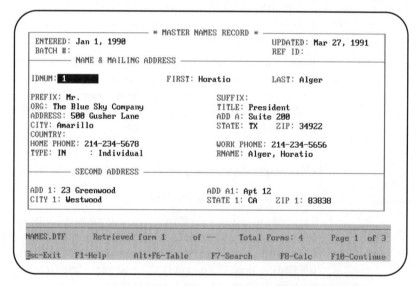

```
                        * MASTER NAMES RECORD * 
    ENTERED: Jan 1, 1990                        UPDATED: Mar 27, 1991
    BATCH #:                                    REF ID:
           NAME & MAILING ADDRESS 

    IDNUM: 1                    FIRST: Horatio       LAST: Alger

    PREFIX: Mr.                        SUFFIX:
    ORG: The Blue Sky Company          TITLE: President
    ADDRESS: 500 Gusher Lane           ADD A: Suite 200
    CITY: Amarillo                     STATE: TX    ZIP: 34922
    COUNTRY:
    HOME PHONE: 214-234-5678           WORK PHONE: 214-234-5656
    TYPE: IN     : Individual          RNAME: Alger, Horatio

           SECOND ADDRESS 

    ADD 1: 23 Greenwood                ADD A1: Apt 12
    CITY 1: Westwood                   STATE 1: CA    ZIP 1: 83838


    NAMES.DTF     Retrieved form 1     of --     Total Forms: 4     Page 1 of 3

    Esc-Exit   F1-Help     Alt+F6-Table    F7-Search     F8-Calc    F10-Continue
```

Figure 3.5   The Names file with screen 1 completely filled in.

All these actions happen because of programming statements placed
in each of the fields. The TYPE field has a programming statement in it that
instructs Q&A to look in the external Codes file (I developed this file to store
your system codes) and find the description associated with the codes IN or
CO and place it in the field next to TYPE. The RNAME field was programmed

to be filled in based on the value in the TYPE field. The programming statement says: If the value in the TYPE field is IN, then place the value from the LAST name field and the value from the FIRST name field in the RNAME field. If anything else is entered in the TYPE field, then place the value from the ORG field (company name) in the RNAME field.

The reason why you didn't have to press Enter to move through the fields is that the programming statements told Q&A to move the cursor to the ADD 1 field when it was through executing the programming statements. All of these concepts will be covered in-depth in Chapter 6.

5. Continue filling in the form. When you are through, press F8. A programming statement will copy the value from the RNAME field to the fields that are found at the top of the second and third screens. The F8 key is the Calc key, and it will be explained in a later chapter.

6. After you are finished filling out the form, either press F10 to save the current form and continue entering new forms or press Shift-F10 to save the last form and exit from Add mode.

Getting Help

While you are using Q&A, you may sometimes find that you aren't sure how to use a particular feature. You would like some help, but you don't want to get out the manual. Q&A provides *on-line context-sensitive help* from most places in the program when you press the F1 key. Context-sensitive help means that the help you receive is specific to the area of the program you are in. For example, to receive help on how to add records, go into Add mode and press F1. A help screen will pop up, explaining how to add records.

In addition to the standard help screens, you can define custom help screens for each field in the database. A custom help screen can be thought of as an electronic "Post-It" attached to a particular field. For example, to tell a data entry operator which codes are available for a given field, you can list them in the custom help screen for that field. Then if the operator is uncertain which codes to use, all that he or she has to do is press F1. The custom help pops up, explaining the available codes. Chapter 5 explains how to develop custom help screens.

Search and Update

This brings us to the most essential concept you need to master in using Q&A—search and update. Once you have entered records into your database, you will need a method of finding and changing them. These changes might be a simple address change, the addition of completely new data to an existing record, or the deletion of an entire record. All of these changes are executed by selecting the Search/Update option from the File menu. Q&A refers to this process as *searching and updating* and entering a *Retrieve spec*. These same concepts are also used when you are selecting records for a report, doing a mass mailing, or printing mailing labels.

When working with an existing Q&A database, you are always in either Search/Update mode or Add mode. In Add mode, you can only add records. In Search/Update mode, you can only change or delete existing records. The screen that directly precedes Update mode is Search mode. This is where you tell Q&A which records you want to retrieve. In other words, to get into Update mode so that you can change a record, you first have to select the records in Search mode.

There are two ways to get into Search/Update mode. The first way is to press **F** for File and **S** for Search, type the filename, and press Enter. Q&A displays a blank form on the screen with the words RETRIEVE SPEC at the bottom of the screen. When you see the words RETRIEVE SPEC at the bottom of the screen, you are in Search mode. It directly precedes Update mode. This is Q&A's way of telling you that you can begin choosing records from the file. The other way to get into Search/Update mode is to do so from Add mode. By pressing F7 while you are in Add mode, you automatically switch to Search/Update mode. When you are viewing a record in Update mode, you can switch back to Add mode by pressing Ctrl-F6.

With Q&A in Search mode, you have to tell it which records to retrieve. This process is known as *executing a search*. When you execute a search, you fill out a Retrieve spec. Q&A then looks to see if any records match the specifications of the Retrieve spec. If any do, Q&A displays them. If they don't, Q&A asks you to make another request. Another way to think about a Retrieve spec is that it is the "restriction" placed on your database—a kind of data filter that filters out all the records except the ones you have specified.

The components of a Retrieve spec are the specifications (the values and operators) and the F10 key. For example, suppose you want to conduct a simple search to find all the companies in your database that have offices in Texas. To do this, move to the STATE field; then type **TX** and press F10.

Q&A searches your database for all the records having TX in the STATE field. If it finds any, the records are displayed. To scroll through the records Q&A found, press F10. When you come to the last record, Q&A gives you the message No more records. Press Esc to exit or F9 for previous form. Then, by pressing F9, you can scroll backward through the records you just looked at.

Here is another example of a simple search. Suppose that you want to find all the people in your database having the last name of "Alger." To do this, move to the LAST name field; type **Alger** and press F10. Q&A retrieves the appropriate records. This type of search is known as an *exact match search*. The most basic search of all is to press F10 without entering any restrictions. Q&A will display ALL the records in the database in random order.

Practice Entering an Exact Match Search

1. Press **F** for File and **S** for Search.

2. Type the filename **Names** and press Enter. This will take you into the form.

3. Move the cursor to the STATE field. Type **CA** and press F10. Since there are three dummy records in the database, and one of them has CA in the STATE field, you will retrieve one record. If you have entered any records with CA in the STATE field, they will also be retrieved.

   Notice that the date has been automatically placed in the UPDATED field and that the cursor has moved to the BATCH # field. This is due to a programming statement in the UPDATED field that places the date in the UPDATED field every time you view or change a record. By looking at the field, you will know when a record was last updated.

4. To perform another search, press F7. Press F3 to clear the last Retrieve spec you entered. You are ready for another search.

5. Practice entering several different Retrieve specs, repeating steps 3 and 4.

Shortcut

Many of the WordStar editing commands work in Q&A, such as the key combinations of Ctrl and *A*, *S*, *D*, *F*, *T*, *Y*, *X*, *W*, etc.

Once you have mastered the exact match search, you are ready to try a *multivariable search*. The only difference between the two is that in the multivariable search you enter criteria into more than one field. For example, say you wanted to list every organization in California who had contacts with the last name of *Smith*. You would switch to Search mode and move to the LAST name field and type **SMITH**, move to the STATE field and type **CA**, and move to the TYPE field and type **OR**. Then you would press F10 to retrieve the records. Figure 3.6 displays this multivariable Retrieve spec.

```
                          ─ * MASTER NAMES RECORD * ─
    ENTERED:                                      UPDATED:
    BATCH #:                                      REF ID:
            ─ NAME & MAILING ADDRESS ─

   IDNUM:                     FIRST:              LAST: SMITH

   PREFIX:                            SUFFIX:
   ORG:                               TITLE:
   ADDRESS:                           ADD A:
   CITY:                              STATE: CA     ZIP:
   COUNTRY:
   HOME PHONE:                        WORK PHONE:
   TYPE: OR        :                  RNAME:

        ─ SECOND ADDRESS ─

   ADD 1:                             ADD A1:
   CITY 1:                            STATE 1:     ZIP 1:


   NAMES.DTF                   Retrieve Spec            Page 1  of 3

   Esc-Exit   F1-Help   F6-Expand   F8-Sort   Alt+F8-List   ↑F8-Save   F10-Continue
```

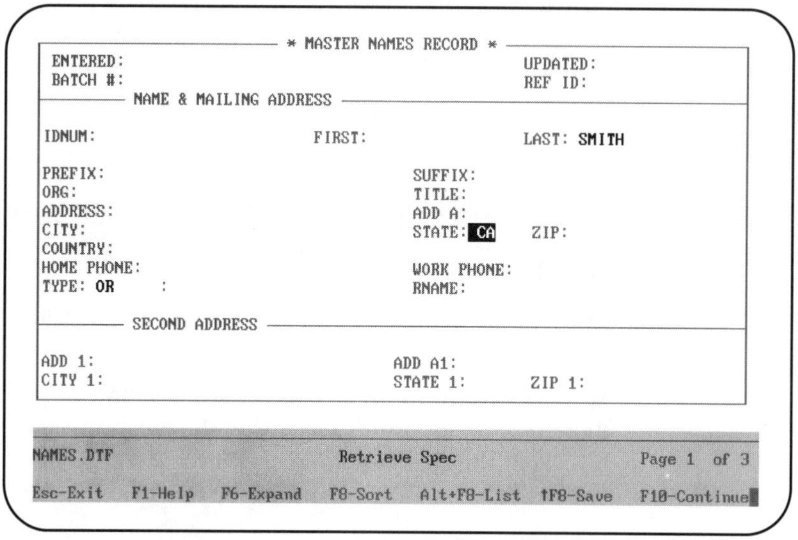

Figure 3.6   Multivariable Retrieve spec.

Q&A provides another tool to add more flexibility to your Retrieve specs—the Search Options menu. By pressing Ctrl-F7 in Search mode after you have entered your Retrieve spec, the Search Options menu appears. This menu, shown in Figure 3.7, lets you change the standard way that Q&A evaluates your Retrieve specs. Q&A's default Search mode is set to find all the records that *do* meet the Retrieve spec and that meet *all* of your restrictions. The Search Options menu lets you change these settings.

For example, you might want to select every organization *not* in California. To do this, you would move to the STATE field, type **CA**, press Ctrl-F7, and change the setting from DO to DO NOT. Then you would press F10. This would select all the records *not* in California. Another way you can use this Search Options menu is to instruct Q&A to find all the records that meet *any* of the conditions of your Retrieve spec. Using the earlier example in Figure 3.6, suppose you wanted to find every organization *and* everyone in California *and* everyone who had the last name of *Smith*. To do this, you would enter the Retrieve spec just as you did in Figure 3.6, press Ctrl-F7 to bring up the Search Options menu, change the Restrictions setting from DO NOT to DO, and press F10. Q&A would search the database and retrieve all the records that met any of the specifications.

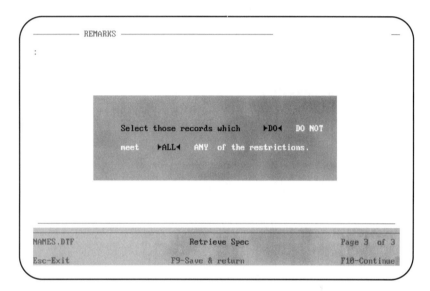

Figure 3.7   Search Options screen.

Another type of Retrieve spec is the *range search*. This search looks for records that fall within a range of values, such as all records entered between January 1 and March 1. To enter a Range Retrieve spec, move to the ENTERED field, press F6 to expand the field (expanding a field will be covered later), type **01/01/90..03/01/90**, and press F10. The dots (**..**) between the two dates act as a range command, instructing Q&A to find all the dates between these two dates. Since the dummy records are contained in the database, three records will be retrieved.

The Range Retrieve spec can be used to search for all types of data except Text and Keyword. For instance, using the Invoice database, you could look for all invoices in which the total invoice amount was between $1000 and $5000. To do this, you would move to the TOTAL field, press F6, type **1000..5000**, and press F10. Experiment with Range Retrieve specs using different types of data.

In addition to the Retrieve specs already covered, there are several advanced options you can use to further refine your Retrieve specs. Figure 3.8 displays many of them, and I will expand on some of the more useful ones. To retrieve a record by a particular field that has a long text value in it, such as an address, you can type the first few characters followed by two periods. The two periods (when used in this manner, as opposed to the range command) are Q&A's wildcard symbol, which is the same as the DOS asterisk (*). For example, by typing **123 No..** in the ADDRESS field, you could look up *123 North Chapple Street* and anything else that started with *123 No.*

This method is also useful if you do not know how an entry is spelled. For instance, by moving to the LAST name field and typing **Sm..**, you could look up *Smyth and Smith.* A variation on this method is to precede the text by the wildcard symbol. Move to the LAST name field again and type **..es**. Q&A would look up *Jones* or anyone else whose last name ended in *es*.

```
┌──────────────────────────────────────────────────────────────────┐
│              HOW TO SEARCH: THE RETRIEVE SPEC        Pg. F-??       │
│                                                                    │
│  Type symbols into individual fields to indicate what information you want. │
│                                                                    │
│   SYMBOL    MEANING                      EXAMPLES                   │
│                                                                    │
│   x         equal to x                   Boston    CA      4/12/85  │
│   /x        not equal to x               /CA       /Sales  /$100    │
│   >x        greater than x               >12:00 pm                  │
│   <x        less than x                  <10,000   <1/1/85          │
│   >=x       greater than or equal to x   >=Jones   >=12:00 am       │
│   <=x       less than or equal to x      <=1000    <=12/31/85       │
│   >x..<y    greater than x and less than y  >10..<100               │
│   x;y;z     x OR y OR z                   red;white;blue  9.99;10.00 │
│   =         empty (i.e., equal to nothing)                          │
│   /=        not empty                                               │
│   MIN n     retrieve n lowest values      MIN 5                     │
│   MAX n     retrieve n highest values     MAX 100                   │
│   x..       begins with x (if text field) pre..                     │
│   ..x       ends with x (if text field)   ..ing                     │
│   ..x..     contains x (if text field)    ..esp..                   │
│                                                                    │
│  Esc-Exit                → PgDn-Using expressions ←           ▮     │
└──────────────────────────────────────────────────────────────────┘
```

Figure 3.8   Advanced Retrieve spec options.

When you are searching for information, you will often want to select records that are less than or greater than some value. For example, to find all the records that you entered after a particular date, say January 1, 1990, you would move to the ENTERED field, type **> 01/01/90**, and press F10. Q&A would then retrieve the desired records.

The symbols preceding the values are known as *operators*: > for *greater than*; < for *less than*; >= for *greater than or equal to*; <= for *less than or equal to*; and <> for *not equal to*. Any of these operators can precede any of these field types: numeric, money, date, or text. Another example of this type of search would be finding all ID numbers greater than or equal to 2. Move to the IDNUM field, type **>=2**, and press F10. Q&A will retrieve records 2 and 3.

Two additional operators are the MIN and MAX commands. They allow you to find either the minimum or the maximum values in a field. By placing a number after the command, you instruct Q&A to find that number of records. To find out the five most recent names you entered in the database, you would move to the ENTERED field, type **MAX 5**, and press F10. To find out the single oldest record you entered, you would move to the ENTERED field, type **MIN**, and press F10. Once again, these commands work on the following field types: numeric, money, date, or text.

You can use the two symbols = and /= to help determine whether a field is empty. By placing the equal sign (=) in a field and pressing F10, you instruct Q&A to search all the available records and look for the ones that have NO value in the specified field. This command is useful if you are not sure whether you filled in a particular field such as the TYPE or ZIP field. The complementary command is the *not empty* (/=) sign. This command is used in the same way as the other one. However, it finds records that *have* any value in a particular field. For example, to find all the records that have a home phone number, you would switch to Search mode, move to the HOME PHONE field, type **/=**, and press F10.

Lastly, the forward slash (/) means "not", and can be used to find records that *do not* match some value. Suppose you need to select all the records that are not in California. You would move to the STATE field, type **/CA**, and press F10. You can use this symbol in front of any value: /$1000, /Mr. Jones, /01/01/90, etc.

If you have erroneously entered a record or found that you no longer need a name in your database, you can easily delete it. Press **F** for File and **S** for Search. Type the filename and press Enter. Retrieve the record using one of the preceding search methods. Once the record is on the screen, press F3. Q&A brings up a warning screen asking if you really want to delete the record. If you do, press Y for Yes. Once you delete a record, it *cannot* be recovered.

Practice Using the Advanced Retrieve Specs

1. Press **F** for File and **S** for search.

2. Type the filename **Names** and press Enter.

3. Enter your first Retrieve spec and press F10.

4. To conduct your next search, press F7. This puts you back in Search mode. Press F3 to clear the old Retrieve spec.

5. You can now enter your next Retrieve spec.

6. Repeat steps 4 and 5 until you feel comfortable using the various types of Retrieve specs.

7. When you are finished, press Shift-F10 to save the last record and exit.

Sort Specs

Often times, just selecting records won't be enough. You will want to display them in some specific order—alphabetically, by date entered, by largest sale, etc. To do this, you will have to *sort* your records. The reason for this is that Q&A stores your records in random order. After you exit Update mode, the records return to random order. If you want to view them in the same order the next time you enter Update mode, you will have to sort them again.

To sort records, you must be in Sort mode. To get into Sort mode, you have to first go through Search mode. That is, once you are in Search mode, simply press F8 and Q&A will indicate that it is ready for you to enter a Sort spec by displaying Sort Spec at the bottom of the screen. A *Sort spec* consists of a number between 1 and 999 followed by either AS for *ascending order*, low to high (A–Z), or DS for *descending order*, high to low (Z–A). The number represents the sort level. You can have up to 999 sort levels, although you will probably never use more than two or three. An easy way to understand sort levels is to think of how phone books are put together. They are first divided by counties into separate books, a level-one sort, and then within each book the names are listed alphabetically, a level-two sort.

To sort the Names file by state and then by zip code, press **F** for File and **S** for Search. Type the filename **Names** and press Enter. Enter an optional

Retrieve spec and press F8 (if you do not enter a Retrieve spec, Q&A will sort all your data). Press F8 to switch to Sort mode, move to the STATE field, and type **1 AS** (first-level sort, low to high). Then move to the ZIP field, type **2 AS** (second-level sort, low to high), and press F10. Q&A will sort all your records first by state and then by zip code and place you in Update mode, ready to view or edit them.

Save Your Retrieve and Sort Specs

A new and very useful feature added to Version 4.0 is the ability to *save your Retrieve and Sort specs*. Without this feature, every time you finished a retrieve or sort, the spec you entered would be lost. This is particularly tiresome if it is a spec you use regularly. But now you can save your most common Retrieve and Sort specs and use them again and again.

To save a Retrieve spec, change to Search mode, enter your Retrieve spec, press Shift-F8, give the spec a name, and press Enter. Now whenever you want to use this spec again, switch to Search mode, press Alt-F8, highlight the spec you want, and press Enter. Q&A will place the Retrieve spec in the appropriate fields. Press F10 to execute the search.

To save a Sort spec for future use, switch to Search mode, press F8, enter your Sort spec, press Shift-F8, give it a name, and press Enter. If you want to use it again, make sure you are in Sort mode; then press Alt-F8, highlight the desired spec, and press Enter. Q&A will place the Sort spec in the proper fields. Just press F10 to execute the sort.

Shortcut

You can add to either the Sort or the Retrieve spec you just selected. Then you can save them with the same name, changing the old spec, or give them a new name, keeping the old spec intact.

Print Current Record

You can print all the screens of a database form from either Add or Update mode. With the record on the screen, press F2. This brings up the File Print Options screen, shown in Figure 3.9. Normally you will not need to change any of these options, so press F10. To print a *blank* form, you must be in Add mode; then press F2 and F10. Techniques for more elaborate form printing are covered in Chapter 4.

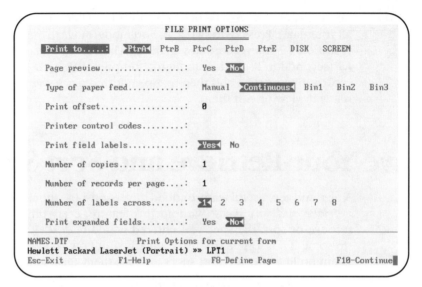

```
                        FILE PRINT OPTIONS

   Print to.....:    ▶PtrA◀  PtrB   PtrC   PtrD   PtrE   DISK   SCREEN

   Page preview.................:    Yes  ▶No◀

   Type of paper feed...........:    Manual  ▶Continuous◀  Bin1   Bin2   Bin3

   Print offset.................:    0

   Printer control codes........:

   Print field labels...........:    ▶Yes◀  No

   Number of copies.............:    1

   Number of records per page...:    1

   Number of labels across......:    ▶1◀  2   3   4   5   6   7   8

   Print expanded fields........:    Yes  ▶No◀
   _____
   NAMES.DTF              Print Options for current form
   Hewlett Packard LaserJet (Portrait) »» LPT1
   Esc-Exit           F1-Help              F8-Define Page          F10-Continue▮
```

Figure 3.9   File Print Options screen.

Beginner's Tip

When you are printing from Update or Add mode, Q&A does not allow you to print only one of the screens of a database form. You have to print all of them.

Print List of Names

Viewing information only on the computer screen is not always practical. Some members of your organization may not have access to the computer. Thus, those people will need the information in printed form. Q&A offers three types of reports: form, cross-tab, and columnar. The specifics of each type of report and how to develop them will be covered in later chapters. However, in this chapter, I will show you how to print an existing report from the Names file that will list all the names in the database. You can see this report in Figure 3.10.

Printing the Master List of Names Report

1. Press **R** for Report.

2. Press **P** for Print. You will notice there are two options for printing, Design/Redesign a Report and Print a Report. If you use the first option to print the report, you permanently change the report. Using the second option, however, changes the settings only temporarily.

```
Nov 7, 1990                          MASTER LIST OF NAMES                                              PAGE 1

    IDNUM  FIRST    LAST       ORG              TITLE            ADDRESS         ADD A     CITY     STATE  ZIP
    -----  -------  -----  ----------------  ---------------  --------------------  ---------  ---------  -----  -----
        1  Horatio  Alger  The Blue Sky Company  President     200 Gusher Lane     Suite 200  Amarillo   TX     34922

        2  Billy    Bob    The Good Health   Chief of Surgery  2398 Golightly Blvd. Suite 234 Podunk     SD     23432
                           Hospital

        3  Sarah    Napier Sacks: Fine Burlap  President        987 Material Lane             New York   NY     12363
                           Clothing

       =====  =======  =====  ======================  ================  ====================  =========  =========  =====  =====
Count:                                          3
```

Figure 3.10   Master List of Names report.

3. Type the filename **Names** and press Enter.

4. Choose Master List of Names and press Enter.

5. Press Yes to make temporary changes.

6. This will bring you to the Retrieve Spec screen. It is here that you choose which records you want to print. Enter your Retrieve spec *exactly* the way you did in Search mode. To print all the names in the database, press F10. Otherwise, enter a Retrieve spec and press F10.

You are now at the Column/Sort spec. It is here that you define how the report is going to look, which fields will appear on the report, how it will be sorted, and if any calculations will be used on any of the columns. Looking at Figure 3.11, you will notice that there are numbers in several of the fields. These are the columns that will appear on the report. The AS after the number 3 in the LAST field means to sort the report in ascending order by last name. The C after the 4 in the ORG field means to count all the names on the list. What the rest of the information means and how to create columnar reports will be covered in-depth in Chapter 5.

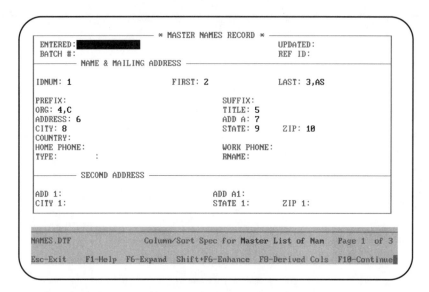

```
                          — * MASTER NAMES RECORD * —
  ENTERED: ████████████████              UPDATED:
  BATCH #:                                REF ID:
  ———————— NAME & MAILING ADDRESS ——————————————————————————

  IDNUM: 1                 FIRST: 2            LAST: 3,AS

  PREFIX:                       SUFFIX:
  ORG: 4,C                      TITLE: 5
  ADDRESS: 6                    ADD A: 7
  CITY: 8                       STATE: 9    ZIP: 10
  COUNTRY:
  HOME PHONE:                   WORK PHONE:
  TYPE:          :              RNAME:

  ——————— SECOND ADDRESS ———————————————————————————

  ADD 1:                        ADD A1:
  CITY 1:                       STATE 1:    ZIP 1:


 NAMES.DTF           Column/Sort Spec for Master List of Nam   Page 1  of 3

 Esc-Exit     F1-Help  F6-Expand  Shift+F6-Enhance  F8-Derived Cols  F10-Continue
```

Figure 3.11   Names screen with Column/Sort spec.

7. For now, you will print the report as it is designed, without making any changes. Press F10 to skip the Column/Sort spec screen.

8. You are at the Print Options menu. Choose the correct printer and press F10.

When the report is finished printing, you will have a list of all the names in the Names database, provided you didn't enter any restrictions.

Direct Mail Macro

You will learn how to replay a macro that I have already developed. It is called the Update Direct Mail Codes macro. This macro automatically updates the direct mail code fields in the Names file. The macro will add a direct mail code of your choice, a mailing date, and a line of remarks to the group of records you select. The records you select are the ones that would normally receive this particular mailing. Figure 3.12 displays these fields with sample data in them.

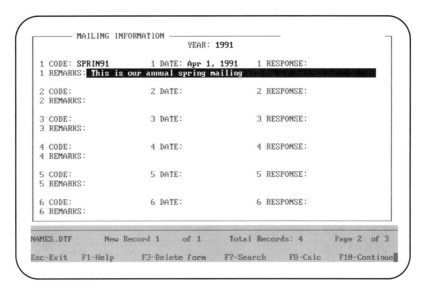

Figure 3.12 Direct mail code fields with sample data.

What is a macro? Recall from Chapter 2 that a *macro* is a series of recorded keystrokes saved under one key combination, called the *macro identifier*, such as Alt-A. When you press the macro identifier, all of the recorded keystrokes are replayed. The main purpose of using macros is to save time by speeding up repetitive tasks. For instance, if you print invoices every week, you have to press the same keys each time. If you recorded these keystrokes in a macro, you could just press the macro identifier each week rather than all the individual keys.

Developing a macro involves nothing more than turning on the macro recording facility, assigning a macro identifier, and typing the keystrokes you want to record. Recording macros is similar to recording music on a tape recorder: Put on your favorite music, press the record button, and turn off the recorder when the song is over. When you want to hear that song again, place the tape in the tape player and press play.

The Update Direct Mail Codes macro allows you to select a group of records, everyone in California for example, and then automatically fill in the mailing codes fields. These codes and dates will be added to *all* the records you select. The first part of the macro goes into the Mass Update feature and pauses at the Retrieve spec. It is here that you specify which records you want to update. The macro then proceeds to the second half of the Mass Update feature, which is the Update spec. Here you tell Q&A which fields you want to update with what information. Lastly, you have the option of updating the records individually or all at once. The Direct Mail macro has already been programmed to perform several tasks. The following instructions will lead you through them.

Running the Update Direct Mail Codes Macro

1. From the Q&A Main menu, press Shift-F2 to bring up the Macro menu.

2. Press **R** for Run a Macro.

3. Highlight the Update Direct Mail Codes macro and press Enter.

> **Caution:** This macro utilizes the *pause* feature. That means that it has been programmed to pause at various places for you to enter variable information. Once you are done entering the variable information, you tell the macro to proceed by pressing Enter. If you press Enter prematurely, however, the macro will malfunction. Therefore, do not use the Enter key to move from field to field. Instead use the Arrow keys and the Tab key to move around the form.

4. The first place that the macro pauses is at the Retrieve spec on the first screen of the Names file in Mass Update. If you have only the dummy data in the database, you can type the Retrieve spec of **CA** in the STATE field and press Enter. Otherwise, type any Retrieve spec you want. *Remember that whatever Retrieve spec you enter, all of those records will be updated.*

5. The next place that the macro pauses is at the first direct mail code field, 1 CODE. Using the Arrow keys, you can position the cursor at the beginning of any of the *groups* of code fields. Whichever group you position the cursor at, is the group that will have the codes placed in them. If you want to update the first group, press Enter.

6. Next, you will notice that the macro expands the CODE field and types #1", leaving the cursor waiting there for you to type a code. Type a code and press Enter to resume the macro playback.

7. The macro will move over to the DATE field and type #2=" (today's date), leaving the cursor waiting there for you to accept the date. To use today's date, press Enter. If you want to type another date, backspace over today's date, type the correct date, and press Enter.

8. The cursor pauses at the REMARKS field and types #3", leaving the cursor waiting there for you to type a line of remarks. Type a line of remarks and press Enter.

9. The cursor will now move back to the CODE field, waiting for you to make any additional changes. If you have none, press Enter.

10. Q&A will search the database for the records you specified. When it finds them, it displays a screen that tells you how many forms will be updated and it asks if you want to update them individually or all at once. The cursor is highlighting the word NO. Press Enter to have all the records changed at once.

11. Q&A will change the records and return you to the Q&A Main menu.

Importing Data

At the beginning of the section "Add Data," I talked about another method of adding data to your database. This method, *importing data*, is used if you have an external data file, such as a list from a mailing house, an existing database, or a spreadsheet file that you want to import into Q&A. For our purposes, the external file will also be referred to as the *source* file and the Q&A file will also be referred to as the *target* file.

Q&A uses a proprietary file format that is not compatible with other databases. This means that in order to import your data into Q&A, it must be translated into a format that Q&A understands. This translation process works the same way as an interpreter works when two people speak different languages. Q&A takes the foreign language, the external file, and translates it into the native language, the Q&A file.

> ▶ **Note:** The procedures in this section are divided into two parts. The procedure, "Getting Ready to Import Data," guides you through the steps preceding the actual import process. The second procedure, "Importing the Sample File IMPORT.ASC," guides you through importing a sample ASCII file.

Getting Ready to Import Data

1. Determine which type of external file format you have. Q&A allows you to import several basic file formats, including ASCII, PFS, IBM Filing Assistant, DIF, dBASE, and Paradox. Figure 3.13 shows you all the different options. If the source file format is on the list, then you are through with step 1. If it is not, you can see if the program that contains the source file can export in one of the supported formats. One format to look for in particular is called ASCII. The ASCII file format is very common and supported by many other programs.

Beginner's Tip

To import a Lotus 1-2-3 spreadsheet (using Lotus Version 2.1), you will need to use the Translate utility and change your spreadsheet to the DIF format.

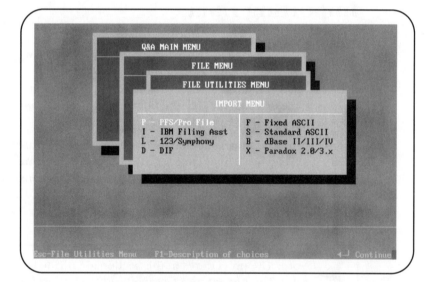

Figure 3.12   File Import Options screen.

Shortcut

If you import a dBASE, Paradox, or PFS file and do not specify a Q&A database where the data can be placed, Q&A will automatically create a Q&A file using the same field names used in the source file format.

2. After you have determined the format of your source file, you must choose which of your Q&A files will be the target file. This is the file that will be receiving the data.

3. Determine the order of the fields in the source database. The reason you need to know this information is because you are going to tell Q&A to place specific fields from your source database into specific fields in your target database.

These first three steps have to be performed each time you do an import. If you import the same type of data, in the same field order, the process will be quite fast. The next set of steps will take you through the actual importing of three dummy records into the Names file. If you do not want to use the dummy data and have your own data to import, simply substitute your data file and field order for the sample ones.

Included on the disk that comes with this book is a standard ASCII file called IMPORT.ASC. The next set of steps will guide you through importing it into the Names file. For simplicity, the fields in this file conform to the order of the fields in the Names file so that your import will go quite smoothly, not requiring you to specify which field from the source file will be placed in which field of the target Q&A file. Normally when you import a file, field order *will not* conform to the Q&A file field format.

Fields in an ASCII file are numbered right to left, beginning with 1. Figure 3.16 shows you what this file looks like. Each of the fields is surrounded by quotes and is separated by a comma. If the field is blank, there is only a comma surrounded by quotes (" , "). Figure 3.14 shows you the ASCII file IMPORT.ASC.

```
"Nov 5, 1990"," ","Test"," ",3,"Sarah","Napier","Ms."," ","Sacks: Fine Burlap Clothing","
President","987 Material Lane"," ","New York","NY","12363"," ","212-238-2211","212-232-2311"," "," "," "
" "," "," "," "," "," "," "," "," "," "," "," "," "," "," "," "," "," "," "," "," "," "," "," "," "," "," "," "," "
" "," "," "," "," "," "," "," "," "," "

"Nov 5, 1990","Nov 5, 1990","Test"," ",2,"Billy","Bob","Mr.","M.D.","The Good Health Hospital","Chief of
Surgery","2398 Golightly Blvd.","Suite 234","Podunk","SD","23432"," ","234-737-3321","234-987-
2321","IN","Individual","Bob, Billy"," "," "," "," "," "," "," "," "," "," "," "," "," "," "," "," "," "," "," "
" "," "," "," "," "," "," "," "," "," "," "," "," "," "," "," "," "

"Oct 18, 1990","Oct 18, 1990","Test"," ",1,"Horatio","Alger","Mr.","JD","The Blue Sky
Company","President","200 Gusher Lane","Suite 200","Amarillo","TX","34922"," ","214-234-5678","214-234-
5656","IN","Individual","Alger, Horatio","23 Greenwood","Apt 12","Westwood","CA","83838"," "," "," "," ","Nov
3, 1990"," "," "," "," "," "," "," "," "," "," "," "," "," "," "," "," "," "," "," "," "," "," "," "," "," "," "," "
```

Figure 3.14   View of ASCII file IMPORT.ASC

Importing the Sample File IMPORT.ASC

1. Press **F** for File, **U** for Utilities, and **I** for Import.

2. Q&A asks for the type of file format you want to import. This must match your source file. Type **S** for Standard ASCII.

3. The next prompt is for the actual source filename. Type **import.asc** (or your filename) and press Enter.

4. Now Q&A wants to know the name of the Q&A target file into which the data will be placed. Type **Names** (or your own filename) and press Enter.

5. The Merge Spec screen appears, waiting for your specs. This is where you tell Q&A which field of the source database you want to place in which field of the Q&A database. You do this by typing a number, which corresponds to a field in the source file, in each field of the target file in which you want data to be imported. IMPORT.ASC already conforms to the Names field order, so press F10 to skip this step.

6. Since you are importing an ASCII file, the ASCII Options screen appears. Here you indicate whether your text is surrounded by quotes and what the field delimiter is. If you were importing another file format, this screen would not appear. Press F10 to continue.

7. You will notice the three records flashing on the screen as they are imported.

8. Press Esc twice to return to the Main menu. This completes the entire importing process.

> ▶ **Note:** After you are through practicing with the dummy data, you can remove it pressing **F** for File and **R** for Remove. Type **Names** and press **S** for Selected Forms. Move to the BATCH # field and type **TEST**. Press F10 and **Y**. Press Esc twice.

Guided Modifications

The next few sections will explain how to use the basic design features of Q&A while guiding you through the modification of the Names database. The features covered are summarized in the "At a Glance" section at the beginning of the chapter.

If the Names file fits your needs in its present format, you can use it exactly as it is, without modification. However, I have found that every organization has different needs and does things a little differently—in short, there is no standard Names file. So you will probably need to change the file.

> ⊘ **Caution:** You may want to make a copy of the Names file before beginning these exercises. Then, if you make any changes you aren't happy with, you still have the original copy on your hard drive.

Suggested Modifications

The amount of information you store on each company or individual depends on your needs. The information you store in the Names file depends on which other databases you will be using. The general rule of thumb is to design your databases so that you *are not typing original information into more than one file.* The Names file normally contains the most general of information, such as name and address, other contacts at the company, etc. For instance, if you are going to use the Personnel application, you would not type the salary information into the Names file, because it is contained in the Staff file.

Shortcut

To determine which other databases you will need, you can complete the exercises in Chapter 1. If you haven't gone through those exercises, I *highly recommend that you do so.* They will help you determine which applications you need and then guide you through designing them.

The applications included with the book use the lookup feature to extract the basic name and address information from the Names file and place it in other files as needed. Remember that the lookup feature uses a common field in two databases, such as the customer ID number, to take information from one file and place it in another one. Which fields are looked up are determined by the programming statements entered in the Program spec, which is accessed through the Customize menu. Programming statements will be covered briefly below, and in-depth in Chapter 6.

If you completed the examples in Chapter 1, you already know which changes you want to make to the Names file. If you did not, here are some suggestions:

- Add a second section for another contact at the organization.

- Add a salutation field.

- Add a fax number field.

- Add six more mailing code fields.

- Add other codes to further classify your records.

Adding a second contact section is a popular change. Often times, particularly in a selling situation, you need room for more than one contact at an organization. Another change, often used by nonprofit organizations, is to add a salutation field. With the widespread use of fax machines, you may need space to record a fax number. Organizations involved in direct mail often mail monthly. To meet this need, you can add six more groups of mailing code fields. Another function to add is one or more code fields to further classify the records in the database, such as sales volume, income, type of business, occupation, etc.

To teach you the design features listed in the "At a Glance" section at the beginning of this chapter, I will guide you through making the following changes: adding a fax number field, adding a second contact section, and adding six more mailing code field groups. If you are making changes different from the ones explained, simply follow the instructions until you reach the part of the instructions that does not apply and substitute your changes for the ones I am suggesting.

You are now ready to begin modifying the Names File. Remember, all instructions assume that you are starting at the Q&A Main menu and have already loaded the application files into the FILE subdirectory. If the instructions start at a menu *other* than the Main menu, you will be guided to the new starting point.

Redesign a File

Q&A uses the term *designing a file* to refer to *creating a new file*. It uses the term *redesigning a file* to refer to *changing an existing file*. When you initially design a file, you start with a blank screen. It is here that you add all the necessary fields, format each field, and customize the database. Since you are using files that have already been designed, you will only be redesigning the file. However, the concepts are the same in both modes of operation.

Here is a brief overview of what you will be doing. Redesigning a file requires several steps, which start at the Design menu. To get there, press **F** for File, **D** for Design, and **R** for Redesign. Type the filename and press Enter. This will place you at the first screen of the file you are redesigning. You then make the necessary changes: add fields, remove fields, or draw lines. When you are through, press F10 to save your design and bring up the Format Spec menu where you define the field types. Press F10 again and the Global Format menu is retrieved. Here you can change the date and other formats. By pressing F10 a final time, you complete the process of redesigning a file.

Add a Fax Number Field

The following procedure will now guide you through adding the FAX NUMBER field to the Names file.

Practice Adding the FAX NUMBER Field to the Names File

1. Press **F** for File, **D** for Design, and **R** for Redesign.

2. Type the filename **Names** and press Enter. You are now at the first screen of the Names file in Redesign mode. It should look like Figure 3.15.

3. Press Home three times.

4. Move down 11 lines.

5. Tab over to the space under the S in the STATE field.

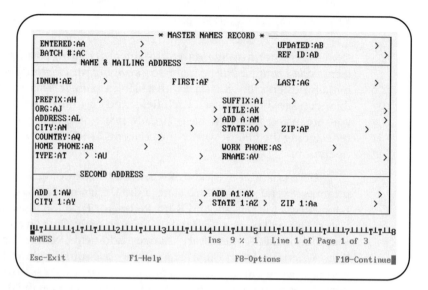

Figure 3.15   Screen 1 of the Names file in Redesign mode.

Beginner's Tip

Remember that a field holds a specific type of information, such as the last name. In Q&A, *field definition* consists of placing a : (colon) to indicate the start of the field and a > (greater-than symbol) to indicate the end of the field. The distance between these two symbols is the amount of space (the number of characters) that you have for entering data.

6. Type **FAX NUMBER:** (13 spaces) >.

This completes the process of adding the FAX NUMBER field. The Names file should now look like Figure 3.16.

Shortcut

You can format the FAX NUMBER and PHONE NUMBER fields to automatically place the dashes between the area code and phone number. To do this, go to the Customize menu, choose Field Template, and follow the instructions on the screen when you press F1.

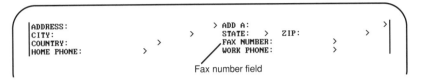

ADDRESS:
CITY: >   > ADD A:
COUNTRY: >   STATE: > ZIP: >   > >
HOME PHONE: >   FAX NUMBER: >
                                              WORK PHONE: >

Fax number field

Figure 3.16   New FAX Number field in Names file.

Add a Second Contact Field

While staying in Redesign mode, you will add a second contact field.

Practice Adding a Second Contact Field

1. Press Home three times.

2. Press PgDn.

3. Turn Insert to ON.

4. Press Enter 22 times to move the Mailing Information section off the second screen.

5. Turn Insert to OFF.

6. Tab over to the second tab marker. Type **CONTACT TWO**.

7. Tab over to the sixth tab marker and place a <. Move 20 spaces and place a >. The < symbol acts in place of the normal colon to start a field. This type of field is referred to as an *invisible field*.

Beginner's Tip

You have created a field at the top of the screen that will be used to hold the name of the company or individual. When you are on page 3 or 4 of a multiscreen form, you cannot always tell whose record you are in. By placing a field at the top of each screen and then placing a programming statement in the field to copy the name to it, you will always know which record you are editing.

8. Move down two lines and tab to the first tab marker.

9. Type all the fields as they appear in Figure 3.17. The number of spaces between the : and > are shown for each field in Figure 3.17.

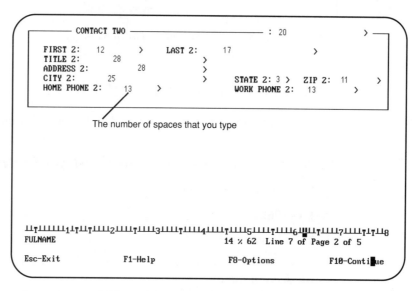

Figure 3.17   Fields with their respective space numbers.

Beginner's Tip

In steps 10 through 12, you will be drawing lines around the fields you just placed on the form. To get to the *Line Draw* facility, you have to open the *Options menu*. To bring up the Options menu, you have to press F8. This menu displays submenus, each with its own set of commands. Some of the commands can be executed only through this menu, while others can be executed by pressing the appropriate function key combinations. If an item appears faint, it is because it is not available in this section of the program. Throughout the chapters, each of the Options menu features will be explained. Figure 3.18 shows you the Options menu.

10. Press F8 to bring up the Options menu.

11. Press **L** for Layout Page and **D** for Draw.

12. Draw lines around the fields as shown in Figure 3.17.

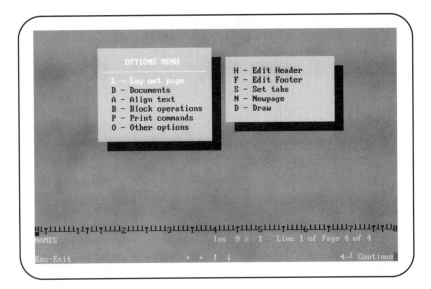

Figure 3.18 Options menu.

To draw single lines, use the Arrow keys. Lines are drawn in the direction of the arrow. If you have a 101 keyboard, press Num Lock and use the arrows on the number pad to draw double lines. To erase a line, press F8 again and use the cursor keys to erase lines. To put the pen back into Draw mode, press F8. Lastly, to move the pen to another spot on the screen without drawing lines, press F6 to pick up the pen. Move to where you want to draw lines and press F6 again to put down the pen and continue drawing.

13. When you are finished drawing, press F10 to return to Design mode.

Add Mailing Code Fields

Continue to stay in Redesign mode while you add another screen of mailing codes.

Practice Adding Mailing Code Fields

1. Press Home three times.

2. Press PgDn twice to move to the next screen.

3. Adjust the Mailing Information section so that it is at the top of the screen. You can use the Del key to pull the section up, or turn Insert to ON and use the Enter key to move the section down.

4. Move the cursor to the upper left corner of the Mailing Information section and press F5 to begin the copy procedure. Move down 20 lines. Then move over to the right side of the screen to highlight the entire section. Press F10 to mark the text you want to copy. Move down to the top left corner of the next screen and press F10. This will copy the entire block.

5. Adjust the second section if necessary so that it is at the top of the screen.

Shortcut

The *Block Copy* command you just used to replicate the Mailing Information section can also be invoked from the Options menu by pressing F8, **B** for Block Operations, and **C** for Copy. When you do this, you will also notice two other block commands very similar to the Copy command. They are *Block Delete* and *Block Move*. These commands can be accessed via the F5 key as well.

Beginner's Tip

To *move a block of text*, move to the beginning of the text that you want to move and press Shift-F5. Then, using the cursor keys, move to the end of the text you want to move and press F10. You will notice that the text is highlighted. Move your cursor to the new location on the form and press F10. The text is relocated. The Delete command works the same way. Move to the beginning of the text you want to delete and press F3. Move to the end of the text and press F10. The text will disappear. To *restore text* after you have deleted it, press Shift-F7. The text will be restored. The Shift-F7 command restores the last text you deleted. For instance, if you delete a block of text and then delete another block of text and then press Shift-F7, only the second block of text will be restored.

6. Because you copied the other Mailing Information section (rather than typing each field individually), all of the fields of the new section have the same field identifier. Q&A does not allow this. You must now remove each of the field identifiers in the new Mailing Information section. The field identifier is the two characters that follow each colon. For example, in 1 CODE:Ad, the Ad is the field identifier.

Turn Insert to OFF. Move to *every* field in the new Mailing Information section and remove the letters immediately after the colon, as shown in Figure 3.19. Place the cursor on the first letter to delete and press the Spacebar twice.

Delete each field
identifier

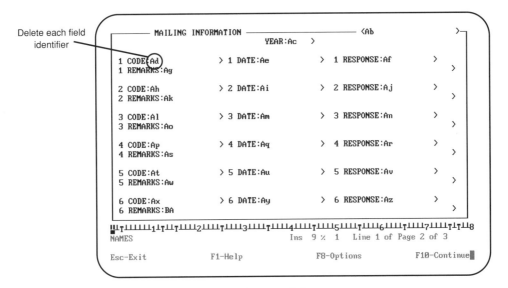

Figure 3.19   Field identifiers to delete.

7. Once you have removed all the field identifiers from the new Mailing Information section, you will need to renumber the field names in the new section to continue the sequence from the previous screen. For example, in the new section 1 CODE becomes 7 CODE, etc. Move to each field and renumber it.

8. After you have renumbered the fields, make sure the new section is properly aligned on the screen.

9. Also check the Remarks screen on the next page to see that it is properly aligned. If you want to make any other changes to the Names file, make them now. These can include adding or removing fields, rearranging the order of the fields, or drawing new lines to create new sections. When you are through with the field design, it is time to move on to save the design.

10. Press F10 to save the design.

Format Fields

The last time you pressed F10, it brought up the *Field Format Options* screen. To format a field, all you have to do is move to each field and type a letter in it that corresponds to one of the field types: N for numeric, T for text, M for money, D for date, T for time, or K for keyword. The default for each field is Text. You can see this menu in Figure 3.20.

The only field type that might need some explanation is the keyword field. This field lets you enter different values into one field separated by semicolons and then search for one or more of these values. For example, if you had a field called HOBBIES, you could enter these values into the field: biking; skiing; hiking; sewing. Then, using the Retrieve spec, you could search for those who sew and hike by typing **sewing;hiking** in the HOBBIES field. Q&A would search your records for anyone who had either of these values in the HOBBIES field and display them.

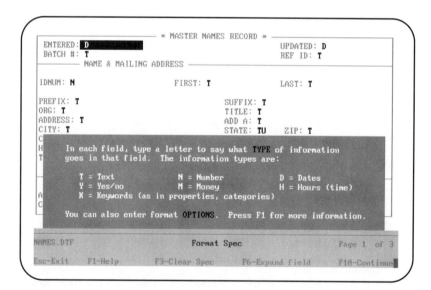

Figure 3.20   Format Spec screen.

Formatting a Field

1. Move to each field and type the letter corresponding to the correct format type. If you press F1 while in the Format screen, you can view the advanced formatting options. These options primarily deal with how the fields are justified. In the Mailing Information section that you just created, each of the DATE fields needs a date designation.

Shortcut

You can generate a Keyword report that takes the headings of all the keywords in a keyword field and then lists all the people who have that keyword in their file.

2. When you are through formatting the fields, press F10.

3. The Global Format Options screen will appear, as shown in Figure 3.21. This screen allows you to change the date, time, and currency formats. Make any changes you want and press F10 to complete the process of adding fields.

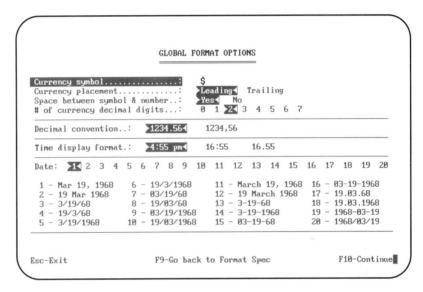

Figure 3.21   Global Format Options screen.

Shortcut

You can access these formatting options without redesigning a file by choosing **F** for file, **D** for design, and **C** for Customize. Type the filename, press Enter, and press **F** for Format Options.

Speed Up Searches

With the fields defined and the formats chosen, it is time to *speed up searches*. This option lets you speed up information retrieval by designating certain fields as *speedy fields*. The fields you designate as speedy are stored in a special presorted file known as an *index file*. You can have up to 115 fields designated as speedy fields. However, too many speedy (indexed) fields will cause a lag time when you are saving new records. This is because Q&A has to place each record in a separate index file. A practical limit is about 7 speedy fields. However, you can experiment with this number.

There are two types of speedy fields. One is regular; the other is unique. The *regular* option is indicated by an S in the field, and the *unique* option is indicated by an SU in the field. The unique option tells Q&A to make sure that every value in that field is unique. For instance, if one record already had number 301 as an ID number and you tried to enter another record with the same ID number, Q&A would instruct you to choose another number.

If you are planning to use the @xlookup option, you must designate the external key field as a speedy field. In all the enclosed applications, the IDNUM field and the Inventory fields are designated as SU and are external key fields.

Practice Designating Unique and Regular Speedy Fields

1. Press **F** for File, **D** for Design, and **C** for Customize.

2. Type the filename **Names** and press Enter.

3. Press **S** for Speed Up Searches.

4. Move to the Contact Two section and place an **S** in the FIRST 2 and LAST 2 fields.

5. Press F10 to save your selections.

Simple Programming Statement

Although programming statements will be covered in-depth in Chapter 6, you need to know how to program a simple statement for the Names file. A programming statement instructs Q&A to perform a task so that you don't have to. In this case, you need to tell Q&A to copy the value from the RNAME field to the fields in the upper right corner of each screen when you press F8 while adding data. The purpose of this field is to let you know which record you are editing when you are not on the first screen. See Figure 3.22 to view where the programming statements are located and what they look like.

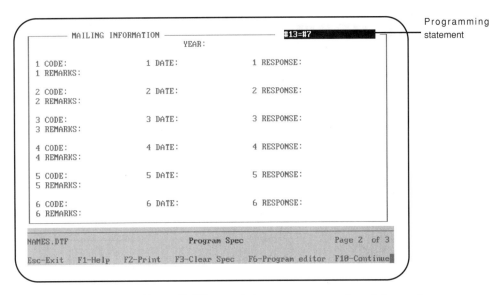

Programming
statement

Figure 3.22   Corner Name field containing a programming statement.

Practice Entering a Simple Programming Statement

1. Press **F** for File, **D** for Design, and **P** for Program.

2. Type the filename **Names** and press Enter.

3. Press **P** for Program Form.

4. You are now inside the Names file. Press PgDn three times. The cursor should be in the upper right field at the top of the new Mailing Information screen.

5. Type **#15=#7**. This tells Q&A that the field you are in is number 15 and that you want it to have the same value as field number 7 (RNAME from screen 1). Repeat this step for each screen that has a field in the upper right corner of the screen, giving a unique number to each field.

6. When you are through, press F10 to save your programming statements.

7. Press **Esc** three times to return to the Main menu.

Summary

At this point you should have completed the suggested modifications or your own modifications. As you learn other design features, you can add more bells and whistles to the Names file, but you do not need to add anything else to use it. If you completed the macro example, you have a macro to automatically mass-update the direct mail fields.

USE APPLICATION FEATURES

Copy/Rename/Delete Files

1. Wherever files are listed, you can press F5 to copy a file, F8 to rename a file, or F3 to delete a file.

Copy/Rename/Delete Report Specs

1. Wherever report names are listed, you can press F5 to copy a file, F8 to rename a file, or F3 to delete a file.

Print Form Reports

1. Press **F** for File and **P** for Print.
2. Type the filename and press Enter.
3. Choose the report and press Enter. Answer Yes to make temporary changes or No to print the report immediately.
4. Enter the Retrieve spec and press F10. Optionally, change the Field spec and press F10.
5. Make any changes at the Print Options screen and press F10 to print the report.

Delete Records

1. Press **F** for File and **R** for Remove.
2. Type the filename and press Enter.
3. Press **S** for Selected Records, enter a Retrieve spec, and press F10.
4. Choose Yes to delete the records.

Delete Duplicate Records

1. Press **F** for File and **R** for Remove.
2. Type the filename and press Enter.
3. Choose **D** for Duplicate Records or **A** for Duplicate Records to ASCII and press Enter. (If you selected **A**, type the filename that the duplicates will be saved to and press Enter.)
4. Type **D** or **DS** into the fields to be used as duplicate checks and press F10.
5. Press Yes to delete the records individually or No to delete them all at once.

DESIGN APPLICATION FEATURES

Set Initial Values

1. Press **F** for File, **D** for Design File, and **C** for Customize a File.
2. Type the filename and press Enter.
3. Press **I** for Set Initial Values, enter the values, and press F10 to save them.

Assign Access Rights

1. Press **F** for File, **D** for Design, and **S** for Secure.
2. Type the filename and press Enter.
3. Press **A** for Assign Access Rights. Type the name of the user or group and press F10.
4. Assign rights and a password. Press F10 to save the spec.

IN
BUSINESS

Personnel Application

The purpose of this chapter is to teach you how to use the Personnel application and the features in the "At a Glance" section. The Personnel application automates the basic record-keeping tasks associated with the personnel process. It does not automate the payroll function.

Overview

Managing your employees is a full-time job with a lot of paperwork. You need all the help you can get in reducing the amount of time spent processing paperwork. This paperwork can be divided into three tasks: basic record-keeping, which includes recording the employee's social security number, home address, dependents, emergency contact, etc.; tracking of sick and vacation time; and the quick generation of reports based on the information you have accrued.

The Personnel application is self-contained and does not make use of the Names file. It contains three databases: Staff, Health, and Holiday. Many of the other applications draw their basic name and address information from the Names file; this one does not. The reason for this is that the personnel department often wants its information kept separate from the rest of the company's data because of the sensitive and private nature of most personnel data. If you wish to use the Names file to store the basic name and address for each staff member, you can do so. But first you will have to place external @xlookup statements in the appropriate fields of the Staff file. How to do this will be covered in a later section.

The heart of the Personnel application is the Staff file. This file automates your basic record-keeping needs. You can store all the standard information such as name and address, birthday, title, social security number, emergency contact, spouse, dependents, insurance plans, and salary information. Personnel systems vary from company to company; thus, this file may require modifications to truly meet your needs.

An auxiliary file used in conjunction with the Staff file is the Health file. This file is used for capturing the sick time each employee accrues and uses. Sick time is calculated for each employee based on a formula. Then as the time is used, it is subtracted from the available time, maintaining a running balance.

The other auxiliary file used in this application is the Holiday file. With this file you can track the vacation time that each employee accrues and uses throughout the year. This file is very similar in structure to the Health file and uses the same type of formula to account for vacation time. It also keeps a running total, so with a quick glance you can know where an employee stands on vacation time.

Each file contains one or more reports to help you manage the personnel process. The Staff file includes reports that list names and addresses, track terminations, and list salaries. The Health and Holiday files have reports that list sick time and vacation time. As with all the applications, you can modify these reports or create your own reports better suited to your specific needs.

The initial step in setting up the Personnel application is to enter basic employee information into the Staff file. One of your key tasks is to assign each employee an ID number. A convenient method, if you don't have many employees, is to use the employee's initials. With the staff record completed, you must next set up health and holiday records for each employee. When you add health and holiday records, you look up the basic information from the Staff file by typing the enployee's ID number and pressing F8. The lookup feature extracts the values from several of the fields in the Staff file and places them in appropriate fields. This obviously saves you the time of retyping the basic information. At the same time that you are adding the health and holiday records, you also fill in the rate at which sick and vacation time accrues.

While you are learning how to use this application, you will also learn how to develop form reports, assign access rights and field-level security, set initial values, delete duplicate records, and delete/copy/rename files with ease.

Application Explained

Here you will learn in detail about each of the three databases making up the Personnel application. The discussion will also cover the fields in the databases and what each field is used for.

The Staff File

The top section of the Staff file has two date fields, one for the date the record was entered and one for the date the record was last viewed or changed. The STATUS field is used to indicate if this person is still an employee. The BATCH # field can be used to indicate who entered this employee or to manually select records that have nothing in common.

In the next section of the Staff file, you enter the employee's name and address. There are also fields for social security number, sex, and birthday. Figure 4.1 shows this section of the Staff file.

Name and Address Fields in Screen 1 of the Staff File

ENTERED	The date the record was entered. It is automatically generated by the system.
UPDATED	The date the record was last viewed or updated. It is automatically generated by the system.
BATCH #	Designates batches of records.
STATUS	Indicates if the employee is still working for the company. Use Active or Terminated.
IDNUM	This is the employee ID number. One option is to use each person's initials. This is the *key field* used to look up the name and address information into the Health and Holiday files.

FIRST	The first name.
LAST	The last name.
PRE	Mr., Mrs., Dr., etc.
SUF	J.D., M.D., Ph.D., C.P.A., etc.
ADDRESS	The street address.
ADD A	The second address line, normally used for the apartment number.
CITY	The city.
STATE	The state.
ZIP	The zip code.
BIRTH DAY	The employee's birthday.
HOME PHONE	The home phone number of the employee.
SOCIAL SECURITY #	The employee's social security number.
SEX	Sex of the employee.

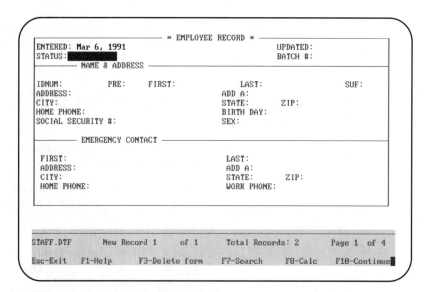

Figure 4.1   Screen 1 of the Staff file.

The Emergency Contact section contains the person to contact in case of an emergency. In the Emergency Contact section, you can type the name of the person whom the company should call in an emergency. This could be a spouse, parent, or friend. Figure 4.1 shows this section.

Emergency Contact Fields in Screen 1 of the Staff File

FIRST — The first name.

LAST — The last name.

ADDRESS — The street address.

ADD A — The second address line, normally used for the apartment number.

CITY — The city.

STATE — The state.

ZIP — The zip code.

WORK PHONE — The emergency contact person's number at work.

HOME PHONE — The emergency contact person's number at home.

Screen 2 of the Staff file, which you can see in Figure 4.2, lets you enter information regarding the employee's spouse and children. There are also fields for insurance, flexible spending plan, number of dependents, and eligibility date for the 401k plan. The last section is for company-issued credit cards and driver's license number.

Fields in Screen 2 of the Staff File

SP FIRST — Spouse's first name.

SP LAST — Spouse's last name.

SP DOB — Spouse's birthday.

CHILD1 — Name of employee's first child.

DOB 1 — First child's birthday.

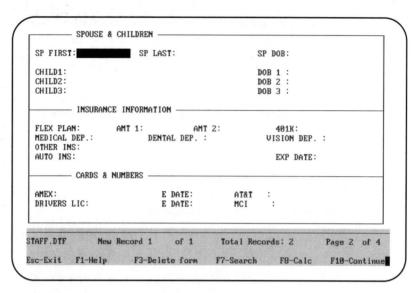

Figure 4.2   Screen 2 of the Staff file.

CHILD2	Name of employee's second child.
DOB 2	Second child's birthday.
CHILD3	Name of employee's third child.
DOB 3	Third child's birthday.
FLEX PLAN	Use this field to indicate if the employee participates in a flexible spending plan. Under section 125 of the Internal Revenue Service code, a portion of an employee's salary can go towards paying child care, medical premiums, and medical reimbursements.
AMT 1	The first amount that the employee defers each month.
AMT 2	The second amount that the employee defers each month.
401K	Use this field to indicate when the employee is eligible for the company's 401k plan. Eligibility is usually based on age and number of years of employment.

MEDICAL DEP.	The number of dependents who are part of the medical insurance plan.
DENTAL DEP.	The number of dependents who are part of the dental insurance plan.
VISION DEP.	The number of dependents who are part of the eye care insurance plan.
OTHER INS	Use this field to indicate if the employee has other medical/dental/eye insurance.
AUTO INS	Auto insurance carrier.
EXP DATE	The date that the employee's auto insurance expires.
AMEX	Company-issued American Express card number.
E DATE	American Express expiration date.
AT&T	Company-issued AT&T calling card.
MCI	Company-issued MCI calling card.
DRIVERS LIC	Employee's driver's license number.
E DATE	Driver's license expiration date.

Screen 3 of the Staff file is for employment information: date of hire, full- or part-time employment, and position in the company. Further, you can record starting salary, current salary, and salary history. In the salary section, all the MONTHLY and HOURLY fields are calculated for you. The final section is for the termination date and termination reason, and has space for comments. You can see all these fields in Figure 4.3.

Fields in Screen 3 of the Staff File

DATE HIRED	The date the employee was hired.
TYPE	A code indicating if the employee is full or part-time.
POSITION	The employee's official title.
ANNUALLY	The employee's starting annual salary.
MONTHLY	The base amount made each month.

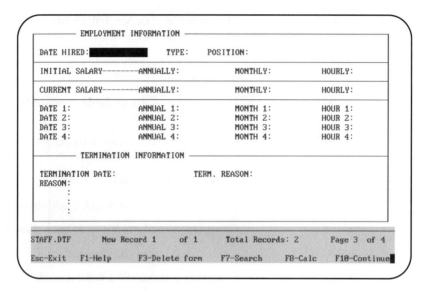

```
┌─────────────────────────────────────────────────────────────────────────┐
│   ┌── EMPLOYMENT INFORMATION ──────────────────────────────────────────┐  │
│   │ DATE HIRED:███████████    TYPE:   POSITION:                         │  │
│   │                                                                     │  │
│   │ INITIAL SALARY────────ANNUALLY:        MONTHLY:        HOURLY:       │  │
│   │                                                                     │  │
│   │ CURRENT SALARY────────ANNUALLY:        MONTHLY:        HOURLY:       │  │
│   │                                                                     │  │
│   │ DATE 1:           ANNUAL 1:       MONTH 1:       HOUR 1:             │  │
│   │ DATE 2:           ANNUAL 2:       MONTH 2:       HOUR 2:             │  │
│   │ DATE 3:           ANNUAL 3:       MONTH 3:       HOUR 3:             │  │
│   │ DATE 4:           ANNUAL 4:       MONTH 4:       HOUR 4:             │  │
│   │      ── TERMINATION INFORMATION ──────────                          │  │
│   │ TERMINATION DATE:              TERM. REASON:                        │  │
│   │ REASON:                                                             │  │
│   │        :                                                            │  │
│   │        :                                                            │  │
│   │        :                                                            │  │
│   └─────────────────────────────────────────────────────────────────────┘  │
│ ───────────────────────────────────────────────────────────────────────── │
│ STAFF.DTF     New Record 1    of 1     Total Records: 2     Page 3  of 4   │
│                                                                             │
│ Esc-Exit  F1-Help     F3-Delete form    F7-Search    F8-Calc   F10-Continue│
└─────────────────────────────────────────────────────────────────────────┘
```

Figure 4.3   Screen 3 of the Staff file.

HOURLY	The base amount made each hour.
ANNUALLY	Current annual salary.
MONTHLY	Current monthly salary.
HOURLY	Current hourly amount.

 Note: The next twelve fields hold the dates and amounts of new salaries.

DATE 1–4	Date of the salary.
ANNUAL 1–4	Annual salary.
MONTH 1–4	Amount made monthly.
HOUR 1–4	Amount made hourly.
TERMINATION DATE	Date of termination.
TERM. REASON	A code to indicate termination. Mostly used for reports.
REASON	Comments about the termination.

The last screen of the Staff file, as shown in Figure 4.4, is for recording the date and comments of each performance review.

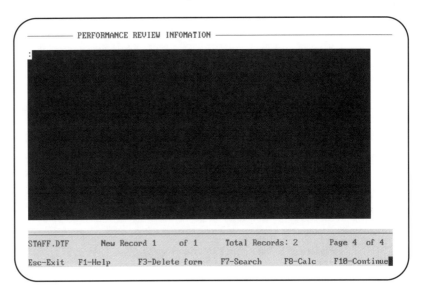

Figure 4.4 Screen 4 of the Staff file.

The Health File

The Health file lets you track an employee's sick time—both accrued sick time and used sick time. In Figure 4.5 you can see the first screen of the Health file. As you will notice, the information is consistent with the Staff file. Recall that when you add a health record, you do not have to retype this information. You simply type the person's ID number and press F8 to look up the information from the Staff file.

All the fields on screen 1 of the Health file are the same as those of the Staff file. The only difference is how the STATUS field is used. In the Staff file, the STATUS field indicates whether the person is still employed by the company. In the Health file, the STATUS field indicates whether this is the current health record. To indicate the status of the health record, you type **Open** or **Closed** in the STATUS field. Then, when an employee's health records accumulate, you can quickly search for and find the current record. To search for the current record, type **Open** in the STATUS field and the person's name in the LAST field.

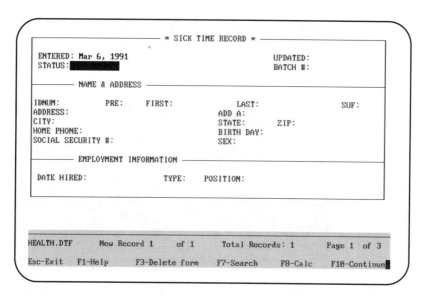

Figure 4.5   Screen 1 of the Health file.

Fields in Screen 1 of the Health File

ENTERED	The date the record was entered. It is automatically generated by the system.
UPDATED	The date the record was last viewed or updated. It is automatically generated by the system.
BATCH #	Used for designating batches of records.
STATUS	Indicates if this is the current health record. Type **Open** or **Closed**.
IDNUM	The employee's ID number. Use this field to look up name and address information from the Staff file.
FIRST	The first name.
LAST	The last name.
PRE	Mr., Mrs., Dr., etc.

SUF   J.D., M.D., Ph.D., C.P.A., etc.

ADDRESS   The street address.

ADD A   The second address line, normally used for
                              the apartment number.

CITY   The city.

STATE   The state.

ZIP   The zip code.

BIRTH DAY   The employee's birthday.

HOME PHONE   The home phone number of the employee.

SEX   The sex of the employee.

SOCIAL SECURITY #   The employee's social security number.

DATE HIRED   The date the employee was hired.

TYPE   A code to indicate if the employee is full or
                              part-time.

POSITION   The employee's official title.

The second screen of the Health file is where the action is. You must fill out the three fields at the top of the form first (without the RATE field, the programming statements won't work). The DATE FROM and TO fields hold the period of time that this health record covers. Since few employees start exactly on January 1, you need a way to track the dates that the health record covers. The RATE field contains the amount of sick time, in hours, that the employee accrues each month.

In Figure 4.6, you can see several columns for information. Below the MONTH column is a title called BALANCE. Moving across the page to the right, you can see that there is room for values under the DATES USED and USED columns. These two fields are for carrying over any comments and hours from the previous health record. The first field under the DATES USED column is for comments regarding the last health record, and the first field under the USED column is for the employee's positive or negative balance of hours.

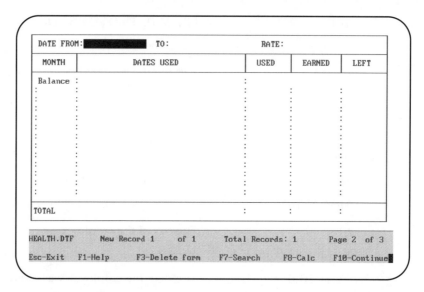

Figure 4.6   Screen 2 of the Health file.

Fields in Screen 2 of the Health File

DATE FROM	The beginning date of the period that the health record covers.
TO	The ending date of the period that the health record covers.
RATE	The number of hours in sick time that an employee accrues each month.
MONTH COLUMN	The abbreviation for the month.
BALANCE COMMENTS	The first field to the right of this title is for comments from the previous health record.
BALANCE HOURS	The first field under the USED column is for the negative or positive hours carried over from the previous health record.
DATES USED COLUMN	Used to record the dates that the employee was away from work during that particular month.

USED COLUMN	Used to record the number of hours that the employee was away from work during that particular month.
EARNED COLUMN	When your cursor travels through this field, a programming statement takes the value in the RATE field and places it in this field to give the number of hours earned this month.
LEFT COLUMN	A programming statement subtracts the EARNED number of hours from the USED number of hours, and places the result in this field.

> ▶ **Note:** At the bottom of each column are the fields for total hours. These give you a running balance of each column. Of particular interest is the number at the bottom of the LEFT column. This tells you if the employee is above or below the allotted time. A negative number indicates that the person has used more sick time than he or she has accrued.

USED TOTAL	The total number of hours used.
EARNED TOTAL	The total number of hours earned.
LEFT TOTAL	The total number of hours remaining.

The final screen, shown in Figure 4.7, is for writing any necessary remarks.

The Holiday File

The Holiday file tracks the amount of vacation time that each employee uses and earns. Figure 4.8 displays the first screen of the Holiday file, which is identical to the Health file's first screen. The Holiday file also operates in the same manner as the Health file. When you add a record, you type the ID number and press F8 to look up the information from the Staff file. All the fields on this screen are the same as they are in the Health file.

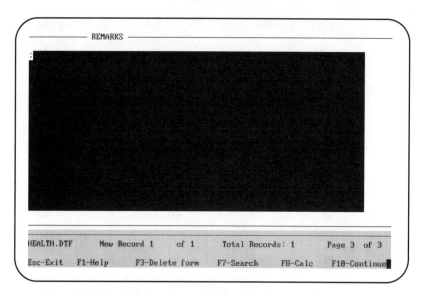

```
┌─ REMARKS ──────────────────────────────────────────────────────────────┐
│ :                                                                        │
│ ███████████████████████████████████████████████████████████████         │
│ ███████████████████████████████████████████████████████████████         │
│ ███████████████████████████████████████████████████████████████         │
│ ███████████████████████████████████████████████████████████████         │
│ ███████████████████████████████████████████████████████████████         │
│ ███████████████████████████████████████████████████████████████         │
│ ███████████████████████████████████████████████████████████████         │
│                                                                          │
│ HEALTH.DTF    New Record 1    of 1     Total Records: 1    Page 3  of 3  │
│ Esc-Exit   F1-Help      F3-Delete form    F7-Search    F8-Calc  F10-Continue│
└──────────────────────────────────────────────────────────────────────────┘
```

Figure 4.7   Screen 3 of the Health file.

```
┌──────────────────────── * VACATION RECORD * ──────────────────────────┐
│                                                                        │
│   ENTERED: Mar 6, 1991                       UPDATED:                  │
│   STATUS: ██████████                         BATCH #:                  │
│   ───── NAME & ADDRESS ──────────────────────────────────────         │
│                                                                        │
│ IDNUM:       PRE:    FIRST:            LAST:              SUF:         │
│ ADDRESS:                              ADD A:                           │
│ CITY:                                 STATE:      ZIP:                 │
│ HOME PHONE:                           BIRTH DAY:                       │
│ SOCIAL SECURITY #:                    SEX:                             │
│                                                                        │
│   ───── EMPLOYMENT INFORMATION ──────────────────────────             │
│                                                                        │
│ DATE HIRED:              TYPE:    POSITION:                            │
│                                                                        │
│                                                                        │
│                                                                        │
│ HOLIDAY.DTF   New Record 1    of 1    Total Records: 1    Page 1  of 3 │
│ Esc-Exit   F1-Help      F3-Delete form   F7-Search   F8-Calc  F10-Continue│
└────────────────────────────────────────────────────────────────────────┘
```

Figure 4.8   Screen 1 of the Holiday file.

Fields in Screen 1 of the Holiday File

ENTERED	The date the record was entered. It is automatically generated by the system.
UPDATED	The date the record was last viewed or updated. It is automatically generated by the system.
BATCH #	Used for designating batches of records.
STATUS	Indicates if this is the current holiday record. Type **Open** or **Closed**.
IDNUM	The employee's ID number. Use this field to look up name and address information from the Staff file.
FIRST	The first name.
LAST	The last name.
PRE	Mr., Mrs., Dr., etc.
SUF	J.D., M.D., Ph.D., C.P.A., etc.
ADDRESS	The street address.
ADD A	The second address line, normally used for the apartment number.
CITY	The city.
STATE	The state.
ZIP	The zip code.
BIRTH DAY	The employee's birthday.
HOME PHONE	The home phone number of the employee.
SOCIAL SECURITY #	The employee's social security number.
SEX	The sex of the employee.
DATE HIRED	The date the employee was hired.
TYPE	A code to indicate if the employee is full or part-time.
POSITION	The employee's official title.

On the second screen of the Holiday file, which can be seen in Figure 4.9, you record the vacation time that the employee earns and uses. There is an extra field on this screen—the HRS YEAR field. This field contains the total vacation hours that the employee is entitled to this year. The HRS MONTH field contains the number of hours earned each month. The FR and TO fields hold the period of time that this holiday record covers.

The columns for recording hours are the same as those in the Holiday file. You can record the hours carried over from the previous year, along with a line of comments.

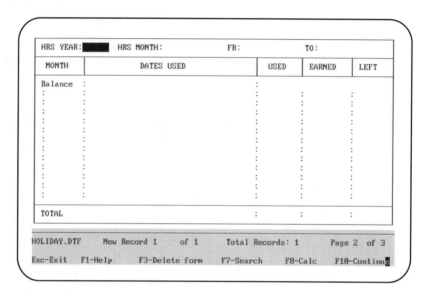

Figure 4.9   Screen 2 of the Holiday file.

Fields in Screen 2 of the Holiday File

HRS YEAR	The total vacation hours that the employee is entitled to this year.
HRS MONTH	The total vacation hours that the employee is entitled to this month. This is the number that is automatically entered into the EARNED column.
FR	The beginning date of the period that the holiday record covers.

TO	The ending date of the period that the holiday record covers.
MONTH COLUMN	The abbreviation for the month.
BALANCE COMMENTS	The first field to the right of this title is for comments from the previous holiday record.
BALANCE HOURS	The first field under the USED column is for the negative or positive hours carried over from the previous holiday record.
DATES USED COLUMN	Used to record the dates that the employee was away on vacation that month.
USED COLUMN	Used to record the number of hours that the employee used for vacation that month.
EARNED COLUMN	When your cursor travels through this field, a programming statement takes the value in the HRS MONTH field and places it in this field to give the number of hours earned this month.
LEFT COLUMN	A programming statement subtracts the EARNED number of hours from the USED number of hours, and places the result in this field.

> ▶ **Note:** The fields at the bottom of each column are total fields. They give you a running balance for each column. Of particular interest is the number at the bottom of the LEFT column. This tells you whether the employee is above or below the allotted time. A negative number indicates that he or she has used too much vacation time to date.

USED TOTAL	The total number of hours used.
EARNED TOTAL	The total number of hours earned.
LEFT TOTAL	The total number of hours remaining.

The final screen of the Holiday file, shown in Figure 4.10, is for writing any necessary remarks.

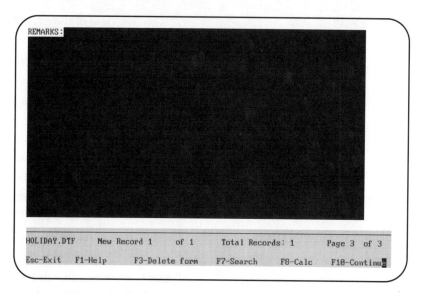

REMARKS:

HOLIDAY.DTF	New Record 1	of 1	Total Records: 1	Page 3 of 3
Esc-Exit	F1-Help	F3-Delete form	F7-Search	F8-Calc	F10-Continue

Figure 4.10   Screen 3 of the Holiday file.

Using the Application

While you are using the Staff, Holiday, and Health files, you will also be exploring more of Q&A's features. This application is ideally suited for managing the basic record-keeping functions of a personnel department. With the Staff file, you can record salary history and performance reviews. The Health and Holiday files let you track vacation and sick time.

Manipulate Files

There are three types of files associated with Q&A. The first type is the program file. Taken together, the program files make up Q&A, and they contain all the instructions necessary to use Q&A's various functions. The next type of file is the database file. These are created every time you develop a new database. When you create a database, two files are actually created, and both must be present for the database to function. The first file has a .DTF extension, and it is where the data and the basic structure of the database are stored. The second file has an .IDX extension and contains the index and Intelligent Assistant information. The final type of file is the word processing file. Q&A has its own proprietary file format and cannot be read by other types of word processors, unless it is converted.

During the installation process, you created a directory on your hard drive to hold each of these types of files. The Q&A program files are in the QA directory. The database files are in a subdirectory under the QA directory called FILE, and the word processing files are in a subdirectory called WORD. The concepts of hard drives, directories, and files are analogous to a file cabinet and its contents. The file cabinet is the hard drive; it contains everything. The hanging file folders are the directories; the manila file folders are the computer files. And the contents of each manila file folder are the same as the contents of the database files.

Just as you have techniques for managing your paper files, you need techniques to manage your electronic files. The main file management tasks you'll perform are listing, copying, renaming, and deleting files. These can be done through a Q&A menu or at the List File Specs option of the Add or Search mode. It is faster to do these things through the Add or Search mode prompt. The first file management method you'll learn involves listing files from the Q&A menus.

Practice Listing Files from the Q&A Menus

1. From the Main menu, press **U** for Utilities, **D** for DOS File Facilities, and **L** for List files. Your screen should look like Figure 4.11.

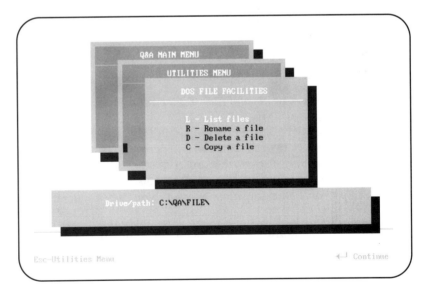

Figure 4.11   DOS File Facilities menu.

You will notice in Figure 4.11 that the menu gives you four choices: listing, renaming, deleting, and copying files. If you look at the rectangular window below the DOS menu, you will see the statement C:\QA\FILE\. This statement indicates which directory (file holder) Q&A is currently looking in. The entire statement is called the *path*, where C is the hard drive (file cabinet), QA is the directory (file holder), and FILE is a subdirectory (file holder).

2. Now press Enter, and you will see the files in the FILE directory—your screen should look like Figure 4.12.

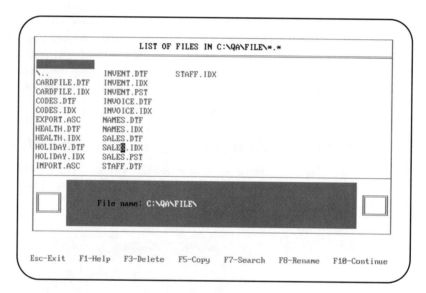

Figure 4.12   List of files in FILE subdirectory.

Looking at the top left side of the screen in Figure 4.12, notice the symbol \ .. (a backslash and two periods). This symbol indicates that there are directories above this one (directories that are under other directories are called *subdirectories*). You will also notice that all the files have either .DTF or .IDX extensions. This tells you they are database files.

3. Move your cursor down one line to the \ .. symbol and press Enter. You will see a listing of all the files in the QA directory. Your screen should look like Figure 4.13.

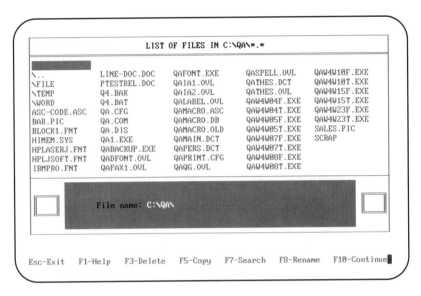

```
              LIST OF FILES IN C:\QA\*.*

▓▓▓▓▓▓       LINE-DOC.DOC   QAFONT.EXE    QASPELL.OVL   QAW4W10F.EXE
\..          PTESTREL.DOC   QAIA1.OVL     QATHES.DCT    QAW4W10T.EXE
\FILE        Q4.BAK         QAIA2.OVL     QATHES.OVL    QAW4W15F.EXE
\TEMP        Q4.BAT         QALABEL.OVL   QAW4W04F.EXE  QAW4W15T.EXE
\WORD        QA.CFG         QAMACRO.ASC   QAW4W04T.EXE  QAW4W23F.EXE
ASC-CODE.ASC QA.COM         QAMACRO.DB    QAW4W05F.EXE  QAW4W23T.EXE
BAR.PIC      QA.DIS         QAMACRO.OLD   QAW4W05T.EXE  SALES.PIC
BLOCK1.FNT   QA1.EXE        QAMAIN.DCT    QAW4W07F.EXE  SCRAP
HIMEM.SYS    QABACKUP.EXE   QAPERS.DCT    QAW4W07T.EXE
HPLASERJ.FNT QADFONT.OVL    QAPRINT.CFG   QAW4W08F.EXE
HPLJSOFT.FNT QAFAX1.OVL     QAQG.OVL      QAW4W08T.EXE
IBMPRO.FNT


        File name: C:\QA\


Esc-Exit   F1-Help   F3-Delete   F5-Copy   F7-Search   F8-Rename   F10-Continue
```

Figure 4.13 List of files in QA directory.

In Figure 4.13, you can see all the Q&A program files, the FILE and WORD subdirectories, and the \.. symbol again. This symbol indicates that there is a directory above the QA directory; in this case, it is the ROOT directory. The ROOT directory is the highest directory on a hard drive. *All* directories are under the ROOT.

> ⊘ **Caution:** NEVER delete any of the files in the QA directory. This will prevent Q&A from functioning.

4. Often, you will want to find one particular file or subset of files. Let's practice these two tasks. With your screen looking like Figure 4.13, type **QAWP.OVL** and press F7 for Search. Your cursor will move to the QAWP.OVL file.

Shortcut

When you are not sure exactly how a filename is spelled, you can type as much of it as you know, followed by two periods. For example, by typing **QA..** and pressing F7, you will find all files that start with QA.

5. Next you'll list all the files with a .OVL extension. Type ***.OVL** and press Enter. Your screen should look like Figure 4.14. The asterisk (*) is the wildcard symbol. You can type it before or after any text.

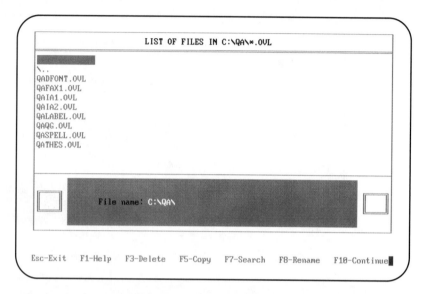

```
              LIST OF FILES IN C:\QA\*.OVL

\..
QADFONT.OVL
QAFAX1.OVL
QAIA1.OVL
QAIA2.OVL
QALABEL.OVL
QAQG.OVL
QASPELL.OVL
QATHES.OVL




         File name: C:\QA\



Esc-Exit   F1-Help   F3-Delete   F5-Copy   F7-Search   F8-Rename   F10-Continue
```

Figure 4.14   List of files with .OVL extensions.

6. Press Enter to list all the files again. Type **QAMAIN.DCT** and press F7. If you look at the second-to-the-last line in Figure 4.15, you will see that several new fields are displayed. They indicate the name of the file your cursor is on, the size of the file, and the date and time it was last edited. The final line at the bottom of the screen lists several function keys. These are the shortcut keys for performing the tasks listed on the DOS File Facilities menu in Figure 4.11.

These same shortcut function keys appear wherever there is a List Files or List Specs function.

Now you are going to use the Copy, Rename, and Delete features.

Practice Renaming a File

1. Press Esc twice to return to the DOS File Facilities menu. Press **C** for Copy and press Enter. This will list the files in the directory.

2. Type **CODES.DTF** and press Enter. Q&A will prompt you for a new filename. Type **NEW** and press Enter.

Every time Q&A displays the File Prompt menu, you can press Enter to list the files in the directory.

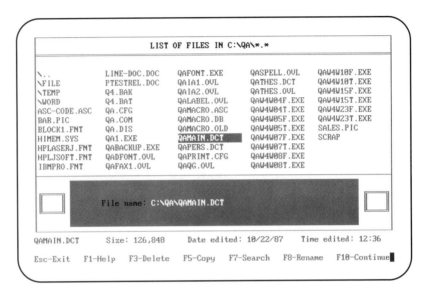

```
                    LIST OF FILES IN C:\QA\*.*

\..              LINE-DOC.DOC    QAFONT.EXE      QASPELL.OVL     QAW4W10F.EXE
\FILE            PTESTREL.DOC    QAIA1.OVL       QATHES.DCT      QAW4W10T.EXE
\TEMP            Q4.BAK          QAIA2.OVL       QATHES.OVL      QAW4W15F.EXE
\WORD            Q4.BAT          QALABEL.OVL     QAW4W04F.EXE    QAW4W15T.EXE
ASC-CODE.ASC     QA.CFG          QAMACRO.ASC     QAW4W04T.EXE    QAW4W23F.EXE
BAR.PIC          QA.COM          QAMACRO.DB      QAW4W05F.EXE    QAW4W23T.EXE
BLOCK1.FNT       QA.DIS          QAMACRO.OLD     QAW4W05T.EXE    SALES.PIC
HIMEM.SYS        QA1.EXE         QAMAIN.DCT      QAW4W07F.EXE    SCRAP
HPLASERJ.FNT     QABACKUP.EXE    QAPERS.DCT      QAW4W07T.EXE
HPLJSOFT.FNT     QADFONT.OVL     QAPRINT.CFG     QAW4W08F.EXE
IBMPRO.FNT       QAFAX1.OVL      QAQG.OVL        QAW4W08T.EXE


          File name: C:\QA\QAMAIN.DCT


QAMAIN.DCT      Size: 126,848     Date edited: 10/22/87     Time edited: 12:36

Esc-Exit    F1-Help    F3-Delete    F5-Copy    F7-Search    F8-Rename    F10-Continue
```

Figure 4.15   File statistics for QAMAIN.DCT.

3. Next you are going to rename the NEW data file. Press **R** for Rename and press Enter. If you look at the list of files, you will see that there are two NEW files. One file has an .IDX extension and the other a .DTF extension. Because a Q&A database needs both of these files to be functional, Q&A treats them as one file.

4. Type **NEW.DTF** and press Enter. Type **OLD.DTF** and press Enter. You have just renamed both of these files to OLD. At the bottom of the screen, Q&A states: C:\QA\Files\OLD.DTF is the new name.

    You are now ready to delete the OLD files.

Practice Deleting Files

1. Press **D** for Delete.

2. Type **OLD.DTF** and press Enter. Q&A will give you a warning sign asking if you really want to delete these files. Answer Yes. Press Esc twice to return to the Main menu.

Finally, here are some shortcuts for managing your files. Press **F** for File and **S** for Search. Press F4 twice to delete any filename that might be listed. If none are listed, pressing F4 does nothing. Otherwise, pressing F4 the first time deletes the filename. Pressing F4 the second time deletes the file extension. Press Enter to see a list of all the database files. If you look at Figure 4.16, you will not see any .IDX files. Q&A has "filtered" them out because it considers .DTF and .IDX files having the same prefix as one file.

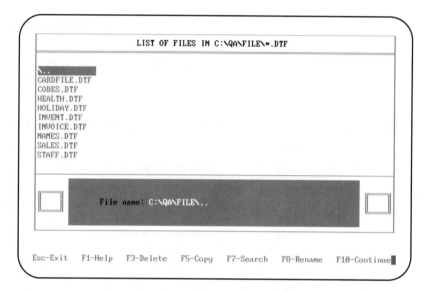

Figure 4.16   Files listed in Search/Update mode.

With your screen looking like 4.16, you are going to perform the same tasks that you performed using the Q&A menus. Move your cursor down to the CODES.DTF file and press F5 for Copy. Type the name **NEW** and press Enter. You will see the file NEW listed. Move your cursor down to the file NEW and press F8 for Rename. Type **OLD** and press Enter. The file is now called OLD. Move your cursor down to the file OLD. Press F3 to delete the file and answer Yes to delete it. Press Esc three times to return to the Main menu. This completes your practice of the file management tools.

All of the preceding file management commands also work in the Write module.

Add Data

To complete the remaining examples, you will need to add a record to each file used in this application. This will also give you the opportunity to learn the specifics of the Personnel application. Start with the Staff file.

Practice Adding a Record to the Staff File

1. Press **F** for File and **A** for Add. Type the filename **STAFF** and press Enter. Fill in the first screen as shown in Figure 4.17. Press PgDn when you are ready to move to screen 2.

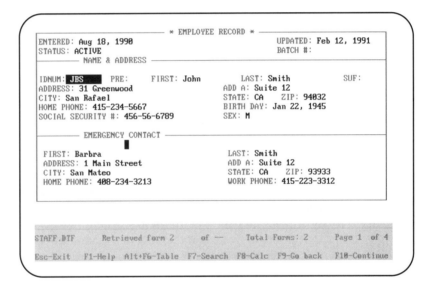

```
                          * EMPLOYEE RECORD *
    ENTERED: Aug 18, 1990                    UPDATED: Feb 12, 1991
    STATUS: ACTIVE                           BATCH #:
           NAME & ADDRESS

    IDNUM: JBS      PRE:      FIRST: John       LAST: Smith          SUF:
    ADDRESS: 31 Greenwood                    ADD A: Suite 12
    CITY: San Rafael                         STATE: CA    ZIP: 94032
    HOME PHONE: 415-234-5667                 BIRTH DAY: Jan 22, 1945
    SOCIAL SECURITY #: 456-56-6789           SEX: M

           EMERGENCY CONTACT

    FIRST: Barbra                            LAST: Smith
    ADDRESS: 1 Main Street                   ADD A: Suite 12
    CITY: San Mateo                          STATE: CA    ZIP: 93933
    HOME PHONE: 408-234-3213                 WORK PHONE: 415-223-3312



    STAFF.DTF      Retrieved form 2     of —      Total Forms: 2      Page 1 of 4

    Esc-Exit   F1-Help  Alt+F6-Table  F7-Search  F8-Calc  F9-Go back   F10-Continue
```

Figure 4.17   Screen 1 of the Staff file.

Shortcut

If you have only a few employees, using their initials is an easy way to remember the ID numbers. If you have many employees, you can use some other numbering scheme. If you want to use just numbers, and you want Q&A to provide the numbers for you, navigate to the Customize menu and the Set Initial Values option and place an @number function in the IDNUM field. Q&A will give a unique number to each employee.

2. With your cursor on page two of the form, fill in the form by following Figure 4.18. Press PgDn to move to page 3 of the form.

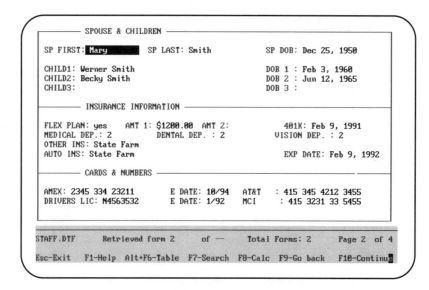

```
┌─── SPOUSE & CHILDREN ──────────────────────────────────────────┐
│                                                                 │
│  SP FIRST: Mary          SP LAST: Smith        SP DOB: Dec 25, 1950 │
│                                                                 │
│  CHILD1: Werner Smith                          DOB 1 : Feb 3, 1960  │
│  CHILD2: Becky Smith                           DOB 2 : Jun 12, 1965 │
│  CHILD3:                                       DOB 3 :              │
│  ──────── INSURANCE INFORMATION ────────────────────────────────── │
│                                                                 │
│  FLEX PLAN: yes    AMT 1: $1200.00  AMT 2:        401K: Feb 9, 1991 │
│  MEDICAL DEP.: 2        DENTAL DEP. : 2        VISION DEP. : 2   │
│  OTHER INS: State Farm                                          │
│  AUTO INS: State Farm                          EXP DATE: Feb 9, 1992 │
│  ──────── CARDS & NUMBERS ──────────────────────────────────────── │
│                                                                 │
│  AMEX: 2345 334 23211      E DATE: 10/94   AT&T : 415 345 4212 3455 │
│  DRIVERS LIC: N4563532     E DATE: 1/92    MCI  : 415 3231 33 5455  │
│                                                                 │
├─────────────────────────────────────────────────────────────────┤
│ STAFF.DTF    Retrieved form 2    of --   Total Forms: 2   Page 2 of 4 │
│ Esc-Exit  F1-Help  Alt+F6-Table  F7-Search  F8-Calc  F9-Go back  F10-Continue │
└─────────────────────────────────────────────────────────────────┘
```

Figure 4.18   Screen 2 of the Staff file.

3. With your cursor on page 3, fill in the screen as it appears in Figure 4.19. However DO NOT fill in the MONTHLY or HOURLY fields. Once you have filled in the ANNUAL salary fields, press F8. Q&A will automatically calculate the MONTHLY and HOURLY fields according to programming statements already provided. The statement in each of the MONTH field divides the ANNUAL salary by 52. The statement in the HOURLY field initially divides the ANNUAL field by 52 and then divides that number by 37.5 hours. You can change this 37.5 figure through the Program Spec menu.

4. Press PgDn to move to the final screen and fill it in according to Figure 4.20. Press Shift-F10 to save the form and exit the Staff file.

   You will now add a record to the Health file.

Practice Adding a Record to the Health File

1. Press **A** for Add, type the filename **HEALTH**, and press Enter.

2. With your cursor in the STATUS field, type **Open** to indicate that this is the current Health record. At the end of the year when you create a new health record for an employee, you will change the STATUS field to Closed and type **Open** in the STATUS field of the new record.

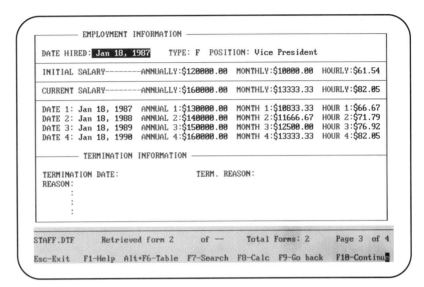

Figure 4.19   Screen 3 of the Staff file.

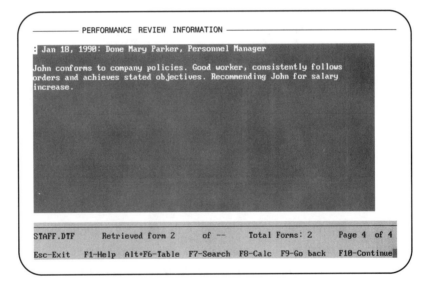

Figure 4.20   Screen 4 of the Staff file.

3. Move to the IDNUM field, type **JBS** and press F8 to look up the information from the Staff file. Your first screen should look like Figure 4.21.

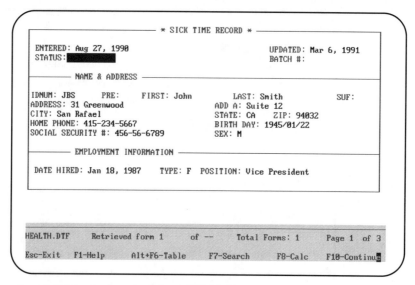

```
 ┌─────────────────────── * SICK TIME RECORD * ───────────────────────┐
 │                                                                     │
 │  ENTERED: Aug 27, 1990                      UPDATED: Mar 6, 1991     │
 │  STATUS:▓▓▓▓▓▓▓▓▓▓▓                          BATCH #:                │
 │  ┌────────── NAME & ADDRESS ─────────────────────────────────────   │
 │                                                                     │
 │  IDNUM: JBS      PRE:       FIRST: John        LAST: Smith      SUF: │
 │  ADDRESS: 31 Greenwood                  ADD A: Suite 12             │
 │  CITY: San Rafael                       STATE: CA    ZIP: 94032     │
 │  HOME PHONE: 415-234-5667               BIRTH DAY: 1945/01/22       │
 │  SOCIAL SECURITY #: 456-56-6789         SEX: M                      │
 │  ┌────────── EMPLOYMENT INFORMATION ─────────────────────────────   │
 │                                                                     │
 │  DATE HIRED: Jan 18, 1987    TYPE: F  POSITION: Vice President      │
 │                                                                     │
 └─────────────────────────────────────────────────────────────────────┘

  HEALTH.DTF    Retrieved form 1      of --     Total Forms: 1    Page 1  of 3

  Esc-Exit   F1-Help      Alt+F6-Table     F7-Search      F8-Calc    F10-Continue▓
```

Figure 4.21   Screen 1 of the Health file.

4. Press PgDn to move to the second screen. The DATE FROM field will contain the beginning of the period that this record covers. The DATE TO field is the last day of the period. The RATE field is the number of hours per month of sick time each employee earns. Fill in these three fields as they appear in Figure 4.22.

5. Move your cursor to the first field under the MONTH column, type **JAN**, press Enter five times to return to the MONTH column. You will notice that the programming statements calculate the LEFT column for you. Now finish filling in the form. Do not type anything in the LEFT column; it will be done for you. Look at the bottom of the screen to see the running totals for each column.

6. Press PgDn to see the Remarks screen. Press Shift-F10 to save the record and exit the file.

   The final step is to fill in the Holiday record.

Practice Adding a Record to the Holiday File

1. Press **A** for Add, type the filename **HOLIDAY**, and press Enter.

2. With your cursor in the STATUS field, type **Open** to indicate that this is the current Holiday record. This field operates identically to the one in the Health file.

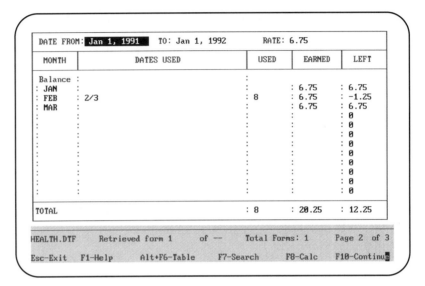

Figure 4.22   Screen 2 of the Health file.

3. Move to the IDNUM field, type **JBS**, and press F8 to look up the information from the Staff file. Your first screen should look like Figure 4.23.

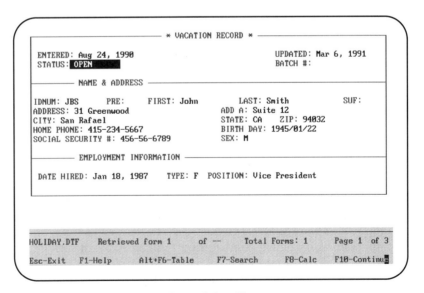

Figure 4.23   Screen 1 of the Holiday file.

4. Press PgDn to move to the second screen. The top of this screen is slightly different from the Health file. The HRS YEAR field is the total vacation hours the employee will earn this year. The HRS MONTH is how many hours earned each month and is the amount that is copied into the EARNED column. The rest of the form works like the Health file. Fill it in according to Figure 4.24.

5. Press Shift-F10 to save the form and exit the file. Press Esc three times to return to the Main menu.

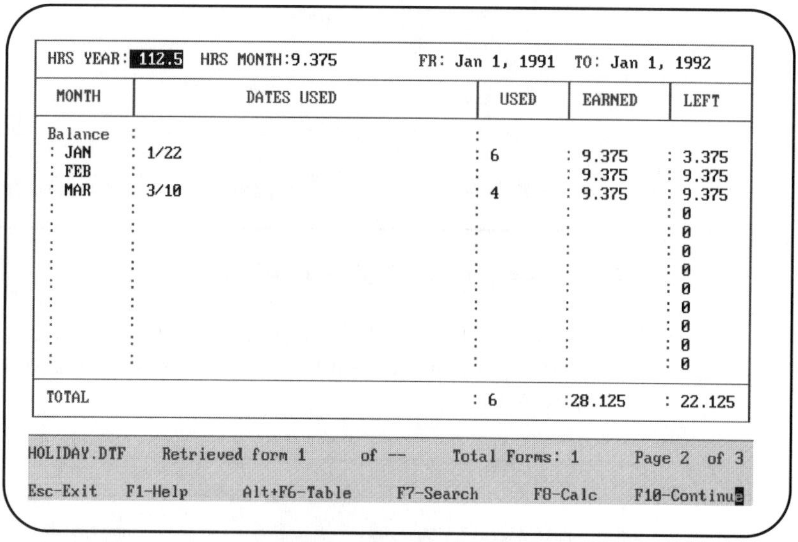

```
HRS YEAR: 112.5  HRS MONTH:9.375       FR: Jan 1, 1991  TO: Jan 1, 1992

 MONTH   |           DATES USED           | USED  | EARNED  |  LEFT
Balance  :                                :       :         :
 : JAN   : 1/22                            : 6     : 9.375   : 3.375
 : FEB   :                                 :       : 9.375   : 9.375
 : MAR   : 3/10                            : 4     : 9.375   : 9.375
 :       :                                 :       :         : 0
 :       :                                 :       :         : 0
 :       :                                 :       :         : 0
 :       :                                 :       :         : 0
 :       :                                 :       :         : 0
 :       :                                 :       :         : 0
 :       :                                 :       :         : 0
 :       :                                 :       :         : 0
 TOTAL                                     : 6     :28.125   : 22.125

HOLIDAY.DTF   Retrieved form 1    of --   Total Forms: 1   Page 2  of 3

Esc-Exit   F1-Help     Alt+F6-Table    F7-Search    F8-Calc   F10-Continue
```

Figure 4.24   Screen 2 of the Holiday file.

Print Existing Reports

Each of the three files already contains one or more columnar reports. The Staff file has reports that will list employee names and addresses, salaries of employees, and the names of terminated employees. Through the Health file, you can print a report that lists all the sick time each employee has taken and whether he or she has exceeded the allotted amount. The report also gives you a total and average of the hours for all employees. With the Holiday file, you can get a similar report on the status of each employee's vacation time. This report will total what each employee is entitled to, has earned so far, has used to date, and has remaining. Like the Health report, it also gives you a company total and average. All of these reports are accessed through the Report menu option off the Main menu.

Printing an Existing Report

1. Press **R** for Report and **P** for Print a Report.

2. Type the filename (Staff, Health, or Holiday) and press Enter.

3. Choose the desired report from the list. Q&A will then ask you if you want to make temporary changes to this report. If you answer No, the report will print exactly as it is defined. If you answer Yes, you can make temporary changes, such as altering the Retrieve spec, Column/Sort spec, and print options.

4. If you pressed Yes, the first screen you will see is the Retrieve Spec. Here you tell Q&A which records you want to print. Type a Retrieve spec (for example, move to IDNUM and type **JBS**).

5. Press F10 to progress to the Column/Sort spec. In this spec you define which fields are to be printed on the report and how the information should be sorted.

Beginner's Tip

When you print a report through the Print a Report selection, remember that any changes you make to the Report spec are temporary. To make permanent changes, you must select the Design/Redesign a Report option.

6. Press F10 to advance to the Print Options menu and make any necessary changes, such as changing the printer.

7. Once you are done with the print options, you can press F8 to go to the Define Page options. With this option, you define the margins, page length, characters per inch (point size), and the headers and footers.

8. When you are through with these two screens, press F10 to print the report. These procedures work identically for each of the files and their respective reports.

Create and Print Form Reports

In the previous section, all the reports were columnar reports. And as the name implies, the information in these reports is printed in columns. However, you will not always want to print information in columns. You will sometimes need to place fields at specific locations on the page. This is when you use the *form report*.

Q&A offers two types of form reports: free-form and coordinate. The only difference between the two is how they are created. Form reports appear in several applications, for example, the invoice in the Invoice file and the name and address report in the Names file. With the *free-form* method, you locate the information on the page by placing a number in the desired field, followed by a command telling Q&A where the field should be placed on the page. Because the free-form method was covered in Chapter 2 and is briefly discussed again at the end of this chapter, this section will focus on the coordinate method.

The *coordinate* method allows you to place fields at specific coordinates on the page by using column/row coordinates (for example, 2,6 signifies two rows down from the top margin and six spaces in from the right margin) or by using inches or centimeters (for example, 2",6" signifies two inches down from the top margin and six inches in from the right margin). Because you can specify exactly where on the page a field should appear, you can often create better-looking reports by using the coordinate method. This method is best for filling in preprinted forms and where accuracy is essential.

Several new features have been added to form reporting. When you place a field on the page, you may sometimes want the field label to print, and sometimes you may not want it to print. With the old version of Q&A, it was all or nothing. Either you placed all the field labels on the report, or you couldn't have any. Well, now you can be selective and use field labels where needed. You can even change the name of the field on the report. The Enhancement menu has also been added. The Enhancement menu lets you highlight any field or header with up to eight fonts, boldfacing, underlining, italics, and more. You can choose to highlight the field label, the data, or both.

Q&A has preselected many of the print settings for you. These are known as the *default print settings*, meaning that if you do not change the settings, these settings remain in force. Default settings are assigned to each database, and depending on your needs, you may want to change some of them.

Changing the Default Settings

1. Press **F** for File and **P** for Print.

2. Type the filename and press Enter.

3. Press **S** for Set Global Default Options. Figure 4.25 displays this menu.

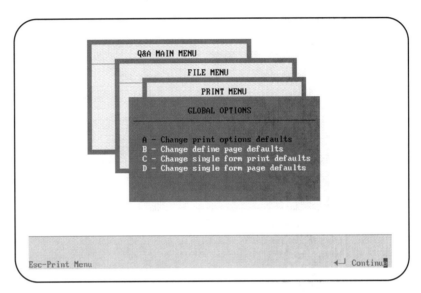

Figure 4.25   Global Options menu for form report.

Options A (print options) and B (define page) are for changing the default settings of the form reports. Options C and D are for changing the default settings when you print a single form through Add or Search mode. Both of the screens are the same. The Print Options default screen can be seen in Figure 4.26, and the Define Page default screen can be seen in Figure 4.27.

4. Press the letter of the option you want and make your changes. Those settings will now be in effect.

You are now ready to begin developing a coordinate form report based on the Staff file. The report will list each employee's name, address, personal information, position, and salary history.

Developing a Coordinated Report Based on the Staff File

1. Press **F** for File and **P** for Print.

2. Type the filename **STAFF** and press Enter.

3. Press **D** for Design/Redesign a Spec and then type the report name **Salary History**. Press Enter.

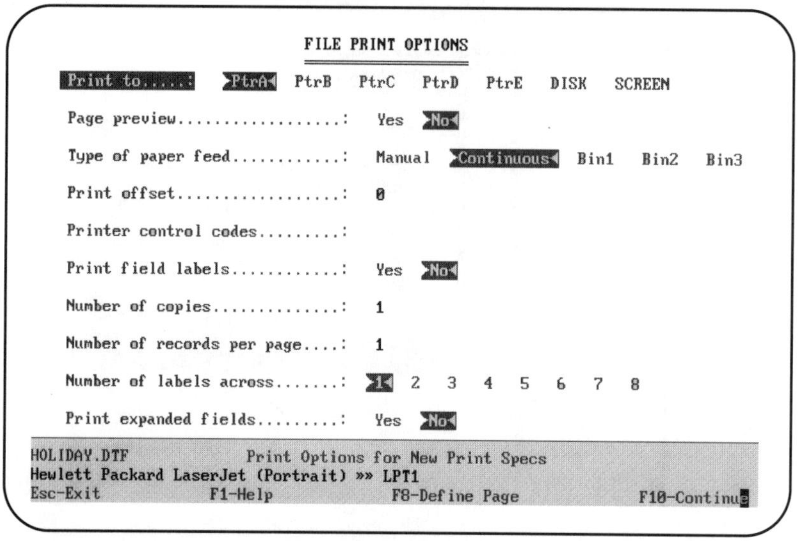

```
                        FILE PRINT OPTIONS

  Print to.....:  ▶PtrA◀  PtrB   PtrC   PtrD   PtrE   DISK   SCREEN

  Page preview.................:    Yes  ▶No◀

  Type of paper feed...........:    Manual  ▶Continuous◀  Bin1   Bin2   Bin3

  Print offset.................:    0

  Printer control codes.........:

  Print field labels............:   Yes  ▶No◀

  Number of copies..............:   1

  Number of records per page....:   1

  Number of labels across.......:   ▶1◀  2   3   4   5   6   7   8

  Print expanded fields.........:   Yes  ▶No◀

HOLIDAY.DTF          Print Options for New Print Specs
Hewlett Packard LaserJet (Portrait) »» LPT1
Esc-Exit          F1-Help              F8-Define Page           F10-Continue
```

Figure 4.26   Default Print Options screen for form report.

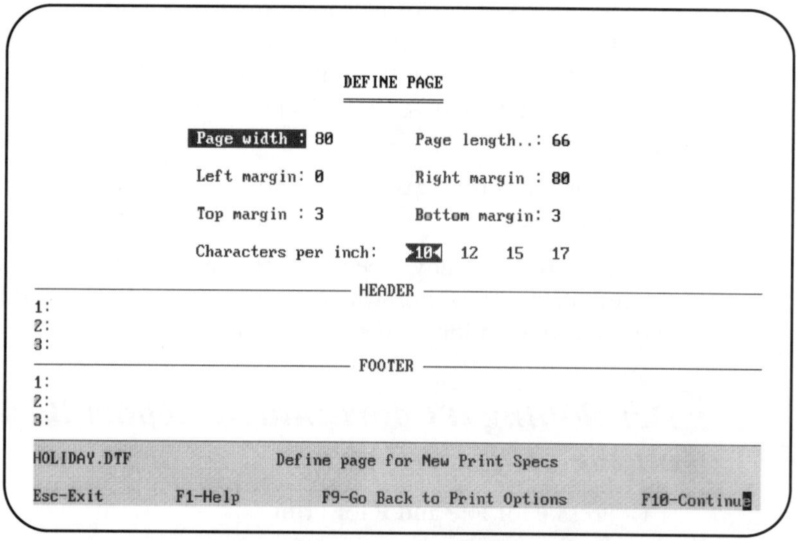

```
                          DEFINE PAGE

         Page width : 80          Page length..: 66

         Left margin: 0           Right margin : 80

         Top margin : 3           Bottom margin: 3

         Characters per inch:   ▶10◀  12   15   17
─────────────────────────── HEADER ───────────────────────────
1:
2:
3:
─────────────────────────── FOOTER ───────────────────────────
1:
2:
3:

HOLIDAY.DTF             Define page for New Print Specs

Esc-Exit     F1-Help      F9-Go Back to Print Options      F10-Continue
```

Figure 4.27   Default Define Page screen for form report.

4. The first screen you will see is the Retrieve Spec. Here you tell Q&A which records you want to print. When you initially added this record, you typed Active in the STATUS field, signifying that the person was still employed with the company. This will be your Retrieve spec. Move to the STATUS field and type **Active**.

Remember, by pressing Shift-F8 you can save a Retrieve spec for future use and by pressing Alt-F8 you can use a previously stored spec.

5. Press F8 to go to the Sort Spec screen. Move to the LAST field and type **1, AS**. Q&A will sort the records by the employee's last name.

Pressing F8 gives you the Sort Spec screen where you designate how you want the report sorted. You have the option of sorting your report by any field you like, even one that will not appear on the report. Q&A offers two sorting options: ascending order (A–Z) and descending order (Z–A). To enter the command, type a number designating which sort should be performed first; then type a comma and an AS or DS. For example, typing **1, AS** in the LAST field will sort the entire report alphabetically (A to Z) by last name.

6. Press F10 to advance to the Field Spec screen.

The Field spec is where you tell Q&A which fields you want to print and where they should be placed on the page. Since you are using the coordinate method, you will be typing specific page coordinates in each of the fields that you want to appear on the report.

To decipher the field codes, look at the FIRST field in Figure 4.28. Notice the code in it of 1,1,L. The first 1 is the number of lines *down* from the top margin, and the second 1 is the number of spaces *in* from the right margin where the field should begin printing. The L says to place the field label before the data, in this case, the FIRST field. Look at the code in the LAST field: 1,30,L. This code says to print this field on the first line down from the top margin and 30 spaces in from the right margin.

To specify the coordinates in inches or centimeters, you must type after each number either a " symbol for inches or the abbreviation cm for centimeters, for example, 1",1",L or 1cm,1cm,L.

If the codes won't fit into a field, press F6 to expand the field. You will have to do this on the STATE and ZIP fields.

7. Press PgDn twice to move to the third screen of the form (the second screen isn't used in this report). Figure 4.29 shows what the Field spec will look like when you are through. You will notice that you cannot read the codes for most of the fields because they are too long. To read a field, move to it and press F6.

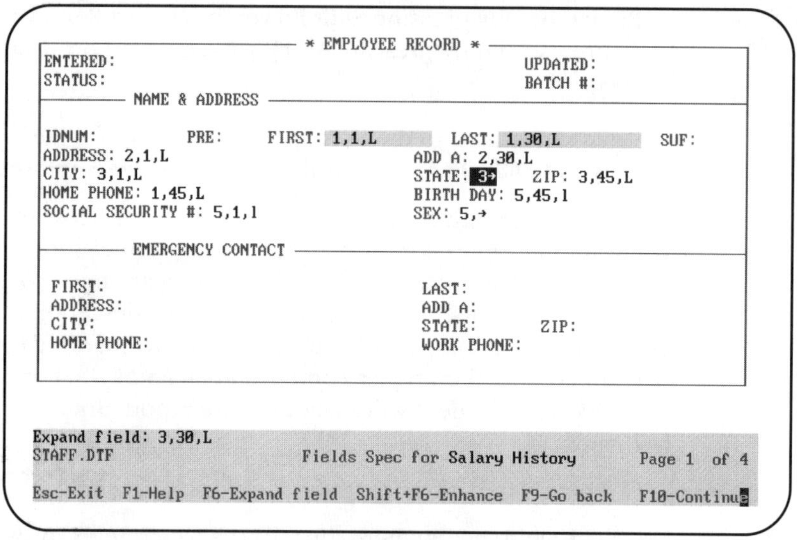

```
┌─────────────────────── * EMPLOYEE RECORD * ───────────────────┐
│ ENTERED:                                          UPDATED:     │
│ STATUS:             ┌── NAME & ADDRESS ──         BATCH #:      │
│                                                                │
│ IDNUM:        PRE:    FIRST: 1,1,L        LAST: 1,30,L    SUF:  │
│ ADDRESS: 2,1,L                     ADD A: 2,30,L               │
│ CITY: 3,1,L                        STATE: 3*    ZIP: 3,45,L    │
│ HOME PHONE: 1,45,L                 BIRTH DAY: 5,45,1           │
│ SOCIAL SECURITY #: 5,1,1           SEX: 5,→                    │
│                  ┌── EMERGENCY CONTACT ──                       │
│   FIRST:                           LAST:                        │
│   ADDRESS:                         ADD A:                       │
│   CITY:                            STATE:       ZIP:            │
│   HOME PHONE:                      WORK PHONE:                  │
└────────────────────────────────────────────────────────────────┘
 Expand field: 3,30,L
 STAFF.DTF                    Fields Spec for Salary History    Page 1 of 4
 Esc-Exit  F1-Help  F6-Expand field  Shift+F6-Enhance  F9-Go back   F10-Continue
```

Figure 4.28   Screen 1 of the Field spec for the Salary History report.

```
┌──── EMPLOYMENT INFORMATION ────────────────────────────────────┐
│ DATE HIRED: 9,1,L        TYPE: →  POSITION: 7,10,1             │
│                                                                │
│ INITIAL SALARY────────ANNUALLY: 9,30,1(I→  MONTHLY:    HOURLY: │
│                                                                │
│ CURRENT SALARY────────ANNUALLY: 16,30,L(→  MONTHLY:   HOURLY:  │
│                                                                │
│ DATE 1: 11,1,L(RAIS→  ANNUAL 1: 11,30,L(→  MONTH 1:   HOUR 1:  │
│ DATE 2: 12,1,L(RAIS→  ANNUAL 2: 12,30,L(→  MONTH 2:   HOUR 2:  │
│ DATE 3: 13,1,L(RAIS→  ANNUAL 3: 13,30,L(→  MONTH 3:   HOUR 3:  │
│ DATE 4: 14,1,L(RAIS→  ANNUAL 4: 14,30,L(→  MONTH 4:   HOUR 4:  │
│              ┌── TERMINATION INFORMATION ──                    │
│ TERMINATION DATE:              TERM. REASON:                   │
│ REASON:                                                        │
│    :                                                           │
│    :                                                           │
│    :                                                           │
└────────────────────────────────────────────────────────────────┘
 STAFF.DTF     Und1          Fields Spec for Salary History    Page 3 of 4
 Esc-Exit  F1-Help  F6-Expand field  Shift+F6-Enhance  F9-Go back   F10-Continue
```

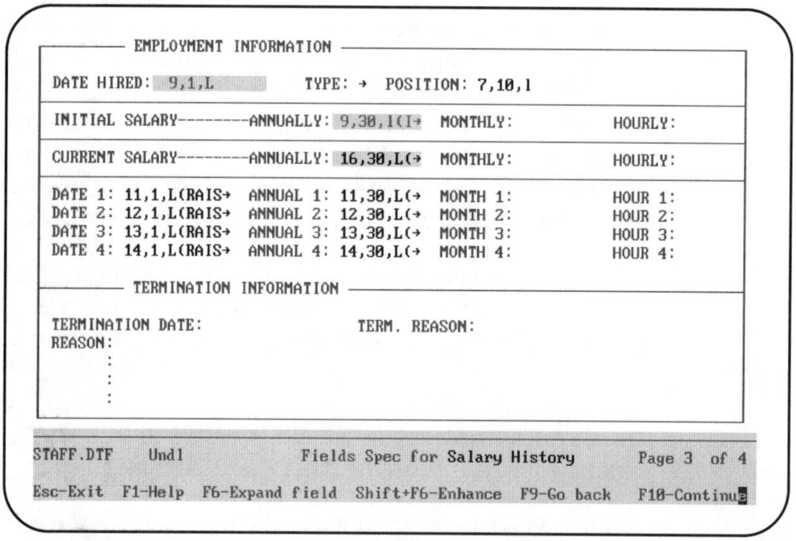

Figure 4.29   Screen 3 of the Field spec for the Salary History report.

8. With the Field specs finished, try enhancing a few of the fields.
   Press Home three times to move to the top of the file (page 1).
   Move your cursor down to the 1 in the FIRST field and press
   Shift-F6. This will bring up the Enhancement menu, which can be

seen in Figure 4.30. Press **B** for Bold and press the End key. This will boldface that field. Press Enter to move to the LAST field. Press Shift-F6, **B** for Bold, and press End. The name will now appear boldfaced on the report. Feel free to experiment with other enhancement features.

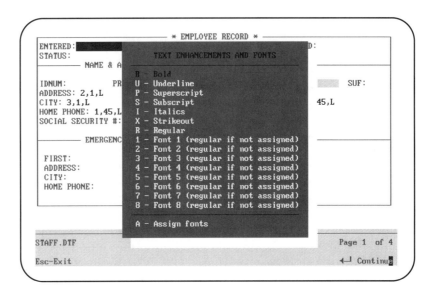

Figure 4.30   Enhancement menu.

In Figure 4.30 notice that eight fonts are possible on the Enhancement menu. Fonts are typefaces. To access different fonts, you must have special Q&A font files (they have .FNT extensions) on your hard drive. These files are placed on your hard drive during the installation process. Even if you have a particular font file installed on your hard drive, you may not be able to print that font. If your printer doesn't support certain fonts, you won't be able to use them. This chapter discusses fonts briefly; they are covered in-depth in Chapter 7 on direct mail.

Shortcut

Before you can print with the new font file, you must change the font file selection in the Install Printer option. To do this, press **U** for Utilities and **P** for Printer. Select the printer and press Enter four times. Press F8 to change the font file, type the new name, and press F10 three times.

To select fonts on the Enhancement menu, press Shift-F6 while in the Field spec. Then press **A** for Assign and press F6 to select the correct font file for your printer. Once you have selected it, your screen should look similar to Figure 4.31. If no font files are listed, you have to install them first.

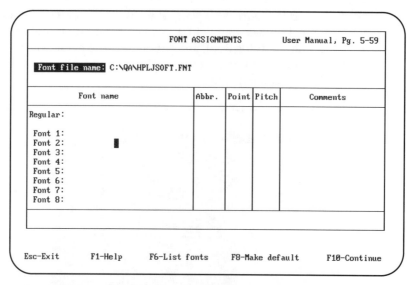

```
                              FONT ASSIGNMENTS         User Manual, Pg. 5-59

    Font file name: C:\QA\HPLJSOFT.FMT

                Font name              Abbr. Point Pitch      Comments
    Regular:

    Font 1:
    Font 2:          ▮
    Font 3:
    Font 4:
    Font 5:
    Font 6:
    Font 7:
    Font 8:


    Esc-Exit      F1-Help      F6-List fonts      F8-Make default      F10-Continue
```

Figure 4.31   Font Assignment screen.

To install fonts on the Enhancement menu, move down to the REGULAR font and press F6 to see a list of the fonts that your printer supports (these can be seen in Figure 4.32). Choose the font you want to be the default font (the one always used) and press Enter. This will select it. Repeat this process until you have selected eight fonts. When you are done, press F8 and F10 to make the changes permanent. Otherwise, when you exit the Report mode, the fonts will be lost.

Beginner's Tip

Font assignments have to be made in Report, File (Form) Report, and Write. Also, the font assignments are saved with each Report spec.

9. Press F10 to advance to the Print Options screen. There are two options on this screen that you should be aware of. The first is the number of records you want to print on each page. The default is one per page. The other option is whether you want the field labels to print. In this case, you want to keep the default settings.

10. Once you have filled in the Print Options spec, press F8 to move to the Define Page Spec screen. Fill it in according to Figure 4.33.

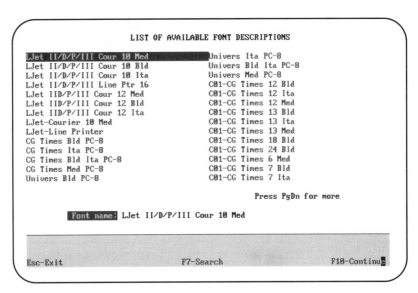

Figure 4.32   List of available fonts.

```
                        DEFINE PAGE
                        ═══════════

            Page width  : 80        Page length..: 66

            Left margin: 0          Right margin : 80

            Top margin  : 3         Bottom margin: 3

            Characters per inch:   ▶10◀  12   15   17
──────────────────────── HEADER ────────────────────────
1: @DATE ! SALARY HISTORY REPORT ! PAGE #
2:
3:
──────────────────────── FOOTER ────────────────────────
1:
2:
3:
```

STAFF.DTF	Define page for Salary History	
Esc-Exit	F1-Help F9-Go Back to Print Options	F10-Continue

Figure 4.33   Define Page Options.

Looking at Figure 4.33, you will notice several options. At the top of the screen, you can change the margins and page width. Below those options is the characters per inch setting. If you increase the characters per inch, you can increase the right margin and width, thus increasing the amount of data that will fit on a page. With the headers and footers, you further describe the report. To center a header or footer, place the text between two exclamation points. Lastly, to enhance headers or footers, press Shift-F6 to bring up the Enhancement menu.

11. Save the Report spec by pressing F10.

12. Press F10 to print the report. It should look like Figure 4.34.

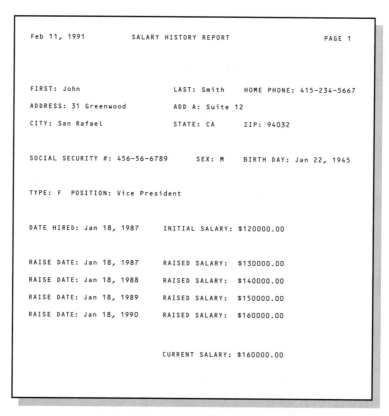

```
Feb 11, 1991              SALARY HISTORY REPORT                    PAGE 1



FIRST: John                   LAST: Smith     HOME PHONE: 415-234-5667

ADDRESS: 31 Greenwood         ADD A: Suite 12

CITY: San Rafael              STATE: CA      ZIP: 94032



SOCIAL SECURITY #: 456-56-6789        SEX: M    BIRTH DAY: Jan 22, 1945



TYPE: F  POSITION: Vice President



DATE HIRED: Jan 18, 1987      INITIAL SALARY: $120000.00



RAISE DATE: Jan 18, 1987      RAISED SALARY:  $130000.00

RAISE DATE: Jan 18, 1988      RAISED SALARY:  $140000.00

RAISE DATE: Jan 18, 1989      RAISED SALARY:  $150000.00

RAISE DATE: Jan 18, 1990      RAISED SALARY:  $160000.00



                              CURRENT SALARY: $160000.00
```

Figure 4.34   Final version of Salary History report.

You have just finished generating a form report by using the coordinate method. As mentioned earlier, you can also use the free-form method. Creating a free-form report is the same as creating a coordinate report except for the commands in the Field spec. When you get to the Field spec, use the next procedure for placing fields on the paper.

Placing Fields in a Free-Form Report

1. Place a number in the field. This designates the order in which the field will appear on the form, starting from top to bottom and left to right.

2. After each number, type either **X** to print this field and then print the next field on the following line; or **+** to print this field, skip one space, and print the next field.

3. Optionally, type a third number to indicate the number of lines or spaces you want to skip. For example, typing **2X,3** means to print this field second (2), move to the beginning of the next line (X), and print three blank lines (3). Typing **4+,5** means to print this field fourth (4), do not move to the next line (+), and print five spaces following this field (5).

4. Follow the instructions in steps 9 through 12 of the preceding procedure for "Developing a Coordinated Report Based on the Staff File."

Rename/Copy/Delete a Report Spec

In the same way that you manipulate files, you can manipulate report names. You can copy one Report spec to another and then modify it. You can rename a Report spec to a more appropriate name, and you can delete a Report spec entirely. Any of these functions can be performed through a menu selection or at the List of Report spec.

Renaming a Report Spec in the Personnel Database

1. Press **F** for File and **P** for Print.

2. Type the filename **STAFF** and press Enter. Press **P** for Print Records.

3. You should see the List of Report specs for this database. Highlight the Salary History report and press F5 to copy the Report spec. Type **New Report** for the new name and press Enter.

4. Highlight New Report and press F8 to rename the report. Type **Old Report** and press Enter. Highlight Old Report and press F3 to delete the Report spec. Answer Yes to delete it. These keys are consistent in all areas of the program: F5 for Copy, F8 for Rename, and F3 for Delete.

Remove Records

Q&A has always allowed mass deletion of records, but in the old versions you were unable to delete duplicate records. Now you can. In Version 4.0, there are three Remove functions, shown in Figure 4.35. The first is the straight remove; you specify a group of records and delete them. The second is the removal of duplicate records. And the third is the copying of duplicate records to an ASCII file, before they are deleted.

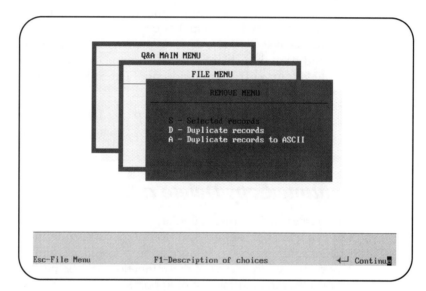

Figure 4.35   The Remove menu.

As you begin using your applications more and more, you will find that at times you want to delete a group of records. The records may be a batch of prospects that didn't pan out or old invoices or purchase orders, or you may just want to clean up your database. Either way, with the Remove feature you are saved from deleting each record individually.

Removing a Group of Records

1. Press **F** for File and **R** for Remove.

2. Type the filename and press Enter.

3. Press **S** for Selected Records, enter a Retrieve spec, and press F10.

4. Q&A will then ask if you really want to delete these records. If you do, press Yes. If you don't, press No.

When you delete duplicate records, you have the option of saving the duplicates into a special file. Since both methods of deleting duplicate records are the same except for the procedure to copy the duplicate records to an ASCII file, I will explain the ASCII method.

Copying Duplicate Records to an ASCII File Before Deleting Them

1. Begin by creating a duplicate record to delete. Press **F** for File and **S** for Search. Type the filename **STAFF** and press Enter. Press F10 to bring up the first record. Press Ctrl-F6 to switch to Add mode. Press Shift-F5 to copy the previous record. Press Shift-F10 to save the record and exit the file.

2. Press **R** for Remove, type the filename **STAFF**, and press Enter.

3. The Remove menu is on the screen, as shown in Figure 4.35. Press **A** for Duplicate Records to ASCII, type the filename **EXTRA.DUP**, and press Enter. Q&A will place the deleted record in the EXTRA.DUP file. The Duplicate Spec screen will appear, as shown in Figure 4.36.

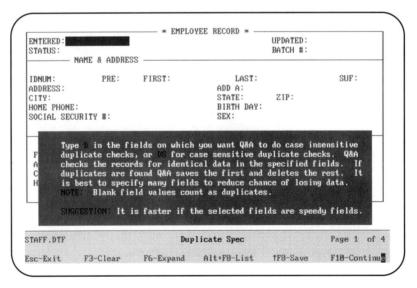

Figure 4.36 Duplicate Spec screen.

It is here that you choose the fields on which you want Q&A to conduct duplicate checks. By placing a **D** in a chosen field, you instruct Q&A to look for duplicate data in that field, save the first occurrence of the record, and delete the rest. All the files used in this book have a unique ID number field. This makes it easy to find duplicates using one field. However, if you didn't have an ID number field, you would need to place a **D** in several fields to check for duplicate records. For instance, if you typed a **D** in the LAST field, Q&A would delete all but one of the records with the same last name. So, you would have to place a **D** in more than one field such as: FIRST, LAST, ADDRESS, and HOME PHONE.

To make your duplicate checking case-sensitive, use a DS in place of the D in each field. Also, the duplicate checking process is faster if the selected fields (containing *D*s) are speedy fields. Lastly, it is important to know that blank field values count as duplicates.

4. Type a **D** in the IDNUM field and press F10. Q&A will give you the option of deleting the records individually or all at once. Press No to delete the records all at once. See Figure 4.37.

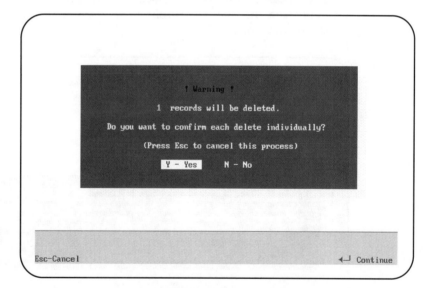

Figure 4.37   Removal Warning screen.

5. Press Esc twice to return to the Main menu.

The record(s) you deleted are now in the file EXTRA.DUP. Use the Write module to look at the file.

Using the Write Module to View the EXTRA.DUP File

1. Press **W** for Write and **G** for Get.

2. Press Shift-F4 to delete the path, type `c:\qa\file\extra.dup`, and press Enter. Press Enter again, since it is an ASCII file. The record should appear on the screen in ASCII format.

3. Press Esc twice to return to the Main menu.

To better analyze the deleted records, make a copy of the file design from which you deleted the records. Then import the deleted records into the new file design.

Guided Modifications

Organizations have varying record-keeping requirements for personnel. These requirements range from writing a name and address on an index card to maintaining extensive personal data. Whatever the needs of your organization, you can modify the Staff file to meet them.

The first change I suggest is to remove all unnecessary fields from the file—the things you'll never use. Then look at your paper records and add any fields from the forms that are appropriate. Finally, since you will probably give several performance reviews during an employee's tenure, I suggest that you add more full-page Performance Review screens to the end of the Staff file.

If you find that you want to store all names associated with your company in the Names file, you can add lookup statements to the Staff file. This lets you place the basic name and address information into the Names file, retrieve it into the Staff file, and then fill in the rest of the form.

Set Initial Values

Often you'll have a database in which the same information is added to every new record. An example is the DATE ENTERED field in the Names file. Every time you add a new record to the Names file, the date is already automatically added. This is accomplished by placing the @date function in the Set Initial Values screen. Two other functions often added to the Set Initial

Values screen are @time and @number. The @time command will place the current time (taken from your computer's internal clock) into the designated field, and the @number command will place the next sequential number into the designated field.

You can also use the Set Initial Values screen to add special codes, tax rates, states, zip codes, etc., to every record. A convenient aspect of setting initial values is the ability to write over any initial value. For instance, if most of your clients are in Texas, you can have TX automatically appear in the STATE field. Then, if a new client isn't from Texas, all you have to do is type the correct value in the field.

Adding Values to the Set Initial Values Screen

1. Press **F** for File, **D** for Design File, and **C** for Customize.

2. Type the filename and press Enter. Press **I** for Set Initial Values.

3. You are now in the Initial Values spec. Move to any field and type the values you want to appear every time a new record is added to this database. Remember that you can type any text you like and use either of the three functions: @date, @time, or @number.

4. Press F10 to save your spec.

Assign Access Rights and Field-Level Security

Q&A lets you restrict access to any aspect of a database's operation. You can let some people change the design, yet allow others to only add data to specific fields. When you *assign access rights* to a file, you type each user's name and password and then specifically select which features the person can access. Thus, when a person wants to use the database, he or she must type the correct name and password before obtaining access to a particular aspect of the file. If the person doesn't have rights to that function, Q&A returns an error message.

> Ø **Caution:** There is one serious drawback to assigning access rights. If a user with full rights uses the database and then doesn't reset the security level, ANYONE can access the data at the same level as the previous user. To reset the security, go to the Q&A Main menu and press Shift-F6. This also works in reverse. If someone with fewer rights opens a file, it must be reset before the person with full rights can access it in the assigned manner.

Used in conjunction with access rights, *field-level security* lets you provide complete protection of your data. You can format fields three different ways: Read & Write, Read Only, and No Access (hidden). The first format, Read & Write, is the default format. The next format, Read Only, allows a user to read the contents of the field but not alter it. The last format, No Access (hidden), actually hides the field from view. In order to assign field-level security, you have to assign access rights to the file first.

For the Personnel application, access rights and field-level security are quite relevant. By using these features, you can allow one person to enter the name and address while salary and personal information remain hidden.

Some applications are less sensitive than others. If you don't need to guard your data, it makes no sense to have users go through the extra steps of typing their names and passwords. But if you do need to protect your data, with these tools you can.

Figure 4.38 shows the default Access Control screen and a listing of all the rights you can restrict. The first option lets you assign password rights; normally the systems supervisor would receive these rights. Next, you can allow only certain people the option of changing the design of the database. Since this is such a potentially destructive function, grant this privilege sparingly. Another potentially damaging feature is mass deletion of records. With access to this feature, someone could eliminate all the records in the database. Deleting individual records, however, is an access right that everyone should have, since a person may enter a record incorrectly and need to remove it. The last three rights are ones that every user should have: run a mass update, design/redesign reports, and enter/edit data.

In the next example, you will create two users for the Staff file. One will be you, and the other will be "John" with the password "DOE." You can delete "John" after you are through with the example.

```
                        ACCESS CONTROL

        Initial Password:  JOY

    Make the selections below to indicate what rights this person has:

        Can assign password rights?........:    ▶Yes◀  No

        Can change design and program?.....:    ▶Yes◀  No

        Can mass delete?...................:    ▶Yes◀  No

        Can delete individual records?.....:    ▶Yes◀  No

        Can run mass update?...............:    ▶Yes◀  No

        Can Design/Redesign reports?.......:    ▶Yes◀  No

        Can enter/edit data?...............:    ▶Yes◀  No

    STAFF.DTF              Access Control Form for DBA

    Esc-Exit                      F1-Help                    F10-Continue
```

Figure 4.38   Access Control screen showing full rights.

Practice Assigning Access Rights

1. Press **F** for File, **D** for Design, and **S** for Secure.

2. Type the filename **STAFF** and press Enter.

3. Type **A** for Assign Access Rights. This is where you assign access rights to each user or group. Initially, you are going to give yourself FULL rights. This way you can alter the database in the future.

> ⊘ **Caution:** Don't forget your password. There is no way to find out what your password is, except by sending it to Symantec's technical support staff.

4. Type your name and press Enter. The screen should look like Figure 4.38. Type a password and press F10 to save the Security spec. By doing this, you have given yourself full rights to the Staff File.

5. Press F10 to add another user. Type **JOHN** and press Enter. Type the password **DOE** and fill in the rest of the screen as it appears in Figure 4.39.

```
                          ACCESS CONTROL

            Initial Password:  TRUST

    Make the selections below to indicate what rights this person has:

        Can assign password rights?........:    Yes  ▶No◀

        Can change design and program?.....:    Yes  ▶No◀

        Can mass delete?...................:    Yes  ▶No◀

        Can delete individual records?......:   Yes  ▶No◀

        Can run mass update?...............:   ▶Yes◀  No

        Can Design/Redesign reports?.......:   ▶Yes◀  No

        Can enter/edit data?...............:   ▶Yes◀  No


    STAFF.DTF           Access Control Form for USER

    Esc-Exit                    F1-Help                    F10-Continue
```

Figure 4.39 User security rights.

6. Press F10 to save JOHN'S rights.

7. Answer No to edit another.

   Now you will add field-level security to the Staff File.

Practice Assigning Field-Level Security

1. Press **F** for Field Level Security. You are now at the screen where you enter the name of the user or group.

2. Type **JOHN** and press Enter.

3. It is here that you designate how you want each field formatted: Read & Write, Read Only, or No Access. Press PgDn to move to the third screen. Type an **R** in the DATE HIRED, TYPE, and POSITION fields. Type an **N** in the CURRENT SALARY fields: ANNUALLY, MONTHLY, and HOURLY. Your screen should look like Figure 4.40.

4. Press F10 to save the Field spec.

5. At the User Selection screen, type **JOHN** and press F10.

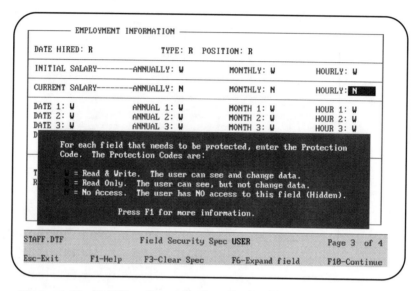

```
┌─── EMPLOYMENT INFORMATION ───────────────────────────────────────┐
│                                                                   │
│  DATE HIRED: R              TYPE: R  POSITION: R                   │
│                                                                   │
│  INITIAL SALARY────────ANNUALLY: W        MONTHLY: W      HOURLY: W│
│                                                                   │
│  CURRENT SALARY────────ANNUALLY: N        MONTHLY: N      HOURLY:▐N▌│
│                                                                   │
│  DATE 1: W         ANNUAL 1: W        MONTH 1: W       HOUR 1: W   │
│  DATE 2: W         ANNUAL 2: W        MONTH 2: W       HOUR 2: W   │
│  DATE 3: W         ANNUAL 3: W        MONTH 3: W       HOUR 3: W   │
│  D╔═════════════════════════════════════════════════════════════╗│
│   ║  For each field that needs to be protected, enter the Protec-║│
│   ║  tion Code.  The Protection Codes are:                       ║│
│  T║                                                              ║│
│  R║   W = Read & Write.  The user can see and change data.       ║│
│   ║   R = Read Only.  The user can see, but not change data.     ║│
│   ║   N = No Access.  The user has NO access to this field (Hidden).║│
│   ║                                                              ║│
│   ║         Press F1 for more information.                       ║│
│   ╚═════════════════════════════════════════════════════════════╝│
│                                                                   │
│  STAFF.DTF            Field Security Spec USER         Page 3 of 4│
│                                                                   │
│  Esc-Exit      F1-Help      F3-Clear Spec    F6-Expand field   F10-Continue│
└───────────────────────────────────────────────────────────────────┘
```

Figure 4.40   Field-level security for the Staff file.

To restrict access, you must go through this same procedure for every database. However, if you use the same user names and passwords, all the databases can be opened when the first database is opened.

Next you are going to reset the security rights and look at the Staff file as if you were the user JOHN.

Practice Resetting the Security Rights

1. Press Esc three times to return to the Main menu.

2. Press Shift-F6 to reset the security rights. A password and user-ID-cleared message appears at the bottom of the screen.

3. Press **F** for File and **S** for Search.

4. Type the filename **STAFF** and press Enter.

5. Type the user name **JOHN** and press Enter. Type the password **DOE** and press Enter.

6. Press F10 to bring up a record. Press PgDn twice to move to the third screen. It should look like Figure 4.41. You'll notice that you cannot place your cursor in the first row of fields or see the third row.

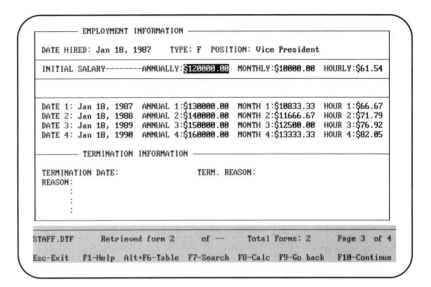

```
┌─────── EMPLOYMENT INFORMATION ───────────────────────────────────┐
│                                                                   │
│  DATE HIRED: Jan 18, 1987    TYPE: F  POSITION: Vice President     │
│ ┌───────────────────────────────────────────────────────────────┐│
│ │ INITIAL SALARY────────ANNUALLY:$120000.00 MONTHLY:$10000.00 HOURLY:$61.54│
│ └───────────────────────────────────────────────────────────────┘│
│                                                                   │
│  DATE 1: Jan 18, 1987  ANNUAL 1:$130000.00  MONTH 1:$10833.33  HOUR 1:$66.67│
│  DATE 2: Jan 18, 1988  ANNUAL 2:$140000.00  MONTH 2:$11666.67  HOUR 2:$71.79│
│  DATE 3: Jan 18, 1989  ANNUAL 3:$150000.00  MONTH 3:$12500.00  HOUR 3:$76.92│
│  DATE 4: Jan 18, 1990  ANNUAL 4:$160000.00  MONTH 4:$13333.33  HOUR 4:$82.05│
│ ─────── TERMINATION INFORMATION ─────────────                     │
│                                                                   │
│  TERMINATION DATE:                  TERM. REASON:                 │
│  REASON:                                                          │
│        :                                                          │
│        :                                                          │
│        :                                                          │
├───────────────────────────────────────────────────────────────────┤
│ STAFF.DTF    Retrieved form 2    of --    Total Forms: 2    Page 3 of 4│
│                                                                   │
│ Esc-Exit   F1-Help  Alt+F6-Table  F7-Search  F8-Calc  F9-Go back  F10-Continue│
└───────────────────────────────────────────────────────────────────┘
```

Figure 4.41   Staff file with field security enabled.

7. Press Shift-F10 to save the record and exit.

Lastly, you are going to delete the user JOHN and, optionally, your name.

Practice Deleting a User

1. Press **F** for File, **D** for Design, and **S** for Secure.

2. Type the filename **STAFF** and press Enter.

3. Type YOUR name and password and press Enter.

4. Type **A** for Assign Access Rights.

5. Move down to the user name JOHN, press F3, and answer Yes. Move down to your name, press F3, and answer Yes. This database is now unprotected.

6. Press Esc three times to return to the Main menu.

Summary

The *Personnel application* automates the basic record-keeping tasks associated with personnel management. It relies on three database files: Staff, Health, and Holiday. Each file contains reports needed in personnel management. All of these reports can be customized to suit your needs. The Personnel application can be expanded to include payroll processing functions, such as the automatic calculation of wages and commissions, payroll taxes, deductions, and the generation of the various state and federal payroll tax forms.

This chapter showed you how to manipulate files, print form reports, and then enhance them. The report you created can be a model for creating other form reports. You also learned how to assign access rights so that only certain people can view specific fields. This concept can be applied to any application where security is an issue. Another useful feature that you explored is how to delete duplicate records. This feature is especially useful if you import data from another system or source and are unsure of the quality of the records.

The next chapter presents another time-saving application—the Sales Management application. With this application, you can automate your sales efforts.

AT A GLANCE

APPLICATION FEATURES

Table View

1. Press **F** for File and **S** for Search.
2. Type the filename and press Enter.
3. Type the Retrieve spec and press F10.
4. Press Alt-F6 to display the data in Table View.

Mass Update

1. Press **F** for File and **M** for Mass Update.
2. Type the filename and press Enter.
3. Type the Retrieve spec and press F10.
4. Type the Merge spec and press F10.
5. Choose Yes to update the records individually or No to update them all at once.

Develop Columnar Reports

1. Press **R** for Report and **D** for Design/ Redesign.
2. Type the filename and press Enter.
3. Type a report name and press Enter.
4. Choose Columnar, type a Retrieve spec, and press F10.
5. Type a Column/Sort spec and press F10.
6. Adjust the print options, press F8, define the page options, and press F10 to save the design.
7. Press F10 to print the report.

Export Records

1. Press **F** for File, **U** for Utilities, and **E** for Export. Choose the type of file you are exporting to—DIF, ASCII, dBASE II, etc.
2. Type the filename and press Enter.
3. Type the filename you want to export the records to and press Enter.
4. Type a Retrieve spec and press F10. Type a Merge spec and press F10 to export the records.

Recover a Database

1. Press **F** for File, **U** for Utilities, and **R** for Recover.
2. Type the filename, press Enter, and press F10 to begin.

DESIGN APPLICATION FEATURES

Custom Help

1. Press **F** for File, **D** for Design, and **C** for Customize.
2. Type the filename and press Enter.
3. Press **D** for Define Custom Help.
4. Type the help screens and press F10 to save your spec.

Field Names

1. Press **F** for File, **D** for Design, and **P** for Program.
2. Type the filename and press Enter.
3. Press **S** for Set Field Names.
4. Type the field names and press F10 to save them.

Sales Management Application

This chapter will teach you how to use the Sales Management application and the features in the "At a Glance" section. This application automates the entire sales management process.

Overview

The Sales Management application can be used to manage your contacts. It acts as a tickler system to remind you when to call someone back or to remind you to perform some action on the customer's behalf. It is ideal if you sell over the telephone. You can easily select all the people you need to contact that day, make your calls, record your remarks, and, if needed, flag any record to receive a personalized letter. The Sales file includes fields for first and last contact, the date you mailed information, the close date, which product the customer is interested in, and room for annotating each conversation. This application works in conjunction with the Names file and the Codes file.

Recall that the *Names file* is often the central repository for all the names used in your applications. As such, you initially have to enter the basic name and address into the Names file and generate an ID number to be used to look up the information into the Sales file.

The Sales Management application also makes use of the *Codes file*, which holds each code and its description. By placing your codes and descriptions into an actual database, you can sort the entries and print them as a handy reference report.

Using the Sales Management application involves three steps. The first is adding your prospects or customers to the Names file. Next is adding to the Codes file any codes that you plan to utilize. Third is adding your records to the Sales file. To add the records, type the prospect's ID number and press F8. Begin entering the specific sales information. When you come to a code field, type the code and the description will automatically be looked up. Now, when needed, you can print two reports: from the Sales file you can print a list of prospects to call today and from the Codes file you can print a list of codes and their descriptions.

In this chapter, you will learn several new and useful features while you are learning how to use the Sales Management application. Initially, you will explore using a file as a lookup file—one that makes use of the `xlookup` statement. Next, you will create a columnar report and use fonts, enhancements, and derived columns, and you will extract information from another file. After that you will learn the Query Programming feature and practice setting up *Restrict specs*, which are pop-up windows containing the allowable values for a field. Using the Table View option, adding custom help screens to fields, and changing a group of records with the Mass Update feature are the final features you will learn about in this feature-packed chapter.

Application Explained

The Sales file is the heart of this application. However, it makes use of the Names and Codes files. Although the Names file is explained in Chapter 3, I will briefly cover it here because it is an integral part of this application.

The Names File

Looking at Figure 5.1, notice that the top section of the Names file contains four fields: one for the date the record was entered, one for the last time it was updated, a batch number field, and a reference ID field. These last two fields can be used for any purpose you choose. A common use for the BATCH # field is to hold a number representing the batch of data you are entering. The REF ID field can be used to manually select a group of records that do not have any field values in common. For example, to mail to ten different customers who have no field values in common in the database, you could manually enter an asterisk in the REF ID field and then print all the records with an asterisk.

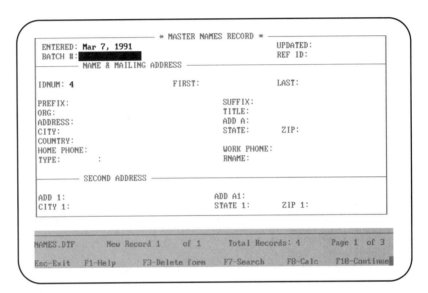

Figure 5.1   Screen 1 of the Names file.

The next section of the Names file, shown in Figure 5.1, is the Name and Mailing Address. Here you enter the primary mailing address.

Name and Address Fields in Screen 1 of the Names File

ENTERED | The date the record was entered. It is automatically generated by the system.

UPDATED | The date the record was last viewed or updated. It is automatically generated by the system.

BATCH # | Used for designating batches of records.

REF ID | User-defined field.

IDNUM | A unique number assigned to each entry in the database. It is used primarily as the *key field* to look up information from the Names file into other files.

FIRST	The first name.
LAST	The last name.
PREFIX	Mr., Mrs., Dr., etc.
SUFFIX	J.D., M.D., Ph.D., C.P.A., etc.
ORG	The organization's name.
TITLE	The title of the person in the database.
ADDRESS	The street address of the individual or organization.
ADD A	The second address line, normally used for suite, building, mail stop, etc.
CITY	The city.
STATE	The state.
ZIP	The zip code.
COUNTRY	Any country outside of the United States.
HOME PHONE	The home phone number of the main contact.
WORK PHONE	The phone number of the organization.
TYPE	A one- to six-character alphanumeric code used to classify the name as a prospect, customer, staff member, etc. This field is programmed to place a description in the field next to the TYPE field. The description is looked up from the Codes file. The programming statement looks at the code in the field and matches it to the code in the Codes file. When it finds a match, it places the code's description in the field next to TYPE.
RNAME	The name of the company or individual. This field is used for reporting for purposes and is created based on the code in the TYPE field. A programming statement placed in the RNAME field says: If the value in the TYPE field is IN for individual, then put the individual's name in the RNAME field. If it is not IN, then put the organization's name in the RNAME field. This field is useful if you have a combination of individuals and organizations in your database and want to use only one name field on a report. This eliminates the need to place the organization name, the FIRST name and the LAST name fields on the same report.

The Second Address section, shown in Figure 5.1, is used to store another address.

Second Address Fields in Screen 1 of the Names File

ADD 1
The second street address. This field can be used for a home address, billing address, or shipping address.

ADD A1
The second part of the street address.

CITY 1
The second city.

STATE 1
The second state.

ZIP 1
The second zip code.

The second screen of the Names file is the Mailing Information section, shown in Figure 5.2. It holds the direct mail codes. These fields can be used to hold codes, dates, and remarks indicating the date on which you mailed material, what was mailed, and a line of remarks elaborating on what was mailed.

Shortcut

By using the Names file in conjunction with the Sales file whenever you send a mailing to a prospect or customer, you can use the Post feature to place the codes into the fields on the second screen of the Names file.

Fields in Screen 2 of the Names File

CODE
A code to represent the mailing, such as Spring91, for the mailing sent during the spring of 1991.

DATE
The date of the mailing.

RESPONSE
The date the customer responded to the mailing.

REMARKS
Additional comments about the mailing.

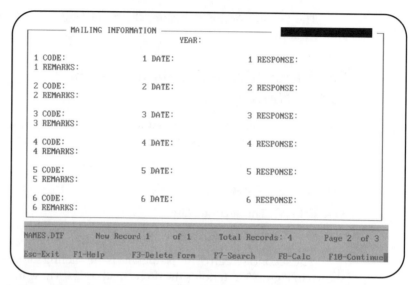

```
┌─────  MAILING INFORMATION ──────────────  ███████████████ ─┐
│                           YEAR:
│  1 CODE:              1 DATE:              1 RESPONSE:
│  1 REMARKS:
│
│  2 CODE:              2 DATE:              2 RESPONSE:
│  2 REMARKS:
│
│  3 CODE:              3 DATE:              3 RESPONSE:
│  3 REMARKS:
│
│  4 CODE:              4 DATE:              4 RESPONSE:
│  4 REMARKS:
│
│  5 CODE:              5 DATE:              5 RESPONSE:
│  5 REMARKS:
│
│  6 CODE:              6 DATE:              6 RESPONSE:
│  6 REMARKS:
└──────────────────────────────────────────────────────────┘
 NAMES.DTF      New Record 1    of 1    Total Records: 4      Page 2  of  3

 Esc-Exit   F1-Help       F3-Delete form    F7-Search      F8-Calc     F10-Continue
```

Figure 5.2   Screen 2 of the Names file.

The Sales File

When you are using this application, you will spend most of your time in the Sales file. Looking at the top section of Figure 5.3, you will see that this section of the Sales file is identical to the top section of the Names file. The second section is where you enter the IDNUM and press F8 to look up the name and address from the Names file. The NEXT CONTACT field holds the date on which you are to call this person again, and the LAST CONTACT field holds the date on which you last contacted this person—whether or not you reached the person.

In the third section, you have room for a few lines of information. In the LAST ACTION field, type a brief synopsis of the last action you took. This could be a phone call, meeting, or mailing. The NEXT ACTION field gives you room to write a brief synopsis of the next action you need to take to keep this sale on track. In the MAIN NEED field, write what primary need the prospect will have fulfilled as a result of using your product or service. The NOTES field gives you room for one line of comments (on another screen there is room for extensive notes). The last field in this section, DEAL, is where you type the basics of the proposed deal between you and your prospect.

The final section on screen 1 contains the person's name and address as it appears in the Names file. The TYPE CODE field can be used for classifying this person as a prospect, customer, vendor, etc. The DESCRIPTION field is automatically filled in based on the value typed in the TYPE CODE field. This is done through a programming statement that searches the Codes file for the code and then places the description in the DESCRIPTION field.

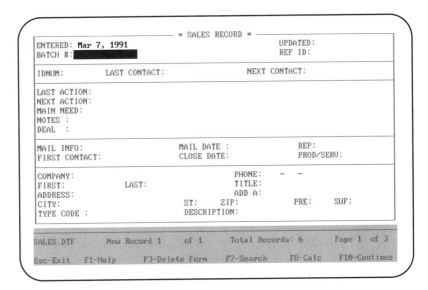

Figure 5.3   Screen 1 of the Sales file.

Fields in Screen 1 of the Names File

ENTERED
: The date the record was entered. It is automatically generated by the system.

UPDATED
: The date the record was last viewed or updated. It is automatically generated by the system.

BATCH #
: Used for designating batches of records.

REF ID
: User-defined field.

IDNUM
: A unique number assigned to each entry in the database. It is used primarily as the *key field* to look up information from the Names file into the Sales file.

213

LAST CONTACT	The date of the last call you made to this person, whether or not you reached the person.
NEXT CONTACT	The date you are to contact this person again.
LAST ACTION	A brief synopsis of the last action you took or conversation you had.
NEXT ACTION	A brief synopsis of the next action you'll take.
MAIN NEED	A synopsis of the prospect's main need.
NOTES	A line of notes.
DEAL	Brief terms of the deal you are discussing.
MAIL INFO	Used to determine which records should receive mail. Type **YES**, **NO**, or a code to indicate a specific mailing.
MAIL DATE	The date you last mailed literature.
REP	The sales rep's name.
FIRST CONTACT	The first date you contacted this person.
CLOSE DATE	The date you expect the sale to close.
PROD/SERV	A code to indicate the product or service the person wants to buy.
COMPANY	The organization's name.
PHONE	The phone number of the organization.
FIRST	The first name.
LAST	The last name.
TITLE	The title of the person in the database.
ADDRESS	The street address of the individual or organization
ADD A	The second address line, normally used for suite, building, mail stop, etc.
CITY	The city.
STATE	The state.
ZIP	The zip code.
PRE	Mr., Mrs., Dr., etc.
SUF	J.D., M.D., Ph.D., C.P.A., etc.

TYPE CODE   A code indicating whether the person is a prospect, customer, etc. The code is contained in the Codes file.

DESCRIPTION   The description associated with the code. Once the code is typed, the description is looked up from the Codes file.

The second screen of the Sales file, shown in Figure 5.4, contains room to record notes regarding your phone conversations. There is currently one screen to do this; you will probably want to add more.

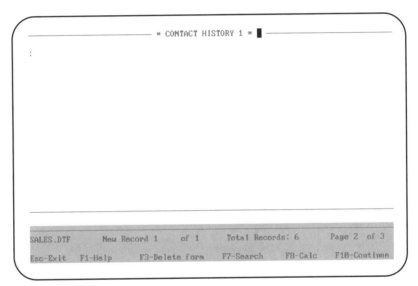

Figure 5.4   Screen 2 of the Sales file.

> **Caution:** There are three fields on the third screen of the Sales file that exist to illustrate the advanced columnar reporting features discussed later in this chapter. Do not remove them until after you have gone through that section.

The Codes File

By utilizing the Codes file, shown in Figure 5.5, you have more flexibility in managing your codes. The top section of the Codes file is the same as that of the Names and Sales files. Looking at the second section of the screen, you will see the first field—the CATEGORY field. This field allows you to segment your codes into logical groups. The CODE field contains the actual code. This field also acts as the *key field* when conducting an external lookup. The DESCRIPTION explains the CODE field and will be placed in your database when you type the code. However, you must correctly utilize the `xlookup` statement or `@xlookup` function for this to occur. The CODE STATUS field indicates whether the field must be used or whether it is optional.

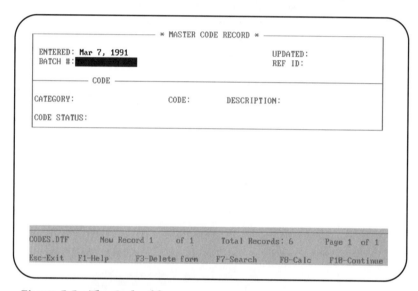

Figure 5.5 The Codes file.

Fields in the Codes File

CATEGORY	Used to segment codes into logical groups.
CODE	The actual code.
DESCRIPTION	The description of the code.
CODE STATUS	Indicates if the code must be used or if it is optional.

Using the Application

In this section you will explore several exciting new features, including Mass Update, Table View, exporting data, Query Programming, recovering damaged databases, and adding records to the Codes, Names, and Sales files.

Suggested Uses

The Sales file is ideally suited as a telemarketing tool. It can support a person who sells primarily over the phone and needs to track and manage sales leads. In a multiuser environment, where several people share the same database, this application can allow a sales manager access to all the sales records while at the same time each sales rep works on his or her own. It also can be used as a contact manager. Used this way, it is a more generic tool for managing all sorts of names and the date when to get back to them.

Examine the Codes and Names Files

To take full advantage of the Sales file's functionality, you must have the necessary codes in the Codes file. A few codes currently exist. However, you may want to add more as you begin to use the Sales Management application and other applications.

Remember, the Codes file is a database just like any other database. As such, all the features you've learned can be utilized in the Codes file. Chapter 6 explains the difference between using the internal lookup table and using a database for lookups. Each database has its own internal lookup table where you can store codes and descriptions. The problem with this method is lack of flexibility—you can't search for specific records, print the codes, or sort them into any particular order. In short, it is a very static environment. A much more useful technique is to use a database as a lookup table. By doing this, you can search for codes, sort them, and print them for reference.

Let's look at a few codes in the Codes file. Press **F** for File and **S** for Search. Press Enter. Type the filename **CODES** and press Enter. Move to the CATEGORY field, type **sales**, and press F10. Continue pressing F10 until you find the Prospect record. It should look like Figure 5.6. From this file, descriptions are looked up based on the value in the TYPE CODE field.

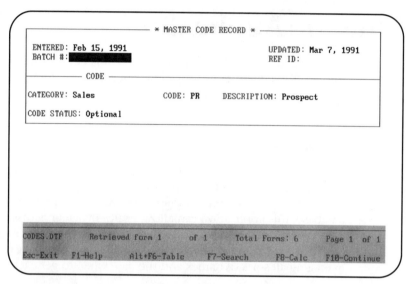

```
┌──────────────────────── * MASTER CODE RECORD * ────────────────────────┐
│                                                                         │
│   ENTERED: Feb 15, 1991                          UPDATED: Mar 7, 1991   │
│   BATCH #:████████████                           REF ID:               │
│   ──────────── CODE ────────────                                        │
│                                                                         │
│  CATEGORY: Sales            CODE: PR      DESCRIPTION: Prospect         │
│                                                                         │
│  CODE STATUS: Optional                                                  │
│                                                                         │
│                                                                         │
│                                                                         │
│                                                                         │
│                                                                         │
│  CODES.DTF      Retrieved form 1     of 1      Total Forms: 6      Page 1  of 1 │
│  Esc-Exit   F1-Help      Alt+F6-Table     F7-Search     F8-Calc    F10-Continue │
└─────────────────────────────────────────────────────────────────────────┘
```

Figure 5.6   Prospect code displayed.

To add additional codes, press Ctrl-F6 to switch to Add mode and begin entering the new records. Press F10 to save each record and press Shift-F10 to save the last record and exit the form.

Shortcut

You can use the Codes file to hold all the codes used with any application.

In order for the examples to work in the following section, there must be at least one record in the Names file. A sample record, Sarah Jones, has been entered for your convenience, or you can add one of your own.

Practice Looking at an Existing Record

1. Press **F** for File and **S** for Search.

2. Type **NAMES** and press Enter.

3. Move to the IDNUM field, type **3**, and press F10. This will retrieve the sample prospect, shown in Figure 5.7. You will use the ID number to retrieve this information into the Sales file. The Names file also makes use of the Codes file by retrieving the description of the code TYPE, found at the bottom of the name and address section.

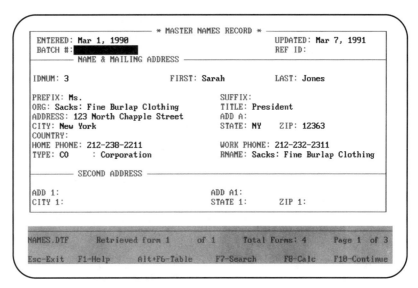

```
┌─────────────── * MASTER NAMES RECORD * ───────────────┐
│  ENTERED: Mar 1, 1990                    UPDATED: Mar 7, 1991  │
│  BATCH #:████████████                    REF ID:              │
│  ─────── NAME & MAILING ADDRESS ──────                        │
│                                                               │
│  IDNUM: 3                FIRST: Sarah        LAST: Jones       │
│                                                               │
│  PREFIX: Ms.                     SUFFIX:                       │
│  ORG: Sacks: Fine Burlap Clothing  TITLE: President           │
│  ADDRESS: 123 North Chapple Street  ADD A:                    │
│  CITY: New York                  STATE: NY    ZIP: 12363      │
│  COUNTRY:                                                     │
│  HOME PHONE: 212-238-2211        WORK PHONE: 212-232-2311     │
│  TYPE: CO     : Corporation      RNAME: Sacks: Fine Burlap Clothing │
│                                                               │
│  ─────── SECOND ADDRESS ──────                                │
│                                                               │
│  ADD 1:                          ADD A1:                      │
│  CITY 1:                         STATE 1:     ZIP 1:          │
│                                                               │
│  NAMES.DTF    Retrieved form 1   of 1    Total Forms: 4   Page 1  of 3 │
│                                                               │
│  Esc-Exit   F1-Help    Alt+F6-Table    F7-Search   F8-Calc   F10-Continue │
└───────────────────────────────────────────────────────────┘
```

Figure 5.7   Names file with Prospect displayed.

Sales File and Table View

By default, Q&A displays your data in *Form View*. That is, one record takes up an entire screen or group of screens. However, at times you will want to view several records at once. To do this, you have to switch to *Table View*, which you can do only from Search/Update mode. Once you have switched to Table View, you can move through the records and edit data in any of the fields.

Table View is particularly useful in the Sales file. You can easily display all your calls for the day by issuing a Retrieve spec in the NEXT CONTACT field of today's date and pressing Alt-F6 to switch to Table View. With all the calls displayed, you can move to your highest-priority calls and press F10 to select the specific record.

Practice Viewing an Existing Sales Record and Adding a New One in Table View

1. Press **F** for File and **S** for Search.

2. Type the filename **SALES** and press Enter.

3. Once inside the file, move to the IDNUM field, type **3**, and press F10. This will retrieve a sample sales record, as shown in Figure 5.8.

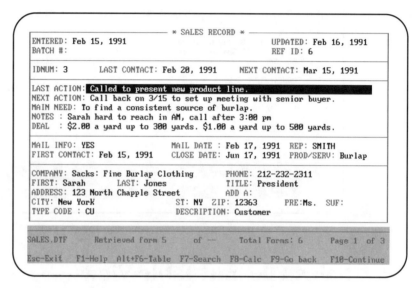

```
                        * SALES RECORD *
ENTERED: Feb 15, 1991                    UPDATED: Feb 16, 1991
BATCH #:                                 REF ID: 6

IDNUM: 3      LAST CONTACT: Feb 20, 1991    NEXT CONTACT: Mar 15, 1991

LAST ACTION: Called to present new product line.
NEXT ACTION: Call back on 3/15 to set up meeting with senior buyer.
MAIN NEED: To find a consistent source of burlap.
NOTES : Sarah hard to reach in AM, call after 3:00 pm
DEAL  : $2.00 a yard up to 300 yards. $1.00 a yard up to 500 yards.

MAIL INFO: YES            MAIL DATE : Feb 17, 1991  REP: SMITH
FIRST CONTACT: Feb 15, 1991   CLOSE DATE: Jun 17, 1991  PROD/SERV: Burlap

COMPANY: Sacks: Fine Burlap Clothing      PHONE: 212-232-2311
FIRST: Sarah       LAST: Jones            TITLE: President
ADDRESS: 123 North Chapple Street         ADD A:
CITY: New York              ST: NY ZIP: 12363    PRE:Ms.  SUF:
TYPE CODE : CU              DESCRIPTION: Customer

SALES.DTF    Retrieved form 5    of —    Total Forms: 6    Page 1 of 3

Esc-Exit  F1-Help  Alt+F6-Table  F7-Search  F8-Calc  F9-Go back  F10-Continue
```

Figure 5.8   Screen 1 of sample Sales Record.

4. As you can see, the record has been filled out for you. Take a look at each of the fields to understand the type of information that goes into them. When you are done looking at screen 1, press PgDn to look at screen 2, shown in Figure 5.9. Here you record any notes associated with your conversations.

5. Now you are ready to try adding a record and displaying and editing records in Table View. Press Ctrl-F6 to switch to Add mode.

6. Move to the IDNUM field, type **1**, and press F8 to look up the name and address. Press Enter to move to the LAST CONTACT field. Go through screen 1 and fill in each of the fields. Stop at the TYPE CODE field.

Shortcut

To quickly enter today's date, press Ctrl-F5. To automatically enter the current time, press Alt-F5 in a TIME field.

7. With your cursor on the TYPE CODE field, press Alt-F7. This will bring up the window shown in Figure 5.10. This window contains the Restrict spec for this field. Every field can have a Restrict spec. When you define a Restrict Spec, which you'll do in a later section, you restrict the options that can be entered into this field.

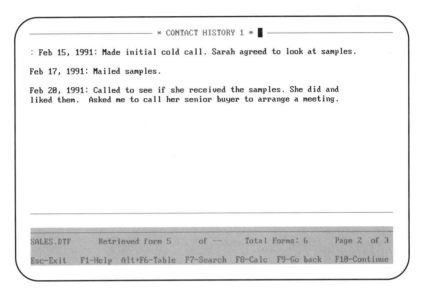

```
──────────────── * CONTACT HISTORY 1 * █ ────────────────

: Feb 15, 1991: Made initial cold call. Sarah agreed to look at samples.

Feb 17, 1991: Mailed samples.

Feb 20, 1991: Called to see if she received the samples. She did and
liked them. Asked me to call her senior buyer to arrange a meeting.




──────────────────────────────────────────────────────────────────

SALES.DTF    Retrieved form 5      of --     Total Forms: 6    Page 2  of 3

Esc-Exit   F1-Help  Alt+F6-Table  F7-Search  F8-Calc  F9-Go back   F10-Continue
```

Figure 5.9   Screen 2 of sample Sales Record.

8. Move your cursor to the code PR and press Enter two times. You will notice that the code was placed in the TYPE CODE field and that the description prospect was looked up from the Codes file.

9. Press PgDn to move to the Contact History screen, enter a few comments, and press F10 to save the record.

10. Display the records in Table View by pressing F7 to switch to Search mode, press F10 to bring up all the records, and move your cursor to the IDNUM field. Press Alt-F6 to switch to Table View. Your screen should look similar to Figure 5.11.

You are now in Table View. You can move to any record and then to any field. Once you are in a field, you can add, change, or delete data. In this example, you have only four records in Table View. However, Table View will display up to seventeen records at a time. Notice that there are only five fields (columns) displayed at a time. As you move your cursor to the right or left, other fields come into view.

Use this opportunity to practice moving around Table View. Some particularly useful keystroke combinations are Ctrl-Right Arrow and Ctrl-Left Arrow. By pressing these keys, you will move five fields at a time. PgUp and PgDn will scroll the screen up or down seventeen rows. Ctrl-Home will take you to the first record, and Ctrl-End will take you to the last record. A Right Arrow in a field indicates that the value is too long to be fully displayed.

Press F6 to expand the field; you will then be able to edit it. Figure 5.12 displays the editing and browsing keys, and Figure 5.13 displays the available function keys.

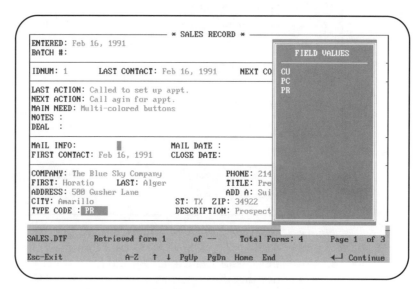

Figure 5.10   Screen 1 with Restrict specs displayed for TYPE CODE field.

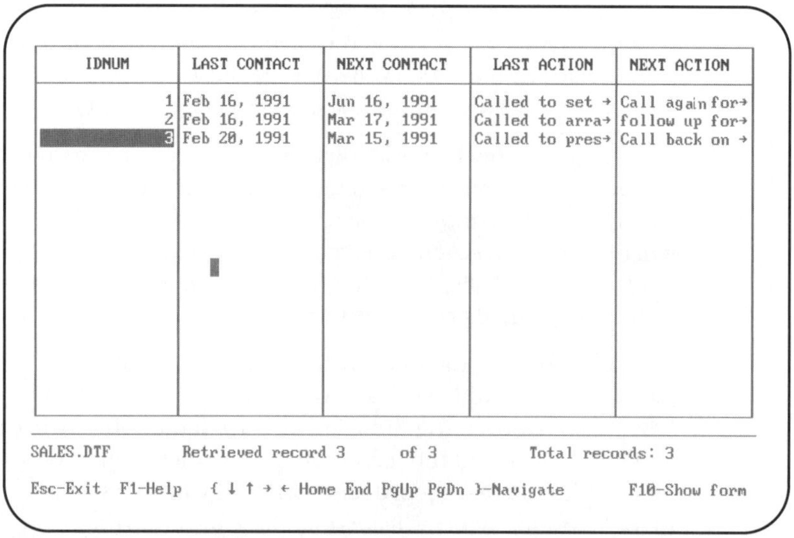

Figure 5.11   Records in Table View.

```
                     BROWSING IN TABLE VIEW

    ↑    Same field, previous record
    ↓    Same field, next record
    →    Next field                   Ctrl →    Scroll right 5 fields
    ←    Previous field               Ctrl ←    Scroll left 5 fields

   Tab   Next field                   Shift Tab  Previous field

  PgUp   Scroll up 17 rows
  PgDn   Scroll down 17 rows
  Home   Top of screen                Ctrl Home  First record
  End    Bottom of screen             Ctrl  End  Last record

   F9    Previous record                  ↵       Next field
   F10   Show form

                   USING THE MOUSE IN TABLE VIEW

  Using the mouse in Q&A's Table View is easy:  Just point and click.
  If you wish to enter a field just move the mouse to the field and press
  the button.

  Esc-Exit                  → PgDn-Function Keys ←
```

Figure 5.12   Editing and browsing keys for Table View.

```
                     FUNCTION KEY ASSIGNMENTS

        F1  Help                       Alt F6    Enter Form View
                                       Ctrl F6   Add records
                                       Shift F6  Define Table View
                                            F6   Enter long values
  Ctrl F2   Print to end of stack
  Shift F2  Macros                     Shift F7  Undo edits
       F2   Print current record            F7   Search for records

       F3   Delete current record


  Ctrl F4   Delete to end of line      Shift F9  Go to Customize specs
  Shift F4  Delete line                     F9   Save & previous record
       F4   Delete word

  Alt F5    Auto-type current time
  Ctrl F5   Auto-type current date     Shift F10 Exit
       F5   Edit field                      F10  Show form


  Esc-Exit                  → PgUp-Moving around ←
```

Figure 5.13   Function keys in Table View.

While you are in Table View, be aware that all your programming statements are still operative. Table View is quite useful for changing common field values in a group of records. However, you will probably need to change the Table View spec to rearrange the order of the fields to match the fields you want to edit. To change the order of the fields in Table View, press Shift-F6 while in either Table View or Form View with a record on the screen. The form will be displayed with numbers in each field. The numbers begin in the top-most left field with the number 10 and increase in increments of ten with each successive field. The fields are numbered from top to bottom and right to left. See Figure 5.14 for the default Table View spec.

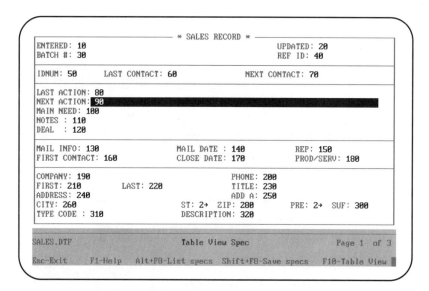

Figure 5.14   Default Table View spec.

In Table View, the fields appear in numerical order, from left to right. In this case, number 10 is the first column to appear, number 20 is the second, and so on. Thus, to make the ENTERED field appear before the DATE UPDATED field, you would switch the numbers. To save a Table View spec for future use, press Shift-F8 and give it a name. In fact, save this complete spec for future use. Then, any time you want to use it, you can retrieve it by pressing Alt-F8. To clear the entire spec, press F3. You can then enter your own custom Table View spec. When you are done rearranging the Table View spec, press F10 to return to Table View.

By combining the actions of retrieving, sorting, and displaying records in Table View, you have a powerful means of quickly accessing a group of records. To do this, access the file in Search mode and enter your Retrieve spec. Press F8 to switch to Sort mode, move to the desired field, and type 1 **AS** (ascending order) or 1 **DS** (descending order). Press F10 and press Alt-F6 to display the records in Table View.

Mass Update

The *Mass Update* feature lets you change an entire group of records all at once rather than one at a time. The changes can be made in minutes rather than hours. The changes can be as simple as altering the prospect code from PR to PROS, granting a bonus of 10 percent if gross sales are greater than $100,000, or executing a lookup into another file. You can execute any programming statement or command except the GOSUB and GOTO commands.

To use the Mass Update feature, choose Mass Update from the File menu, type a Retrieve spec to select the desired records, and press F10 to advance to the Update spec. Once in the Update spec, type the programming statements or update commands that will alter the data. Press F10 again, and Q&A gives you the opportunity to update each record individually or update all the records at once.

The real work of mass update takes place in the Update spec, where you type the statements that will alter your data. Every Update spec statement must start with the number sign (#) and a unique number (#1). The numbers are executed in sequential order. This is important. Suppose you had a programming statement in field #3 that depended on the result of programming statement #1. If you reversed the numbers, the statement would fail.

The next part of the statement is the expression. The simplest expression is known as a *direct change expression*. For example, to change all PR codes to PROS, you would type #1="PROS" in the field that contains the PR code. You can also use most programming statements, such as IF...THEN. As an example of an IF...THEN statement, suppose you wanted to place the number $1000 in field #1 (bonus) if the value in field #2 (gross sales) were greater than 100,000. The statement would read: BONUS: #2: if #1 100,000 then #2 = 1000. In this new version of Q&A, you can execute the existing programming statements already in the form by pressing F8 and choosing that option. By pressing Shift-F5 in the Update spec, you can recall all the existing programming statements and then use them as is or modify them accordingly. In the next example, you will explore several of these examples and execute one of them.

Practice Using the Mass Update Feature

1. Press **F** for File and **M** for Mass Update. Type the filename **SALES** and press Enter.

2. The first screen you see is the Retrieve Spec screen. Here you tell Q&A which records you want to change. In this example, you are going to change all the records, so press F10 to advance to the Update Spec screen.

3. The Update Spec screen contains the programming statements and commands used to change your data. Before you enter the final Update specs, you will retrieve the Programming specs that are already in the form. Press Shift-F5. Your screen should look like Figure 5.15. By using this feature, you can make use of some or all of the programming logic you have already programmed into the form.

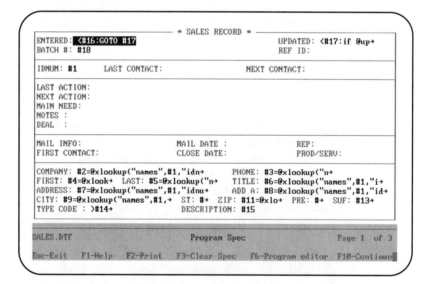

```
ENTERED: <#16:GOTO #17                        UPDATED: <#17:if @up→
BATCH #: #18                                  REF ID:

IDNUM: #1     LAST CONTACT:                 NEXT CONTACT:

LAST ACTION:
NEXT ACTION:
MAIN NEED:
NOTES :
DEAL  :

MAIL INFO:              MAIL DATE :            REP:
FIRST CONTACT:          CLOSE DATE:            PROD/SERV:

COMPANY: #2=@xlookup("names",#1,"idn→     PHONE: #3=@xlookup("n→
FIRST: #4=@xlook→  LAST: #5=@xlookup("n→    TITLE: #6=@xlookup("names",#1,"i→
ADDRESS: #7=@xlookup("names",#1,"idnu→       ADD A: #8=@xlookup("names",#1,"id→
CITY: #9=@xlookup("names",#1,→  ST: #→  ZIP: #11=@xlo→  PRE: #→  SUF: #13→
TYPE CODE : >#14→              DESCRIPTION: #15

SALES.DTF                    Program Spec                Page 1  of 3

Esc-Exit  F1-Help  F2-Print  F3-Clear Spec  F6-Program editor  F10-Continue
```

Figure 5.15   Existing Programming specs.

4. Save this spec for future use. First remove the Navigation specs in the ENTERED and DATE UPDATE fields. Then move to each field, press F6, and press Shift-F4 to clear the contents. Then press F10. Press Shift-F8 to save the spec. Type the name **Existing Programming Spec** and press Enter. Clear the Update spec by pressing F3.

5. Now look at the Auto Program Recalc screen. This is an easier way to execute the existing programming statements. Press F8 to display the options, as shown in Figure 5.16. Press F9 to return to the Update spec.

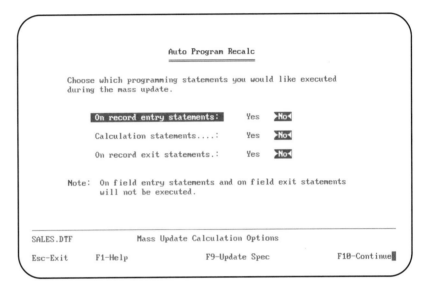

```
                        Auto Program Recalc
                        ═══════════════════

        Choose which programming statements you would like executed
        during the mass update.


            On record entry statements:      Yes  ▶No◀

            Calculation statements....:      Yes  ▶No◀

            On record exit statements.:      Yes  ▶No◀


        Note:  On field entry statements and on field exit statements
               will not be executed.



   ─────────────────────────────────────────────────────────────────
   SALES.DTF            Mass Update Calculation Options

   Esc-Exit     F1-Help            F9-Update Spec         F10-Continue█
```

Figure 5.16 Auto Program Recalc screen.

6. Now type the Update spec that you will execute. The first one is an IF...THEN programming statement. Move to the REF ID field and press F6 to expand the field. Type the statement **#2:if #1>1/1/91 then #2= "Call Now"**. Move to the LAST CONTACT field and type **#1**. This statement says: If the Last Contact date is greater than January 1, 1991, then place the words *Call Now* in the REF ID field.

7. Next you are going to type a direct field change statement. Move to the TYPE CODE field and press F6. Type **#3="CU"** and press F10. Move to the DESCRIPTION field, press F6, and type **#4="Customer"**. Press F10. The preceding statement will change the codes in these records from Prospects to Customers. Your screen should look like Figure 5.17.

8. Press F10 to save the Update spec and proceed to the Execute screen. If you answer No, all the records will be updated automatically. If you answer Yes, Q&A gives you the option to update the records individually. Answer No.

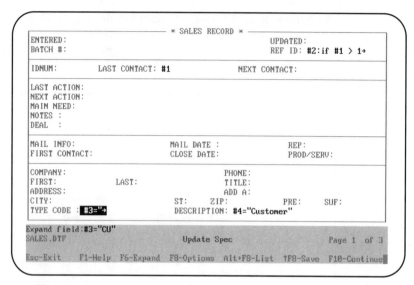

```
┌──────────────────── * SALES RECORD * ─────────────────┐
│ ENTERED:                                  UPDATED:     │
│ BATCH #:                                  REF ID: #2:if #1 > 1→
│                                                        │
│ IDNUM:        LAST CONTACT: #1        NEXT CONTACT:     │
│                                                        │
│ LAST ACTION:                                           │
│ NEXT ACTION:                                           │
│ MAIN NEED:                                             │
│ NOTES  :                                               │
│ DEAL   :                                               │
│                                                        │
│ MAIL INFO:            MAIL DATE :          REP:         │
│ FIRST CONTACT:        CLOSE DATE:          PROD/SERV:   │
│                                                        │
│ COMPANY:                       PHONE:                  │
│ FIRST:        LAST:            TITLE:                   │
│ ADDRESS:                       ADD A:                  │
│ CITY:                 ST:   ZIP:      PRE:    SUF:      │
│ TYPE CODE : #3="     DESCRIPTION: #4="Customer"         │
├────────────────────────────────────────────────────────┤
│ Expand field:#3="CU"                                   │
│ SALES.DTF                  Update Spec      Page 1  of 3│
│ Esc-Exit  F1-Help F6-Expand F8-Options Alt+F8-List ↑F8-Save F10-Continue│
└────────────────────────────────────────────────────────┘
```

Figure 5.17   Update spec in Mass Update.

9. You have finished the example on using the Mass Update feature. Press Esc to return to the Main menu.

Query Programming

The conventional method of retrieving data may not always be adequate. To supplement the normal methods of retrieving data, in Version 4.0 you can now use programming expressions in the Retrieve spec. This method is referred to as *Query Programming* or *Retrieve Spec Programming*.

All the programming functions are allowed except @number, @total, @average, @count, @maximum, @minimum, @cvar, @cstd, @help, and @ditto. In general, you can use any of the programming functions that are allowed in derived columns, which are covered in the next section.

You can use the @date function in a date field rather than typing the entire date. This function could also be used to retrieve all the records you entered in the last seven days by typing **@date-7**. Where this function really becomes useful is when you save it in a Retrieve spec. Then all you have to do is get the Retrieve spec; you don't have to continually type today's date.

Another example of Query Programming would be to retrieve all the records in which a sales rep's bonus factor equals the salary divided by 10 (10 percent of the salary). In the YEAR END BONUS field, you would enter the statement =`{Salary/10}`. You could also use this feature to retrieve all the records in one database that exist in another database. The ID numbers or names would have to match. To do this, you would type in the IDNUM field the statement = `{@xlookup ("file#2",idnum,"idnum", "idnum") }`.

All Query Programming statements are written in this order: an equal sign (=), a left brace ({), the expression, and a right brace (}), for example, DATE ENTERED: = `{@date}`. This statement would find all the records entered today. Programming expressions can be used anywhere a Retrieve spec is used.

Shortcut

When you are issuing a Retrieve spec and you are unsure of an item's exact spelling, you can do a *sounds-like* search. With a sounds-like search, you can find any records that sound like the one you are looking for. To do this, place the tilde (~) before the word you are searching for, for example, ~ `Smyth`. This statement would find *Smith, Smyth,* and *Smither*.

Columnar Reports

The Report option offers two different types of reports: columnar and cross-tab. This section will cover columnar reports; Chapter 10 will cover cross-tab reports. *Columnar reports* display in columns information from your database. The columns can be arranged in any order you choose. Besides listing the information, you can also calculate the data with a variety of functions. These functions can include counting, totaling, averaging, etc. Once you have selected the columns and applied the desired functions, you can enhance the columns with boldfacing, underlining, italics, or different fonts. Just prior to printing, you can view the report on the screen to make sure that it looks the way it is supposed to. The final step is to print the report to a printer or disk file.

The steps needed to create a columnar report are almost identical to those for a form report. You begin by choosing the Report option—Design/Redesign a Report. You select the file you want to base the report on. The first screen you see is the Retrieve Spec screen. Type a spec and press F10 to advance to the Column/Sort Spec screen. At the Column/Sort Spec screen, you decide which fields you want to print and how you want the report sorted. To add functions or enhancements to any of the columns, press Shift-F6 and use the special codes available here. After you are done entering the Column/Sort spec, press F10 to advance to the Print Options.

Make your selections and press F8 to set up your margins, headers, and point size. Pressing F10 two more times will print the report.

In the next example, you will go through all the steps of creating and printing a columnar report. However, before you begin, let's look at three fields on the last screen of the Sales file. These fields illustrate advanced features of columnar reporting. Press **F** for File and **S** for Search. Type **SALES**, press Enter, and press F10 to bring up the first record. Press PgDn two times to move to the third screen. It should look like Figure 5.18.

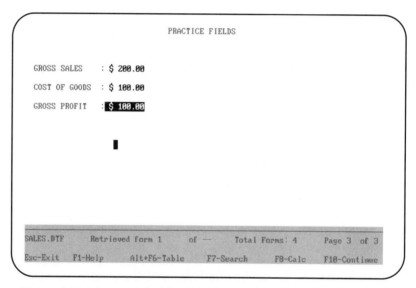

Figure 5.18   Practice fields in the Sales file.

Next use the Table View to make sure that the correct data exists in the Sales file. Press Alt-F6 and move to the last set of five fields by pressing Ctrl-Right Arrow. Once you get to these fields, make sure that your fields have the same values in them as Figure 5.19. If they don't, add the correct values. When you are through, press Shift-F10 to save the records and exit the file.

Practice Creating and Printing a Columnar Report

1. Press **R** for Report and **D** for Design. Type the filename **SALES** and press Enter.

2. Choose the Sample Columnar Report and press Enter.

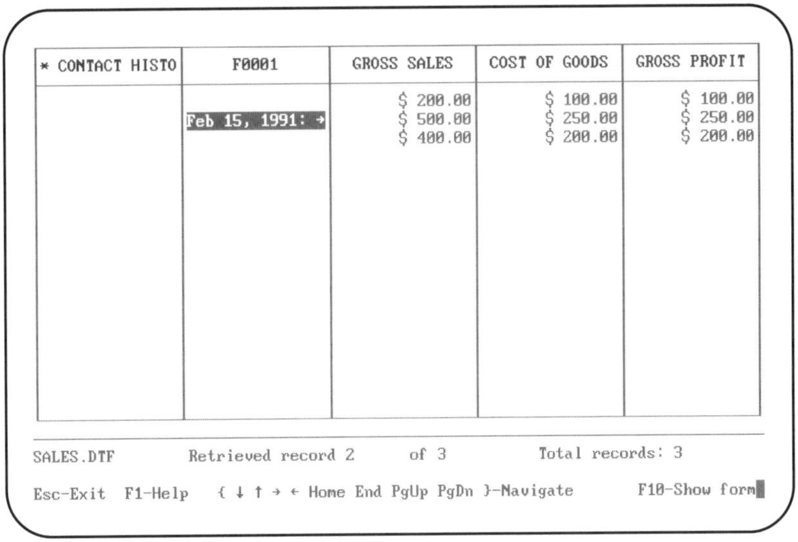

```
┌─────────────────────────────────────────────────────────────────────────┐
│ * CONTACT HISTO │    F0001    │ GROSS SALES │ COST OF GOODS │ GROSS PROFIT │
│                 │             │  $  200.00  │   $  100.00   │  $  100.00   │
│                 │Feb 15, 1991:→│ $  500.00  │   $  250.00   │  $  250.00   │
│                 │             │  $  400.00  │   $  200.00   │  $  200.00   │
│                 │             │             │               │              │
│                 │             │             │               │              │
│                 │             │             │               │              │
│                 │             │             │               │              │
│                 │             │             │               │              │
│                 │             │             │               │              │
│ ─────────────────────────────────────────────────────────────────────────│
│ SALES.DTF    Retrieved record 2      of 3          Total records: 3        │
│ Esc-Exit  F1-Help  { ↓ ↑ → ←  Home End PgUp PgDn }-Navigate    F10-Show form│
└─────────────────────────────────────────────────────────────────────────┘
```

Figure 5.19   Values to type into the new fields.

3. You are at the Retrieve Spec screen. This is where you tell Q&A which records you want included in the report. Normally you would enter one, but in this case you are going to print all the records, so press F10 to advance to the Column/Sort spec.

4. The Column/Sort spec is where you do most of your work. It is here that you choose the fields to include in the report and how they will be formatted and calculated. Since you are viewing a pre-made report, the codes are already in the fields (see Figure 5.20). With a new report, this screen would be blank. Stop here for now and read the following discussion, which explains in detail all aspects of creating a Column/Sort spec. Then continue with step 5 at the end of the discussion.

When you enter a Column/Sort spec, the first thing you do is type numbers into those fields that you want to appear on the report. The order of the numbers is the order in which the fields will appear on the report, from left to right. In this case, number 4 will be the first column. Notice that I started with the number 4 and jumped to 6, then 8, and so on. There is a good reason for this. Should you later decide to add a field between two existing fields, you can do so without renumbering all the fields. Selecting columns by placing numbers in the fields is the minimum you need to do to develop a report. The numbers must always appear first in a statement. All the codes that follow the numbers are separated by a comma and have some effect on the data or the column heading, for example, 1 ,AS.

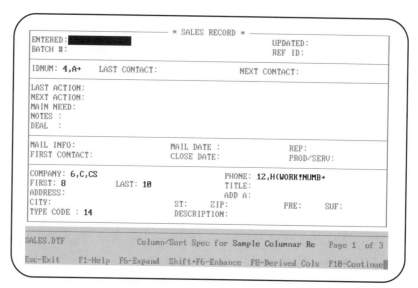

Figure 5.20   Column/Sort spec on screen 1.

Once you have chosen the fields, you have to decide how to sort them. Sorting is indicated by typing **AS** for ascending order or **DS** for descending order into the fields you want to sort by. In the example you have been working on, there is an AS after the 4 in the IDNUM field. You can sort your report in multiple levels. For instance, to end up with a report that is sorted alphabetically by state, zip code, and ID number, place an AS in the STATE, ZIP, and IDNUM fields. To sort by a field that you do not want to appear on the report, place a number in the field followed by an AS or DS and then an I for invisible, for example, 5,AS,I.

To make reports more readable, you may want to start a new page when a particular value changes. This is known as *breaking your report on field change*. You can place any or all of these commands in the sorted field: Year (YB), Month (MB), Day (DB), or Alphabet (AB). When the page breaks, any subcalculations you have in other fields will also be performed, for example, 1,AS,MB.

Some field names are not very descriptive and may need to be changed for a printed report. In this report, you know what the field name IDNUM means, but someone unfamiliar with the application may not. To remedy this situation, you can use the **H** for Heading command to give the column a different heading. The syntax for this command can be found in the IDNUM field: 4,AS,H(ID Number). The text inside the parentheses is what the new column heading will be.

Q&A offers several ways of calculating numeric and money fields. The calculating functions are divided into two types. This first type works on the entire column and will calculate whether the report is sorted or not. These commands include: count (C), total (T), average (A), minimum (MIN), maximum (MAX), variance (VAR), and standard deviation (STD). The second type works only if you sort your columns. These commands include: subcount (SC), subtotal (ST), subaverage (SA), subminimum (SMIN), submaximum (SMAX), subvariance (SVAR), and substandard deviation (SSTD). All these commands can be viewed in Figure 5.21.

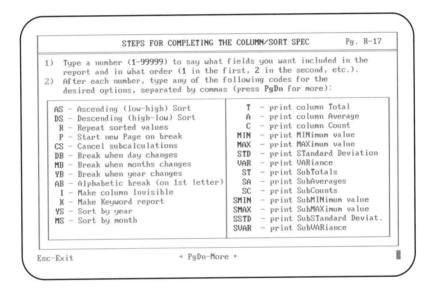

Figure 5.21   Function codes.

In order for the subcalculation commands to work, you must sort your data. Subcalculation commands will not execute on a field that contains a sort code (AS or DS). The subcalculation codes must be placed in fields that are to the right of the sort commands. In this report, the IDNUM field has a sort command in it, and the COMPANY field has the Count (C) and Subcount (SC) commands in it. If you place the subcalculation codes in several fields and you have several sort levels, the subcalculations will occur at every sort level. To cancel subcalculations on selected fields, type **CS** in the field that contains the AS or DS commands.

Press PgDn two times to see most of the calculation commands used in these fields. They can also be viewed in Figure 5.21. The GROSS SALES field, as shown in Figure 5.22, has this set of commands: 16,ST,SA,A,MIN,MAX,T,VAR,STD. The Subtotal (ST) and Subaverage (SA) commands total and average the amounts for each new ID number. The Average, Minimum, Maximum, Total, Variance, and Standard Deviation are calculated on the entire column.

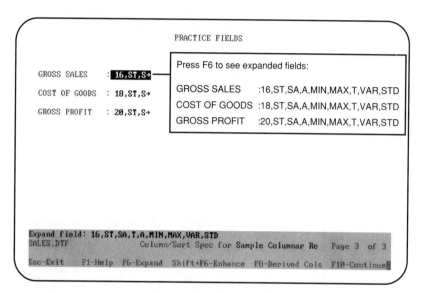

Figure 5.22   Page 3 of the Column/Sort spec.

Q&A also gives you the option of changing how a field is formatted, particularly money and date fields. To change the format of a field, type **F ( )** in the field. Between the parentheses, type the code. For example, typing **1,F (JR,U)** would justify the field left and make the text uppercase. You can see a table of all the codes in Figure 5.23.

Derived columns add another dimension to your columnar report. A *derived column* derives its values from one or more fields in the current database or from fields in an external database via a lookup statement. Press F8 to view the derived columns and F9 to return to the Column/Sort spec. Figure 5.24 shows the derived columns used in this report.

There are three parts to a derived column (we'll use the column DERIVED TOTAL as our sample). The first part is the *heading*. Whatever is typed in this section will appear at the top of the column. The second part is the *formula*. Here you "derive" the value for the column. You can use any of the math functions along with most of the programming expressions. In this example, columns 16, 18, and 20 were added. The last part is the *Column spec*. All the standard report codes can be used here. In this case all I did was give the spec a field number. In the HOME PHONE field's formula,

I used the @xlookup statement to retrieve the Home Phone number from the Names file. With this function, you can retrieve information from several files.

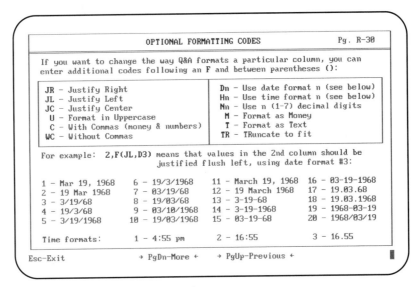

```
                    OPTIONAL FORMATTING CODES                Pg. R-30

If you want to change the way Q&A formats a particular column, you can
enter additional codes following an F and between parentheses ():

  JR - Justify Right            Dn - Use date format n (see below)
  JL - Justify Left             Hn - Use time format n (see below)
  JC - Justify Center           Nn - Use n (1-7) decimal digits
   U - Format in Uppercase       M - Format as Money
   C - With Commas (money & numbers)  T - Format as Text
  WC - Without Commas           TR - TRuncate to fit

For example:  2,F(JL,D3) means that values in the 2nd column should be
                       justified flush left, using date format #3:

  1 - Mar 19, 1968     6 - 19/3/1968     11 - March 19, 1968   16 - 03-19-1968
  2 - 19 Mar 1968      7 - 03/19/68      12 - 19 March 1968     17 - 19.03.68
  3 - 3/19/68          8 - 19/03/68      13 - 3-19-68           18 - 19.03.1968
  4 - 19/3/68          9 - 03/10/1968    14 - 3-19-1968         19 - 1968-03-19
  5 - 3/19/1968       10 - 19/03/1968    15 - 03-19-68          20 - 1968/03/19

  Time formats:     1 - 4:55 pm       2 - 16:55        3 - 16.55

Esc-Exit             → PgDn-More ←    → PgUp-Previous ←
```

Figure 5.23   Justification codes.

```
                         DERIVED COLUMNS


 Heading: DERIVED TOTAL
 Formula: #16+#18+#20
 Column Spec: 22

 Heading: HOME PHONE
 Formula: @XLOOKUP("names",#4,"idnum","home phone")
 Column Spec: 24

 Heading:
 Formula:
 Column Spec:

 Heading:
 Formula:
 Column Spec:

 SALES.DTF           Derived Columns for Sample Columnar Repo    Page 1 of 4

 Esc-Exit       F1-Help      F9-Go back to Column/Sort Spec    F10-Continue
```

Figure 5.24   Derived columns.

You can use the financial functions in a derived column to calculate data that exists in another column. For instance, to obtain the total of the GROSS SALES column, #16, type the command `@total (#16)` in the formula section of a derived column. You can see a complete list of derived column functions in Figure 5.25. Now resume creating and printing a columnar report, beginning with step 5.

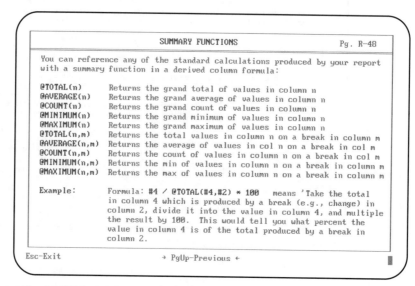

```
                       SUMMARY FUNCTIONS                    Pg. R-48

You can reference any of the standard calculations produced by your report
with a summary function in a derived column formula:

@TOTAL(n)       Returns the grand total of values in column n
@AVERAGE(n)     Returns the grand average of values in column n
@COUNT(n)       Returns the grand count of values in column n
@MINIMUM(n)     Returns the grand minimum of values in column n
@MAXIMUM(n)     Returns the grand maximum of values in column n
@TOTAL(n,m)     Returns the total values in column n on a break in column m
@AVERAGE(n,m)   Returns the average of values in col n on a break in col m
@COUNT(n,m)     Returns the count of values in column n on a break in col m
@MINIMUM(n,m)   Returns the min of values in column n on a break in column m
@MAXIMUM(n,m)   Returns the max of values in column n on a break in column m

Example:        Formula: #4 / @TOTAL(#4,#2) * 100    means 'Take the total
                in column 4 which is produced by a break (e.g., change) in
                column 2, divide it into the value in column 4, and multiple
                the result by 100.  This would tell you what percent the
                value in column 4 is of the total produced by a break in
                column 2.

Esc-Exit                    → PgUp-Previous ←
```

Figure 5.25   Derived column functions.

Press F10 to advance to the Print Options screen. This screen is used to control printing. To view your report on the screen before it is sent to the printer, answer Yes to Page Preview. Go through each option. When you are through, press F8 to advance to the Define Page screen.

At the Define Page screen, you can set the page width, margins, point size, headers, and footers. Since these are already defined for you, press F10 to save the design and press F10 to print the report.

This concludes your practice in creating and printing columnar reports. The next section will cover how to export records for use in other programs.

Export Records

With Q&A you can easily export data from one of your databases for use in another program. This feature is handy when, for example, you want to give your data to an associate who doesn't have access to Q&A or you want to do a mail merge with another word processor. Whatever the reason, Q&A makes it quite easy. You can export to any of these file formats: DIF, which is used for spreadsheets; dBASE II/III/IV; standard ASCII, which is the most common format; fixed ASCII; and Paradox 2.0. In the next exercise, you will export all the records in the Sales database into a dBASE III file.

Practice Exporting into a dBASE III File

1. Press **F** for File, **U** for Utilities, **E** for Export, and **3** for dBASE III.

2. Type the filename **SALES** and press Enter.

3. Type the filename **EXPORT.DBF** (DBF is the dBASE file extension) and press Enter.

4. You are at the Retrieve Spec screen. Here you specify which records you want to export. Press F10 to export them all.

5. The next screen is the Merge Spec screen, where you specify which fields you want to export. Do this by typing a number in the fields you want to export, starting with the number 1. The exported file will have the fields placed in the order of the field numbers. Press F10 to export all the records. You can now read this file with dBASE III.

Recover Database

Q&A offers a feature designed to fix a database if it fails to function correctly. This feature is called *recover a file*. The chief cause of a database malfunction is turning off the computer without properly exiting the database. This could be the result of a power outage or because someone inadvertently turned off the computer. Either way, losing power before the database has been properly exited is the worst thing that can happen to your database.

There are many subtle and mysterious signs that can alert you to the fact that your database has been corrupted. The most obvious sign that your database has gone south is receiving an error message from Q&A. Other signs include such situations as: data that you know you entered is gone, sorting the data doesn't reorder the file, and "things that always worked before" suddenly don't. If any of these situations happens, make a backup of your database and follow these instructions.

Recovering a Database

1. Press **F** for File, **U** for Utilities, and **R** for Recover.

2. Type the filename and press Enter.

3. Press F10 to begin the recovery process. It is done in several steps. Whether the recovery is successful will be indicated by a message at the bottom of the screen.

 Caution: Even though you get a message that says the recovery was successful, it may not have been.

Guided Modifications

This section will cover several features that might be considered bells and whistles. They will give your application that extra dimension of usefulness and friendliness. These features include customizing help screens, specifying Restrict specs, defining field names, and using field templates.

Suggested Modifications

To make this application really useful, you may want to add some new fields. For example, you could add a field to indicate how "hot" this prospect is or to indicate which stage of the sales cycle the prospect is in. If you have more than one contact at an account, you could add more name-contact fields. Most likely, you will need to add more contact history screens so that you can record the results of more than one conversation. Lastly, you may want to add a group of fields to hold the dates and contents of everything you have mailed to this prospect.

Custom Help

Create *custom help screens* to help those people using your applications who may not know what each field is used for. A custom help screen can be created for every field. Each help screen can contain instructions on how to fill in a field or use a portion of the application. The help screen is invoked by pressing the F1 key on the desired field. To view an existing custom help screen and then create your own, follow these instructions.

Viewing a Custom Help Screen and Creating Your Own Custom Help

1. Press **F** for File, **D** for Design, and **C** for Customize.

2. Type the filename **SALES** and press Enter.

3. Press **D** for Define Custom Help. The first field will be highlighted, and a corresponding help box will be open as well.

4. Use F8 to move forward through the fields and stop at the IDNUM field, as shown in Figure 5.26. Use F6 to move back through the fields.

5. When you are through defining help screens, press F10.

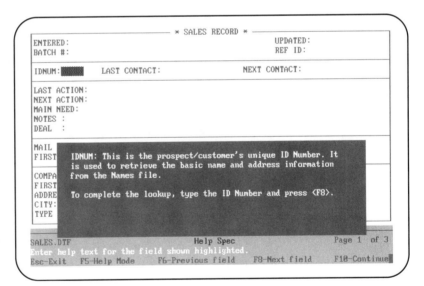

Figure 5.26   Custom help screen for IDNUM field.

Restrict Spec

The *Restrict Spec option* lets you place restrictions on any field; the restrictions are the only valid options for that particular field. You can place two types of restrictions on a field: requested and required. Placing a *requested* Restrict spec option on a field means that if you enter a value that is not part of the Restrict spec, you will get the error message Value not in specified range. But if you press Enter, you will be able to enter the value anyway. Placing a *required* Restrict Spec option on a field means that if you enter a value that is not part of the spec, you will not be able to exit the field or save the form until you enter one of the correct values or erase the field.

To display a window containing all the correct entries, simply press Alt-F7. To select an entry, move the cursor to the correct one and press Enter. Q&A places it in the field. Figure 5.27 shows the Restrict Spec pop-up window.

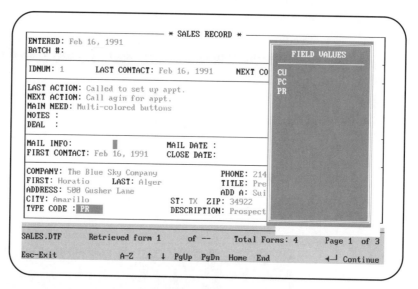

Figure 5.27   Restrict Spec pop-up window.

Defining a Restrict Spec for a Field

1. Press **F** for File, **D** for Design, and **C** for Customize.

2. Type the filename **SALES** and press Enter.

3. Press **R** for Restrict Values.

4. Move to the TYPE CODE field and press F6 to inspect the existing spec. You will notice the values PR;CU;PC. Each item you place in the spec needs to be separated by a semicolon. This spec is a requested spec. To make it a required spec, type an exclamation

mark (!) before all the values, for example, ! PR;CU;PC. You can also use the spec to indicate a range of acceptable values. For instance, 100..10000 would allow only values between $100 and $10,000. To request that a user enter a value into a field, use the code /=. To require that a user type a value into a field, use the code !/=.

5. When you are done entering your Restrict specs, press F10 to save and exit the file.

Field Template

A *field template* allows you to speed data entry and to further restrict what type of values can be entered into a field: text, numbers, or both. You can even create a template that lets you type only five characters into the middle of a twenty-character field. Telephone fields can have the dashes automatically entered. Part-number fields can be formatted to accept numbers for the first two digits and letters for the last five digits. With this feature, you can format a field any way you want to.

Using the Field Template Feature

1. Press **F** for File, **D** for Design, and **C** for Customize.

2. Type the filename **SALES** and press Enter.

3. Type **T** for Field Template. Move down to the PHONE field where you see a phone number template (###-###-####). The # sign allows you to enter only numbers into the field. Move to the ST field where you see the alphabet-only restriction (@@). The $ code lets you enter any symbol except numbers. You can even combine the two. For instance, ###-$$-##-$$$$ could end up like this: 111-aa-22-bbbb. Figure 5.28 shows a table of acceptable options.

```
   TYPE     NAME                      MEANING

   --------------------------------------------------------------
     $       Text         Any character can be entered.

     @       Alphabetic   Only characters A-Z or a-z can be entered.

     #       Numeric      Any number (0-9) can be entered.

     9       Numeric      Any number (0-9) can be entered.
```

Figure 5.28   Field Template options.

4. When you are through entering your templates, press F10 to save them.

Field Names

When you create large files, you may have fields with no names or with names that are too long. This poses no problem unless you want to address these fields by name in programming statements. If the field name is too long, typing it all the time becomes tiresome. If the field does not have a name, Q&A calls it F0001, F0002, and so on—not very descriptive names. The *Field Names feature* lets you change the internal name of the field without changing the name on the screen.

Using the Field Names Feature

1. Press **F** for File, **D** for Design, and **P** for Program.

2. Type the filename **SALES** and press Enter.

3. Press **S** for Set Field Names. You will see that Q&A has made the internal field name the same as the name on the screen. If for any reason you gave two fields the same name, such as PHONE, Q&A will call the first one Phone and the second one Phone1. Press PgDn to see how Q&A labels a field without a name (F0001). This can also be seen in Figure 5.29. To give the field a new name, simply move to the field and type a unique name. All your internal field names must be unique.

4. When you are through making or changing field names, press F10 to save the spec.

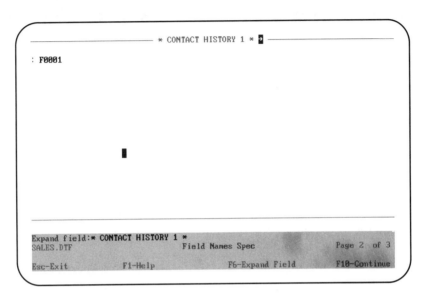

Figure 5.29   Field Name spec.

Summary

You have just completed using all aspects of the *Sales Management application*. In doing so, you examined three useful Q&A features: Table View, Mass Update, and Query Programming. *Table View* lets you view several records at once and is convenient for editing data. For example, you can arrange your sales calls for the day. In the Invoice file, you can use Table View to display all of a client's sales.

The *Mass Update* feature can expedite changing data. If you need to change one or more fields in several records, this is the feature to use. You can change an entire group of records all at once, rather than one at a time. Lastly, *Query Programming* lets you retrieve records by using programming expressions in the Retrieve spec.

As you utilize the Sales Management application on a daily basis, you will discover ways of changing it to meet your needs exactly. By customizing this database to capture all the necessary data on a prospect and then using it on a regular basis, you can improve your sales effectiveness. In the next chapter you will explore how to use the Invoice and Inventory databases.

USE APPLICATION FEATURES

Print a Form Report

1. Press **F** for File and **P** for Print.
2. Type the filename and press Enter.
3. Press **P** for Print Records. Choose the report name and answer Yes or No for temporary changes.
4. Enter the Retrieve spec and press F10. If necessary, modify the Column/Sort spec and press F10.
5. Adjust the Print options and press F10 to print the report.

Post Records

1. Press **F** for File and **T** for Post.
2. Type the *source* (FROM) filename and press Enter. Type the *target* (TO) filename and press Enter.
3. Enter the Retrieve spec and press F10. Enter the Post spec and press F10.
4. Choose Yes to post records individually or No to post records all at once.

Switch from Search to Special Programming Menu

1. While in Search/Update mode and with a record on the screen, press Shift-F9 to invoke the special Programming menu. Make your selection.
2. To return to Search/Update mode, press F7.

DESIGN APPLICATION FEATURES

Enter Programming Statements

1. Press **F** for File, **D** for Design, and **P** for Progam.
2. Type the filename and press Enter.
3. Type **P** for Program form. Enter your programming statements.
4. Press F10 to save them when you are done.

Enter Navigation Statements

1. Press **F** for File, **D** for Design, and **P** for Program.
2. Type the filename and press Enter.
3. Type **N** for Field Navigation. Enter your navigation statements.
4. Press F10 to save them when you are done.

Copy Database Design

1. Press **F** for File and **C** for Copy.
2. Type the name of the file you want to copy and press Enter.
3. Press **D** for Copy Design only or **I** for Copy Design with IA/QG. Type the name of the new file and press Enter.

Inventory/Invoicing Application

This chapter will teach you how to use the Inventory/Invoicing application and the features in the "At a Glance" section. With the Inventory/Invoicing application, you will be able to automate the entire inventory/invoicing and accounts receivable process.

Overview

The focus of this chapter is on product invoicing and inventory. The concepts that you will learn here apply equally well to service invoicing. In fact, a later section of this chapter explains how you can adapt the product invoicing and inventory databases for service invoicing and inventory. One of the main differences between the two applications is that the service inventory database will be used only for storing descriptions of services and their corresponding rates, and there is no actual inventory to maintain. The other difference is that the service invoice database will have larger description fields. Other than these differences, everything else in the two applications is the same.

Shortcut

If a single line is sufficient for the description of each service, you can use the product inventory and invoicing databases, as they are, for a service organization.

The Inventory/Invoicing application makes use of three database files (or *files* for short): Names, Invent (Inventory), and Invoice. The Names file is thoroughly covered in Chapter 3 and must be used in conjunction with this application. From the Names file, you draw the customer name and address information that is used for the BILL TO address, and from the Inventory file, you draw the product descriptions and prices. This process of reading information from one file into another file is known as conducting an *external lookup*. Figure 6.1 shows the relationship among the files used in this application.

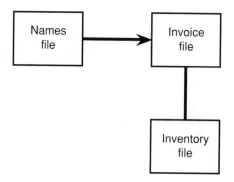

Figure 6.1   Files used in Inventory/Invoicing application.

For most organizations, the Names file is the heart of their applications and is used in conjunction with many applications. This is because most applications need to access information stored in the Names file. If you have read Chapter 3, you learned which information is best stored in the Names file, and which information is best stored in other files.

The Invoice file is the heart of the Inventory/Invoicing application and the primary component. It looks up information from both the Names file and the Inventory file. It is from the Invoice file that you print invoices, generate receivables lists, enter payments, and analyze sales.

The Invent (Inventory) file is where you store all information pertaining to your inventory. This file contains descriptions of your products, wholesale and retail prices, units on hand, units sold, units purchased, and the value of each of these unit fields. Information is stored so that it can be easily retrieved into the Invoice file when you type a part number and press F8. A large array of reports can be created to give you the status of your inventory.

The next components of this application are the various reports. Reports take the raw data and translate it into useful information. Included with this application are two reports that will help you manage your receivables and inventory.

The three database files we have been discussing will be used in the following order. First you will fill in the Invent file with the pertinent data about your inventory: wholesale and retail prices, current number on hand, the minimum and maximum numbers you want on hand, and period-to-date sales and purchases. With this done, each time you acquire a new customer you will fill out a new record in the Names file. The system will assign the customer a unique ID number. Then, each time the customer buys something, you will go to the Invoice file and type the customer's ID number and press F8 to place the name and address information in the BILL TO fields. Next you will fill in the product ID numbers and quantities for each item and press F8 to look up all the product descriptions and retail prices. The next task is to print the invoices. Once they are printed, you will run the posting procedure to remove the units you just sold from inventory.

In this chapter you will learn several powerful and useful features. On the design side, you will learn how to do advanced programming—specifically how to program external lookups and IF...THEN statements. These statements are used extensively in this application. You will also learn how to copy a database design and copy selected records from one database to another.

The most significant feature you will learn is how to do posting. *Posting* is a new feature that lets you post information from a record in one database file to a record in another database file. For example, with posting you could change addresses in a group of records and then post all those changes to the corresponding records in another file. The posting feature will be used to take the products from each invoice and post them to the PRODUCTS SOLD field in the Invent file. Along with these items, you will also continue to practice many other Q&A features.

Application Explained

This section will explain how each file works and define each of the fields. The Names file is covered in detail in Chapter 3. However, the Inventory/Invoicing application makes extensive use of the Names file so some of the information is repeated here, specifically information regarding the first screen.

Figure 6.2 shows the first screen of the Names file. This screen is used to enter the basic name and address information for each of your customers. The top section of the screen contains a field for the date the record was entered, a field for the last time it was updated, a batch number field, and a reference ID field. If you begin using the posting process in earnest, the batch number field will play an increasingly important role in your data processing activities. If you have outstanding invoices for several customers who have changed addresses, you will have to update the BILL TO fields in the Invoice records. With Version 3.0, you had to update each of them manually. However, with Version 4.0, you can assign a batch number to each record that you change and then post that entire batch to the Invoice file, automatically changing their addresses.

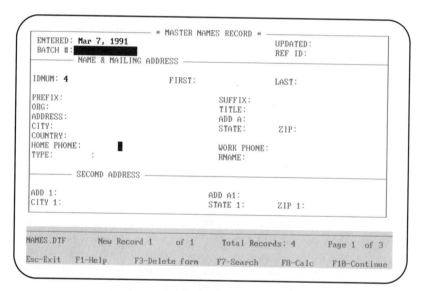

Figure 6.2   Screen 1 of the Names file.

The second section of the Names file contains the basic name and address information. It is where you enter the primary mailing address. The TYPE field contains a lookup statement that instructs Q&A to retrieve a description from the Codes file based on the code you type in that field. Depending on the code in the TYPE field, the RNAME field is filled in with either the individual's name or the name of the company. The Code file contains two codes and descriptions: IN for Individual and CO for Corporation. Use one of these codes to designate whether a record is for an individual or a corporation.

Shortcut

The Codes file is a regular database that you can use to hold *all* the codes you might use in *all* your application's files. To extract information from the Codes file, you have to place an @xlookup statement in the appropriate fields. This file can be accessed the same as all other files.

Name and Mailing Address Fields in Screen 1 of the Names File

ENTERED	The date the record was entered. It is automatically generated by the system.
UPDATED	The date the record was last viewed or updated. It is automatically generated by the system.
BATCH #	Used for designating batches of records.
REF ID	User-defined field.
IDNUM	A unique number assigned to each entry in the database. It is used primarily as the *key field* to look up information from the Names file.
FIRST	The first name.
LAST	The last name.
PREFIX	Mr., Mrs., Dr., etc.
SUFFIX	J.D., M.D., Ph.D., C.P.A., etc.
ORG	The organization's name.
TITLE	The title of the person in the database.
ADDRESS	The street address of the individual or organization.
ADD A	The second address line, normally used for suite, building, mail stop, etc.
CITY	The city.
STATE	The state.
ZIP	The zip code.
COUNTRY	Any country outside of the United States.

HOME PHONE   The home phone number of the main contact.

WORK PHONE   The phone number of the organization.

TYPE   A one- to six-character alphanumeric code used to classify the name. Currently the two options are: IN for individual or CO corporation. This field is programmed to place a description in the field next to the TYPE field. The description is looked up from the Codes file. The programming statement looks at the code in the field and matches it to the code in the Codes file. When it finds a match, it places the code's description in the field next to TYPE.

RNAME   Contains the name of the company or individual. Used for reporting purposes. It is created based on the code in the TYPE field. A programming statement has been placed in the RNAME field that says: If the value in the TYPE field is IN for individual, then put the individual's name in the RNAME field. If it is not IN, then put the organization's name in the RNAME field. This field is useful if you have a combination of individuals and organizations in your database and want to use only one name field on a report. With this field, you do not have to place the organization name, the first name, and the last name fields on the same report.

The lower portion of screen 1 of the Names file is the Second Address section. You can use it to store another address, such as the home address of a customer or a special billing or shipping address.

Second Address Fields in Screen 1 of the Names File

ADD1   The second street address. This section can be used for a home address, billing address, or shipping address.

ADD A1   The second part of the street address.

CITY 1   The second city.

STATE 1   The second state.

ZIP 1   The second zip code.

Before you can begin using the Inventory/Invoicing application, you must enter your inventory into the Invent file. This file is used to store product descriptions, prices, and various quantity numbers. The Invoice database extracts much of its information from the Invent file. This database file has only one screen, as shown in Figure 6.3.

Beginner's Tip

If you are using this database as a service inventory database, you will only be entering the description of the service and placing the hourly rate in the UNIT PRICE field.

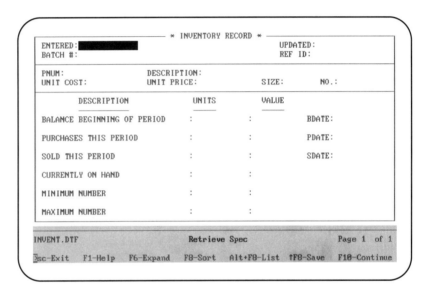

```
                           ─── * INVENTORY RECORD * ───
   ENTERED:▮▮▮▮▮▮▮▮▮▮▮▮            UPDATED:
   BATCH #:                       REF ID:

   PNUM:               DESCRIPTION:
   UNIT COST:          UNIT PRICE:            SIZE:      NO.:

            DESCRIPTION          UNITS        VALUE

   BALANCE BEGINNING OF PERIOD    :            :        BDATE:

   PURCHASES THIS PERIOD          :            :        PDATE:

   SOLD THIS PERIOD               :            :        SDATE:

   CURRENTLY ON HAND              :            :

   MINIMUM NUMBER                 :            :

   MAXIMUM NUMBER                 :            :

 INVENT.DTF              Retrieve Spec                Page 1  of 1
 Esc-Exit   F1-Help   F6-Expand   F8-Sort   Alt+F8-List   ↑F8-Save   F10-Continue
```

Figure 6.3   The Invent file screen.

Fields in the Invent File

ENTERED	The date the record was entered. It is automatically generated by the system.
UPDATED	The date the record was last viewed or updated. It is automatically generated by the system.
BATCH #	Used for designating batches of records.
REF ID	User-defined field.
PNUM	The ID number of the inventory item.

251

DESCRIPTION | The description of the inventory item.

UNIT COST | The wholesale cost of the inventory item.

UNIT PRICE | The retail price of the inventory item.

SIZE | The size of the item: case, quart, crate, pallet, etc.

NO. | The number of individual units per size, e.g., 12 per case.

> ▶ **Note:** In the second section of the Invent database, the fields for UNITS and VALUE are located under the appropriate column heading, just to the right of the colons following the DESCRIPTION.

BAL BEGIN OF PERIOD UNITS | The number of units you started with when you originally entered the inventory record.

VALUE OF BEG BAL UNITS | The value of the units you began with. This is created by a programming statement that multiplies the UNIT COST by the BEGINNING BALANCE UNITS.

BEG BAL DATE | The date you entered the beginning balance.

PURCHASES THIS PERIOD | The number of units you added to inventory this period.

VALUE OF PURCHASES | The value of the units you purchased this period.

PURCHASES DATE | The date you added to the purchases total.

UNITS SOLD THIS PERIOD | The number of units you sold this period.

VALUE UNITS SOLD | The value of the units sold this period.

DATE OF LAST UNITS SOLD | The date you last posted the sold units to inventory.

CURRENTLY ON HAND | The number of units currently in inventory.

VALUE OF ON HAND	The value of the units you currently have on hand.
MINIMUM NUMBER	The minimum number of units you should keep in stock.
VALUE OF MIN UNITS	The value of the minimum units you should keep on hand.
MAXIMUM NUMBER	The maximum number of units you should keep on hand.
VALUE OF MAXIMUM	The value of the maximum units kept on hand.

While you are working with the Inventory/Invoicing application, you will spend most of your time in the Invoice file. Figure 6.4 displays the first screen of the Invoice file. The top section of the screen is the same as the Names file. In the second section, the basic name and address information is retrieved from the Names file by typing an ID number in the ID NUMBER field and pressing F8 (the Calc key). There are four lines under the SHIP TO heading that can hold the shipping address or remarks. The last section of the screen holds other important invoice information: sales rep, purchase order #, invoice #, invoice date, days until invoice is due, ship date, and due date.

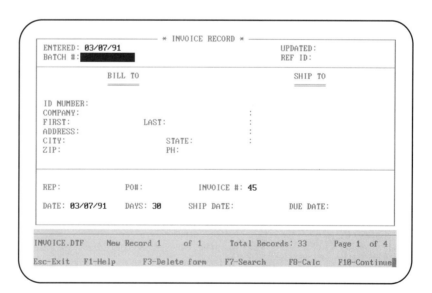

Figure 6.4   Screen 1 of the Invoice File.

Fields in Screen 1 of the Invoice File

ENTERED   The date the record was entered. It is automatically generated by the system.

UPDATED   The date the record was last viewed or updated. It is automatically generated by the system.

BATCH #   Used for designating batches of records.

REF ID   User-defined field.

ID NUMBER   A unique number assigned to each entry in the Names database. It is used to look up information from the Names file into this file.

FIRST   The first name.

LAST   The last name.

COMPANY   The company's name.

ADDRESS   The street address of the individual or organization.

CITY   The city.

STATE   The state.

ZIP   The zip code.

PH   The work phone number.

REP   The sales rep who sold this invoice.

PO#   The customer's purchase order number.

INVOICE #   The invoice number. It is automatically assigned by the system.

DATE   The date the invoice was created. It is automatically assigned by the system.

DAYS   The number of days before the invoice is due. The default is 30 days.

SHIP DATE   The day the product was shipped.

DUE DATE   The date the invoice is due. It is generated by a programming statement that adds the DAYS field to the DATE field.

The second screen of the Invoice file contains fields for the product ID number (PNUM) and the quantity (QTY). Press F8 to look up the description and the unit price from the Invent file. This screen also contains fields to record payments, interest rate, sales tax rate, and the total fields. These can be seen in Figure 6.5.

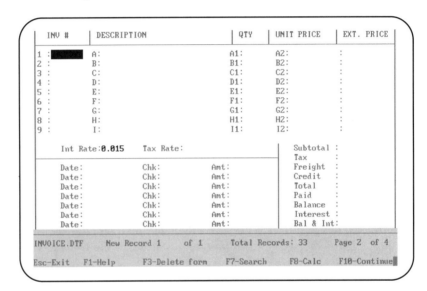

Figure 6.5   Screen 2 of the Invoice file.

Fields in Screen 2 of the Invoice File

INV #	This column of fields holds the product ID number.
DESCRIPTION	This column of fields holds the product description.
QTY	This column of fields holds the number of units purchased.
UNIT PRICE	This column of fields holds the price of the product.
EXT. PRICE	This column of fields holds the total of the quantity multiplied by the unit price.
INT RATE	The monthly interest rate you want to charge on past due invoices.
TAX RATE	The sales tax rate.

The next three fields are for payments made towards this invoice.

DATE	The date of the payment check.
CHK	The number on the check.
AMT	The amount of the check.
SUBTOTAL	The total of the values in the EXT.PRICE column.
TAX	The amount of sales tax. It is calculated by the value in the TAX RATE field multiplied by the SUBTOTAL field.
FREIGHT	The cost of shipping.
CREDIT	A credit against this invoice.
TOTAL	The sum of the SUBTOTAL, FREIGHT, and TAX, less any CREDIT.
PAID	The sum of the values in the payment fields.
BALANCE	The balance still due before interest.
INTEREST	Interest calculated 30 days after the invoice date by multiplying the value in the INT RATE field by the BALANCE field.
BAL & INT	The sum of the BALANCE and INTEREST.

The next two screens, as shown in Figures 6.6 and 6.7, contain special fields needed to generate the invoice. The fields are filled in automatically for every record and contain all the necessary field labels and titles. They are necessary because Q&A's form-reporting features are lacking.

Using the Application

In this next section, you will learn several new features and will practice using the entire application. You will complete an entire inventory/invoicing cycle.

Suggested Uses

The Inventory/Invoicing application is pretty straightforward. There are not a lot of other uses for it, other than maintaining inventory and generating invoices. The uses described here are standard ones, but feel free to be innovative.

```
!!!!!!!!!! WARNING DO NOT ALTER THE VALUES IN THESE FIELDS--EVER!!!!!!!!!

                    IT WILL RENDER THE REPORTS USELESS


Bill To: BILL TO    Ship To/Remarks: SHIP TO/REMARKS    Subtotal: SUBTOTAL
                                                        Tax: TAX
Item #: ITEM #   Description: DESCRIPTION               Freight: FREIGHT
                                                        Credit: CREDIT
                                                        Total: TOTAL
Unit: UNIT   Extended: EXTENDED    Qty: QTY             Paid: PAID
                                                        Balance: BALANCE
Rep: REP    Ship Date: SHIP DATE                        Interest: INTEREST
                                                        Bal & Int: BAL & INT
Invoice #: INVOICE #    Date: DATE    Due Date: DUE DATE    PO#: PO#

Line: -----------------------------------------------------------------
Line: -----------------------------------------------------------------
Line: -----------------------------------------------------------------
Line: -----------------------------------------------------------------

INVOICE.DTF    New Record 1    of 1    Total Records: 33    Page 3 of 4

Esc-Exit  F1-Help    F3-Delete form   F7-Search   F8-Calc   F10-Continue
```

Figure 6.6   Screen 3 of the Invoice file containing special fields used for the invoice.

```
Please Remit To: PLEASE REMIT TO:
The Famous ABC Company: The Famous ABC Company
123 Glamor Avenue: 123 Glamor Ave
Hollywood, CA 94960: Hollywood, CA 94960

Thank You for Your Business !: THANK YOU FOR YOUR BUSINESS !
You Are Sincerely Appreciated !: YOU ARE SINCERELY APPRECIATED !
1.5 % Per Mo. Will Be Charged On Overdue Amount
: 1.5% Per Mo. Will be Charged on Overdue Amount




INVOICE.DTF    New Record 1    of 1    Total Records: 33    Page 4 of 4

Esc-Exit  F1-Help    F3-Delete form   F7-Search   F8-Calc   F10-Continue
```

Figure 6.7   Screen 4 of the Invoice file containing special fields used for the invoice.

The Invent file will maintain your product inventory, storing the amount and cost of each item. Many useful reports can be generated from the Invent file including current value of inventory, products in stock, items below minimum levels, items above maximum level, etc.

The Invoice file can help you analyze which products are hot sellers and which ones are laggards. It can help you find out who your top customers are and which products they buy most often. The aged accounts receivables report can help you collect your overdue invoices.

The Calc Key in the Invent File

The essence of using a database is data entry. Recall that the Inventory/ Invoicing application requires that you enter data into three separate databases, the first being the Invent file. Before you can generate an invoice, you must have entered product descriptions and prices in the Invent file. It is from this file that you will extract the product descriptions and retail prices. You will now open the Invent file and add an inventory record.

Practice Opening the Invent File and Adding an Inventory Record

1. Press **F** for File and **A** for Add.

2. Type the filename **INVENT** and press Enter.

3. Your cursor should be in the BATCH # field (a programming statement inserts the date and moves the cursor to this field). Fill in your screen as shown in Figure 6.8 and press F8 to calculate the financial values.

4. Your screen should now look like Figure 6.9. Press F10 to save the record.

In Figure 6.9, notice the BALANCE BEGINNING OF PERIOD field. This field holds the number of units you started with when you began using this system. The BDATE field opposite the BALANCE BEGINNING OF PERIOD field is the date you entered the inventory. The last two fields on the form, MINIMUM NUMBER and MAXIMUM NUMBER, refer to the least amount of this item you want in stock and the most of this item you want in stock. In the upcoming section on posting, you will automatically fill in the SOLD THIS PERIOD field.

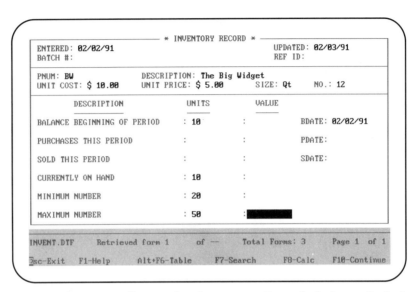

Figure 6.8   Partially completed Inventory Record—before calculating.

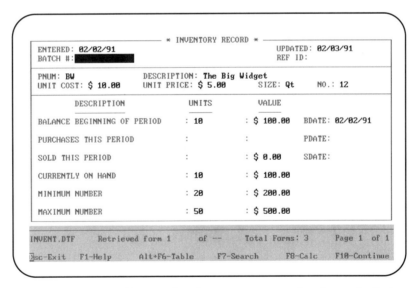

Figure 6.9   Partially completed Inventory Record—after calculating.

Programming statements are needed in order to have the VALUE fields automatically calculated when you press F8. These programming statements multiply the UNIT COST field by each of the UNITS fields. When you pressed F8, also known as the Calc key, in the preceding exercise, you caused these programming statements to calculate (execute).

You can designate when you want this calculation to occur: when your cursor enters a field, when it exits a field, or when you press F8. To have a statement calculate when your cursor enters or exits a field, place a < (less-than) or > (greater-than) symbol at the beginning of the programming statement. If you place a < (less-than) symbol at the beginning of the statement, the calculation happens when your cursor enters the field. If you place a > (greater-than) symbol at the beginning of the statement, the calculation happens after your cursor leaves the field. These concepts are fully covered in Chapter 2.

If you omit the < or > symbols from the statement, it can be calculated only through the manual or automatic mode. The Manual Calculation mode is invoked by pressing the F8 key. The automatic method calculates every programming statement every time your cursor leaves every field. Switching between the two modes can be accomplished by pressing Shift-F8 in either Add mode or Search/Update mode (in Search mode, you must have a record on the screen). Figure 6.10 displays the menu that appears when you press Shift-F8. Notice that the default setting of Manual is highlighted.

Q&A gives you the option of executing one programming statement when you enter the form and executing another when you exit the form. The second line of the menu asks Main program before field exit? This selection lets you choose whether you want the On Exit field programming statements executed before or after all the other programming statements are executed. These concepts will be covered later in the chapter under "Programming."

Add Data to Names

With an inventory record in the Invent file, you are ready to add a customer record to the Names file. You need at least one customer in the Names file to follow the examples.

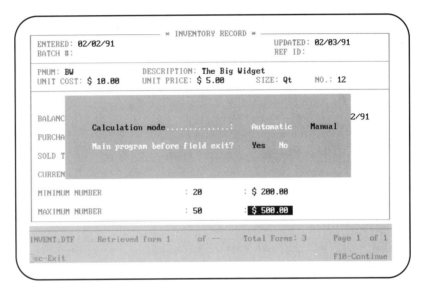

Figure 6.10 Invent screen with Calculation menu.

Practice Adding a Customer Record to the Names File

1. Press **F** for File and **A** for Add.

2. Type the filename **NAMES** and press Enter.

3. Your screen should look like Figure 6.11. Fill it in as shown in Figure 6.12 (the only difference will be the ID number).

4. Write down the ID number and press Shift-F10 to save the record and exit the form.

Generate an Invoice and Conduct a Lookup

You are now ready to create and print an invoice. The next procedure shows you how.

Creating and Printing an Invoice

1. Press **F** for File and **A** for Add.

2. Type the filename **INVOICE** and press Enter.

3. Your cursor should be in the BATCH # field shown in Figure 6.13. Type the number **1** in the field and press the Down Arrow.

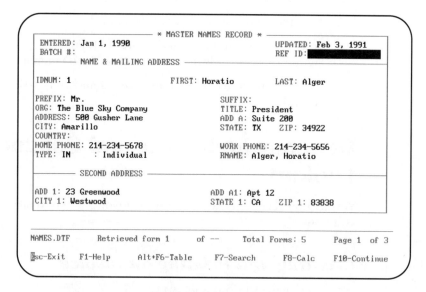

```
                    ──────── * MASTER NAMES RECORD * ────────
  ENTERED: Mar 7, 1991                              UPDATED:
  BATCH #:                                          REF ID:
             ──── NAME & MAILING ADDRESS ────

  IDNUM: 1                      FIRST:          LAST:

  PREFIX:                               SUFFIX:
  ORG:                                  TITLE:
  ADDRESS:                              ADD A:
  CITY:                                 STATE:      ZIP:
  COUNTRY:
  HOME PHONE:                           WORK PHONE:
  TYPE:       :                         RNAME:

       ──── SECOND ADDRESS ────

  ADD 1:                                ADD A1:
  CITY 1:                               STATE 1:     ZIP 1:

─────────────────────────────────────────────────────────────────
NAMES.DTF       New Record 1    of 1     Total Records: 4      Page 1 of 3

Esc-Exit    F1-Help       F3-Delete form     F7-Search     F8-Calc    F10-Continue
```

Figure 6.11   Screen 1 of the Names file—empty.

```
                    ──────── * MASTER NAMES RECORD * ────────
  ENTERED: Jan 1, 1990                               UPDATED: Feb 3, 1991
  BATCH #:                                           REF ID:
             ──── NAME & MAILING ADDRESS ────

  IDNUM: 1                      FIRST: Horatio       LAST: Alger

  PREFIX: Mr.                           SUFFIX:
  ORG: The Blue Sky Company             TITLE: President
  ADDRESS: 500 Gusher Lane              ADD A: Suite 200
  CITY: Amarillo                        STATE: TX   ZIP: 34922
  COUNTRY:
  HOME PHONE: 214-234-5678              WORK PHONE: 214-234-5656
  TYPE: IN    : Individual              RNAME: Alger, Horatio

       ──── SECOND ADDRESS ────

  ADD 1: 23 Greenwood                   ADD A1: Apt 12
  CITY 1: Westwood                      STATE 1: CA   ZIP 1: 83838

─────────────────────────────────────────────────────────────────
NAMES.DTF       Retrieved form 1    of --     Total Forms: 5      Page 1 of 3

Esc-Exit    F1-Help      Alt+F6-Table      F7-Search      F8-Calc     F10-Continue
```

Figure 6.12   Screen 1 of the Names file—filled in.

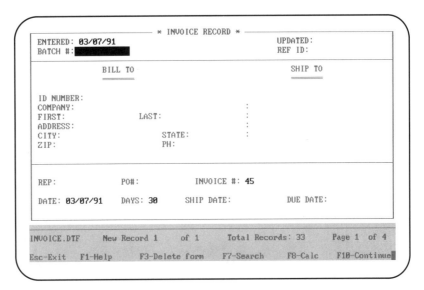

```
                          ──── * INVOICE RECORD * ────
  ENTERED: 03/07/91                                UPDATED:
  BATCH #:███████████                              REF ID:

                  BILL TO                              SHIP TO
                  ═══════                              ═══════

  ID NUMBER:
  COMPANY:                                  :
  FIRST:              LAST:                 :
  ADDRESS:                                  :
  CITY:                     STATE:          :
  ZIP:                      PH:


  REP:             PO#:           INVOICE #: 45

  DATE: 03/07/91   DAYS: 30    SHIP DATE:         DUE DATE:
─────────────────────────────────────────────────────────────
 INVOICE.DTF    New Record 1     of 1   Total Records: 33   Page 1  of 4

 Esc-Exit   F1-Help      F3-Delete form    F7-Search    F8-Calc    F10-Continue
```

Figure 6.13   Screen 1 of the Invoice file.

Beginner's Tip

Always use a batch number when entering invoices. This number will be used to post the items sold to the Invent file. You can always use the number 1 because you will erase it from all records after each use.

4. With your cursor in the ID number field, type the customer's ID number and press F8 to place the name and address data in the BILL TO fields. Your screen should look like Figure 6.14.

5. Fill in the other fields on the first screen. Type initials into the REP field. Type the number **22343** into the PO# field; type **30** into the DAYS field. Press F8 again. Q&A will execute the programming statement that adds the DAYS field to the DATE field to obtain the DUE DATE field.

6. Press PgDn to move to the second page as shown in Figure 6.15.

7. Fill in the product ID numbers and quantity numbers in each of the fields. Model your screen after Figure 6.16.

8. To look up the description and price for each item, press F8. Your screen should look like Figure 6.16.

263

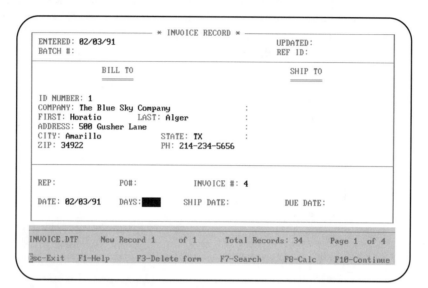

```
 ┌─────────────────────── * INVOICE RECORD * ───────────────────────┐
 │  ENTERED: 02/03/91                              UPDATED:          │
 │  BATCH #:                                       REF ID:           │
 │                                                                   │
 │              BILL TO                        SHIP TO               │
 │              ━━━━━━━                        ━━━━━━━               │
 │                                                                   │
 │  ID NUMBER: 1                                                     │
 │  COMPANY: The Blue Sky Company                  :                 │
 │  FIRST: Horatio       LAST: Alger               :                 │
 │  ADDRESS: 500 Gusher Lane                       :                 │
 │  CITY: Amarillo          STATE: TX              :                 │
 │  ZIP: 34922              PH: 214-234-5656                         │
 │                                                                   │
 │                                                                   │
 │  REP:          PO#:            INVOICE #: 4                       │
 │                                                                   │
 │  DATE: 02/03/91   DAYS:███    SHIP DATE:        DUE DATE:         │
 └───────────────────────────────────────────────────────────────────┘
 │ INVOICE.DTF   New Record 1   of 1    Total Records: 34   Page 1 of 4 │
 │ Esc-Exit   F1-Help      F3-Delete form   F7-Search   F8-Calc  F10-Continue │
```

Figure 6.14   Invoice screen after lookup.

```
 ┌──────────────────────────────────────────────────────────────────┐
 │   INV #   │ DESCRIPTION        │ QTY   │ UNIT PRICE │ EXT. PRICE   │
 │ 1 : █████    A:                  A1:      A2:          :           │
 │ 2 :          B:                  B1:      B2:          :           │
 │ 3 :          C:                  C1:      C2:          :           │
 │ 4 :          D:                  D1:      D2:          :           │
 │ 5 :          E:                  E1:      E2:          :           │
 │ 6 :          F:                  F1:      F2:          :           │
 │ 7 :          G:                  G1:      G2:          :           │
 │ 8 :          H:                  H1:      H2:          :           │
 │ 9 :          I:                  I1:      I2:          :           │
 │                                                                    │
 │      Int Rate:0.015    Tax Rate:            Subtotal :             │
 │                                             Tax      :             │
 │      Date:        Chk:        Amt:          Freight  :             │
 │      Date:        Chk:        Amt:          Credit   :             │
 │      Date:        Chk:        Amt:          Total    :             │
 │      Date:        Chk:        Amt:          Paid     :             │
 │      Date:        Chk:        Amt:          Balance  :             │
 │      Date:        Chk:        Amt:          Interest :             │
 │      Date:        Chk:        Amt:          Bal & Int:             │
 └────────────────────────────────────────────────────────────────────┘
 │ INVOICE.DTF   New Record 1   of 1    Total Records: 33   Page 2 of 4 │
 │ Esc-Exit   F1-Help      F3-Delete form   F7-Search   F8-Calc  F10-Continue │
```

Figure 6.15   Screen 2 of the Invoice file before lookup.

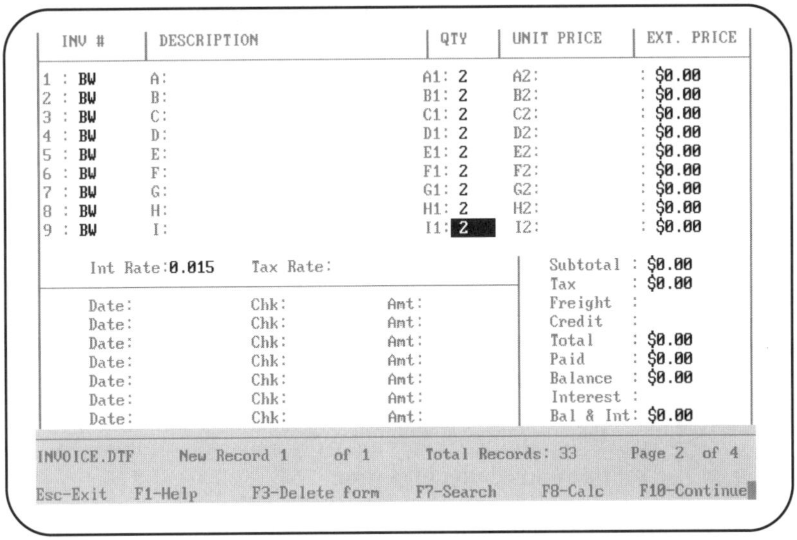

```
┌─────────────────────────────────────────────────────────────────────────┐
│  INV #    DESCRIPTION                      QTY    UNIT PRICE   EXT. PRICE  │
│                                                                           │
│ 1 : BW    A:                              A1: 2   A2:          : $0.00     │
│ 2 : BW    B:                              B1: 2   B2:          : $0.00     │
│ 3 : BW    C:                              C1: 2   C2:          : $0.00     │
│ 4 : BW    D:                              D1: 2   D2:          : $0.00     │
│ 5 : BW    E:                              E1: 2   E2:          : $0.00     │
│ 6 : BW    F:                              F1: 2   F2:          : $0.00     │
│ 7 : BW    G:                              G1: 2   G2:          : $0.00     │
│ 8 : BW    H:                              H1: 2   H2:          : $0.00     │
│ 9 : BW    I:                              I1:[2]  I2:          : $0.00     │
│                                                                           │
│     Int Rate:0.015    Tax Rate:                    Subtotal : $0.00       │
│                                                    Tax      : $0.00       │
│     Date:          Chk:          Amt:              Freight  :             │
│     Date:          Chk:          Amt:              Credit   :             │
│     Date:          Chk:          Amt:              Total    : $0.00       │
│     Date:          Chk:          Amt:              Paid     : $0.00       │
│     Date:          Chk:          Amt:              Balance  : $0.00       │
│     Date:          Chk:          Amt:              Interest :             │
│     Date:          Chk:          Amt:              Bal & Int: $0.00       │
│                                                                           │
│ INVOICE.DTF    New Record 1    of 1    Total Records: 33    Page 2 of 4   │
│                                                                           │
│ Esc-Exit   F1-Help      F3-Delete form     F7-Search     F8-Calc   F10-Continue │
└─────────────────────────────────────────────────────────────────────────┘
```

Figure 6.16   Screen 2 of Invoice file with product ID numbers and quantities.

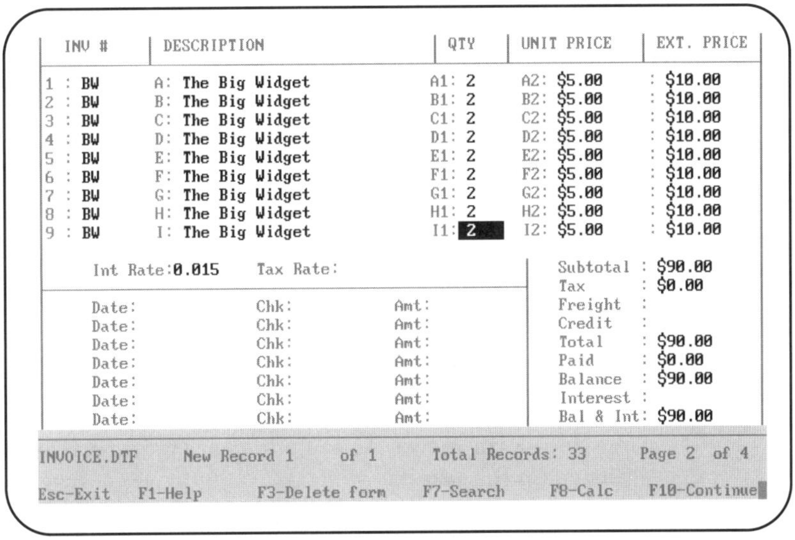

```
┌─────────────────────────────────────────────────────────────────────────┐
│  INV #    DESCRIPTION                      QTY    UNIT PRICE   EXT. PRICE  │
│                                                                           │
│ 1 : BW    A: The Big Widget               A1: 2   A2: $5.00   : $10.00     │
│ 2 : BW    B: The Big Widget               B1: 2   B2: $5.00   : $10.00     │
│ 3 : BW    C: The Big Widget               C1: 2   C2: $5.00   : $10.00     │
│ 4 : BW    D: The Big Widget               D1: 2   D2: $5.00   : $10.00     │
│ 5 : BW    E: The Big Widget               E1: 2   E2: $5.00   : $10.00     │
│ 6 : BW    F: The Big Widget               F1: 2   F2: $5.00   : $10.00     │
│ 7 : BW    G: The Big Widget               G1: 2   G2: $5.00   : $10.00     │
│ 8 : BW    H: The Big Widget               H1: 2   H2: $5.00   : $10.00     │
│ 9 : BW    I: The Big Widget               I1:[2]  I2: $5.00   : $10.00     │
│                                                                           │
│     Int Rate:0.015    Tax Rate:                    Subtotal : $90.00      │
│                                                    Tax      : $0.00       │
│     Date:          Chk:          Amt:              Freight  :             │
│     Date:          Chk:          Amt:              Credit   :             │
│     Date:          Chk:          Amt:              Total    : $90.00      │
│     Date:          Chk:          Amt:              Paid     : $0.00       │
│     Date:          Chk:          Amt:              Balance  : $90.00      │
│     Date:          Chk:          Amt:              Interest :             │
│     Date:          Chk:          Amt:              Bal & Int: $90.00      │
│                                                                           │
│ INVOICE.DTF    New Record 1    of 1    Total Records: 33    Page 2 of 4   │
│                                                                           │
│ Esc-Exit   F1-Help      F3-Delete form     F7-Search     F8-Calc   F10-Continue │
└─────────────────────────────────────────────────────────────────────────┘
```

Figure 6.17   Screen 2 of Invoice file after lookup.

Lookups are used extensively in this application and many of the other applications. There are two primary types of lookups: internal and external. *Internal lookups* utilize the lookup table that is part of each Q&A database.

265

External lookups extract information from other Q&A databases. The lookups you just performed were external lookups—they extracted information from the Names and Invent databases. The upcoming section on programming will explain in detail the different types of lookup statements and how to use them.

9. In this example, you did not enter freight or credit. However, if you had entered them, you would have had to press F8 again to calculate the totals fields.

Beginner's Tip

The most efficient way to enter an invoice is to type the customer ID number and press F8. This way you can tell if you have the correct customer. Next, type all product ID numbers and quantities. Fill in the sales tax, freight, and credit. Then press F8 to calculate all the remaining programming statements. This will reduce your data entry time.

10. Press Shift-F10 to save and exit the form.

11. Press Esc twice to return to the Main menu.

Print the Invoice

After all the invoices have been added, you can print them. The invoice is a form report, designed and maintained in the File Print menu. Since the invoice form is already designed, all you are going to do is print it.

Practice Printing an Invoice

1. Press **F** for File and **P** for Print.

2. Type **INVOICE** and press Enter.

3. Type **P** for Print records.

4. Type **SALES INVOICE** and press Enter. This is the name of the invoice form report. As you add other form reports, they will be listed on this screen.

The main difference between the Design/Redesign a Spec and the Print Records options is that you can create a report and print it in the Design/Redesign a Spec option, but you can only print in the Print Records option. Any changes you make to a report spec while in the Print Records option are not permanently saved.

Shortcut

Use the Print Records option to print reports, particularly when you develop a macro to print a report. This way any accidental changes will not be saved.

5. Type **Y** for Yes to make temporary changes.

6. You are at the Retrieve spec. Move to the BATCH # field and type **1** and press F10.

The Retrieve spec is where you specify which invoices you want to print. When you added the invoice record, you typed batch number 1 in the BATCH # field. Use this number to retrieve the invoices you want to print each time.

7. The Column/Sort spec is on the screen. Take a minute to look at it because it is the most complex form report used in any of the applications. Press PgDn to view each page. When you are through viewing the spec, press F10 to proceed to the Print Options screen. Chapter 4 covers form reports in-depth.

8. The Print Options are on the screen. Press F10 to proceed.

9. Press F10 to print the invoice.

10. Press Esc three times to return to the Main menu.

Let's summarize what you have done so far: you have created an inventory record for The Big Widget, added a customer to the Names file, and printed an invoice. To complete the cycle, you will now post the products sold to the Invent file and blank out the BATCH # field.

Post Products to the Invent File

Posting is probably the most significant new feature added to Version 4.0. In previous versions of Q&A, the biggest drawback to using Q&A for "sophisticated" applications was the fact that you could not make changes in one file and automatically transfer those changes to another file. Well now you can!

Figure 6.18 displays the posting path between the Invoice file and the Invent file. When you post information from one file to another, you designate which fields from the source file should be posted into which fields of the target file. You can specify whether you want the values replaced, added, subtracted, multiplied, or divided by the fields from the source file. Also, the programming statements you have in the target file can be made to execute after the post is completed.

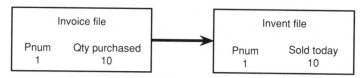

Figure 6.18   Posting path from Invoice to Invent file.

For the post to work, you must have a field common to both database files that has been designated as a *speedy field*. This is the field that the Posting spec uses to match the source file and the target file. An example of a speedy field is the customer ID number or, in the case of this application, the product ID number.

In the next example, you will be posting the number of widgets sold on the sample invoice into the SOLD THIS PERIOD field of the Invent file. The *Key field* will determine if a match is made, and the record updated is the PNUM field. This field is common to both files.

Practice Posting to the Invent File

1. Press **F** for File and **T** for Post.

2. Type **INVOICE** and press Enter. This is the source file—the file you will be posting FROM.

3. Type **INVENT** and press Enter. This is the target file—the file you will be posting TO.

4. The Retrieve Spec screen is displayed. You will be posting the invoice that has a 1 in the BATCH # field. Move to the BATCH # field and type **1**. Press Shift-F8 to save the Retrieve spec for future use. Give it the name Batch Number 1. Your screen should look like Figure 6.19. Now press F10 to save the spec and press F10 to proceed to the Posting spec.

Beginner's
Tip

By saving the Retrieve spec in this process, you can reuse it over and over, anywhere a Retrieve spec is called for.

5. You are at the Post Spec screen, where you indicate which fields you want to post to the Invent file. For every field you want to post, you have to fill out a Post spec. The first field you will post is the date from the ENTERED field into the SDATE field in the Invent file. This date is used to indicate when you last posted records to this

file. Your cursor should be in the ENTERED field. Press F7 to bring up the Post Spec option, shown in Figure 6.20. The cursor should move to the field `into external field` of the Post spec.

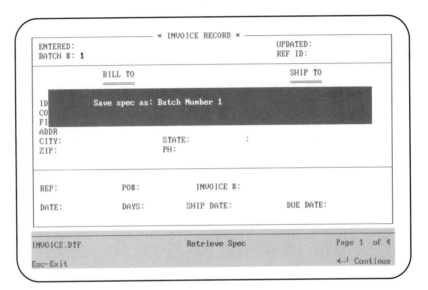

Figure 6.19   Save Retrieve Spec screen.

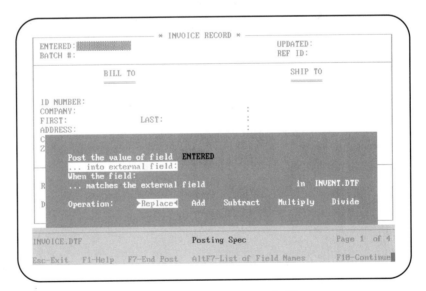

Figure 6.20   Blank Post spec for ENTERED field.

6. Press Alt-F7 to bring up the list of fields in the Invent file. Press **S** for SDATE and press Enter to select it. Press Enter to move to the field `When the field` and press Alt-F7 to list the fields in the Invoice file.

7. Press Enter to place field **1** in the spec. Press Enter to move to the field `matches the external field`. Press Alt-F7 and select pnum by pressing Enter.

8. Press Enter to move to the `Operation` line. Use the Right Arrow key to move to the Add selection.

9. Your screen should look like Figure 6.21. Press F10 to save the spec.

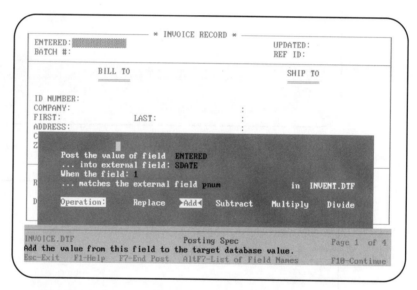

Figure 6.21   Sub-Post spec for the field ENTERED.

10. Press PgDn and press Tab twice. Your cursor is now at the first QTY field. You will be entering Post specs for each of the QTY fields in this column. Press F7 to bring up the Post spec for this field. Fill in the Post spec as shown in Figure 6.22. Press F10 when you are done.

11. Use the Down Arrow key to move to the next QTY field and press F6. Fill it in as shown in Figure 6.23. Press F10 when you are through.

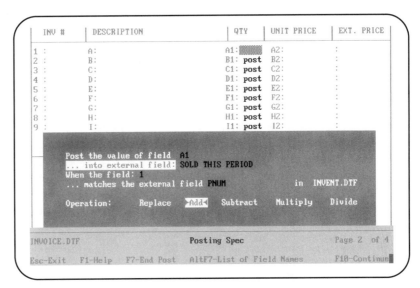

Figure 6.22   Post Spec options for first QTY field.

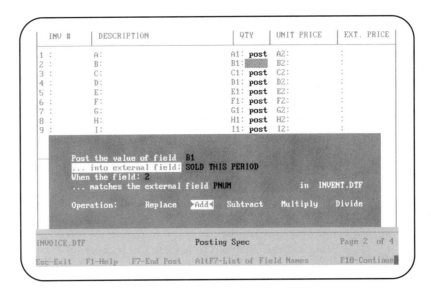

Figure 6.23   Post Spec options for second QTY field.

12. Fill out the rest of the fields in the QTY column. Change the field
    When the field to the corresponding number in the INV # (this
    is the PNUM field in the Invent file) column. For example, the
    corresponding INV # for the next QTY field is 3, and so on. Also
    check to make sure that the Operation on each one is Add.

13. When you are through with all the Post specs, your screen should look like Figure 6.24.

```
┌─────────┬──────────────────────┬─────────┬────────────┬────────────┐
│  INV #  │ DESCRIPTION          │   QTY   │ UNIT PRICE │ EXT. PRICE │
│         │                      │         │            │            │
│ 1 :     │  A:                  │ A1: post│ A2:        │      :     │
│ 2 :     │  B:                  │ B1:▐post│ B2:        │      :     │
│ 3 :     │  C:                  │ C1: post│ C2:        │      :     │
│ 4 :     │  D:                  │ D1: post│ D2:        │      :     │
│ 5 :     │  E:                  │ E1: post│ E2:        │      :     │
│ 6 :     │  F:                  │ F1: post│ F2:        │      :     │
│ 7 :     │  G:                  │ G1: post│ G2:        │      :     │
│ 8 :     │  H:                  │ H1: post│ H2:        │      :     │
│ 9 :     │  I:                  │ I1: post│ I2:        │      :     │
│         │                      │         │            │            │
│   Int Rate:        Tax Rate:                │ Subtotal :            │
│                                             │ Tax      :            │
│    Date:        Chk:        Amt:            │ Freight  :            │
│    Date:        Chk:        Amt:            │ Credit   :            │
│    Date:        Chk:        Amt:            │ Total    :            │
│    Date:        Chk:        Amt:            │ Paid     :            │
│    Date:        Chk:        Amt:            │ Balance  :            │
│    Date:        Chk:        Amt:            │ Interest :            │
│    Date:        Chk:        Amt:            │ Bal & Int:            │
├─────────────────────────────────────────────────────────────────────┤
│ INVOICE.DTF                    Posting Spec              Page 2 of 4 │
│                                                                     │
│ Esc-Exit  F1-Help   F7-Make post   F8-Calc  ↑F8-Save Alt+F8-Get  F10-Continue▐│
└─────────────────────────────────────────────────────────────────────┘
```

Figure 6.24   Completed Post spec.

14. Now tell Q&A whether you want the Programming specs in the target database (Invent file) to be executed after you post the values to the PNUM field. These Programming specs calculate the total products on hand and the value of each of the different unit fields. Press F8 to bring up the Auto Program ReCalc menu seen in Figure 6.25. Press Enter to move to the Calculation Statements option and change it to Yes. Press F9 to return to the Programming spec.

15. Press F10 to begin the post.

16. You will see the Update Warning screen, as shown in Figure 6.26. Q&A gives you the option of updating each record individually or all at once. Press No to update the records all at once.

17. Lastly, view how the posting procedure changed the inventory record. Press **S** for Search/Update, type **INVENT**, and press Enter. Use the Down Arrow to move to the PNUM field, type **BW**, and press F10 to retrieve the record. Look at the value in the SOLD THIS PERIOD and the SDATE fields. Your screen should look like Figure 6.27, except for the dates. When you are through looking at the record, press Shift-F10 to save the record and exit the file.

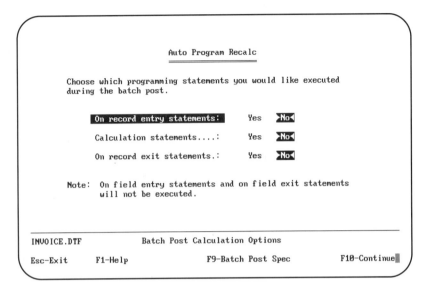

Figure 6.25   Auto Program ReCalc menu.

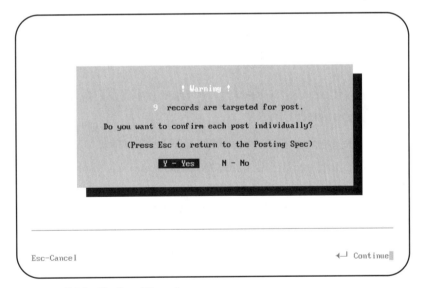

Figure 6.26   Update Warning screen.

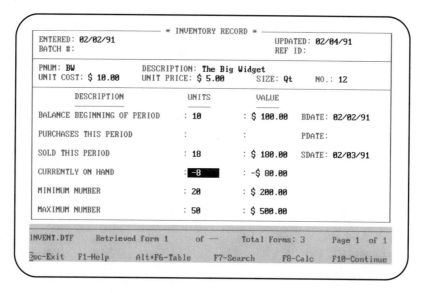

┌─────────────────────────────── * INVENTORY RECORD * ───────────────────────────┐

```
                              ──── * INVENTORY RECORD * ────
   ENTERED: 02/02/91                                    UPDATED: 02/04/91
   BATCH #:                                             REF ID:

   PNUM: BW                  DESCRIPTION: The Big Widget
   UNIT COST: $ 10.00        UNIT PRICE: $ 5.00      SIZE: Qt    NO.: 12

           DESCRIPTION              UNITS          VALUE
           ───────────              ─────          ─────
   BALANCE BEGINNING OF PERIOD    : 10         : $ 100.00    BDATE: 02/02/91

   PURCHASES THIS PERIOD          :            :             PDATE:

   SOLD THIS PERIOD               : 18         : $ 180.00    SDATE: 02/03/91

   CURRENTLY ON HAND              : -8         : -$ 80.00

   MINIMUM NUMBER                 : 20         : $ 200.00

   MAXIMUM NUMBER                 : 50         : $ 500.00

   INVENT.DTF    Retrieved form 1      of —     Total Forms: 3    Page 1  of 1
   Esc-Exit   F1-Help     Alt+F6-Table     F7-Search     F8-Calc    F10-Continue
```

Figure 6.27   Inventory Record after post.

18. Press Esc to return to the Main menu.

The final step is to clear the BATCH # field in the Invoice file. To do this, you will use the Mass Update feature (covered in Chapter 5).

Practice Clearing the BATCH # Field in the Invoice File

1. Press **F** for File and **M** for Mass Update.

2. Type the filename **INVOICE** and press Enter.

3. You will see the Retrieve Spec screen. Select all records with a 1 in the BATCH # field. Move to the BATCH # field and type **1**.

4. Press F10 to proceed to the Update Spec screen. Here is where you will clear the BATCH # field. Move to the BATCH # field and type **#1=" "**. The " " is Q&A's signal to clear the field. Press F10 to save the spec.

5. Press **N** for No because you do not want to manually update each record. Do this each time you use a batch number in any file.

Calculate Interest

Billing a customer does not always ensure payment. To encourage payment, you can add interest to invoices on a case by case basis.

Adding Interest to Invoices

1. Press **F** for File and **S** for Search.

2. Type the filename **INVOICE** and press Enter.

3. Retrieve all the records in which the due date is less than today's date. Type **@date** in the DUE DATE field. This will retrieve all the delinquent invoices.

4. With the first record on the screen, press PgDn and press F8 to calculate the interest. Press F10 to save the record and bring up the next one. If you do not want to charge interest for a particular client, do not press F8; just press F10 to advance to the next record. Continue this process until you are done.

The interest is calculated by a programming statement in the INTEREST field. This statement says: If the date in the DUE DATE field is less than today's date, multiply the value in the INT RATE field by the value in the BALANCE field and add any existing interest to this amount as well. In Figure 6.28, you can see the DUE DATE field, and in Figure 6.29 you can see the INT RATE and INTEREST fields. The INT RATE field holds the monthly interest that you charge each customer. You can set this rate differently for each client. The default rate is 1.5 percent a month. To change the default rate, navigate to the Set Initial Values option of the Customize menu and type a new number in the INT RATE field.

Shortcut

You can create a macro to charge interest on *all* overdue invoices. Use the Mass Update feature. When you get to the Update Spec screen, use the same formula in the INTEREST field.

Print Aged A/R Report

In business, it is essential to stay current on your outstanding receivables, particularly the ones that are over 60 days old. To facilitate this process, you can print an aged accounts receivables report. This columnar report is based on the Invoice file.

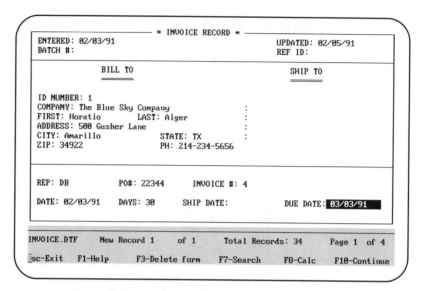

```
 ┌─────────────────────── * INVOICE RECORD * ───────────────────────┐
 │  ENTERED: 02/03/91                              UPDATED: 02/05/91  │
 │  BATCH #:                                       REF ID:           │
 │  ─────────────────────────────────────────────────────────────── │
 │                  BILL TO                         SHIP TO          │
 │                  ═══════                         ═══════          │
 │                                                                   │
 │  ID NUMBER: 1                                                     │
 │  COMPANY: The Blue Sky Company                  :                 │
 │  FIRST: Horatio        LAST: Alger              :                 │
 │  ADDRESS: 500 Gusher Lane                       :                 │
 │  CITY: Amarillo            STATE: TX            :                 │
 │  ZIP: 34922                PH: 214-234-5656                       │
 │  ─────────────────────────────────────────────────────────────── │
 │                                                                   │
 │  REP: DB        PO#: 22344        INVOICE #: 4                    │
 │                                                                   │
 │  DATE: 02/03/91    DAYS: 30    SHIP DATE:        DUE DATE: 03/03/91│
 └───────────────────────────────────────────────────────────────────┘
 INVOICE.DTF    New Record 1    of 1      Total Records: 34   Page 1  of 4
 Esc-Exit   F1-Help      F3-Delete form   F7-Search    F8-Calc    F10-Continue
```

Figure 6.28   Due Date field in Invoice file.

```
┌──────┬────────────────────┬───────┬─────────────┬──────────────┐
│ INV #│ DESCRIPTION        │  QTY  │  UNIT PRICE │  EXT. PRICE  │
├──────┼────────────────────┼───────┼─────────────┼──────────────┤
│1 : BW│ A: The Big Widget  │ A1: 2 │ A2: $5.00   │ : $10.00     │
│2 : BW│ B: The Big Widget  │ B1: 2 │ B2: $5.00   │ : $10.00     │
│3 : BW│ C: The Big Widget  │ C1: 2 │ C2: $5.00   │ : $10.00     │
│4 : BW│ D: The Big Widget  │ D1: 2 │ D2: $5.00   │ : $10.00     │
│5 : BW│ E: The Big Widget  │ E1: 2 │ E2: $5.00   │ : $10.00     │
│6 : BW│ F: The Big Widget  │ F1: 2 │ F2: $5.00   │ : $10.00     │
│7 : BW│ G: The Big Widget  │ G1: 2 │ G2: $5.00   │ : $10.00     │
│8 : BW│ H: The Big Widget  │ H1: 2 │ H2: $5.00   │ : $10.00     │
│9 : BW│ I: The Big Widget  │ I1: 2 │ I2: $5.00   │ : $10.00     │
└──────┴────────────────────┴───────┴─────────────┴──────────────┘

        Int Rate:0.015    Tax Rate:              Subtotal : $90.00
                                                 Tax      : $0.00
    Date:        Chk:        Amt:                Freight  :
    Date:        Chk:        Amt:                Credit   :
    Date:        Chk:        Amt:                Total    : $90.00
    Date:        Chk:        Amt:                Paid     : $0.00
    Date:        Chk:        Amt:                Balance  : $90.00
    Date:        Chk:        Amt:                Interest : $4.05
    Date:        Chk:        Amt:                Bal & Int: $94.05
 INVOICE.DTF    Retrieved form 1    of --     Total Forms: 33   Page 2  of 4
 Esc-Exit   F1-Help      Alt+F6-Table   F7-Search    F8-Calc    F10-Continue
```

Figure 6.29   Int Rate and Interest fields in the Invoice file.

Printing an Aged A/R Report

1. Press **R** for Report and **P** for Print a Report.

2. Type the filename **INVOICE** and press Enter.

3. Choose the Aged Accounts Receivables report and press Enter.

4. The default Retrieve spec for this report is `Print all invoices that have a balance greater than zero`. To view this Retrieve spec, press PgDn and look at the BAL & INT field. Press F10 to advance to the Column/Sort spec and press F10 to advance through this screen.

5. Press F10 to advance through the Print Options screen. Press F10 to print the report. If you printed the report with the sample data, your report should look like Figure 6.30.

```
02/05/91                    AGED ACCOUNTS RECEIVABLE REPORT                         Page 1


COMPANY                 INVOICE   DUE DATE   DAYS 0-30   DAYS 31-60   DAYS 60 PLUS   GRAND TOTAL
- - - - - - - - - - -   - - - -   - - - -    - - - - -   - - - - -    - - - - -     - - - - - -

The Blue Sky Company 2            03/02/91   $94.05                                  $94.05

                                             - - - - -   - - - - -    - - - - -     - - - - - -

     Total:                                  $94.05      $0.00        $0.00

= = = = = = = = = = = = = = = = = = = = = = = = = = = = = = = = = = = = = = = = = = = = = =

     Total:                                  $94.05      $0.00        $0.00          $94.05
```

Figure 6.30   Aged Accounts Receivables report.

Shortcut

If you want to add the first and last name or the phone number to this report, you can do so in the Column/Sort spec. Choose Report and Design/Redesign a Report.

Guided Modifications

In this section you will learn more about programming statements, conducting lookups, and copying database designs and selected forms.

Suggested Modifications

One of the modifications you might want to make is to add more lines to the Invoice database. In one of the upcoming examples, you will add one line to the Invoice form. If you need more, add them at that time. Another modification you can make is to create invoice and inventory files for a service organization. In a later example, you will make copies of these files, which you can then use as a starting point. You will likely need to increase the size of the description fields in both files and remove fields inappropriate to a service organization.

Programming

Elementary programming concepts were covered in Chapter 2. This section will focus on more advanced programming statements and functions. Q&A does not have a programming language. It requires that you place specific programming statements in the actual fields of the database—in the *Program spec*. This Program spec contains all the commands that affect the form's operation.

The other portion of the Program spec is known as the *Navigation spec*. This spec is where you place the statements that control the movement of the cursor throughout the form. You can combine both of these statements in the Program spec, but, if you do, you will not be able to use the databases with other special versions of Q&A, such as Q&A for the Macintosh.

The primary purpose of programming is to automate tasks that you would otherwise have to do manually. For instance, in the Invoice file, you could manually calculate the interest due on the outstanding invoices and type the value in the INTEREST field. But by utilizing a simple programming statement, you can press F8 instead and have Q&A do it for you.

There are five basic steps to writing programming statements. The first step is to decide what you want to accomplish—what action do you want Q&A to perform. Once you have determined this, you can proceed with step 2—conceptualize the statements. Mark which fields on the database will be involved in the various programming statements and in what order they will be executed. To do this, print a blank copy of a database form by opening the database in Add mode and pressing F2 and F10.

With the statements designed, you can type the programming statements in the Program spec. This is step 3. In step 4, you'll need to test them to make sure they work as intended. If you find any errors, you will need to debug (fix) them. Once you have them operating the way you want, you can do the last step—put the database into use.

To make room for an additional programming statement, you need to add another line to the Invoice file. The next exercise will show you how to do this.

Practice Adding a Line to the Invoice File

1. Press **F** for File, **D** for Design File, and **R** for Redesign a File.

2. Type the filename **INVOICE** and press Enter.

3. Press PgDn and press the Down Arrow ten times so that your cursor is on the 9 in line 9. Press Ctrl-F4 to delete the line and Shift-F7 to restore it.

4. Move down one line and place the cursor below the 9. Press Shift-F7 to restore the line again. Change the 9 in the last line to a 10, the I to a J, and the I1 to a J1.

5. Press Home to move to the other side of the screen and then delete each of the field identifiers in line 10. The field identifiers are the two letters after the colon in each field. Once they are deleted, make sure that the line is adjusted correctly. There should be no space between line 10 and the INT RATE field. When you are through, your screen should look like Figure 6.31.

6. Press F10 four times to save your Design spec.

Work Through the Programming Process

This section will guide you through the programming process outlined previously. You will use the Inventory/Invoicing application for illustration purposes and imagine that you are creating it from scratch.

Suppose you just finished developing the Invoice database. You realize that unless you put programming statements in the database the invoices could probably be generated faster by hand. The first question you ask yourself is "Which tasks could Q&A automate in this form?" Q&A could look up name and address information, look up inventory information, multiply the quantity by the unit price, total all the numbers, calculate interest on overdue invoices, and automatically generate the date and the invoice number. With all these tasks automated, the form would be much faster than the manual method.

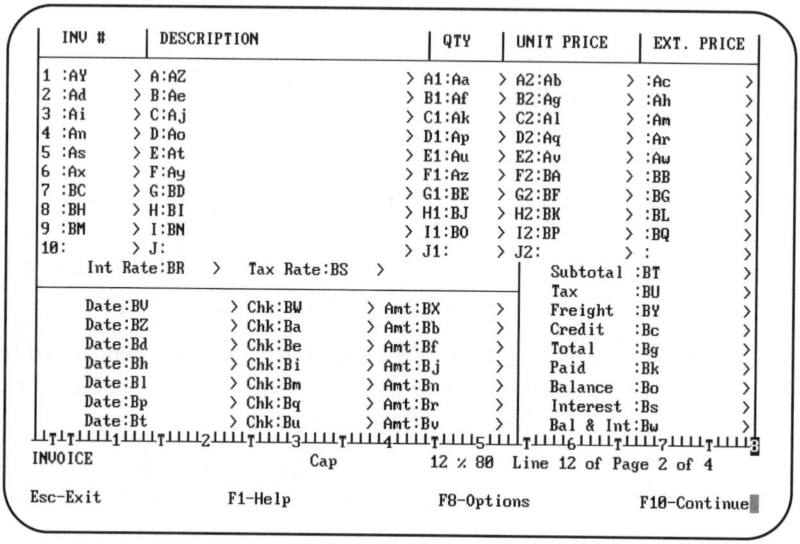

```
┌─────────────────────────────────────────────────────────────────────────┐
│  INV #    │ DESCRIPTION           │ QTY  │ UNIT PRICE │ EXT. PRICE │      │
│ 1 :AY    > A:AZ                    > A1:Aa  > A2:Ab   >    :Ac     >       │
│ 2 :Ad    > B:Ae                    > B1:Af  > B2:Ag   >    :Ah     >       │
│ 3 :Ai    > C:Aj                    > C1:Ak  > C2:Al   >    :Am     >       │
│ 4 :An    > D:Ao                    > D1:Ap  > D2:Aq   >    :Ar     >       │
│ 5 :As    > E:At                    > E1:Au  > E2:Av   >    :Aw     >       │
│ 6 :Ax    > F:Ay                    > F1:Az  > F2:BA   >    :BB     >       │
│ 7 :BC    > G:BD                    > G1:BE  > G2:BF   >    :BG     >       │
│ 8 :BH    > H:BI                    > H1:BJ  > H2:BK   >    :BL     >       │
│ 9 :BM    > I:BN                    > I1:BO  > I2:BP   >    :BQ     >       │
│10:       > J:                      > J1:    > J2:     >    :       >       │
│      Int Rate:BR  >   Tax Rate:BS  >          Subtotal :BT       >         │
│                                                  Tax      :BU    >         │
│      Date:BV    > Chk:BW   > Amt:BX   >     Freight  :BY        >          │
│      Date:BZ    > Chk:Ba   > Amt:Bb   >     Credit   :Bc        >          │
│      Date:Bd    > Chk:Be   > Amt:Bf   >     Total    :Bg        >          │
│      Date:Bh    > Chk:Bi   > Amt:Bj   >     Paid     :Bk        >          │
│      Date:Bl    > Chk:Bm   > Amt:Bn   >     Balance  :Bo        >          │
│      Date:Bp    > Chk:Bq   > Amt:Br   >     Interest :Bs        >          │
│      Date:Bt    > Chk:Bu   > Amt:Bv   >     Bal & Int:Bw        >          │
│ INVOICE                   Cap        12 % 80  Line 12 of Page 2 of 4       │
│                                                                           │
│ Esc-Exit          F1-Help          F8-Options          F10-Continue       │
└─────────────────────────────────────────────────────────────────────────┘
```

Figure 6.31   Invoice file with line 10 added.

Next, you print a copy of the Invoice form and design the programming statements. From Add mode, press F2 and F10. Here are some suggestions for designing statements:

- Place a **K** (for key field) in any field that will be used as the basis to look up information from another file.

- In each field that will have a lookup statement in it, place an **L** and the first letter of the file that the data will be looked up from.

- Place a **CS** in all the fields that require a calculation statement.

- Place an **S** in any field that is part of a calculation statement.

- Place an **N** in any field that needs a navigation statement. Figures 6.32 and 6.33 show you an example using the Invoice file.

```
┌──────────────────────── * INVOICE RECORD * ────────────────────────┐
│ ENTERED:  N                                    UPDATED: CS N        │
│ BATCH #:                                       REF ID:              │
├─────────────────────────────────────────────────────────────────────┤
│              BILL TO                              SHIP TO           │
│              ───────                              ───────           │
│                                                                     │
│  ID NUMBER:  K                                                      │
│  COMPANY: LN                                              :         │
│  FIRST: LN          LAST: LN                              :         │
│  ADDRESS: LN                                              :         │
│  CITY: LN               STATE: LN                         :         │
│  ZIP: LN                PH: LN                                      │
├─────────────────────────────────────────────────────────────────────┤
│  REP:          PO#:             INVOICE #:  @number                 │
│                                                                     │
│  DATE:  S      DAYS:  S     SHIP DATE:          DUE DATE:  CS        │
└─────────────────────────────────────────────────────────────────────┘
 INVOICE.DTF                  Retrieve Spec              Page 1  of 4

 Esc-Exit   F1-Help   F6-Expand   F8-Sort   Alt+F8-List  ↑F8-Save   F10-Continue
```

Figure 6.32   Screen 1 of the printed Invoice file used for programming statements.

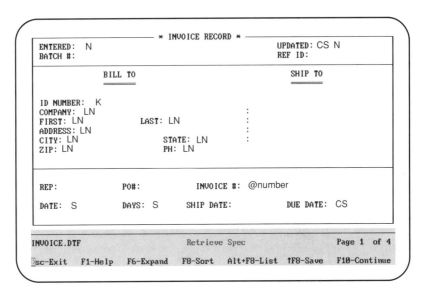

```
    ┌────────┬──────────────────────┬─────┬────────────┬──────────┐
    │ INV #  │  DESCRIPTION         │ QTY │ UNIT PRICE │ EXT. PRICE│
    ├────────┼──────────────────────┼─────┼────────────┼──────────┤
    │ 1 :█████│  A: LI               │ A1: │ A2: LI     │ : CS     │
    │ 2 : K  │  B: LI               │ B1: │ B2: LI     │ : CS     │
    │ 3 : K  │  C: LI               │ C1: │ C2: LI     │ : CS     │
    │ 4 : K  │  D: LI               │ D1: │ D2: LI     │ : CS     │
    │ 5 : K  │  E: LI               │ E1: │ E2: LI     │ : CS     │
    │ 6 : K  │  F: LI               │ F1: │ F2: LI     │ : CS     │
    │ 7 : K  │  G: LI               │ G1: │ G2: LI     │ : CS     │
    │ 8 : K  │  H: LI               │ H1: │ H2: LI     │ : CS     │
    │ 9 : K  │  I: LI               │ I1: │ I2: LI     │ : CS     │
    ├─────────────────────────────────────────────┬──────────────┤
    │   Int Rate:  S    Tax Rate:  S              │ Subtotal : CS │
    │                                             │ Tax      : CS │
    │   Date:        Chk:        Amt:             │ Freight  : S  │
    │   Date:        Chk:        Amt:             │ Credit   : S  │
    │   Date:        Chk:        Amt:             │ Total    : CS │
    │   Date:        Chk:        Amt:             │ Paid     : CS │
    │   Date:        Chk:        Amt:             │ Balance  : CS │
    │   Date:        Chk:        Amt:             │ Interest : CS │
    │   Date:        Chk:        Amt:             │ Bal & Int: CS │
    └─────────────────────────────────────────────┴──────────────┘
 INVOICE.DTF                  Retrieve Spec              Page 2  of 4

 Esc-Exit   F1-Help   F6-Expand   F8-Sort   Alt+F8-List  ↑F8-Save   F10-Continue
```

Figure 6.33   Screen 2 of the printed Invoice file used for programming statements.

Feel free to use whichever method works for you. If you want to number the fields and develop the statements first, do so.

With the programming statements designed, you begin entering them. Since they are all done, you will only be adding one new statement, analyzing the others, and exploring programming concepts.

Practice Entering a Programming Statement

1. Press **F** for File, **D** for Design File, and **P** for Program a File.

2. Type the filename **INVOICE** and press Enter.

3. Press **P** for Program Form. Move to the DUE DATE field. Your screen should look like Figure 6.34. You will notice that many of the fields have programming statements in them.

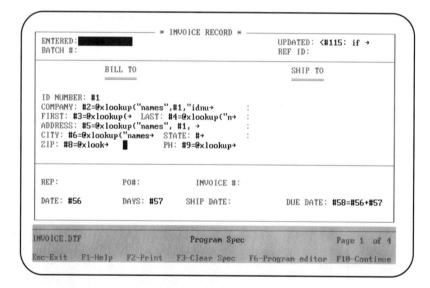

Figure 6.34   Invoice file in Program spec.

Let's analyze the simple programming statement in the DUE DATE field: #58=#56+#57. Field #56 is the DATE field, and field #57 is the DAYS field. This statement adds the DAYS field to the DATE field to obtain the DUE DATE field.

You can add, subtract, multiply, and divide any numeric or money field by another field or another number. Some examples are: #1=#2+50, #1=#2-#3, #1=#2/#3, and #1=#2*10. You can combine fields to make other fields. In the case of a first name (#3) and last name (#2), the combined field would be #1=(#2+", "+#3). This would place the last name first, a comma, and then the first name (Jones, John).

4. Move back up to the UPDATED field. In this field, you will notice that there is a → on the right side of the field. This means that to access the statement you have to open the Program Editor by pressing F6 because the statement is too large to fit into the field.

5. Press F6 to open the Program Editor. The Program Editor is where you type your programming statements. A programming statement can contain a maximum of 32,000 characters of text, with a total of 64,000 characters for all statements in the form.

6. With the Program Editor open, press F8 to open the Options menu. Move through the menu options and look at each of the submenus. Notice in particular the Block Operation and the Document menus. With these options, you can copy a programming statement to a separate file and then insert it into another field. Figure 6.35 shows the opened Program Editor and the Options menu.

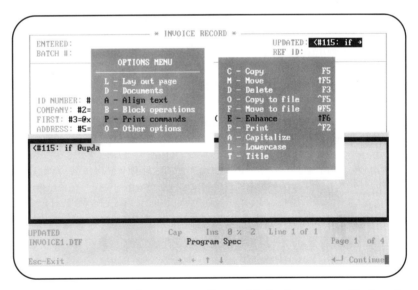

Figure 6.35   Opened Program Editor with Options menu displayed.

7. Press Esc to remove the Options menu and look at the programming statement in the UPDATED field. It reads: `<#115: if @update then #115 = @date`. Translated to English, it says: IF you are in Search/Update mode, THEN place today's date in the UPDATED field. This statement is the reason that the date is placed in this field when it is retrieved.

The preceding programming statement utilizes several programming expressions. The first is the < symbol at the beginning of the field. This tells Q&A to execute the statement when the cursor *enters* the field. If the symbol > had been used, the statement would have executed when you exited the field. If there is no symbol, you must press F8 to execute the statement.

The next element is a conditional statement. It is an called an *IF...THEN statement*. An IF...THEN statement tells Q&A to check whether something is true and, if it is true, to then perform some action. In this case, Q&A checks to see IF you are in Update mode, and if you are, THEN it places the date in this field. The last two items are functions: `@update` and `@date`. The `@update` function is used when you want some action performed only when you are in Search/Update mode. The `@date` command is used to indicate today's date.

The other conditional statement is the *IF...THEN...ELSE statement*. This statement checks to see if something is true, and if it is, it performs one action. If it is false, then it does another action. For instance, you could change the statement in the UPDATED field to an IF...THEN...ELSE statement with `<#115: if @update then #115 = @date else #115=@date-30`. This statement now says: If you are in Update mode, place the current date in this field; if you are not in Update mode, place the date minus 30 days in this field.

You also have the option of having several IF...THEN statements in one field, for example, `#10: IF #8 = "Large Dog" THEN BEGIN; #10="German Shepherd"; #11="Great Dane"; END ELSE BEGIN #10="Cocker Spaniel"; #11="Poodle"; END`. This statement says: IF the value in field #8 is Large Dog, THEN do each of these statements: place German Shepherd in field #10 and Great Dane in field #11. If field #8 is NOT Large Dog, then do these statements: place Cocker Spaniel in field #10 and Poodle in field #11.

You can combine statements by using the AND, OR, and NOT commands. Here are three examples: `#1: if #2="YES" AND #4="YES" then #5="ALWAYS"`, `#1: if #2="YES" OR #4="NO" then #5="MAYBE"`, and `#1: if #2="NO" AND NOT #4="YES" then #5="NEVER"`.

8. Press F10 to close the Program Editor window. Stay in the Program spec. You will be adding more programming statements.

The ON ENTRY and ON EXIT Fields

At times you may want a programming statement to execute as soon as you enter a record. For example, if your database calculates mortgage rates, the ON ENTRY field could automatically read in today's interest rates. Using this same example, you could automatically calculate the mortgage payments as you were saving the record. This would require setting that field to ON EXIT calculation.

To set which field should be the ON ENTRY field or ON EXIT field, press F8 while in the Progam Spec and type the field number in the correct option.

Programming Lookups

This section will explore the different types of lookup statements, focusing on the xlookup statement and the @xlookup function. There are two basic types of lookup statements: *lookup* and *xlookup*. The lookup statement retrieves information from the internal lookup table. Every database has its own lookup table. You can store all types of information in this table, such as tax rates, company codes, county codes, etc. In the lookup table, you place a key value and assign a description to that key value. Then, whenever that key value is typed, the description is placed into the field you designated. For more information on lookups using the internal lookup table, see Chapter 2.

The xlookup statement and the @xlookup function each retrieve information from an external (other) database. Information is retrieved from the external database when you type the key value and Q&A finds an exact match in the external database. Previously, when you added an invoice, you typed the customer's ID number. The xlookup statement went to the Names file, found the ID number, and placed the corresponding name and address information into the BILL TO fields. You also used the same type of lookup when you typed the PNUM (product ID number) to retrieve product descriptions and prices.

To use either the xlookup statement or the @xlookup function, you need at least two fields in your database. One field is the key field, and the other field contains the xlookup statement. The key value must be a speedy field.

When you type either of the xlookup statements, you have to follow a specific syntax. The syntax for the xlookup statement is

```
#1: xlookup ("filename","key","xkf","lf","df")
```

where,

Filename is the name of the external database that contains the data you want to look up.

Key is the key field. This is the value you type to initiate the lookup. Q&A looks in the external database for a match. This is the field that must be a speedy field in both the target and the external database.

XKF is the external key field. This is the field on which Q&A does its match.

LF is the lookup field. The value of this field will be retrieved from the external database and placed in the target database.

DF is the destination field. This is where, in the target database, you want to place the value of the lookup field.

The syntax for the @xlookup function is

```
#1=@xlookup ("filename","key","xkf","lf",)
```

where,

Filename is the name of the external database that contains the data you want to look up.

Key is the key field. This is the value you type to initiate the lookup. Q&A looks in the external database for a match. This field must be a speedy field in both the target and the external database.

XKF is the external key field. This is the field on which Q&A does its match. It must be a speedy field.

LF is the lookup field. The value of this field will be retrieved from the external database and placed in the target database. With this statement, you do not specify a destination field. The lookup field value is placed in the field that contains the programming statement.

The main difference between the xlookup statement and the @xlookup function is that in the xlookup statement you must specify a destination field, and in the @xlookup function the destination field is the field containing the lookup statement. The other difference, which can be significant, is that if the xlookup statement does not find a match for the key value in the external database, it will do nothing to the destination field; it will leave the existing value intact. If the @xlookup function does not find a match, it will blank out the value in the destination field. You have to determine which statement is correct for your particular applications.

Shortcut

If you plan to use a lookup statement while mass-updating some records, use the xlookup statement.

If you wish, you can have one xlookup statement retrieve information from several fields in the external database and place the information in several destination fields in the target database. For example, you could use this statement to replace all the lookup statements in the BILL TO fields. This example is a partial statement, and you would need to add the other name and address fields to make it useful for the purposes of this application.

The syntax for a multifield lookup is

```
#2:xlookup("names",#1,"idnum","org",#2,"first",#3,"last", #4,)
```

You can also use the @xlookup statement in a derived column in a columnar report. This would allow you to look up information from several databases and pull them into one report. Try adding an @xlookup statement to line 10 of the Invoice file.

Adding an @xlookup Statement to the Invoice File

1. While still in the Invoice file, press PgDn to move to the second screen. Move down to the first field in line 10.

2. Type **#56** in the first field, INVOICE #, and press Enter. Type **#57** and press Enter. Type **#58** and press Enter. Type **#59** and press Enter. Type **#60**. Your screen should look like this:

```
10: #56     J: #57           J1: #58   J2: #59      : #60
```

3. Press Shift-Tab to move back to field #57, and press F6 to open the Program Editor.

4. Type this statement in the field:

```
#57=@xlookup ("invent",#56,"pnum","description")
```

5. Press F10 to close the window. Press Enter to move to field #59 and press F6.

6. Type this statement in the field:

```
#59=@xlookup ("invent",#56,"pnum","unit price")
```

7. Press F10 to close the window. Press Enter to move to field #60 and press F6.

8. Type **#60=#58*#59**.

9. Press F10 to close the window. Your screen should like Figure 6.36.

10. Stay in the Program spec.

```
 INV #    DESCRIPTION                     QTY    UNIT PRICE    EXT. PRICE

1 : #11   A: #12=@xlookup("invent",#1→  A1: #13  A2: #14=@xl→  : #15=#13×→
2 : #16   B: #17=@xlookup("invent",#1→  B1: #18  B2: #19=@xl→  : #20=#18×→
3 : #21   C: #22=@xlookup("invent",#2→  C1: #23  C2: #24=@xl→  : #25=#23×→
4 : #26   D: #27=@xlookup("invent",#2→  D1: #28  D2: #29=@xl→  : #30=#28×→
5 : #31   E: #32=@xlookup("invent",#3→  E1: #33  E2: #34=@xl→  : #35=#33×→
6 : #36   F: #37=@xlookup("invent",#3→  F1: #38  F2: #39=@xl→  : #40=#38×→
7 : #41   G: #42=@xlookup("invent",#4→  G1: #43  G2: #44=@xl→  : #45=#43×→
8 : #46   H: #47=@xlookup("invent",#4→  H1: #48  H2: #49=@xl→  : #50=#48×→
9 : #51   I: #52=@xlookup("invent",#5→  I1: #53  I2: #54=@xl→  : #55=#53×→
10: #56   J: #57=@xlookup("invent",#5→  J1: #58  J2: #59=@xl→  : #60=#58×→
    Int Rate: #156    Tax Rate: #147              Subtotal : #146=@sum→
                                                  Tax      : #148=#147→
   Date:         Chk:         Amt: #150           Freight  : #149
   Date:         Chk:         Amt: #151           Credit   : #157
   Date:         Chk:         Amt: #152           Total    : #153=@sum→
   Date:         Chk:         Amt: #300           Paid     : #154=@sum→
   Date:         Chk:         Amt: #301           Balance  : #155=#153→
   Date:         Chk:         Amt: #302           Interest : #159: if →
   Date:         Chk:         Amt: #303           Bal & Int: #160=#155→
Expand field:#146=@sum(#15,#20,#25,#30,#35,#40,#45,#50,#55,#60)
INVOICE1.DTF                    Program Spec                 Page 2  of 4

Esc-Exit  F1-Help  F2-Print  F3-Clear Spec  F6-Program editor  F10-Continue
```

Figure 6.36   Completed Program spec.

Let's summarize what you have done. You have added a statement in field #57 that retrieves the DESCRIPTION and a statement in field #59 that retrieves the UNIT COST from the Invent file. The other statement that you added in field #60 multiplies the QTY by the UNIT COST.

@Functions

Functions are expressions that perform some action on your data. All functions are preceded by the @ symbol and fall into these categories: date, numbering, financial, math, text string, typecasting, context, comparison, numbering, and lookup functions (which have already been covered). Figures 2.24 through 2.27 in Chapter 2 list the various commands for these functions. Here are some of the more common functions:

@date   Lets you use today's date in a programming statement or place the date in a field.

@update   Executes programming statements only when updating data.

> **Note:** Both the @date and @update functions are used in the UPDATED field.

@add   Executes the programming statement only when adding data.

@number   Returns a unique number always 1 greater than the last one.

> **Note:** The @number function is used to automatically generate invoice numbers.

@crg   Calculates the compound growth rate.

@sum   Produces the sum of values in the list.

@msg   Displays a user-defined message at the bottom of the screen.

The preceding functions are just a few of the many available. In the next example, you will modify the @sum function used in the TOTAL field of the Invoice file.

Practice Modifying the @sum Function

1. While still in the Program spec, move to the SUBTOTAL field and press F6.

2. The Program Editor should contain this statement:

   ```
   #146=@sum(#15,#20,#25,#30,#35,#40,#45,#50,#55)
   ```

   Press the End key and the Backspace key to delete the) (right parenthesis). Type **,#60)** and press F10.

3. You have just added field #60 to the list of values to be summed. The statement should now look like this:

   ```
   #146=@sum(#15,#20,#25,#30,#35,#40,#45,#50,#55,#60)
   ```

   Press F10 to save your Program spec.

Navigation Spec

With the *Navigation spec*, you can change the normal movement of the cursor through the fields. For example, you may want to progress to a specific field based on the value in another field, or you may have programming statements that you want automatically calculated as soon as you enter the form. To accomplish these and similar tasks, you create *navigation commands*. These commands can be added to your existing Program spec, or they can be put in a separate Navigation spec.

The Navigation spec is a separate option of the Program menu. It holds nothing but navigation statements that tell the cursor when and where to move. The only reason for placing your navigation programming statements in the Navigation spec is to make the databases compatible with special versions of Q&A, such as Q&A for the Macintosh. If you do not plan to use your databases on different types of Q&A, you can put all your statements in the Program spec. These are the navigation commands available:

Command	Cursor Movement
GOTO n	Move directly to field n, where n is a field identifier.
CNEXT	Move to the next field.
CPREV	Move to the previous field.
CHOME	Move to the first field in the form.
CEND	Move to the last field in the form.
PgDn	Move to the first field on the next page.
PgUp	Move to the first field on the previous page.

Figure 6.37 shows the navigation commands used in the Invoice file. These commands advance the cursor through the first two fields. As the cursor is advancing through the fields, the programming statements are executing because they begin with < symbols.

To add navigation commands to programming statements in the Program spec, place a semicolon (;) at the end of the statement followed by the appropriate navigation command, for example:

```
<#115: if @update then #115 = @date; goto #1
```

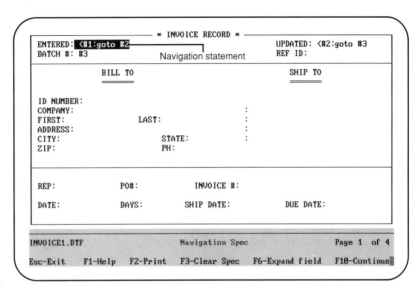

Figure 6.37   Navigation spec in Invoice file.

Debugging

If a programming statement fails to work correctly, you will need to *debug* (fix) it. Q&A doesn't offer any debugging tools, other than a warning when you try to save a spec; it alerts you that the spec isn't in the proper syntax. You can, however, print your Programming and Navigation specs. To assist in the debugging process, you can move quickly from Search mode to Programming mode (see the following steps).

To print the Programming specs for a particular database, you must have that file on-screen and be in the Program Spec mode. Once you are there, press F2 to print, move down to the field that says PRINT EXPANDED FIELDS and answer Yes, and press F10 to print the spec. This works identically for Navigation specs.

Practice Switching from Search Mode to Program Spec Mode

1. Press **F** for File and **S** for Search.

2. Type **INVOICE** and press Enter.

3. Press F10 to bring a record onto the screen.

4. Press Shift-F9 to bring up the special Programming menu. Press **P** for Program. You are now in the Program Spec.

5. To return to Search mode, press F6.

Note that you must have a record on the screen to bring up the special Programming menu. Here is a description of each item on the special Programming menu.

Menu Item	Description
F-Frmt	Format field options.
R-Rstrct	Restrict field options.
I-Initl	Set initial field specification.
M-Masks	Set field masks.
P-Prgrm	Program spec.
L-Lkup	Lookup table.
H-Help	Define custom help.
N-Nav Prog	Navigation spec.

Change the Invoice File

To use the Invoice file, you will have to change screen 4 of the file. You will need to change the field names in Redesign a File and change the initial specifications in Set Initial Specs. You can see what you have to change in Figure 6.38.

The fields on this screen hold values that are used in the printing of the invoice. Every time you add an invoice, these fields are automatically filled in by the Initial Values spec. To make the necessary changes, redesign the file and change these fields to your company name and address. Then select Set Initial Values from the Customize menu and change the values in these fields to your company's information.

Copy Design

The final features that you are going to use in this chapter are Copy Design and Copy Selected Forms. There are three major reasons for copying the design of a database. The first is to fix structural problems with a bad database. Databases can become corrupted in various ways, such as the power being turned off while they are open; the existence of bad tracks on your hard disk; or a surge of electricity into your computer when a file is open. Copying the design can fix some of these problems.

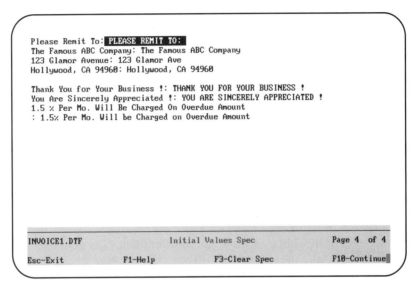

Figure 6.38   Screen 4 of the Invoice file with fields used for address.

The second reason to copy the design and then copy the forms to the new design is to reduce file size. When you delete a record from a database, the record is not actually removed. It is simply marked for deletion. If you delete only a few records, the space taken up by the old records is negligible. However, if you delete hundreds of records, you can reduce the file size considerably by doing the Copy Design/Copy Selected Records procedures.

The last reason why you might copy the design of a database is so that you can create a new database based on the old one. If the old database had many of the fields you needed in the new one, you could copy the design and then modify the new file.

In the next example, you are going to copy the Invoice file to a new design called Service, which will be modified for use in producing service invoices.

Practice Copying the Invoice File to the Service File

1. Press **F** for File and **C** for Copy.

2. Type **INVOICE** and press Enter.

3. Press **D** for Copy Design only, type **SERVICE**, and press Enter. You will receive a message that asks you to wait while Q&A is copying.

Beginner's Tip

If you have set up a file to work with the Query Guide or the Intelligent Assistant, it has had special features added to it. You have the option of copying a design with or without the IA/QG features.

4. Now you will copy the records in the Invoice file to the new Service database file. Press **S** for Copy Selected Records and press Enter to accept the filename SERVICE.

5. You are at the Retrieve Spec screen. In future copying operations, you may not want to copy all the records of a database. You may want to copy only a selected few. For this example, press F10 to copy all the sample records.

6. The Merge Spec is the next screen that appears. Press F10 to skip this screen because the database forms match exactly.

If you ever have to transfer data between two databases having different file structures, you *must* use the Merge spec. With the Merge spec, you tell Q&A which fields you want to copy from the source database (the one on the screen) to the target database (the new design). You do this by placing a number equal to the field number of the target database in the field you want copied in the source database. To determine the field number, count the fields in the database from top to bottom and left to right. See Figure 6.39 for a sample.

Beginner's Tip

To ensure that you do not miss any fields when numbering them for use in a Merge spec, enter a record in the target database that contains the field numbers. That is, start with the first field on the first screen and begin numbering, using the Enter key to move to each field in order.

7. The forms will flash on the screen as they are copying. When they stop, you will have a new database called SERVICE with the same records as the Invoice file.

8. Press Esc twice to return to the Main menu.

Beginner's Tip

Copying records will take varying amounts of time. The main factors that add to copying time are the number of screens in the file and the number of records to copy. Also the speed of your computer is a major factor. As a rule of thumb, it takes approximately one hour of copying time for every 1,000 records with a 10-screen database using a 286 12-MHz computer.

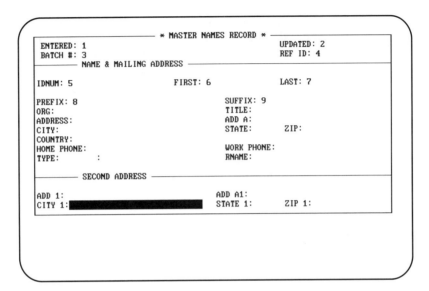

Figure 6.39   Invoice form with field numbers.

If you need a service invoice file, you have the basic format ready to be modified. The main thing you will need to change is the size of the description field so that it can hold large text descriptions. Also, you will want to follow the preceding procedure to make a copy of the Invent file. You can use the copied file to store the descriptions of your services.

Summary

The *Inventory/Invoicing application* can help you automate your entire inventory/invoicing and accounts receivable process. This application relies on three database files: Names, Invent (Inventory), and Invoice. The Names file provides the customer name and address information that is used for the billing address. The Invent file provides product descriptions, prices, and information about your inventory. The Invoice file lets you print invoices, generate receivables lists, enter payments, and analyze sales. The application also includes reports that will help you manage your receivables and inventory.

The Q&A features covered in this chapter are some of the most powerful and complex available in Q&A. One feature that greatly expands the usefulness of Q&A and closes the gap between relational and flat-file databases is the *posting feature*. With this feature, you can create applications that act similarly to relational database application. Another feature that offers a lot of possibility is *programming statements*. By mastering progamming statements, you can transform ordinary applications into dynamic programs.

In the next chapter, you will begin using the Write module. With this tool you will be able to create letters, reports, proposals, and any other documents you need. You will also practice merging data with a form letter to create personalized letters that can be used for direct sales, invitations, stock reports, etc.

Get a Document

1. Press **W** for Write and **G** for Get.
2. Type the filename and press Enter.

Define Page

1. At the document screen, press Ctrl-F6.
2. Make your changes and press F10.

Print a Document

1. At the document screen, press F2.
2. Make your selections and press F10 to print.

Save a Document

1. At the document screen, press Shift-F8.
2. Type the filename and press Enter.

Spell-Check a Document

1. Press the Home key three times.
2. Press Shift-F1 and follow the prompts.

Use the Thesaurus

1. Place your cursor on the word you want to look up and press Alt-F1.
2. Move to the new word and press F10.

Access the Options Menu

1. From anywhere in the document, press F8 and make your selections.

Import/Export a Document

1. Press **W** for Write and **U** for Utilities.
2. Press **I** for Import or **E** for Export. Choose the type of file you are importing or exporting (ASCII, MultiMate, DCA, etc.).
3. Type the filename and press Enter.
4. Type the name of the new file and press Enter.

Print a Merge Letter

1. Press **W** for Write and **G** for Get.
2. Type the filename and press Enter.
3. Press F2 to advance to the Print Options screen and make your selections.
4. Press F10 to advance to the Retrieve Spec screen and type your spec.
5. Press F8 to switch to the Sort Spec screen and type your Sort spec.
6. Press F10 twice to print the letters.

Print Mailing Labels

1. Press **W** for Write and **M** for Mailing Labels.
2. Choose the label format and press Enter.
3. Press F2 to advance to the Print Options screen and make your selections.
4. Press F10 to advance to the Retrieve Spec screen and type your spec.
5. Press F8 to switch to the Sort Spec screen and type your Sort spec.
6. Press F10 twice to print the labels.

IN
BUSINESS

Direct Mail Application

The purpose of this chapter is to teach you how to use the Write module while you develop the components needed to do direct mail. The components needed for direct mail include a merge letter, label definition, and a macro.

Overview

This chapter does not have a design section because all the features are accessed from the Write module. Thus, after the "Application Explained" section, you will begin exploring how the application works and many of the Write module's features.

Mailing information to prospects, customers, and associates is one of the most frequent tasks an organization performs and one that should be completely automated. In this chapter, you will learn how to create regular letters and then transform them into merge letters. You will also be guided through the process of developing mailing labels and creating a macro to automate the printing of letters and labels.

The word processor in Q&A is called the *Write module* and is considered an excellent "executive" word processor. It does not have all the features of some high-end word processors, but it does have most of the features you'll probably need. It contains a full set of page formatting features, fonts, spelling checker, thesaurus, import/export capabilities, search and replace, and of course mail merge. There are also a host of lesser features that make generating documents quite easy.

Q&A's mail merge feature is perhaps the best that is available in any word processor. This is because Q&A's word processor and database are seamlessly linked, and the programmers did an excellent job of implementing this feature, making it powerful and easy to use.

Mailing labels are also easy to produce. Q&A has set up and defined many of the most popular Avery label formats. All you have to do is link a label format to a database, select which fields you want on the label, and print the labels.

The word processing features are divided between this chapter and Chapter 8. In this chapter, you will learn how to set margins and tabs; develop and print labels; develop and print a merge letter; print a single letter and envelope; use the spell checker and thesaurus; import and export a document to another word processor; enhance the document with fonts, boldfacing, and underlining; use programming expressions; and, lastly, develop a macro to print the letters and labels for you.

Application Explained

The Direct Mail application has four basic components: the merge letter, the label, a database, and a macro. The merge letter and label each extract their information from a database based on the Retrieve spec you specify. Figure 7.1 shows the relationship of the merge letter and label to the database. To illustrate the merge examples, I will be using the Names database. However, these principles apply to any Q&A database.

The Merge Letter

The *merge letter* is created in the same manner as any other word processing document. The only difference is that you place merge codes in the document. These merge codes correspond to fields in the database and can be seen in the merge letter in Figure 7.2. The asterisk (*) on either side of a word signifies a merge code. The text between the asterisks must be a valid field name within the specified database. If it is not, Q&A will alert you.

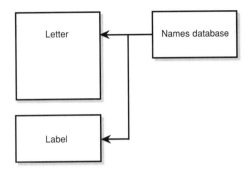

Figure 7.1   Overview of merge feature.

```
      *@DATE(n)*


      *FIRST*  *LAST*
      *TITLE*
      *ORG*
      *ADDRESS*
      *ADD A*
      *CITY*, *STATE* *ZIP*

      Dear *FIRST*:

      This is a sample letter used to illustrate the mail merge
      feature. It makes sending one or one hundred letters very
      easy.


      Sincerely,

      Wrangler Bob
      President
|||||||||1||s||T|||||2|||||T|||3|||||T|||4|||||T||||5|||||||||||6|||||||||17|||||||||
DIRECT.LET                          Ins  0 %  1   Line 18 of Page 1 of 1

Esc-Exit  F1-Help  F2-Print  Shift+F7-Restore   F7-Search  F8-Options  ↑F8-Save
```

Figure 7.2   Sample merge letter.

Fields in Sample Merge Letter

`*@DATE(n)*`	A print command that automatically inserts the date into your document. The (n) is used to specify the format of the date.
`*FIRST*`	The first name field.
`*LAST*`	The last name field.
`*TITLE*`	The title field.

`*ORG*`	The company name field.
`*ADDRESS*`	The first address field.
`*ADD A*`	The second address field.
`*CITY*`	The city field.
`*STATE*`	The state field.
`*ZIP*`	The zip code field.
`*FIRST*`	You can place a field in your document more than once. This is the first name field again.

The Label Definition

Q&A has already set up mailing labels for many of the most popular formats. Since Q&A's label file cannot be shipped, this label will not be on your system. In a later example, you will create this label. Figure 7.3 shows the fields in the sample label.

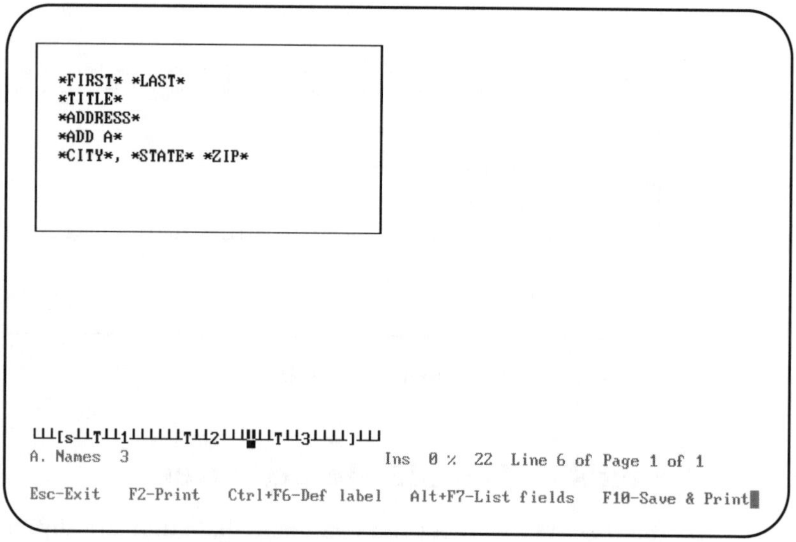

Figure 7.3   Label definition.

Fields in Sample Label

FIRST	The first name field.
LAST	The last name field.
TITLE	The title field.
ORG	The company name field.
ADDRESS	The first address field.
ADD A	The second address field.
CITY	The city field.
STATE	The state field.
ZIP	The zip code field.

Using the Application

When you are using the Write module, you can access some of its features through the Write menu. Within the document, you can access these same features (and many more) by using the Options menu or the function keys, such as Ctrl-F8. Keep in mind that some of the features can be accessed only through one of these modes. As you use the Write module regularly, you will develop your own preferences for accessing the various features. In the examples, I have accessed them in the manner most effective and efficient.

The remaining sections will explore the various features of the Write module, using sample letters to illustrate the examples. The first sample letter, covered in this section, is a regular letter. The second one, the merge letter, will be used for the remaining examples. After you have used many of the features, you will create and print a merge letter and labels.

Suggested Uses

You can use the Write module to create memos, reports, letters, proposals, or any type of written correspondence. *Boilerplate*, or standardized, forms can be set up for any of these documents so that you can quickly create them and maintain a consistent style. The *mail merge feature*, merging letters with names in your database, can be used to generate collection letters, thank you letters, invitations, sales letters, and more.

The Write Menu and the Simple Letter

Here, you will develop and print a simple letter and envelope by using the Write menu for each task. Start by looking at the Write menu, shown in Figure 7.4. The Define Page option is where you set up margins, page length, characters per inch, and the page where headers and page numbering should begin. Selecting the Type/Edit option takes you to a blank document screen, where you can begin composing a document.

After the document is composed, you can use the Print command to print it. This command works only with documents that are currently on the screen. Once the document is printed, you can save it by using the Save selection. Then you can clear the screen by using the Clear option. With the Get command, you can retrieve another document from your directory.

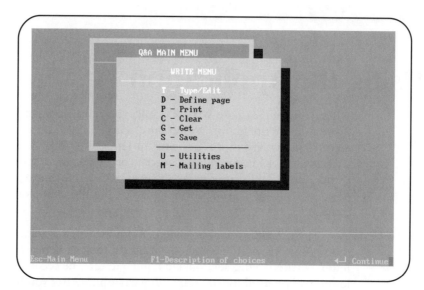

Figure 7.4 Write menu.

The Utilities menu, shown in Figure 7.5, allows you to change the global defaults, import or export a document from another word processor, fix a damaged file, and use several DOS features. The final selection of the Write menu, Mailing Labels, is where you define and print labels.

In the next example, you are going to get an existing letter, add a line, change the right margin, print it, print the envelope, save the letter, and clear the screen. All these features are accessed from the Write menu.

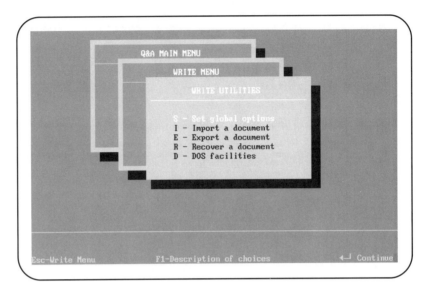

Figure 7.5 Write Utilities menu.

Practice Retrieving and Printing a Single Letter

1. Press **W** for Write and **G** for Get.

2. Press F4 twice to clear any existing file and press Enter to list the files in the directory. Use your cursor to move down to SINGLE.LET and press Enter.

3. You now have the document on the screen. Use the Down Arrow to move below the only paragraph and type the line **Please send the designs by overnight mail**. Your letter should look like the one in Figure 7.6.

4. Press Esc to return to the Write menu. Press **D** for Define Page. Move to the Right Margin setting, type **58**, and press Esc.

5. Press **P** for Print Options and press F10 to print the letter.

6. Load an envelope into your printer and press **P** again. This time move to the Line Spacing option and select Envelope. Press F10 to print the envelope. Q&A will take the inside address from your letter and print an envelope.

```
      ┌─────────────────────────────────────────────────────────────┐
      │   May 12, 1991                                               │
      │                                                             │
      │                                                             │
      │   Mary Miller                                               │
      │   Creative Director                                         │
      │   Totally Alive Fashions                                    │
      │   4523 Fifth Avenue                                         │
      │   New York, NY  12934                                       │
      │                                                             │
      │   Dear Mary:                                                │
      │                                                             │
      │   Just a brief reminder to let you know we need your winter │
      │   designs by June 15th to make the August deadline. Please  │
      │   send the designs by overnight mail.                       │
      │                                                             │
      │                                                             │
      │   Sincerely,                                                │
      │                                                             │
      │   Willy Wonka                                               │
      │   Production Manager                                        │
      └─────────────────────────────────────────────────────────────┘
   SINGLE.LET                          Ins  0 %  37  Line 15 of Page 1 of 1

   Esc-Exit  F1-Help  F2-Print  Shift+F7-Restore   F7-Search  F8-Options  ↑F8-Save
```

Figure 7.6   Single letter.

7. Press **S** for Save and then press Enter to save the changes you made to the letter.

8. Now clear the screen and return to the Write menu by pressing **C** for Clear and pressing Esc. You have just finished a basic letter-writing cycle using the Write menu. All of these operations can be performed using the Options menu or function keys.

Set Global Options

Before you begin editing the merge letter, try changing some of the Global Options. These options are shown in Figure 7.7. The changes you make will become the new default settings and will remain in force until you change them again. In this example, you will change the first option—the Editing options.

Although you will be working with the first option only, you should be aware of the three other options. The Print Defaults option controls the Print Options screen. Here you can select another printer as the primary printer, set Page Preview to on, and change many other functions. The Page Defaults option defines the margins, characters per inch, page width, and other selections. The final option, Import Defaults, regulates how a document other than a Write document is retrieved.

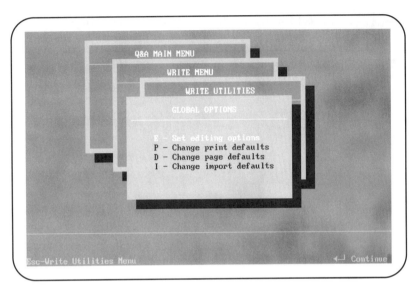

Figure 7.7   Global Options menu.

Changing the Editing Options

1. Press **W** for Write, **U** for Utilities, **S** for Set Global, and **E** for Set Editing Options. You can see these options in Figure 7.8.

2. Change the first option to Insert and make any other changes you want.

3. When you are through, press F10 to save the changes and press Esc three times to return to the Main menu.

Options Menu

Many of the commands you will be using are accessed through the Options menu, which is invoked by pressing F8. Recall that you can also perform most of these commands by using the function keys. But if you are new to the Write module, you will probably want to start by using the Options menu. In the following example, you will simply call up the Options menu and look at each of its submenus.

Shortcut | Press F1 to learn what each function key controls.

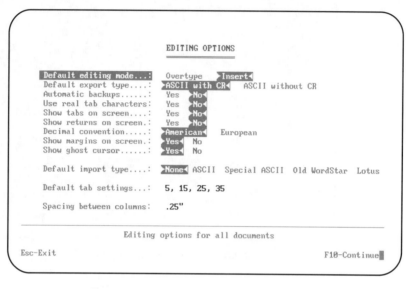

Figure 7.8   Editing Options.

Accessing the Options Menu and Submenus

1. Press **W** for Write and **T** for Type/Edit.

2. You are at a blank document screen. Press F8 to invoke the Options menu shown in Figure 7.9. Notice that the Lay Out Page submenu also appears. As you move your cursor down the Options menu or press the first letter of the selection, the submenu appears. Go through each menu selection and look at each option.

3. When you are through looking at the menu, press Esc. Throughout this chapter and the next one, you will go through most of these options.

Retrieve and Insert a Document

You are now ready to explore the various features of the Write menu by using a merge letter. Start by using the Options menu to retrieve the merge letter.

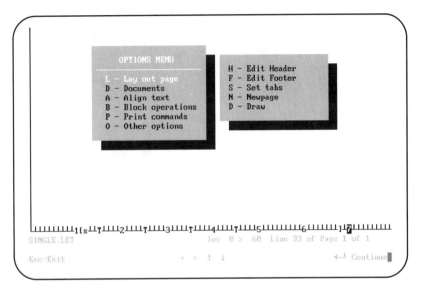

Figure 7.9   Options menu and Lay Out Page submenu.

Practice Retrieving a Merge Letter with the Options Menu

1. You should still be at the blank document screen. Press F8 to invoke the Options menu. Press **D** for Document and **G** for Get.

2. Type the filename **DIRECT.LET** and press Enter.

3. Notice in Figure 7.10 that the Document menu holds the last twelve documents you have edited. Select one of these documents by pressing the corresponding number or letter. Your screen should look like Figure 7.2 at the beginning of the chapter.

Beginner's
Tip

If you delete a letter from your subdirectory, it will still appear on this list of documents, even though it is gone.

The last two options on the Document submenu allow you to retrieve documents other than these twelve. The Get a document option works the same way as it does from the Write menu. It lets you retrieve a document from any subdirectory. If you use this option and you have a document on-screen, the document will be replaced as long as it has been saved first. The Insert a document option lets you insert a document into an existing document without displacing the current one. You are going to use the Insert command to insert a paragraph containing a programming expression (which will be covered later in the chapter) into the letter.

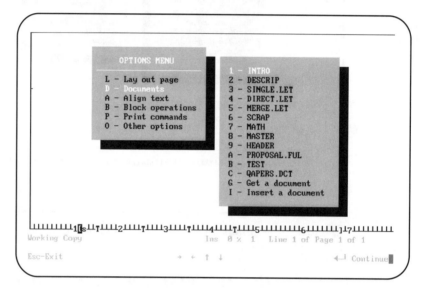

Figure 7.10   Document submenu.

Practice Using the Insert a Document Option

1. Move your cursor underneath the last sentence in the paragraph and press Enter to make space between the paragraph and the signature block.

2. Press F8 to invoke the Options menu. Press **D** for Documents and **I** for Insert a document.

3. Type the filename **INSERT** and press Enter. Your screen should look like Figure 7.11.

Define and Lay Out Page Options

The Define Page and Lay Out Page options are usually set when you initially open a document. You'll begin by setting the Define Page options, shown in Figure 7.12.

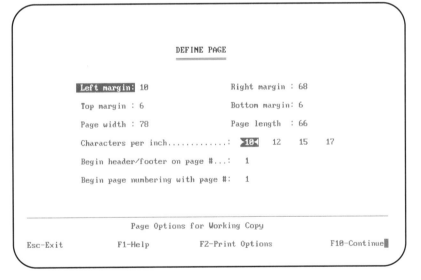

```
      Dear *FIRST*:

      This is a sample letter used to illustrate the mail merge
      feature. It makes sending one or one hundred letters very
      easy.

      A new feature that was added in version 4.0 is called
      Programming Expressions. This feature allows you to use
      programming statements in your document. One of them lets
      you look up data from several databases such as the Annual
      4 field in the Staff file that has the value *program
      {@xlookup ("staff", #1, "idnum", "annual 4")}* in it.


      Sincerely,


      Wrangler Bob
      President

└┴┴┴┴┴┴┴┴┴1┃s┴┴T┴┴┴2┴┴┴┴T┴┴┴┴3┴┴┴T┴┴┴┴4┴┴┴┴T┴┴┴5┴┴┴┴┴┴┴┴6┴┴┴┴┴┴┴┴7┴┴┴┴┴┴┴┴
DIRECT.LET                        Ins  0 %  1   Line 30 of Page 1 of 1

Esc-Exit  F1-Help  F2-Print  Shift+F7-Restore   F7-Search  F8-Options  ↑F8-Save
```

Figure 7.11   Merge letter after document insert.

```
                              DEFINE PAGE
                              ═══════════


             Left margin: 10              Right margin : 68

             Top margin : 6               Bottom margin: 6

             Page width : 78              Page length  : 66

             Characters per inch.............:   ►10◄   12   15   17

             Begin header/footer on page #...:   1

             Begin page numbering with page #:   1


─────────────────────────────────────────────────────────────────────────
                    Page Options for Working Copy

 Esc-Exit            F1-Help        F2-Print Options         F10-Continue
```

Figure 7.12   Define Page options.

Practice Setting the Define Page Options

1. Press Ctrl-F6 to bring up the Define Page options. As you can see, the default margins are left 10, right 68, top 6, and bottom 6. The page length is 66.

2. To alter any of these settings, move to the appropriate field and type your new settings. The characters per inch (CPI) setting determines the size of your print—how many characters will print within each inch. Ten CPI is the default setting for most printers and typewriters. The 16 CPI setting is the smallest print and is known as *condensed* or *line printer mode* on a laser jet. You can print these different settings only if your printer supports them.

Very few printers support the 15 CPI setting, but most support all the others.

Q&A's page numbering and header/footer features are not flexible. Your only choice is whether or not to use them and on which page they will start. You cannot have different headers and footers in the same document or start and stop them on various pages. The same holds true for page numbering.

The Lay Out Page options are accessed through the Options menu. Figure 7.9, shown earlier, displays the Lay Out Page submenu on the right. With this menu you can define headers and footers, set tabs, establish a new page, and draw lines around your text. In the next example, you will do all of these except draw lines.

Practice Using the Lay Out Page Option

1. Press F8, press Enter, and press **H** for Edit Header. Notice that the header says `Direct Mail Merge Letter: Header`. To change it, simply delete it and type a new one. When you are through, press F10.

2. Press F8 again, press Enter, and press **F** for Edit Footer. Notice that the footer says `Direct Mail Merge Letter: Footer`. To change it, simply delete it and type a new one. When you are through, press F10.

3. The default tab settings are set every five spaces. To change them, press F8, press Enter, and press **S** for Set Tabs. Your cursor is now at the bottom ruler line and is slightly larger. Move to the location

where you want to place a tab marker and type **T**. To delete a tab setting, press the Del key while on the T. When you are through setting tabs, press F10.

The last feature you are going to explore in this section is the New Page option.

Practice Using the New Page Option

1. To force a new page, place your cursor where you want the new page to begin. Press F8, press Enter, and press **N** for New Page.

2. Notice that a small code appears on the right side of your screen indicating the new page. To remove the new page that you inserted in step 1, simply remove the code.

Adding, Deleting, Restoring, and Moving Around the Text

The essence of word processing is typing. However, once a document is created, you need to be able to move around the document, delete text, and restore text. Take some time now to practice moving around the document.

Practice Moving Around the Document

1. With the merge letter still on the screen, press End three times to move to the end of the document. Press Enter four times to make some room at the end of the document. Type three lines of text. You will notice as you reach the end of line 1 that the text automatically wraps to the next line.

2. Once you have finished typing, practice moving around the document. Some of the more common ways are to move one word at a time right or left by using Ctrl-Right Arrow and Ctrl-Left Arrow. To move to the end of a line, press End, and to move to the beginning of the line, press Home. Press F9 to scroll a document up the screen one line at a time, and press Shift-F9 to scroll back down again one line at a time. Figure 7.13 displays the basic cursor movement keys.

```
┌─────────────────────────────────────────────────────────────────┐
│                  HOW TO MOVE AROUND THE DOCUMENT                  │
├──────────────────────┬──────────────────────┬────────────────────┤
│ ↑  Up one line        │ PgUp    Previous screen │ Ctrl PgUp  Previous page │
│ ↓  Down one line      │ PgDn    Next screen     │ Ctrl PgDn  Next page     │
│ ←  Left one column    │ Ctrl ←  Previous word   │ Ctrl Home  Top of doc    │
│ →  Right one column   │ Ctrl →  Next word       │ Ctrl End   Bottom of doc │
├──────────────────────┴──────────┬───────────────────────────────┤
│ Home(1)   Beginning of line      │ End(1)    End of line          │
│ Home(2)   Top of screen          │ End(2)    Bottom of screen     │
│ Home(3)   Top of page            │ End(3)    Bottom of page       │
│ Home(4)   Top of document        │ End(4)    Bottom of document   │
└──────────────────────────────────┴───────────────────────────────┘
```

Figure 7.13   Basic cursor movement keys.

Shortcut

Q&A supports many of the WordStar editing and cursor movement keys: combinations of the Ctrl key with the *A, S, D, F, E, X, T,* and *Y* keys.

Besides knowing how to move around a document, you need to know how to delete and restore text. You can practice these techniques on the text you just added in the preceding exercise.

Practice Deleting and Restoring Text

1. With the merge letter on the screen, delete one word to the right by placing your cursor just before the word and pressing F4. To delete to the end of the line, press Ctrl-F4, and to delete the entire line, press Shift-F4.

2. Restore the last text you deleted by pressing Shift-F7. When you are through, delete all the text.

> ▶ **Note:** When you are through with these examples, DO NOT SAVE the merge letter. Press Esc and answer Yes to continue without saving your changes.

Enhancing a Document

Q&A now has a separate Enhancement menu, shown in Figure 7.14, that contains Bold, Underline, Superscript, Subscript, Italics, Strikeout, and Fonts options. All of these features work within the body of the text and with the headers and footers.

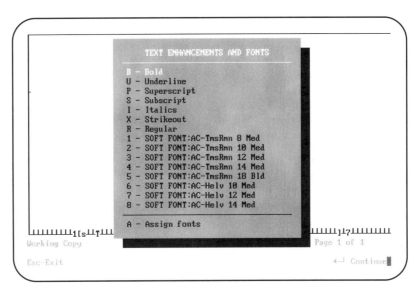

Figure 7.14   Enhancement menu.

To assign any of these enhancements, move to the beginning of the text and press Shift-F6 to invoke the Enhancement menu. Choose an enhancement. Use your cursor to highlight the desired text and press F10. This text will appear enhanced. If you move your cursor to the first paragraph of the merge letter and then move through the lines of text, you will notice that several enhancement codes appear at the bottom of your screen. Depending on your monitor, the codes should also appear enhanced on-screen. In the first half of the first sentence, the Bold code appears, indicating that the first half of the sentence is boldfaced. Then the Bold Ital code appears, indicating that the text is boldfaced and in italics. Lastly, the Undl code appears, indicating that the text is underlined.

Assigning Fonts

Before you can use fonts in your document, you must perform these steps: set up the correct font file in the printer setup; download soft fonts (if you are using them); and place the fonts on the Enhancement menu. Q&A will allow you to place up to eight fonts in any one document. A *font* is a particular typeface. Some of the more popular fonts are Courier, Times Roman, and Helvetica.

If you have a dot matrix printer, you are limited to the fonts that are supplied with your printer. If you have a laser printer, you can use either cartridge fonts or soft fonts. *Cartridge fonts* are contained in separate cartridges and are physically inserted into your printer. They are sold separately by either the manufacturer or a third party vendor. Each cartridge contains a certain number of fonts, which can be placed on the Enhancement menu.

Soft fonts are contained in files that reside on your hard drive and are sold by the printer manufacturers and third party vendors. The big difference between cartridge fonts and soft fonts is that you must download your soft fonts to the printer before they are available. *Downloading* is the process of copying the fonts from your hard drive to the printer's memory. Once they are in memory, they reside there until you turn off the printer. This makes downloading a daily process. The vendors of the soft fonts provide a method of downloading their fonts; Q&A does not provide one.

The most common laser printer and soft font combination is made by Hewlett-Packard. The only HP printers that support soft fonts are the LaserJet Plus, Series II, and Series III. These printers contain memory that the older models do not. The next example—how to load soft fonts—is based on using a LaserJet Plus printer and the HP soft fonts Times Roman and Helvetica.

Beginner's
Tip

If you do not have a LaserJet Plus printer and the HP soft fonts Times Roman and Helvetica, you will have to check with Symantec to see if your printer and soft fonts are supported.

Loading Soft Fonts

1. Provided you have a supported printer and soft font combination, download your fonts by using the vendor's downloading program.

2. Once that is done, change the font file in the printer configuration option. This needs to be done only once, whereas the downloading procedure has to be done each time you turn the printer on. To change the printer font file, press **U** for Utilities and **P** for Printer. Select the desired printer and press Enter four times. Press F8 and change the font filename at the bottom of the screen to the correct one. Figure 7.15 shows the Special Printer Options screen that you have to modify.

```
                    SPECIAL PRINTER OPTIONS


   Use this screen if you have problems with your printer or want to
   change your default font file.

      ┌──────────────────────────────────────┐
      │ Check for printer timeout?.......:    │  ►Yes◄  No

        Length of timeout (in seconds)..:     15

        Check for printer ready signal?.:      Yes   ►No◄

        Check for paper out?............:      Yes   ►No◄

        Formfeed at end of document?....:      Yes   ►No◄

        Font file name..................:     HPLJSOFT.FNT ─────────── Font



   Esc-Exit                 F9-Reselect printer            F10-Continue█
```

Figure 7.15   Special Printer Options.

3. With the correct font file chosen, you are ready to place the fonts
   on the Enhancement menu. To do this, press **W** for Write and **T** for
   Type/Edit. Press Shift-F6 to bring up the Enhancement menu. Press
   A for Assign fonts. You will be at the Font Assignments screen.
   Select the correct font file by pressing F6. Press Enter. In this
   example, it is HPLJSOFT.FNT. Move down to the Regular font and
   press F6. This is the font that your documents will always print in.
   Highlight the font and press Enter. Repeat this process for the
   other eight fonts. Figure 7.16 shows you a completed Font Assignments screen. When you are through, press F8 to make these fonts
   the default fonts for all documents. Press F10 when you are
   through.

Pressing F8 will make these fonts appear in the report Enhancement menu.

   Any of these fonts can be easily assigned to text by moving to the
beginning of the text and pressing Shift-F6 to invoke the Enhancement
menu. Choose the font, highlight the desired text, and press F10. The text
should appear enhanced on your screen. To find out which font you
assigned, move your cursor onto the text in question and a font code will
appear at the bottom of your screen.

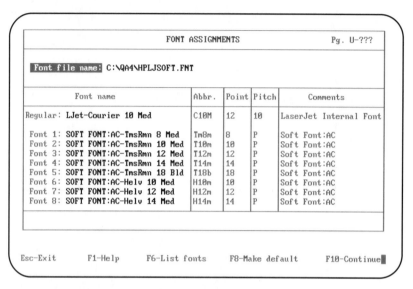

```
                        FONT ASSIGNMENTS                    Pg. U-???

    Font file name: C:\QA4\HPLJSOFT.FNT

    Font name                    Abbr. Point Pitch      Comments

Regular: LJet-Courier 10 Med     C10M   12    10    LaserJet Internal Font

Font 1: SOFT FONT:AC-TmsRmn 8 Med   Tm8m   8    P     Soft Font:AC
Font 2: SOFT FONT:AC-TmsRmn 10 Med  T10m  10    P     Soft Font:AC
Font 3: SOFT FONT:AC-TmsRmn 12 Med  T12m  12    P     Soft Font:AC
Font 4: SOFT FONT:AC-TmsRmn 14 Med  T14m  14    P     Soft Font:AC
Font 5: SOFT FONT:AC-TmsRmn 18 Bld  T18b  18    P     Soft Font:AC
Font 6: SOFT FONT:AC-Helv 10 Med    H10m  10    P     Soft Font:AC
Font 7: SOFT FONT:AC-Helv 12 Med    H12m  12    P     Soft Font:AC
Font 8: SOFT FONT:AC-Helv 14 Med    H14m  14    P     Soft Font:AC



Esc-Exit      F1-Help      F6-List fonts     F8-Make default      F10-Continue
```

Figure 7.16   Completed Font Assignments screen.

Developing a Merge Letter

The heart of the Direct Mail application is the merge letter. Any standard letter can become a merge letter. All you need to do is link a database to it, place the proper merge codes in the body of the text, select the records you want to mail to, and print the letter.

Shortcut

While you are going through the next example, keep in mind that you can merge data with any type of document.

There are two components to any mail merge operation: the database and the document with merge codes. You have to develop the database first. Once it is done, you can write the letter and insert the merge codes. For this example, use the database Names and the merge letter Direct.let.

Developing a Merge Letter

1. Press **W** for Write and **G** for Get. Type the filename **DIRECT.LET** and press Enter. Press Home three times to go to the top of the document.

2. When you create a merge document from scratch, the first thing you have to do is link a database to it. This is done by pressing

Alt-F7 and typing the database name (in this example it has already been done for you). Then you type the letter.

Looking at the merge document, you will notice that each field has an asterisk (*) before and after it. This is how Q&A knows that these are merge codes. To insert a database field into your document, you can type the field name enclosed in asterisks or you can select it from a list of fields in the database.

3. To select a field, position your cursor in the document where you want the field to appear. Press Alt-F7 to bring up a list of fields in the database. Your screen should look like Figure 7.17. Type the first character of the field you want; Q&A will take you to that field. If more than one field starts with that letter, Q&A takes you to the first occurrence. Then use your cursor to move to the correct field and press Enter. Repeat this process until you are through.

Shortcut

You can position any field anywhere in a document. For instance, to write a dunning letter, you could use the Invoice file as the database and place the amount owed on the invoice in the body of the text.

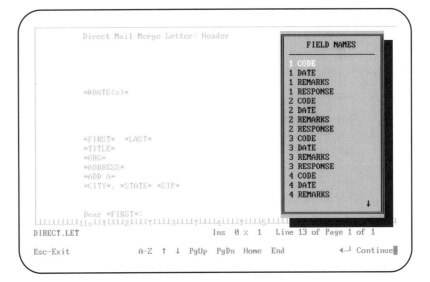

Figure 7.17   Merge letter with database field names.

4. When you are finished adding fields to the letter, it is a good idea to save the letter by pressing Shift-F8 and giving it a name (or accepting the existing name) and pressing Enter.

5. Press F2 to advance to the Print Options screen shown in Figure 7.18. Before you print the letters, read the following explanation of the fields in the Print Options.

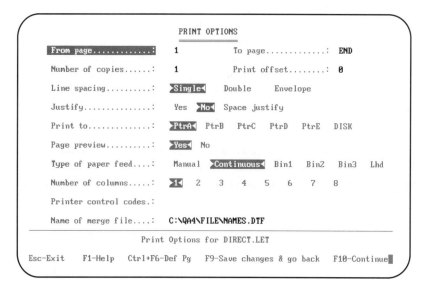

Figure 7.18   Print Options screen.

At the top of the screen are fields to control which pages of the document you want to print. For example, to print from page 3 to page 7, you would type these values in the top fields. You can also indicate how many copies of this document you want printed. The next two fields let you change the line spacing or the way the text is justified. You also have the option of printing to any of your defined printers or to a disk file in IBM or Macintosh ASCII.

A new and very useful feature is Page Preview, which allows you to view your document exactly as it will print. When you are at the Page Preview screen, you can zoom in and out on the document. Press F2 to return to the Print Options screen and print the document. The next option lets you control how the paper is fed. If you have a laser printer, you can even print to a different bin. This is useful when you have letterhead in one bin and second sheets in another.

To format your text into columns, you can select the number in the Number of columns field. This will wrap the text through each column. The next field allows you to type special printer control codes, though you will probably never use this field. The last field indicates the name of the database to which this document is linked. You can change the link by simply typing another database name. If you are printing a regular document, this field will be blank.

6. Set Page Preview to No and press F10 to advance to the Retrieve spec.

7. The Retrieve spec operates here exactly as it does throughout the program. You will send letters to all four people in the database. Press F8 to switch to the Sort spec. Move to the LAST field and type **1 AS**. This will sort the letters by last name in alphabetical order. Press F10 to save the Sort and Retrieve specs.

8. Make sure your printer is on and press F10 to begin printing four personalized letters.

9. Once the printing is finished, you will be returned to the document. If you haven't saved the document, you can do so by pressing Shift-F8. You can leave the document screen by pressing Esc.

Programming Expressions

At times, the action you want to perform can be accomplished only by using programming expressions. For example, you may want to merge data from more than one database into one document, or you may want to sum a range of values in a database and place the total in the document. In the next exercise, you will add to the merge letter a programming expression that looks up the salary from the Staff file.

Practice Adding a Programming Expression

1. Press **W** for Write and **T** for Type/Edit. Press F8 for the Options menu and press **D** for Documents. You should see the file DIRECT.LET listed on the menu. If it isn't, press **G** for Get and type **DIRECT.LET**.

2. Move below the second paragraph and insert some space. Press F8, press **D** for Document, and press **I** for Insert. Type the filename **INSERT** and press Enter.

In the paragraph you just inserted, the programming expression will place a salary in the body of the text. The programming expression reads:

```
*program{@xlookup ("staff", #1, "idnum", "annual 4")}*
```

All programming expressions must start with `*program{` and must end with `}`. The text between the `{` and `}` must be a valid programming expression. This example used the `@xlookup` statement.

3. Press F2 to advance to the Print Options screen. Press F10 to accept the options.

4. At the Retrieve Spec screen, move to the IDNUM field and type the number **1** and press F10 twice. You should have a letter that includes a salary of $90,000.

5. Leave the document on the screen for the next example.

Spell Checker and Thesaurus

Q&A offers two tools to improve the quality of your writing. The first is the spell checker, and the other is the thesaurus. The *spell checker* is used to correct misspellings and typographical errors. The *thesaurus* is used to provide alternate word choices.

Starting the Spell Checker

1. To use the spell checker after you are done writing a document, press the Home key three times to move to the top of the document. You should start at the top of the document because the spell checker begins checking words from the spot where your cursor is located in the document.

2. There are two ways to access the spell checker. You can invoke the Options menu by pressing F8 and then pressing **O** for Other and **S** for Spell check (this submenu can be seen in Figure 7.19), or you can press Shift-F1.

Once you have begun the spell check, each word in your document is compared to the internal dictionary. If the spell checker finds a word in the document that is not in the dictionary, it presents a list of choices, which are shown in Figure 7.20. However, even though the spell checker doesn't find the word in the dictionary, the word isn't necessarily misspelled. The dictionary won't contain technical terms, many proper names, locations, and the plurals of many words.

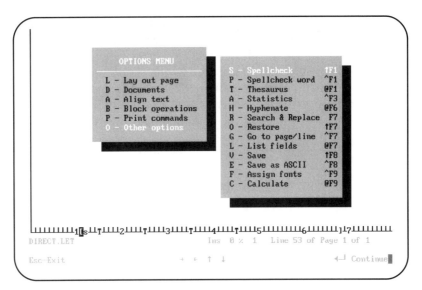

Figure 7.19   Other Options submenu.

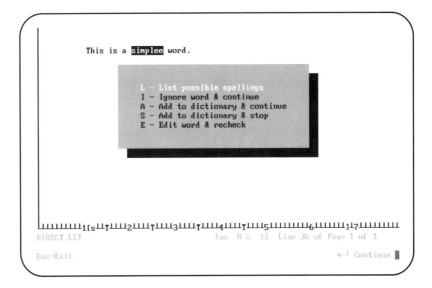

Figure 7.20   Spell check options.

The first choice on the menu is to list the possible correct spellings of the word. To invoke this option, press **L** for List Possible Spellings. You will get a list like that in Figure 7.21. If you know that the word is spelled correctly, press **I** to Ignore the Word and Continue. The next option allows you to add a correctly spelled word to the Personal Dictionary, which is contained in the file QAPERS.DCT. This file can be edited in Write. Thus, if you want to add a number of words at once, you can do so. To invoke this option, press **A** for Add Word to Dictionary and Continue. You can also add a word to the dictionary and stop the spell check by pressing **S**. The final option lets you edit the word manually by pressing **E**.

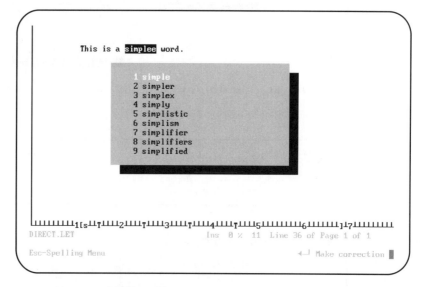

Figure 7.21   List of possible words.

If a word doesn't properly express your thoughts, you can use the thesaurus to replace it with a better one.

Starting the Thesaurus

1. Move to the word in question and press Alt-F1.

2. If the word is in the thesaurus, Q&A will give you a list of options similar to those shown in Figure 7.22. Once this list appears, move your cursor to one of the words and press F10 to replace the word. To look up one of the words in the list, press Alt-F1.

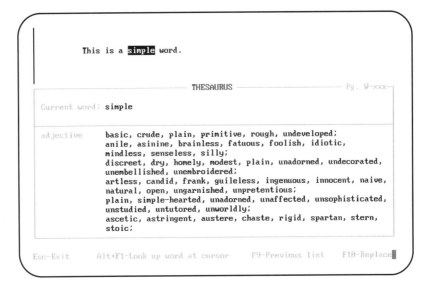

This is a **simple** word.

```
┌──────────────────── THESAURUS ────────────────── Pg. W-xxx─┐
│                                                            │
│ Current word: simple                                       │
│                                                            │
│ adjective    basic, crude, plain, primitive, rough, undeveloped;│
│              anile, asinine, brainless, fatuous, foolish, idiotic,│
│              mindless, senseless, silly;                   │
│              discreet, dry, homely, modest, plain, unadorned, undecorated,│
│              unembellished, unembroidered;                 │
│              artless, candid, frank, guileless, ingenuous, innocent, naive,│
│              natural, open, ungarnished, unpretentious;    │
│              plain, simple-hearted, unadorned, unaffected, unsophisticated,│
│              unstudied, untutored, unworldly;              │
│              ascetic, astringent, austere, chaste, rigid, spartan, stern,│
│              stoic;                                        │
└────────────────────────────────────────────────────────────┘
Esc─Exit      Alt+F1-Look up word at cursor    F9-Previous list   F10-Replace
```

Figure 7.22   Thesaurus.

Import and Export to Another Word Processor

If you share documents with associates that use different word processors, you can do so without losing the document's formatting. You can import or export any of these file formats: ASCII, Special ASCII, Microsoft Word, WordPerfect, Macintosh ASCII, MultiMate, DCA, Professional Write, and WordStar. The ASCII file format is a universal format. If you do not have one of these formats, you can always transfer to ASCII. However, if you do use the ASCII format, you will lose all your page formatting, such as boldface, fonts, italics, etc.

Importing a Document

1. Press **W** for Write, **U** for Utilities, and **I** for Import a document.

2. Choose a file format. Type the name of the file you want to import and press Enter. Then type the name of the new file and press Enter. The file is now in Q&A Write format. Q&A will use its best efforts to save boldfacing, fonts, and other special characteristics of the document.

Exporting a Document

1. Press **W** for Write, **U** for Utilities, and **E** for Export a document.

2. Choose a file format. Type the name of the file you want to export and press Enter. Then type the name of the file you want to export to and press Enter. Your Q&A Write file is now in the format you selected and can be directly read by that word processor.

Shortcut

When you are inside the Write module, with a document on the screen, you can save a file directly to ASCII by pressing Ctrl-F8 and giving the file a name.

Printing Labels

The final component of the Direct Mail application is printing labels. You can print a list of labels sorted in the same order as your letters for easy collating. The procedures for printing labels are the same as for mail merge. To print labels, you select a label format, add the field merge codes, type a Retrieve spec, type a Sort spec, and print the labels. To make generating labels even easier, Q&A provides several predefined Avery label formats.

These steps in the following example will guide you through the label definition and printing process. The example uses the Pin Fed $3^1/_2$-by-$1^7/_{16}$-inch, 1-up format.

Practice Defining and Printing a Label

1. Press **W** for Write and **M** for Mailing labels. The first screen you see lists the available label formats. Press PgDn to see the rest of the list.

2. Rather than using the actual label definition, you are going to make a copy of it and give it another name. You can choose any label format you want; just make the appropriate substitutions to the example. Press PgDn and move to the second page of labels. Move the cursor to the label titled: `Pin Fed 3 1/5" x 1 7/16" - 1 up` and press F5. Type the new name: **A. Names 3 1/5" x 1 7/16" -1 up** and press Enter. Your screen should look similar to Figure 7.23.

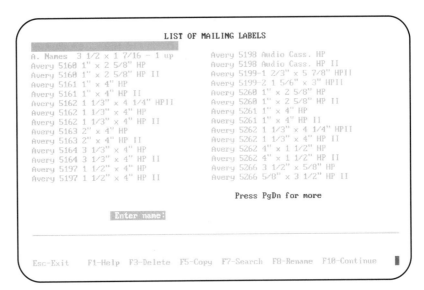

Figure 7.23 List of label formats.

3. Move to the new label format and press Enter. Press Home three times to move to the top of the format. Press Ctrl-Y five times and delete the default settings.

4. Press Alt-F7 and type the filename **NAMES**. Press Enter to link the database to this label.

5. Press the first letter of each field. Move the cursor down to the field and press Enter to place it in the label. Repeat this process until you have the necessary fields in the label. When you are done, your screen should look similar to Figure 7.24.

6. To change the dimensions of a label, press Ctrl-F6. This screen controls margins, label width, and characters per inch.

7. Once your label is defined, press F2 to advance to the Print Options screen. Here you can select which printer to send the labels to, the number of labels across the page, the space between labels, the blank lines at the top and bottom of the label, and Page Preview. If you want to change the database to which this file is linked, you can do so at the bottom of this screen.

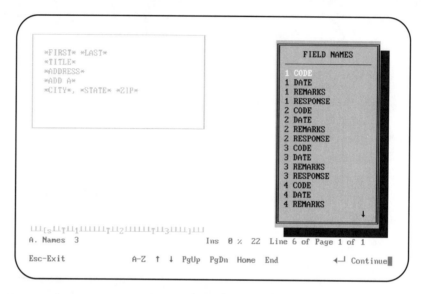

Figure 7.24 Completed label format with list of fields.

8. Press F10 to advance to the Retrieve Spec screen. Type the desired spec and press F8 to advance to the Sort Spec screen. Move to the LAST field and type **1 AS**. This will sort the labels in the same order as the letters.

9. Press F10 twice to print the labels.

10. After the labels are printed, press Shift-F8 to save the label definition and then press Esc to exit.

Printing Letters and Labels with a Macro

An optional step is to create a macro that will automatically print the letters and the labels. This is particularly useful if you plan to print letters and/or labels on a regular basis. This example will guide you through the steps of creating such a macro. If you are not familiar with creating macros, read Chapter 10 first.

Creating a Macro to Print Letters and Labels

1. If you do not already have them, prepare a finished merge letter and label format.

2. With these completed, navigate to the Q&A Main menu and press Shift-F2. Press **D** for Define macro. Type a macro identifier (for example, Alt-L) and press Enter. Every keystroke you type will now be recorded.

3. Press **W** for Write and **G** for Get. Type the filename of the merge letter and press Enter.

4. Press F2 to advance to the Print Options menu. Press Alt-F2 twice to cause the macro to pause at this menu on playback. Press F10 to advance to the Retrieve Spec screen.

5. At the Retrieve Spec screen, press the Home key three times and press Alt-F2. Type a Retrieve spec and press Alt-F2 to cause the macro to pause at the Retrieve spec on playback. The spec you typed will not be recorded.

6. Press F8 to switch to the Sort Spec screen. Press the Home key three times and press Alt-F2. Move to the desired field by using the Tab or Arrow keys. Type a Sort spec and press Alt-F2 to cause the macro to pause at the Sort spec on playback. This Sort spec will not be saved with the macro.

7. Press F10 to print the letters. When the Print screen appears, press Alt-F2 twice to cause the macro to pause here on playback. Press Enter to print the letters.

8. Back at the letter, press Shift-F8 to save the letter and press Esc to exit to the Write menu.

9. Press **M** for Mailing labels. Type the entire name of the label definition and press Enter. Do not use the cursor to move to it.

10. Press Alt-F2 twice at the Label Definition screen and press F2 to advance to the Print Options menu. Press Alt-F2 twice to cause the macro to pause at this menu on playback.

11. Press F10 to advance to the Retrieve Spec screen. Press the Home key three times and press Alt-F2. Type a Retrieve spec and press Alt-F2. Use the Tab or Arrow keys to move to the desired field.

12. Press F8 to switch to the Sort spec. Press the Home key three times and press Alt-F2. Type a Sort spec and press Alt-F2.

13. Press F10 to print the labels. When the Print screen appears, press Alt-F2 twice to cause the macro to pause here on playback. Press Enter to print the labels.

14. You will be returned to the Label Definition screen. Press Shift-F8 to save the label and press Esc four times to return to the Main menu.

15. Press Shift-F2 to bring up the Macro menu. Choose **S** for Save macros. Type a name for the macro. Press F10 and Enter to save the macro.

You now have a custom macro that will print labels and letters anytime you want. Remember to always start this macro from the Q&A Main menu.

Summary

With the *Direct Mail application*, you can automate the mailing of information to prospects and clients. This application has four components: the merge letter, a label, a database, and a macro. The merge letter and the label each extract their information from a database, based on the Retrieve spec that you specify.

In this chapter, you explored approximately half of the Write module's features. You will explore the second half in Chapter 8. Of particular significance is the expanded *Options menu*. This feature places all available commands in one central location and allows you to select them quite easily. Two other features that are very useful are the *Enhancement menu*, used to enhance your text, and *mail merge*, used to merge data and form letters. You learned how to combine printing letters and labels into one macro for easy playback.

In the next chapter, you will learn how to create proposals from several different documents. This is done by creating a master document and using the Join command to link several other files. Then, at the time of printing, Q&A prints each of the subdocuments within the context of the master document.

Block Operations

1. From within a document, move to the beginning of the desired text.
2. Press F8 and press **B** for Block.
3. Choose the desired operation. Highlight the text. (If you are copying or moving to a file, type the filename and press F10.) Press F10.

Search and Replace

1. From within a document, press F7.
2. Press PgDn for advanced options. Type in the value you want to search for and press Enter. Type in the value you want to replace it with and press Enter.
3. Select your other options and press F7 to begin the operation.

Align Text

1. From within a document, move to the desired text.
2. Press F8 and press **A** for Align text.
3. Choose the alignment function, highlight the text, and press F10.

Line Draw

1. From within a document, press F8, Enter, and **D** for Draw.
2. Begin drawing. To erase, press F8. To move the pen, press F6.
3. When you are through, press F10.

Page Numbering

1. From within a document, press F8 and press Enter.
2. Choose header or footer. Type the number sign (#) anywhere on the line and press F10.

Math Functions

1. From within a document, type either a row or a column of numbers.
2. If you typed a row, move to the right of the last number. If you typed a column, move onto the last number. Press Alt-F9 and choose the desired operation.
3. Move your cursor to the spot where you want the result to appear and press F10.

Print Commands

1. Position your cursor where you want the commands to appear.
2. Press F8 and press **P** for Print Commands.
3. Choose the appropriate command and press Enter.
4. Press F2 and F10 to print the document.

Recover a File

1. Press **W** for Write, **U** for Utilities, and **R** for Recover.
2. Type the filename and press Enter. Press F10.

IN
BUSINESS

Proposal Generation Application

The purpose of this chapter is to teach you how to easily create propos-als (multipart documents) while you learn many of the Write module's features.

Overview

Like the previous chapter, this one does not have a design section because all the features can be found in the Write module. The previous chapter, "Direct Mail Application," contained the first half of the Write module's features. This one contains the second half.

The focus of this chapter is on creating a proposal from several different subdocuments. By using Q&A's Join command in a master docu-ment, you can assemble several subdocuments into one master document at the time of printing. The premise is that you have several logical sections that are self-contained and aren't used in every proposal. Thus, you can mix and match the various sections based on your specific needs. You can also insert a Lotus spreadsheet or graph into the document. This concept works equally well for developing reports, bids, contracts, estimates, or any other type of printed matter that has subsections.

While exploring the Proposal Generation application, you will be exposed to the following features: block operations, search and replace, calculation of rows and columns, page numbering, line spacing, print codes, justification commands, line draw, text alignment, and document recovery. And remember that you can issue these commands through the Options menu, the F8 key, or the appropriate function keys.

Application Explained

The Proposal Generation application assembles several subdocuments into one document, based on the commands in the file named Master. In this example, the subdocuments are Intro, Descrip, Options, and a Lotus spreadsheet called Estimate.wk1. Figure 8.1 shows the file Master. The top of the file contains information used in every proposal: title, sender, recipient, subject, and date code. Three Join commands contain the names of the files that assemble the documents at the time of printing. The final command is the Spreadsheet command. It places the spreadsheet Estimate.wk1 in the document.

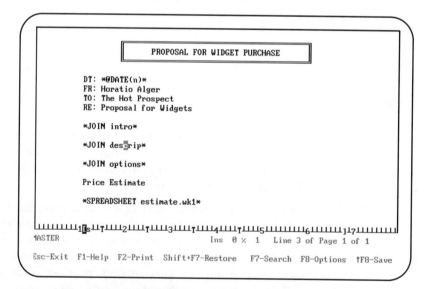

Figure 8.1   Master document.

Fields in the Master File

`*@DATE(n)*`	Places today's date in the document. You can replace the n with a specific date format.
`*JOIN intro*`	Prints the file Intro.
`*JOIN descrip*`	Prints the file Descrip.
`*JOIN options*`	Prints the file Options.
`*SPREADSHEET estimate.wk1*`	Prints the Lotus spreadsheet Estimate.wk1.

This example uses three subdocuments. They can be seen in Figure 8.2. The Lotus spreadsheet can be seen in Figure 8.3. When the file Master prints, it looks like Figure 8.4.

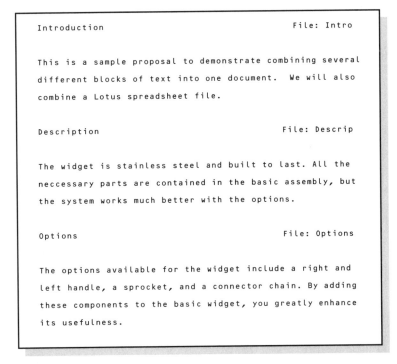

Figure 8.2   Subdocuments.

	Qty1-10	Qty 11+
Basic Assembly	$100.00	$75.00
Left Handle	$24.00	$22.00
Right Handle	$29.00	$25.00
Main Sprocket	$34.00	$30.00
Connector Chain	$12.00	$8.00
Total Cost Each	$199.00	$160.00

Figure 8.3   Lotus spreadsheet.

Using the Application

In this application, you will use the Insert command to place subdocuments into one main document. Then you will practice using the search and replace and block operations. After that, you will utilize the Calculate command to do math inside the text of the document. Next you will explore page numbering, line spacing, line draw, and aligning text. You will finish up the chapter with print codes and document recovery.

Suggested Uses

The Proposal Generation application can be used to assemble any type of document that has logical sections: contracts, bids, estimates, reports, or proposals.

Block Operations

Recall from Chapter 7 that there are three ways to access the Write module's features. You can use the main Write menu, you can press F8 to invoke the Options menu, or you can use the function keys. The following examples will use the Options menu and the function keys.

```
DT: Feb 28, 1991

FR: Horatio Alger

TO: The Hot Prospect

RE: Proposal for Widgets


Introduction

This is a sample proposal to demonstrate combining several

different blocks of text into one document. We will also

combine a Lotus spreadsheet file.


Description

The widget is stainless steel and built to last. All the

neccessary parts are contained in the basic assembly, but

the system works much better with the options.


Options

The options available for the widget include a right and

left handle, a sprocket, and a connector chain. By adding

these components to the basic widget, you greatly enhance

its usefulness.


Price Estimate      Qty 1-10   Qty 11+

Basic Assembly       $100.00    $75.00

Left Handle           $24.00    $22.00

Right Handle          $29.00    $25.00

Main Sprocket         $34.00    $30.00

Connector Chain       $12.00     $8.00

Total Cost Each      $199.00   $160.00
```

Figure 8.4   Final printed Master file.

Practice Performing Block Operations

1. Before you begin the block operations, you will need to retrieve several documents into the Main Document screen. To do this, press **W** for Write and **T** for Type/Edit. This will place you at a blank document screen.

2. Now you are going to insert three subdocuments into this screen. Press F8 to invoke the Options menu. Press **D** for Document and **I** for Insert. Type the filename **Intro** and press Enter three times. Repeat this process for the files Descrip and Options. When you are done, you should have three sections on your screen.

All the block commands work basically the same: Using either the Options menu or the function keys, you invoke a block command. With your cursor, you highlight the text. You press F10 to complete the action. Figure 8.5 displays the Block menu. Notice that next to each command is its function key equivalent. In the block operation examples, you will be using the function keys.

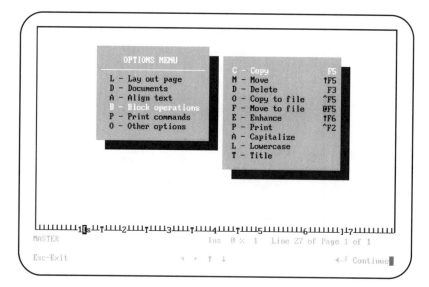

Figure 8.5   Block menu.

The first command you are going to use is the *Copy* command. This command allows you to make an exact duplicate of the highlighted data anywhere in your document.

3. Move your cursor to the I in the header `Introduction` and press
    F5. Move your cursor to the end of the paragraph and press F10.
    The highlighted text can now be placed anywhere in the document.
    Move down one line and press F10. You should now have two
    copies of this section.

A related Copy command, *Copy to file*, allows you to copy a block of
text to a separate file. This is particularly useful if you are creating an
application like the one explained in this chapter. You can create the master
document and then go through the text and save various sections to their
own file, but still leave the master document intact.

4. Move your cursor to the I in the header `Introduction` in the
    newly copied section. Press Ctrl-F5, move your cursor to the end of
    the paragraph, and press F10. Type the filename **Scrap** and press
    Enter. You now have a new file named Scrap containing this
    paragraph.

During editing, you may want to move text around in your document.
Many times a document reads better if sections are rearranged. With the
Move and the *Move to file* commands, you can easily move sections around
in the document.

5. Move your cursor to the I in the header `Introduction` and press
    Shift-F5. Highlight the paragraph and press F10. Press the End key
    three times and the Enter key three times. Press F10. This section
    now appears at the end of your document.

6. Next, move this section to a separate file. Move your cursor to the I
    in the header `Introduction` and press Alt-F5. Highlight the para-
    graph and press F10. Type the filename **Scrap1** and press Enter.
    The paragraph is removed from the screen and placed in its own
    file.

Another useful block feature is the *Delete* command. It allows you to
quickly delete a block of text.

7. Move your cursor to the I in the header `Introduction` and press
    F3. Highlight the paragraph and press F10. The section is now
    deleted. To restore the text that you just deleted, press Shift-F7.
    Your document should have the same three sections you started
    with.

When you want to print only a portion of a document, you can use the
block *Print* command.

8. Turn your printer on and move your cursor to the I in the header `Introduction` and press Ctrl-F2. Highlight the paragraph and press F10. This block will now be sent to the printer.

The final block commands are *Capitalize, Lowercase,* and *Title.* They let you change a block of text to all capital letters, to all lowercase letters, or to the title format, respectively.

9. Move to the I in `Introduction` and press F8. Press **B** for Block Operations and press **A** for Capitalize. Press the End key to high-light the entire word and press F10. The word is in all caps.

10. Press F8, press **B** for Block, and press **L** for Lowercase. Press the End key to highlight the word and press F10. The word is all lowercase.

11. Press F8, press **B** for Block, and press **T** for Title. Press the End key to highlight the word and press F10. The word is back to title format.

This completes the block operations. Leave the text on the screen if you want to go through the examples in the next section.

Search and Replace

As you develop more and more documents, similarities will develop between them, especially if you are generating contracts, estimates, sales letters, or proposals. With the Search and Replace command, you can retrieve an existing document and change all the occurrences of *type 1* to *type 2*, where *type 1* and *type 2* represent a specific word, person, project or deal. You can also search and replace more obscure items, like carriage returns, boldfaced text, fonts, and more. You can use this same menu to search for only text or numbers; simply leave the replace field blank. The search feature is particularly handy in finding text buried deep in your document. This section will give you practice in three kinds of searches: simple, advanced, and pattern.

The basic Search and Replace menu is invoked by pressing F7. You can see this menu in Figure 8.6. The first line of the menu is where you type what you want to search for. If you want to replace the text with something else, type it on the second line. The third line controls whether you want the replacement to happen manually, automatically, or in fast automatic. In *manual method*, Q&A stops at each instance of the searched-for word and asks if you want to replace the word. In *automatic method*, Q&A automatically replaces the words, and you can see the replacements happen on-screen. In the final method, *fast automatic*, you do not even see the replacements happen. This final mode is the fastest. Now try a basic search.

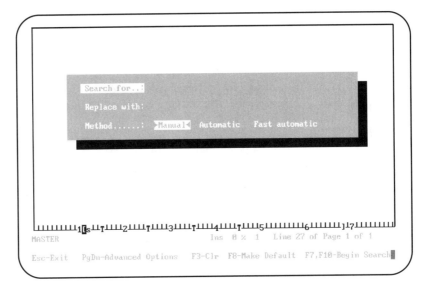

Figure 8.6   Basic Search and Replace menu.

Practice Doing a Basic Search

1. Have on-screen the three files you retrieved in the previous section. Press the Home key three times and press F7 to invoke the Search menu.

2. Type **Sprocket** into the Search for field and press F10. The word should be highlighted in the third section. Press F7 again.

3. Now search for all the boldface codes. Type **@BD** in the Search for field and press F7. Press F7 three more times. Each time you press F7, you are taken to the next bold code until you see the message at the bottom of your screen Manual Search COMPLETED After 3 Matches. Figure 8.7 displays all the special codes for which you can search.

```
@CR - Carriage returns    @BD - Bold text        @XO - Strikeout text
@CT - Centered lines      @IT - Italicized text  @SP - Superscript text
@NP - New pages           @UL - Underlined text  @SB - Subscript text
@Fn - Fonts (1-8)         @RG - Regular text     @TB - Real Tabs

Example:  @BD@ITcat  finds all bold, italicized "cat"s in the document.
```

Figure 8.7   Function codes.

Shortcut

You can replace any of these special codes with others. For instance, you can search for all boldface codes (@BD) and replace them with italics codes (@IT).

After you gain familiarity with the basic search techniques, you can start using the advanced features. If you are not exactly sure how a word is spelled, you can use the ? to fill in the missing letters. For example, to find the reference to a name that begins with "Bell" and has a total of seven characters, you can type **bell???** in the Search For field. If you aren't sure how long the name is, you can type **bell..** (two periods). This would find all words that started with *Bell*.

The following characters are *reserved characters:* ?, .., and \. To search for a reserved character, precede the character with a backslash (\). If you type \?, Q&A will find all question marks in your document

To access the advanced search options, press F7 and then press PgDn. This will bring up the other half of the Search Options menu, as shown in Figure 8.8. The first option is Type. Here you can choose whole words (the default), text, or patterns. With Whole Words selected, if you searched for "TEST," you would not find "TESTING." If you choose Text, you would find both "TEST" and "TESTING." The Patterns option lets you search for any text/number pattern, such as a social security number. The Case selection lets you make your searches sensitive or insensitive to case. For instance, with this option set to Sensitive, if you searched for "IN," Q&A would not find "in." The Range option lets you search the entire document (all) to the end of the document or backward to the beginning of the document. The final option extends your searches into files that are designated in *Join*, *Queue*, or *QueueP* commands, such as the ones used in this application.

Now try an advanced search. In the next example, you are going to replace all the occurrences of the word "widget" with "Big Widget."

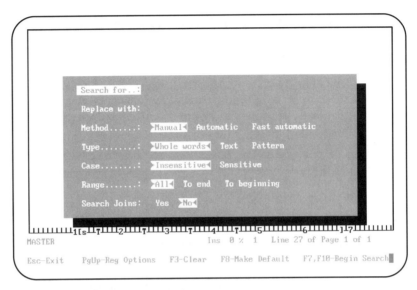

```
   Search for..:
   Replace with:
   Method......:  ▶Manual◀  Automatic   Fast automatic
   Type........:  ▶Whole words◀  Text   Pattern
   Case........:  ▶Insensitive◀  Sensitive
   Range.......:  ▶All◀  To end   To beginning
   Search Joins:  Yes  ▶No◀

MASTER                        Ins  0 %  1   Line 27 of Page 1 of 1

Esc-Exit    PgUp-Reg Options   F3-Clear   F8-Make Default   F7,F10-Begin Search
```

Figure 8.8   Advanced Search Options.

Practice Doing an Advanced Search and a Pattern Search

1. Try an advanced search. Press F7 and type **Widget**. Press Enter and type **Big Widget**. Make sure that Case is set to Insensitive and Method is set to Automatic. Press F10 to replace the text.

Beginner's Tip

To delete the occurrence of a word, type a backslash (\ ) in the `Replace with` field.

The final type of search is known as a pattern search. To conduct a pattern search, you have to set the Type selection to Pattern and then you can use any of these commands in your search: a *9* will find any single numeral, an *A* finds any single alphabetic character, a *?* finds any single alphanumeric character, and a *~* (tilde) finds any single nonalphanumeric character. For example, typing **99999** would find any five-character number, and **AA 99** would find any five-character phrase that begins with two letters, followed by a space and two numbers.

2. Try a pattern search. Press F7 and type **AAAAAAAAAA**. Change the type to Pattern. Press F10. You will find three occurrences of a ten-letter word.

Align Text, Line Draw, and Page Numbering

The Align Text menu, shown in Figure 8.9, allows you to justify your text, set temporary margins, and set line spacing. There are three justify commands: Left, Center, and Right. You can justify text as you type it, or you can justify existing text.

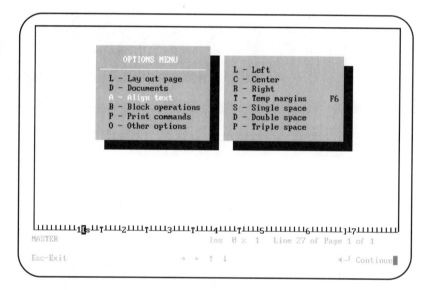

Figure 8.9   Align Text options.

Practice Justifying Text

1. To justify new text, move to a blank line on your screen and press F8. Press **A** for Align Text and **C** for Center. Type **this is the center line**. The line will automatically justify as you type. You cannot automatically justify more than one line at a time. If you keep typing onto the next line, the second line will be left-justified.

2. To right-justify some existing text, move to the I in the header `Introduction` and press F8. Press **A** for Align and **R** for Right.

3. To change from right to left justification, place your cursor on the word and press F8. Press **A** for Align and **L** for Left.

If a section in a document needs to be set off with bullet points or hanging paragraphs, you can set temporary margins.

Practice Creating a Hanging Paragraph by Setting Temporary Margins

1. To create a hanging paragraph, move your cursor to the position on the left side of the page where you want the hanging paragraph to begin and press F6. Press **L** for Left.

2. Move to the position on the right side of the page where you want the hanging paragraph to end and press F6. Press **R** for Right. Type your paragraph.

3. To reset the margins to the normal settings, press F6 and **C** for Center. You can also reset an existing hanging paragraph to regular by moving to the first word in the paragraph and pressing F6 and **C** for Center.

Practice Changing the Default Single Line Spacing

1. To change the line spacing from the default of Single to Double or Triple, press F8. Press **A** for Align and then choose Double or Triple Space.

2. To reset the spacing to Single, move one line below the double or triple space code and set a single space code.

Line Draw

With the Line Draw command, you can use the cursor to draw lines in and around the text in your document. Two common uses for the Line Draw command are to draw organizational charts and to enhance the title page of a report.

Using Line Draw

1. Press F8, Enter, and **D** for Draw.

2. You are now in Line Draw mode. To draw single lines, use the cursor keys. If you have a keyboard with a separate number pad, you can draw double lines by pressing the Num Lock key and using the cursor keys on the number pad.

3. To erase lines, press F8 and use the Arrow keys. To start drawing again, press F8.

4. To move the pen to another part of the document without drawing a line, press F6 to turn the pen up. When you are ready to begin drawing, press F6.

5. When you are finished drawing, press F10.

Inserting Page Numbers

1. You can place page numbers in headers or footers only. To insert page numbers, press F8 and Enter. Choose either Header or Footer. Then place the number sign (#) anywhere in the header or footer. Wherever the number sign appears, the actual numbers will print. You can precede the number sign with the word *Page* if you like. When you are through, press F10.

2. You cannot stop and start page numbering. You can only control on which page it begins. To specify the beginning page number, press Ctrl-F6 and choose which page you want the numbering to begin on.

Calculate Numbers in Text

The Calculate commands are handy when you have simple math to perform in the body of a document. You can calculate numbers in rows or columns. The operations performed can include total, average, count, multiply, and divide. Using the Proposal Generation application in this chapter, you could replace the *spreadsheet* command with the math command. The next example will guide you through using the Calculate commands. You will be using a document called Math, which contains the basic math format.

Practice Calculating Numbers in Text

1. Begin by clearing the screen. Press Esc, press **C** for Clear, and answer Yes. Retrieve the Math document by pressing F8, **D** for Document, and **G** for Get. Type the filename **MATH** and press Enter.

In the file you just retrieved are two numbers at the top of the page. These will be used in your calculation. There are also several words down the left of the page. These words correspond to all of the math operations. They are only listed so that you have a location on the page where you can place the results of your calculation. They are not necessary for the math functions to work properly.

2. If you are going to calculate a column of numbers, it is best to set a Decimal tab. Press F8, Enter, and **S** for Set Tabs. Move to the location where you want the numbers to be and type a **D**. Then press F10. By setting a decimal tab, all your numbers will line up correctly.

3. To perform calculations on a column of numbers, type your numbers and then place your cursor *on the last number*. Press Alt-F9 to bring up the Calculate menu. Choose the operation and move your cursor where you want the first number of the result to appear. Press F10.

4. To calculate a row of numbers, type your numbers and place your cursor to the *right of the last number*. Press Alt-F9 to bring up the Calculate menu. Choose the operation and move your cursor where you want the result to appear. Press F10.

5. Now practice each of the operations. Move your cursor to the last number (200.30) and press Alt-F9 to invoke the Math menu. Notice that Q&A highlights the two numbers. Press **T** for Total. Move down to the line that has the label TOTAL on it and press F10. Continue this for each of the remaining operations, placing the results next to the appropriate title. When you are done, your screen should look like Figure 8.10.

6. To save your results, press Shift-F8 and press Enter. Then press Esc and **C** for Clear to clear the screen.

Printing the Proposal and Print Codes

In this section you will print the sample proposal and explore the various print codes. *Print codes* allow you to perform specific operations at the time of printing. Many of the commands are quite esoteric and you will probably never use them, so the discussion will cover only the ones you are likely to use.

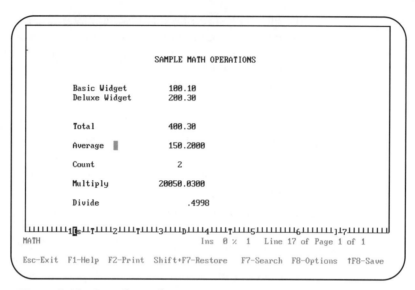

Figure 8.10   Sample math operations.

Print commands are always embedded in a document and are activated at the time of printing. Print commands can be placed in a document in one of two ways: through the Print Commands menu (shown in Figure 8.11) or by typing them. If you type them, make sure that they are enclosed in asterisks (*). The next example will show you how to print the file Master.

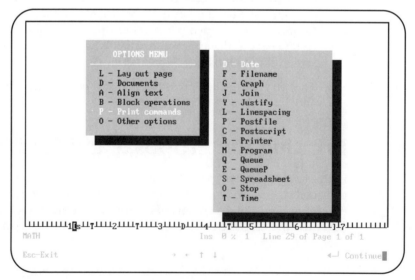

Figure 8.11   Print Commands menu.

Practice Printing the Master File

1. Retrieve the file Master. Press F8, **D** for Document, and **G** for Get. Type the filename **MASTER** and press Enter.

   In this file, shown in Figure 8.12, there are three common print commands: Date, Join, and Spreadsheet. The Date command automatically places the date in the document. It is taken from your computer's internal clock. Each Join command prints the file listed next to it, and the Spreadsheet command prints the Lotus spreadsheet next to it.

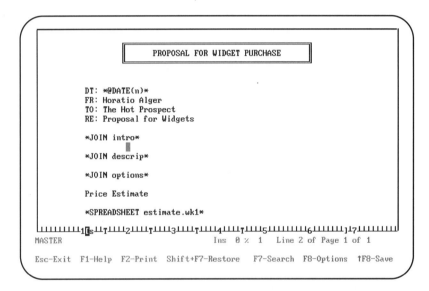

Figure 8.12   The Master file with print commands inserted.

2. To print the document, press F2 and F10.

   Some of the other print commands you might use are Queue and QueueP. The Queue command lets you specify through a master document a series of files to print. Each file will print as if you printed it individually. The syntax is

   ```
   *Queue filename*
   ```

where filename is the name of the document you want to print.

The QueueP command works similarly to the Queue command except that it will continue the pagination across each of the documents. If you have developed a Lotus, Symphony, or PFS graph, you can place it in your document by using this syntax:

```
*Graph, filename, density*
```

where `filename` is the name of the graph and the `density` is **S** for Single, **D** for double, or **Q** for Quadruple.

When printing a Lotus or Symphony .PIC file, you add fonts, width, height, and rotation. The syntax is

```
*Graph, filename, density, font1, font2, width, height, rotation*
```

The *Linespacing N* command lets you change the line spacing at the time of printing. The letter N is equal to the number of lines you want. The *@Time* command will place the time in your document.

3. Save your document by pressing Shift-F8 and Enter. Clear your screen by pressing Esc. Then press Esc again to exit.

Document Recovery

Occasionally a Write file may become damaged. If this should happen, you may be able to recover it using the Recover utility.

Using the Recover Utility

1. Press **W** for Write, **U** for Utilities, and **R** for Recover a document.

2. Type the filename, press Enter, and press F10 to begin the recover process. If the recovery is successful, Q&A will let you know by displaying a message at the bottom of the screen.

Summary

The *Proposal Generation application* was the focus of this chapter. It assembles several subdocuments into one document. You can use this application for any document that has logical sections, such as contracts, reports, bids, and estimates, that will be mixed and matched. After you have created several of these multipart documents, you can use the search and replace feature to change references to specific projects, clients, etc. By using this handy feature, you save yourself the time needed to recreate the documents.

In the next chapter, you will learn how to analyze your business by using cross-tab reports and the Intelligent Assistant. Mastering the principles in Chapter 9 can help you in your decision-making process because you will be able to get timely, summarized information on any aspect of your business that is automated.

Design and Print Cross-Tab Report

1. Press **R** for Report. Type the filename and press Enter. Type the report name and press Enter.

2. Type a Retrieve spec and press F10. Enter a Cross-Tab spec, using the Col, Row, and Sum commands. Press F7 to change the Groupings spec. Press F9 to go back and press F8 to create any derived fields.

3. Press F10 to advance to the Print Options spec. Press F8 to Define the Page and press F10 to save the Report spec.

4. Press F10 to print the report.

Use the Intelligent Assistant

1. Press **A** for Assistant (you have to teach your database before asking questions). Press **A** for Ask Me to Do Something, type the filename, and press Enter.

2. Type your request and press Enter.

Use the Query Guide

1. Press **A** for Assistant (you have to teach your database before asking questions). Press **Q** for Query Guide, type the filename, and press Enter.

2. Make your request.

IN
BUSINESS

Business Analysis Application

The purpose of this chapter is to teach you how to use the cross-tab reporting and the Intelligent Assistant features to analyze the results of your business.

Overview

Like the two previous chapters, this chapter has no design section. It explores two features that you can use with any of your applications. These two features are cross-tab reporting and the Intelligent Assistant. The Invoice database will be used to illustrate the examples in this chapter. However, all the principles can be applied equally to any of the applications.

Before you begin, you should understand what the term "business analysis" means in this chapter and how to choose what should be analyzed. *Business analysis* is the act of examining your business operations in order to identify ways to run the business more effectively. If you read Chapter 1, you remember that it talked about the importance of a Strategic System and that a Strategic System consisted of two parts: process automation systems and decision support systems. So far, 80 percent of the work you have done has been in the process automation area. Now, you will focus on decision support systems.

A *decision support system* (this could also be called a business analysis system) extracts selected information from a database and, optionally, performs calculations on that data. Then it prints the information in an easily readable format. A decision support system is intended to help your decision-making process by giving you *summarized, timely,* and *useful* information. These terms are subjective and only you can define them. But here are some guidelines. "Summarized" is not detail; it is a total of the month's sales, not each invoice. It is the percentage of sales increase for the quarter, not each day. "Timely" is not late; the end-of-the-month sales reports should be delivered by the first day of the following month. You should know *before* an item is out of stock. For a report to be "useful," it has to give you information you don't already have and present it in a format that is easy to interpret. Good data is of no use if you can't understand the report.

To determine what information you need, examine the important decisions you make on a regular basis and see if your applications contain data that can help you with these decisions. Some examples of questions that could be answered with data extracted from your applications are

- What amount of raw materials should we purchase this month?

- Are the sales reps selling the right mix of products?

- Are salaries increasing equal to the norm in our industry?

- What are the sales trends for each product?

- What percentage of our revenue is coming from services?

As you can see, the possibilities are endless, but you can probably apply the *80/20 rule* to determine what data you want to extract from your applications. In other words, focus on getting the top 20 percent of your questions answered and you will most likely derive 80 percent of the benefit. As you progress through this chapter, look for ways to apply these two features to your decision support needs.

Shortcut

A decision support system can be of real value in analyzing how each product or service is selling. Suppose that your sales are increasing each month but that the sales of your top product are decreasing. Without adequate reports, you may not spot this trend until it is too late and you are faced with a big problem.

Application Explained

Cross-tab reporting and the Intelligent Assistant are the two features you will use to construct decision support systems and do business analysis. The purpose of a *cross-tab report* is to cross-tabulate information. In Figure 9.1, you can see that sales are cross-tabulated by company and date and that the date is segmented by month. This report is based on the Invoice database.

```
03/08/91                    Total Sales Grouped by Month                    page 1

                                          Invoice Date
                                 - - - - - - - - - - - - - -
COMPANY                              Jan 91      Feb 91      Mar 91    Total Sale
- - - - - - - - - - - - - - - - - -  - -    - - - -    - - - - - - - - - -  ==========
Brazilian Lumber                Avg  $3996.00   $9144.00   $3816.00    $5859.00
                                Tot  $7992.00  $27432.00  $11448.00   $46872.00

Sacks: Fine Burlap Clothing     Avg  $1196.37   $2028.33    $585.00    $1355.51
                                Tot  $3589.10   $6085.00   $1170.00   $10844.10

The Blue Sky Company            Avg   $993.41   $3467.70   $1742.70    $1647.63
                                Tot  $5960.48   $6935.40   $5228.10   $18123.98

The Good Health Hospital        Avg   $547.20    $322.43    $385.88     $455.97
                                Tot  $1641.61    $322.43    $771.76    $2735.80
==============================  ===  =========  =========  =========  ==========
Total Sale                      Avg  $1370.23   $4530.54   $1861.79    $2381.09
                                Tot $19183.19  $40774.83  $18617.86   $78575.88
```

Figure 9.1   Sample cross-tab report.

Any cross-tab report is based primarily on one database and contains three basic specifications: Row, Col (Column), and Summary. In the example shown in Figures 9.2 and 9.3, the COMPANY field was given the Row code, the DATE field was given the Col (Column) code, and the BAL & INT field was given the Summary code. Within the Summary field, there are codes to calculate the Total and Average amounts of sales.

Q&A provides two different assistants to help you make requests of your database. The original assistant is called the *Intelligent Assistant* (IA), and the new assistant is called the *Query Guide* (QG). These assistants allow you to make plain English requests of your database, such as "List all invoices greater than $1,000 sold by John in January." You can also use assistants to run reports, add forms, perform calculations, etc. Many of the File mode features can be accessed through the assistants. As you gain experience with using the assistants, you will find which tasks are better performed in File mode and which are better performed in IA and QG.

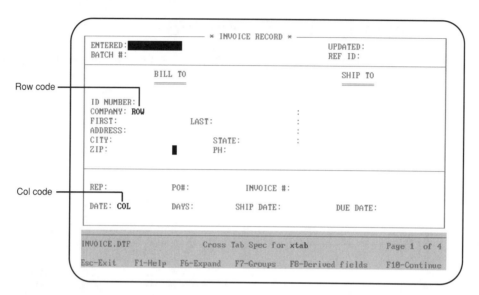

Figure 9.2 Cross-Tab Report spec shown on screen 1 of the Invoice file.

```
  INV #  │ DESCRIPTION                │ QTY   │ UNIT PRICE  │ EXT. PRICE
  ───────┼────────────────────────────┼───────┼─────────────┼────────────
  1 :    │     A:                     │ A1:   │ A2:         │      :
  2 :    │     B:                     │ B1:   │ B2:         │      :
  3 :    │     C:                     │ C1:   │ C2:         │      :
  4 :    │     D:                     │ D1:   │ D2:         │      :
  5 :    │     E:                     │ E1:   │ E2:         │      :
  6 :    │     F:                     │ F1:   │ F2:         │      :
  7 :    │     G:                     │ G1:   │ G2:         █   :
  8 :    │     H:                     │ H1:   │ H2:         │      :
  9 :    │     I:                     │ I1:   │ I2:         │      :

        Int Rate:        Tax Rate:                        Subtotal :
                                                          Tax      :
        Date:            Chk:           Amt:              Freight  :
        Date:            Chk:           Amt:              Credit   :
        Date:            Chk:           Amt:              Total    :
        Date:            Chk:           Amt:              Paid     :
        Date:            Chk:           Amt:              Balance  :
        Date:            Chk:           Amt:              Interest :
        Date:            Chk:           Amt:              Bal & Int: SUM,T,A,M→
  Expand field: SUM,T,A,MIN,MAX
  INVOICE.DTF              Cross Tab Spec for X-Sales by Month    Page 2  of 4
  Esc-Exit    F1-Help    F6-Expand    F7-Groups    F8-Derived fields    F10-Continue
```

Expanded field

Figure 9.3 Cross-Tab Report spec shown on screen 2 of the Invoice file.

The two assistants provide basically the same functions but use a slightly different methodology. The main difference between the two is that the Intelligent Assistant requires that you type your requests using a natural language, whereas the Query Guide allows you to build your requests from selections on a menu. For the novice user, the Query Guide is easier to use. Figure 9.4 shows the initial Intelligent Assistant screen, and Figure 9.5 shows a sample request and answer.

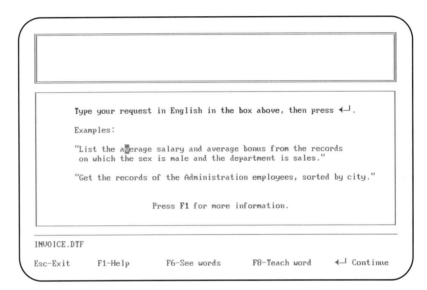

Figure 9.4   Initial Intelligent Assistant screen.

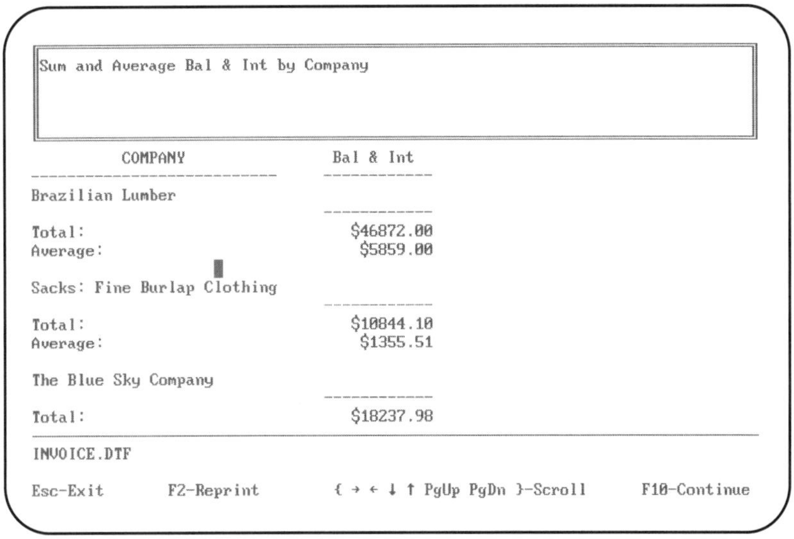

Figure 9.5   Intelligent Assistant request and answer.

The fact that the Query Guide allows you to build your requests from selections on a menu is a big benefit. The menu makes it easier to construct requests with the proper syntax. Figure 9.6 shows the initial Query Guide screen, and Figure 9.7 shows a sample request and answer.

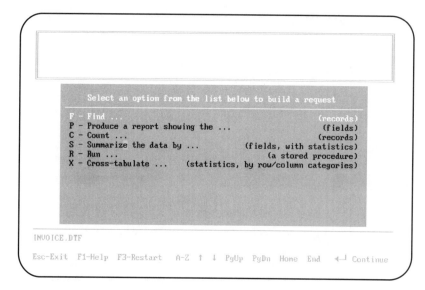

Figure 9.6   Initial Query Guide Request screen.

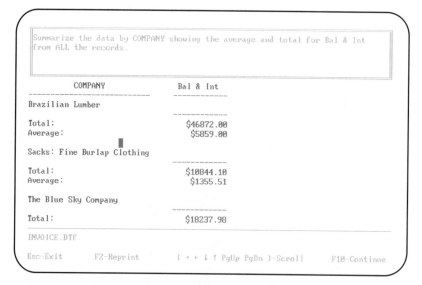

Figure 9.7   Query Guide request and answer.

Using the Application

The two features—cross-tab reporting and Intelligent Assistant—that make up this chapter are not considered an application per se. Rather, they would be used as a part of an application. So as you are learning how to use them, consider ways to apply them to your applications.

Suggested Uses

Cross-tab reporting is ideally suited for creating reports from databases that contain numbers, money, people, organizations, and things. A cross-tab report shows the relationship between items, such as total sales to reps, memberships to districts, inventory costs to products, salaries to employee type, sales calls to appointments, etc.

The Intelligent Assistant is particularly useful for the infrequent user who wants to get some basic information from the database but doesn't want to learn how to use the File module.

Cross-Tab Reporting

The first step in developing a cross-tab report is deciding what information you want to cross-tabulate. The easiest way to do this is to formulate the question in English first. For example, you might ask: What is the average, total, minimum, and maximum amount of each sale for each client in the first quarter of the year? Once your question is formulated, you have to determine which database contains the information you need. In the case of this question, it is the Invoice file. The final step is to create the report.

Creating a cross-tab report is similar to creating a columnar report, and the report is selected from the same menu. The only difference between creating the two reports is the spec used to designate which rows and columns appear. In a columnar report, you select which fields you want to appear as columns of information. In a cross-tab report, you have both columns and rows to contend with.

Creating a Cross-Tab Report

1. Press **R** for Report and **D** for Design. Type the filename and a report name. Then select Cross-Tab Report.

2. The first spec you come to is the Retrieve spec. Just type it as you would in any other area of the program.

3. Press F10 to advance to the Cross Tab Spec screen. Here you select fields for the Col (Column), the Row, and the Summary.

4. Press F10 again to select print options. Press F8 to define the page.

5. Press F10 to save your report design and F10 again to print the report.

In the following pages, you will explore the majority of the features used to construct a cross-tab report. I have already created a report, based on the Invoice file, that cross-tabulates the sales of each client by the month and displays the client's total, average, minimum, and maximum sales for each month. This report is called X-SALES BY MONTH and you will be using it in the following example.

Practice Using the Cross-Tab Report Features

1. Press **R** for Report and **D** for Design. Type the filename **INVOICE** and press Enter.

2. Before you begin working on this *existing* report, look at the screen that appears when you create a *new* report. Type the report name **NEW** and press Enter. Here you choose whether you want to create a cross-tab or a columnar report. Press Esc to abandon this report.

3. Press **D** for Design again and press Enter. Highlight the report X-SALES BY MONTH and press Enter.

<table>
<tr><td>**Beginner's Tip**</td><td>Precede each of your cross-tab reports with an *X*. This will differentiate them from the columnar reports.</td></tr>
</table>

4. The first spec you come to is the Retrieve spec. It is here that you tell Q&A which records you want included on the report. For this example, you will use all the records in the database, so press F10. You should now arrive at the Cross-Tab spec.

The Cross-Tab spec is similar to the Column/Sort spec in a columnar report. Before you go on to step 5, you should understand the components that make up the Cross-Tab spec. Since the spec has already been created for you, all you have to do is understand what each code does.

Three elements make up a *Cross-Tab spec*: the Col (Column), Row, and Summary codes. You must use all three to produce a report. You type the codes into fields on the form. Placing the Row code in a field causes these values to appear down the left side of the page. Placing the Col code in a field causes the values to appear across the top of the report. Placing the Summary code in a field causes these values to appear at the "intersection" of the Row and Column fields—the body of the report. It is due to this intersection that the report is called a *cross-tab report*. In Figure 9.8 you can see the Row code in the COMPANY field and the Col code in the DATE field.

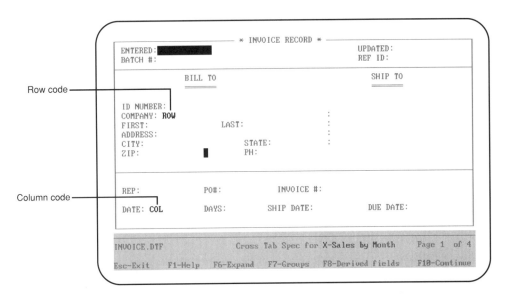

Figure 9.8   Row and Col codes.

You can combine the Summary code with either the Col or the Row code in the same field. This makes the Column or Row fields also the Summary field. A report exists with these specifications—the X-NUMBER OF COMPANIES GROUPED BY STATE report. This report counts the number of companies in each state. It was created by placing the Row code in the COMPANY field and the Col and Summary codes in the STATE field. To prevent the Summary column from printing (the Summary column is the right-most column that totals everything horizontally), you would place the NS code (no summary) after the Col code: COL,NS,SUM.

Shortcut

To view the Cross-Tab spec that combines the Col and Summary codes, select the report X-Number of Companies Grouped by State. This report also makes use of some special Grouping commands (which are covered later).

You can make your reports much more useful by using Calculation codes with the Summary code. These codes perform calculations on the values in the fields. The available codes are **T** for total, **A** for Average, **MIN** for finding the minimum value in a field, **MAX** for finding the maximum value in a range, **STD** for finding the standard deviation, and **V** for finding the variance. Some examples are: counting all the companies in each state, finding the average sale for each client, and totaling all commissions for each sales rep. The choice of codes is dependent on the field type. For instance, you cannot calculate the average value of a text field, but you can calculate the average value of a numeric or money field. In Figure 9.9 you can see the Summary and Calculation codes in the BAL & INT field used in this report. Figure 9.10 lists all the available codes.

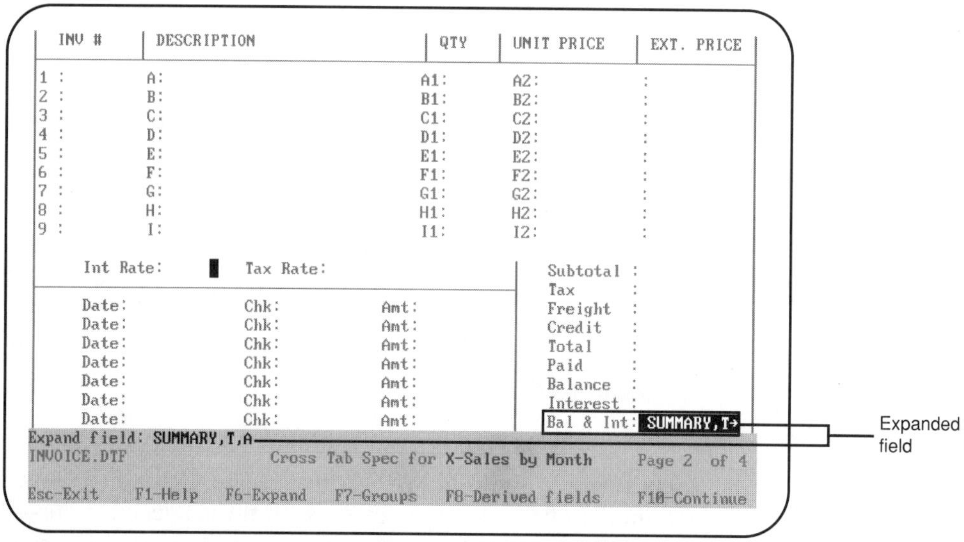

Figure 9.9   Summary and Calculation codes in BAL & INT field.

5. To make the report more useful, you have the option of grouping the Column and Row headings in many variations. The grouping you use depends on the field type. Figure 9.11 shows the Grouping spec. To access the Grouping spec, press F7 at the Cross-Tab spec.

Figure 9.11 shows how Q&A places the field name under the appropriate heading. In this case, COMPANY is under the Row heading and DATE is under the Column heading. Within the box under the Row heading, notice the command @ALL. This is the default setting for all fields. In this report the @ALL code is correct because you want to list all the companies. But in the

Column heading, you don't want to see the detail, so the invoices are grouped by month using the @MONTH command. If you left the Column heading (Invoice Date) grouped by @ALL, your report would display too much detail to be useful.

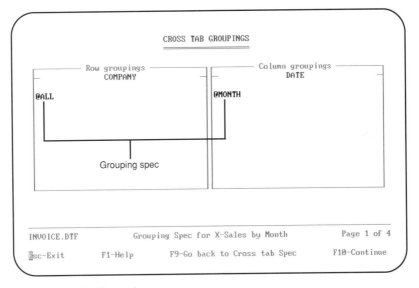

```
                    CALCULATION CODES

       T - Total the summaries.
       A - Average the summaries.
       C - Count the summaries.
     MIN - Get the MINimum of the summaries.
     MAX - Get the MAXimum of the summaries.
     STD - Get the STandard Deviation of the summaries.
       V - Get the Variance of the summaries.
```

Figure 9.10   Summary Calculation codes.

```
                    CROSS TAB GROUPINGS
                    ═══════════════════

      ┌──── Row groupings ────            ┌──── Column groupings ────
             COMPANY                                DATE

      @ALL                               @MONTH



                   Grouping spec



 INVOICE.DTF           Grouping Spec for X-Sales by Month      Page 1 of 4

 Esc-Exit      F1-Help        F9-Go back to Cross tab Spec      F10-Continue
```

Figure 9.11   Grouping spec.

Q&A offers ten of these predefined grouping functions: six for date fields, one for all fields, one for alpha text fields, and two for numeric and money fields. They make using the Cross-Tab Grouping spec easier. Table 9.1 shows the functions for each grouping.

Table 9.1   Q&A's Predefined Grouping Functions

Function	Purpose
	Groupings for All Field Types
@ALL	To include each unique value of the row or column field as a row or column heading. This is Q&A's default.
	Groupings for Money and Number Fields
@RANGE(x,y,z)	To group data into a set of regular, predefined ranges, where x is the number the range starts from, y is the size of the interval, and z is the number of intervals. Example: @RANGE(0, 10000, 10)
@INTERVAL(x)	To group data into a predefined number of intervals, where the ranges are determined automatically by Q&A and x is the number of ranges desired. Example: @INTERVAL(5)
	Groupings for Dates
@DAY	To group data by days of the year. This is the same as using @ALL.
@DOW	To group data by days of the week. This would produce a maximum of seven groupings, one for each day of the week (all Mondays would be grouped together, etc.).
@DOM	To group data by days of the month. This would produce a maximum of 31 groupings, one for each day of the month.
@MONT	To group data by months of the year. This would produce a maximum of 12 groupings, one for each month.
@MO	To group data by months. This would group all the data for each month.
@YEAR	To group data by years. There would be as many groupings as there are years in the retrieved forms.
	Groupings for Text
@ALPHA	To group data by the first letter, *A* through *Z*.

Some of these functions are particularly useful. The @RANGE and @INTERVAL functions are good for segmenting dollar amounts or numbers into various ranges. It is important to assign groupings that match the data type of the field. If you don't, you will print unreadable reports.

6. In addition to the predefined groupings, you can optionally use *Range and Match groupings*, which are shown in Figure 9.12. The syntax for Range and Match groupings is similar to the Retrieve spec.

SYMBOL	MEANING	EXAMPLES		
x	equal to x	Boston	CA	4/12/85
/x	not equal to x	/CA	/Sales	/$100
>x	greater than x	>12:00 pm		
<x	less than x	<10,000	<11/13/65	
>=x	greater than or equal to x	>=Jones	>=12:00 am	
<=x	less than or equal to x	<=1000	<=12/31/90	
x..y	between x and y	10..1000	a..f	
>x..<y	greater than x and less than y	>10..<1000		
x;y;z	x OR y OR z	red;white;blue	5.00;10.00	
=	empty			
/=	not empty			
x..	begins with x (if text field)	pre..		
..x	ends with x (if text field)	..ing		
..x..	contains x (if text field)	..esp..		

Figure 9.12   Syntax for Range and Match Groupings.

Figure 9.13 shows an example of this type of Grouping spec. Looking at the Row Groupings spec, you will see two lines of text. Each line of text represents a row. These codes will make two groups of companies: one group whose names start with the letters *A, B,* and *C,* and another group whose names start with *S* and *T.* Looking at the Column Groupings spec, you will see three rows of text. These codes will create three columns: one from January through April, the second from May through September, and the third from November through December. The semicolon (;) is the command to join entries on the same line.

Like the columnar report, the cross-tab report lets you create derived columns. *Derived columns* "derive" their value from other fields in the current database or other databases. You can use the @xlookup statement to look up values from other databases. You can also create columns or rows by combining fields in the database.

7. To display the full name associated for each company as a Row heading, use a derived column. Place **#1** in the FIRST field and **#2** in the LAST field. Press F8 to switch to the Derived Field spec and enter the spec as it appears in Figure 9.14. The Heading field is the title of the row or column. The Formula is how you create the row or column, and the Cross tab spec contains either Row, Col, or Sum.

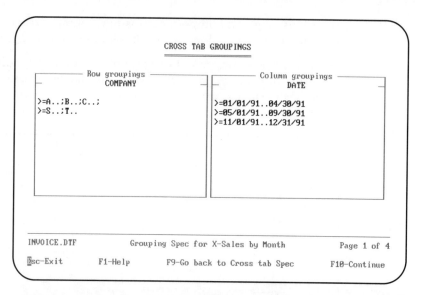

CROSS TAB GROUPINGS

┌─ Row groupings ─┐   ┌─ Column groupings ─┐
          COMPANY   DATE

>=A..;B..;C..;   >=01/01/91..04/30/91
>=S..;T..   >=05/01/91..09/30/91
                           >=11/01/91..12/31/91

INVOICE.DTF   Grouping Spec for X-Sales by Month   Page 1 of 4

Esc-Exit   F1-Help   F9-Go back to Cross tab Spec   F10-Continue

Figure 9.13   Sample of a user-defined Grouping spec.

DERIVED FIELDS

Heading: **FULL NAME**
Formula: #1+" "+#2
Cross tab spec: **ROW**

Heading:
Formula:
Cross tab spec:

Heading:
Formula:
Cross tab spec:

INVOICE.DTF   Derived Fields for X-Sales by Month   Page 1 of 1

Esc-Exit   F1-Help   F9-Go back to Cross tab Spec   F10-Continue

Figure 9.14   Sample Derived Field spec.

There are several other miscellaneous features that you should be aware of, and you can try these out in the remaining steps. The first feature is the heading code: H(n), where n is the new name of the field. Try out this code in step 8.

8. To change the field label from COMPANY to ORGANIZATION, type **ROW** or **COL, H(Organization)** in the COMPANY field. If you have sales in the millions of dollars, you can use the `Scale(1000)` command to lop off three zeros. This code can be placed with the Col, Row, or Sum codes, for example, `SUM, scale(1000)`.

9. To apply a different font or enhancement to a Row, Column, Summary, Derived, or Grouping code, press Shift-F6 to bring up the Enhancement menu, select the enhancement, highlight the text, and press F10.

10. After you have created the Cross-Tab spec, advance to the Print Options screen, shown in Figure 9.15. To do this, press F10 at the Cross-Tab spec. Notice that the `Show Results` as field gives you the choice of displaying the values in the SUM field as: Numbers (the default), a percent of the Total, a percent of the ROW field, or a percent of the COL field. You also have the choice of Normal, which displays the results as some amount above or below average, where the average is represented by 100. At the Print Options screen, you may wish to change the line spacing; the default is single.

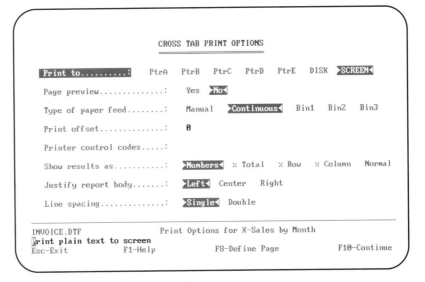

Figure 9.15   Print Options screen.

11. Press F8 to change to the Define Page screen. This screen controls the margins and characters per inch, and allows you to add footers and headers.

12. Press F10 to save the Report spec and F10 to print the report.
Figure 9.16 shows the finished report.

```
03/10/91              SALES BY COMPANY AND MONTH                      PAGE 1


                                      Invoice Date

                             ----------------------------

COMPANY                             Jan 91      Feb 91      Mar 91   Total Sale
-------------------------   --     --------    ---------   ---------  ==========

Brazilian Lumber            Avg     $3996.00    $9144.00    $3816.00    $5859.00

                            Tot     $7992.00   $27432.00   $11448.00   $46872.00

                            Min     $3888.00    $1944.00    $1728.00    $1728.00

                            Max     $4104.00   $21384.00    $5184.00   $21384.00


Sacks: Fine Burlap Clothing Avg     $1196.37    $2028.33     $585.00    $1355.51

                            Tot     $3589.10    $6085.00    $1170.00   $10844.10

                            Min      $585.00     $225.00     $135.00     $135.00

                            Max     $1969.10    $3385.00    $1035.00    $3385.00


The Blue Sky Company        Avg      $993.41    $3467.70    $1742.70    $1647.63

                            Tot     $5960.48    $6935.40    $5228.10   $18123.98

                            Min       $92.70    $3017.70     $542.70      $92.70

                            Max     $1982.70    $3917.70    $3692.70    $3917.70


The Good Health Hospital    Avg      $547.20     $322.43     $385.88     $455.97

                            Tot     $1641.61     $322.43     $771.76    $2735.80

                            Min       $90.00     $322.43      $48.38      $48.38

                            Max     $1008.23     $322.43     $723.38    $1008.23
=========================== ===    =========   =========   =========  ==========
Total Sale                  Avg     $1370.23    $4530.54    $1861.79    $2381.09

                            Tot    $19183.19   $40774.83   $18617.86   $78575.88

                            Min       $90.00     $225.00      $48.38      $48.38

                            Max     $4104.00   $21384.00    $5184.00   $21384.00
```

Figure 9.16   Finished cross-tab report.

Like the columnar and form reports, the cross-tab report lets you change the global defaults. The default settings control Headings, Page Format, Print options, and the Define Page options. Two of these options have been changed for this report. They are the cross-tab Headings and the Format options. The cross-tab Headings spec lets you change your field labels and can be used in place of the Heading command described earlier. The changes you make here become the new defaults but can be overridden by the Heading command.

Practice Changing the Cross-Tab Headings

1. Press **R** for Report and **S** for Set Global Options. Type the filename **INVOICE** and press Enter.

2. Select **X** for Cross Tab Global Options and **C** for Set Col/Row headings. If you move to the DATE field, you can see that the heading has been changed to INVOICE DATE, and in the BAL & INT field you can see that the heading has been changed to TOTAL SALE. Make your changes.

3. When you are done, press F10 to save your changes.

The other item that has been changed is in the Format Options. I have told Q&A to print "no entry" columns or rows. If a column or row has no entry, Q&A will still print the column or row heading. Suppose that you want to check the number of clients from each state. With this setting on NO, you would not see the title for Florida if there were no entries.

Practice Changing the Format Options

1. Press **R** for Report and **S** for Set Global Options. Type the filename **INVOICE** and press Enter.

2. Press **X** for Cross Tab Global Options and **F** for Set Format Options. You can see that the No Entry option is now set to Yes; the default is No. Make your changes.

3. Press F10 to save your changes.

This concludes the section on cross-tab reporting. This is a very powerful feature, so take some time to experiment with it.

Intelligent Assistant Module

There are two assistants in the Intelligent Assistant module: the original one, called the Intelligent Assistant (IA); and a new one, called the Query Guide (QG). To avoid confusion when I refer to the two assistants together, I will call them the Intelligent Assistant module. When I refer to the portion of the module that uses the natural language, I will refer to it as the Intelligent Assistant, or IA, and when I refer to the other assistant, I will call it the Query Guide, or QG.

The *Intelligent Assistant* lets you make requests of your database by using a natural language interface. These requests can be any question in the form of who, what, where, or how many. You can change all the values in a field; add, change, or delete any record; print predefined reports; create new reports; and more. In short, you can do almost all of the tasks that you can do in the File module and many that you can't.

The *Query Guide* performs the same function as the IA except that your requests are built by selecting options from a menu. This limits some of your options but makes it more likely that your request will follow the proper syntax. Most of what you will want to do can be done by using the QG, but not everything.

You will need to gain familiarity with the File module, the Intelligent Assistant, and the Query Guide. Then you can determine which module is best suited for which type of task. You will learn some of these distinctions as you go through the examples in the next two sections.

The Intelligent Assistant

Before you can begin using the IA, you have to teach it about your database. This is a two-part process: the first part is done by Q&A, and the second part is done by you when you answer the IA's questions about the information in your database. These questions are referred to as *lessons* and are divided into basic and advanced. You can complete as many of the lessons as you like. However, the more you complete, the faster and easier your requests will be fulfilled.

In order to use the IA, you have to run the *teaching process*. The Invoice database has already been "taught," but you should go through the process anyway so that you gain an understanding of how it works. During the teaching process, Q&A reads all the records in your database and adds the information to the index (.IDX) file. This process increases the size of that file. The increase is dependent on how many of the lessons you go through. In the next example, the index file was increased by a factor of three. You should be aware that after you have taught a database, data entry will be slowed somewhat, and the time it takes to copy a record from one database to another will double. In smaller databases (under 1,000 records), these issues generally aren't much of a factor. However on large databases (over 5,000 records), the speed and file size issues could be a nuisance.

Running the Teaching Process and Exploring the Basic Lessons Menu

1. Press **A** for Assistant and **T** for Teaching.

2. Enter the filename. Since the teaching process has already been done, Q&A will move almost immediately to the Basic Lessons menu, shown in Figure 9.17. If the database had been a new one, the teaching process would have taken considerably longer. In fact, it is *always* a good idea to teach the database with only a few records in it, since the teaching process can take a long time if you have many records in the database.

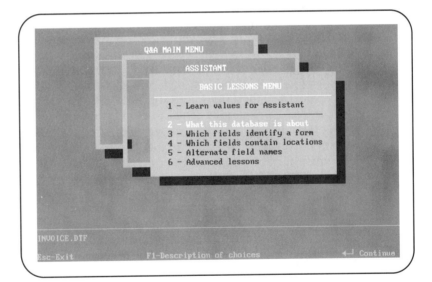

Figure 9.17   Basic Lessons menu.

3. Move to the first option, What this database is about, and press Enter. Answer the question Each record contains information about a particular X. As you can see in Figure 9.18,

371

this question has been answered with Invoices and Sales. Type definitions in singular form (*invoice,* not *invoices*). Press F10 to save your changes.

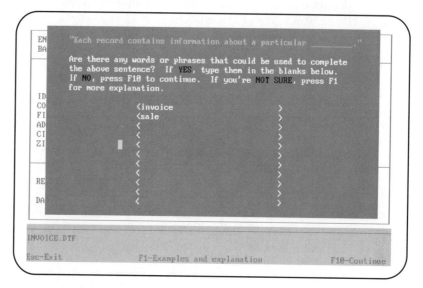

Figure 9.18   The first lesson.

4. Press the Down Arrow and press Enter to select Which fields identify a form. The fields you specify here will be displayed even if a request does not explicitly say that it uses these fields. For example, if you say "list all sales" and you have not specified the company field here, you will get a list of all the sales with no company name attached. In this lesson, I chose COMPANY. You can make further selections, but too many will clutter up the requests. Press F10 to save your selections.

5. The lesson, Which fields contain locations, is used to specify which fields are associated with locations. In this case, the fields are ADDRESS, CITY, STATE, and ZIP. As you will see, I did not fill in this option. I will show you later how to accomplish this same task by using a "synonym." Press F10 to exit this lesson.

6. The next option allows you to assign alternate field names to your fields. This affords two benefits. The first is that you can call a field by some other term, meaning that you can abbreviate the field to

shorten your requests. If you look at Figure 9.19, you can see that I added `total sale` and `ts` to the BAL & INT field. Select this option and use the F8 key to move forward through the fields and the F6 key to move backward. When you are through, press F10.

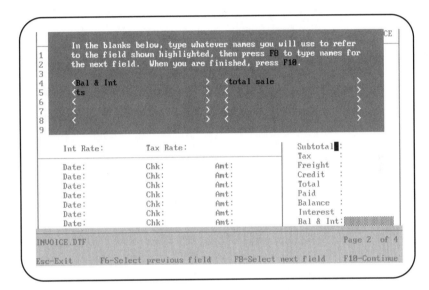

```
     In the blanks below, type whatever names you will use to refer
1    to the field shown highlighted, then press F8 to type names for
2    the next field.  When you are finished, press F10.
3
4    <Bal & Int          >  <total sale              >
5    <ts                 >  <                        >
6    <                   >  <                        >
7    <                   >  <                        >
8    <                   >  <                        >
9
     Int Rate:        Tax Rate:                    Subtotal :
                                                   Tax      :
     Date:       Chk:          Amt:                Freight  :
     Date:       Chk:          Amt:                Credit   :
     Date:       Chk:          Amt:                Total    :
     Date:       Chk:          Amt:                Paid     :
     Date:       Chk:          Amt:                Balance  :
     Date:       Chk:          Amt:                Interest :
     Date:       Chk:          Amt:                Bal & Int:

INVOICE.DTF                                        Page 2  of 4

Esc-Exit    F6-Select previous field   F8-Select next field   F10-Continue
```

Figure 9.19   Alternate field names for BAL & INT.

Exploring the Advanced Lessons Menu

1. Select the Advanced Lessons menu by highlighting it and pressing Enter. You can see the options in Figure 9.20. Each of these lessons works the same way as the basic lessons: select the option and fill in the blanks.

2. The first lesson, `Which fields contain people's names`, allows you to designate which fields contains proper names. To do this, place a number (for each person) in the field, followed by an **F** for first name, **L** for last name, and **M** for middle name. For example, the FIRST field would contain the code 1F, and the LAST field would contain 1L.

3. The next option, `Units of measure`, lets you tell Q&A the unit of measure for each numeric field. For example, you could designate a WEIGH field as pounds, and a GAS field as gallons.

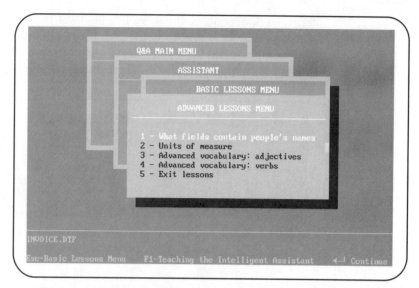

Figure 9.20   Advanced Lessons menu.

4. The Advanced vocabulary: adjectives lesson is where you
    assign adjectives to describe money and numeric fields. Each field
    should have two adjectives, one for the high value and one for the
    low value. For example, you could assign Huge and Tiny to the BAL
    & INT field and make a request like "List all Huge sales." You
    would get all the largest sales. Q&A already understands these
    adjectives: big, few, great, high, large, little, low, many, much, and
    small.

5. The Advanced vocabulary: verbs permits you to assign a verb to a
    particular field. In this case, I assigned the word *buy* to the field
    BAL & INT. So now you can ask "What did everybody *buy* in 1990?"

    Before you begin making requests, you should look at Q&A's built-in
    words and learn how to define synonyms.

Looking at Q&A's Built-in Words

1. If you are at the Advanced Lessons menu, press Esc twice. Press **A**
    for Ask, type the filename, and Enter. You are now at the main
    Request screen.

2. Press F6 to see the words that Q&A already knows. Press Enter
    to select the built-in words option and press Esc when done.
    Figure 9.21 shows the built-in vocabulary.

Screen 1

BUILT-IN VOCABULARY

A	ANY	BELOW	COME	DECREASE	ENTRY
ABOUT	ANYONE	BEST	COMMENCING	DEFINE	EQUAL
ABOVE	APPEAR	BETTER	CONCERN	DEFINITION	ERASE
ACCORDING	APRIL	BETWEEN	CONSTRAINT	DELETE	EVERY
ADD	ARE	BIG	CONTAIN	DESCENDING	EVERYBODY
AFTER	AS	BLANK	COULD	DETAIL	EVERYTHING
AGAIN	ASCENDING	BOTH	COUNT	DEVIATION	EXCEED
AGAINST	ASSIGN	BOTTOM	CREATE	DIFFERENCE	EXCLUDE
AGO	AT	BREAK	CROSSTAB	DISPLAY	EXCLUSIVE
ALL	AUGUST	BUT	CROSSTABULATE	DIVIDE	EXIST
ALONG	AVERAGE	BY	CURRENT	DO	F
ALPHABETICAL	AWAY	CALCULATE	CUT	DURING	FALSE
ALSO	B	CAME	DAILY	EACH	FEBRUARY
AM	BE	CAN	DATA	EARLY	FETCH
AMONG	BEEN	CHANGE	DATABASE	EITHER	FEW
AN	BEFORE	CHRISTEN	DATE	EMPTY	FIELD
AND	BEGIN	CHRISTMAS	DAY	END	FILE
ANNUAL	BEING	COLUMN	DECEMBER	ENTER	FILL

Esc-Exit   PgDn-View More Definitions

Screen 2

FIND	HIM	LARGE	MINIMUM	NULL	PRESENT
FOLLOWING	HIS	LAST	MINUS	NUMBER	PREVIOUS
FOR	HOUR	LATE	MINUTE	OCTOBER	PRINT
FORM	HOW	LEAST	MONTH	OF	PRODUCE
FOUND	I	LESS	MORE	OK	PRODUCT
FROM	ID	LET	MOST	ON	PROGRESSION
GET	IDENTIFICATION	LIKE	MUCH	ONE	PUT
GIVE	IF	LIST	MULTIPLY	ONLY	QUOTIENT
GOOD	IN	LITTLE	MUST	OR	RAISE
GOT	INCLUDE	LOOK	MY	ORDER	RANK
GRAND	INCLUSIVELY	LOW	N	OUT	RATIO
GREAT	INCREASE	M	NAME	OVER	RECENT
HAD	INFORMATION	MADE	NEGATIVE	OVERALL	RECORD
HALF	IS	MAKE	NEITHER	PAST	REDUCE
HALLOWEEN	IT	MANY	NEW	PATTERN	REMOVE
HAS	JANUARY	MARCH	NEXT	PERCENT	REPLACE
HAVE	JULY	MATCH	NO	PLUS	REPORT
HE	JUNE	MAXIMUM	NON	POOR	RESET
HELP	JUST	MAY	NOT	PORTION	RESPECT
HER	K	ME	NOVEMBER	POSITIVE	RESTRICTION
HIGH	KNOW	MEAN	NOW	PRECEDING	RETRIEVE

Esc-Exit   PgDn-View More Definitions

Screen 3

REVERSE	STANDARD	TABLE	TO	WHAT	YEAR
RUN	START	TAKE	TODAY	WHEN	YES
SAME	STATISTICS	TELL	TOMORROW	WHERE	YESTERDAY
SEARCH	STILL	THAN	TOP	WHETHER	YOU
SEE	SUBAVERAGE	THANK	TOTAL	WHICH	YOU'LL
SELECT	SUBCALCULATION	THAT	TRUE	WHO	YOUR
SEPTEMBER	SUBCOUNT	THE	TWICE	WHOM	Z
SEQUENCE	SUBMAXIMA	THEIR	UNDER	WHOSE	
SET	SUBMAXIMUM	THEM	UP	WILL	
SHALL	SUBMINIMA	THEN	US	WITH	
SHE	SUBMINIMUM	THERE	USE	WNEC	
SHOULD	SUBTOTAL	THESE	VALUE	WNIC	
SHOW	SUBTRACT	THEY	VARIANCE	WNRC	
SINCE	SUBVARIANCE	THING	VERSUS	WON'T	
SMALL	SUCCEEDING	THINK	WANT	WORSE	
SOME	SUM	THIS	WAS	WOULD	
SORT	SUMMARY	THOSE	WE	WRITE	
SOUND	SYNONYM	THROUGH	WELL	WRT	
SOUNDEX	T	TIME	WERE	Y	

% ( ) * + , - / /= ; < <= <> = > >< >=

Esc-Exit   + PgUp-More +

Figure 9.21   Q&A's built-in word list.

375

A very useful feature is defining synonyms. This option lets you define new words based on Q&A's built-in words or on fields in the database. Choose the Synonym option (shown in Figure 9.22), and you will see the synonyms I have defined. The first one defines CLIENT as the field name COMPANY, the second one defines FETCH as GET, and the last one defines OFFICE as the fields ADDRESS, CITY, STATE, and ZIP. Press Esc twice to return to the Request screen.

There are two ways to define synonyms. The first is at the Request screen. You type **DEFINE X as** Y, where X is the synonym and Y is either a word from the built-in list or one or more fields.

The other way to define synonyms is to press F8 from the main Request screen and press **S** for A Synonym. Type the synonym in the left box and the words or fields in the right boxes. Press F10 to save your changes.

Practice Defining Synonyms

1. Let's define two synonyms. Type **DEFINE good as well-behaved** and press Enter twice. Then type **DEFINE well-behaved as BAL & INT 5000** and press Enter twice.

2. Now ask the question **List all well-behaved clients** and press Enter twice. This will create a report listing all your well-behaved clients.

3. Press F10 when you are through viewing the report.

Asking a Question of the IA

1. Type the question in the box and press Enter.

2. Press Enter again to print the report to the screen. If it is a long report, you will have to press Enter or the Down Arrow key until you come to the End of Report message and then press F10 to make another request.

3. You can press Shift-F7 to bring up the last request or type a follow-up question to the previous request. If you want to cut the report short and make another request, press Esc.

4. To reference a specific value in a field, you must enclose it in quotes, for example, "Smith". If you make a request that Q&A doesn't understand, it will ask you to clarify it. When this occurs, you have the option of editing the unknown word or defining it.

5. To send a report to the printer, press F2, select the correct printer, and press F10.

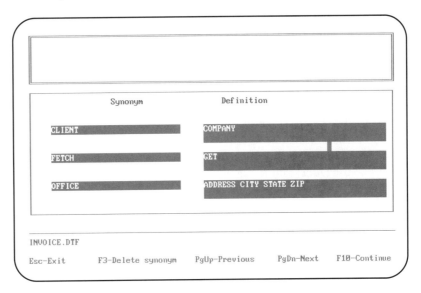

Figure 9.22   Existing synonyms.

Practice making requests of your own by typing the requests in the following list. Simply type the question and press Enter twice to begin the request. Keep pressing Enter until you reach the End of Report message. Then press F10 to begin the next request.

> List all clients.
>
> List all clients sorted by client.
>
> What is the average sale for client.
>
> Show company and sum total sale where company="braz..".
>
> Count clients where state="CA".
>
> Change BATCH # to "2" where company="braz..".
>
> Show BATCH # where company="braz..".
>
> Show sales where DUE DATE 02/15/91 sorted by DUE DATE.
>
> Add a new record with "1" as IDNUM and PO#="11111".

Press F8 to complete the lookup and F10 to save the record.

> Show all clients sum BAL & INT where STATE="CA" or BAL & INT 1500 or 1="BW and sorted by COMPANY.

When you are through practicing, press Esc three times to return to the Main menu.

If you add fields to your database, you will have to give your IA a refresher course by running the teaching process again and going through any appropriate lessons.

The Query Guide

The *Query Guide* is a menu-driven method of asking common questions of the Intelligent Assistant. It supports your requests by presenting the essential building blocks of the natural language used by the IA. Like the IA, the Query Guide needs to be taught; however, there is only one step to the process and it is quite easy. Once the QG is taught, all you have to do is select options from the menu and build your request—with almost no typing. This makes it ideal for the occasional user who just wants to ask questions.

Practice Teaching the Query Guide

1. Press **A** for Assistant and **E** for Teach Query Guide.

2. Type the filename **INVOICE** and press Enter. This file has already been taught for you. You can tell because there is a Q in several of the fields. The Q indexes the fields, presenting you with a list of the field values when you make the appropriate request. For instance, if you made the request "Show all records where city equals X," and you had a Q in the CITY field, the QG would let you choose from all the cities in your file.

3. When you are through teaching the QG, press F10 to save your changes. Figure 9.23 shows the Teach screen.

Practice Using the Query Guide

1. Press **Q** for Query Guide.

2. Type the filename **INVOICE** and press Enter.

You are now at the main Query screen, shown in Figure 9.24. You will explore each option by making sample requests.

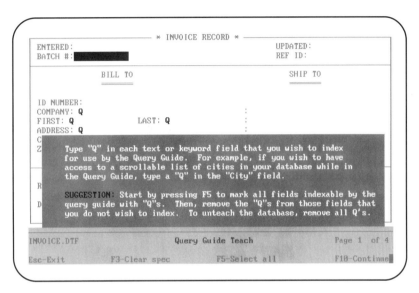

Figure 9.23   Teach screen for the Query Guide.

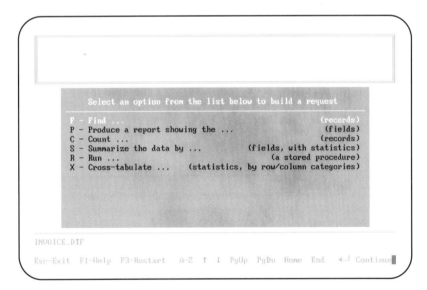

Figure 9.24   Main Query Guide Request screen.

The first option, Find, is for finding and displaying records in Form View. This option is identical to the Search/Update process. You are going to make this request: Find the records where CITY equals Podunk sorted by INVOICE #.

3. Press **F** for Find. You will see three suboptions. The first one allows you to choose exact matches or ranges of records, the second option retrieves all records in the database, and the last option brings up the last record you entered. You are going to do a selected search, so press **R** for The Records Where, type **CITY**, and press Enter.

4. You are now at the Constraints screen, shown in Figure 9.25. This is where you make your choices for selecting records. At the top of the screen, you can see your request being built statement-by-statement. Press Enter to select equals. A list of cities in the database will pop up because a Q was placed in the CITY field during the teaching process. Press **P** for Podunk and press Enter.

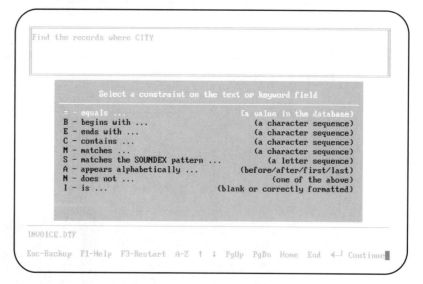

Figure 9.25   Constraint screen in Find mode.

5. This places you at another screen (shown in Figure 9.26), where you can continue making your request more specific by selecting the and the or the or command.

Shortcut

If you press Esc, you can retrace your steps in the request and make changes. The screens will move back one at a time. If you want to start over, press F3.

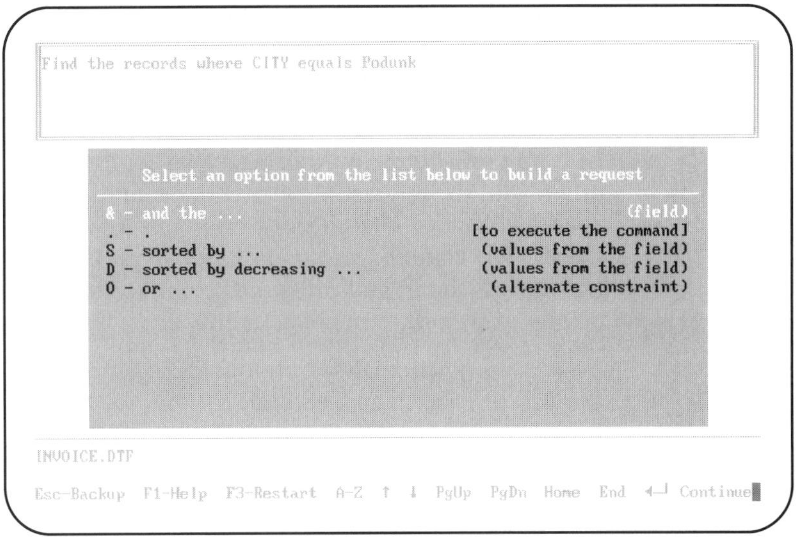

```
 Find the records where CITY equals Podunk



        Select an option from the list below to build a request

 & - and the ...                                     (field)
 . - .                              [to execute the command]
 S - sorted by ...                  (values from the field)
 D - sorted by decreasing ...       (values from the field)
 O - or ...                         (alternate constraint)




 INVOICE.DTF

 Esc-Backup  F1-Help  F3-Restart  A-Z ↑ ↓  PgUp  PgDn  Home  End  ←⌐ Continue█
```

Figure 9.26   Additional Constraints and Sorting options.

6. Press **S** for Sorted By, type **INVOICE #**, and press Enter. To execute the command, press the period (**.**). You are now in Form View, looking at all the records where the CITY field is Podunk and all the records are sorted by INVOICE #. You can make any changes to these records.

7. When you are done, press Shift-F10 to exit and return to the Query Guide screen. The request sequence you just completed is the same for all the other options on the menu.

The next option on the main Query screen is `Produce a report showing the`. It allows you to construct columnar reports from fields in the database. You can place any fields from the database on a report, sort it any way you want, and add any of the calculation options. You are going to create a report showing the company name and the invoice total, and use the average, count, and total calculation options. The request you will end up with is `Produce a report showing the COMPANY and the Bal & Int with average and total and count of values from ALL the records sorted by COMPANY`.

8. Press **P** for Produce a Report, type **COMPANY**, press Enter, press **&**, type **BAL & INT**, and press Enter. Press **A** for Average, **T** for Total, **C** for Count, and **F** for From. Select **A** for All and **S** for Sorted By.

Type **COMPANY** and press the period (**.**). To scroll through your report, use the Down Arrow. To send the report to the printer, press F2 and select your printer. When you are done viewing the report, press Esc.

9. To count the records in a database, use the Count option. You will end up with the request: Count the records where COMPANY begins with "t". Press **C** for Count and **R** for The Records Where. Type **COMPANY** and press Enter. Type **B** for Begins With, type **T**, press Enter, and press the period (**.**) to initiate the count. Press Esc to return to the Main menu.

You can do quick analyses of your data with the next option. The request will be: Summarize the data by COMPANY showing all statistics for Bal & Int from ALL the records.

10. Press **S** for Summarize The Data By, type **COMPANY**, and press Enter. Press **A** for Showing All Statistics For, type **BAL & INT**, and press **A** for All Records. These are all the statistics you can display on your numeric and money fields. Press Esc to return to the Query main menu.

The Run command lets you print a pre-existing form, columnar, or cross-tab report. In step 11, you will issue the command "Run the report X-Number of Companies by State."

11. Press **R** for Run and **R** for Report. Choose the report X-# of Companies By State and press Enter. Answer No to print the report as is. (If you answered Yes, you would be taken through all the standard report options.) Press Esc to return to the Main menu.

The final option allows you to build your own cross-tab reports. You will build the same report illustrated in the cross-tab section. The request will end up as: Cross-tabulate the average and the total for Bal & Int by COMPANY and by DATE grouped by month from ALL the records.

12. Press **X** for Cross Tab, **A** for Average, **T** for Total, and **F** for Field. Type **BAL & INT** and press Enter. Press Enter on **B** for By, type **COMPANY** for Row and press Enter. Press **&**, type **DATE**, press Enter, type **M** for Month, and type **A** for All Records. Press Esc when you are through viewing the report.

This completes the examples. You may wish to practice using other variations of these commands. When you are through practicing, press Esc twice to return to the Q&A Main menu.

Summary

Now would be a good time to give some thought to how you can apply these features to the other applications you are using. Remember, these two features form the heart of your decision support systems and can provide you with a quick and easy way to analyze your data.

When designing a cross-tab report, start out by formulating the report into a plain English question, for example, "What are the average and total sales by company, by month?" Once this is done, you can design the report, keeping in mind that you must have one Row, Col, and Sum code for each report. The Groupings command lets you further segment your data, and you can apply any of the statistical codes to the SUM field.

The Intelligent Assistant now consists of two parts: the original Intelligent Assistant (IA) and the Query Guide (QG). Both of these assistants need to be "taught" before you can use them. The IA has a more elaborate teaching process, along with two menus of lessons. The QG requires only that you place a Q in each field you want indexed. Both assistants let you make requests of your database. The IA uses a natural language interface, and the QG uses a menu. Both let you ask questions, run reports, summarize data, change records, and more.

In the final chapter, you will learn how to combine all your files and macros in an easy-to-use new system.

Run a Macro

1. Press Alt-F2.
2. Highlight the macro and press Enter.

Record a Macro

1. Press Shift-F2 and press **D** for Define. Type a macro identifier.
2. Record your keystrokes and press Shift-F2.
3. Type the macro name and choose Yes or No to show the screen.
4. Press F10 and then Enter to save the macro.

Create a Custom Menu

1. Press Shift-F2. Press **M** for Create Menu and press Enter on the new menu selection.
2. Fill in the Macro Menu Options form. Press F10 and Enter to save the menu.
3. Press Esc to return to the Q&A Main menus.

IN
BUSINESS

Menu/Macro Application

This chapter will teach you how to use the features of the Macro and Custom menus so that you can integrate files, reports, and procedures into seamless applications.

Overview

This chapter varies from previous chapters because the "Application Explained" and the "Use Application" sections have been combined. The features in the Menu/Macro application are so easy to use that explaining them tells you how to use them. Thus, the majority of your work will be done in the Design section.

The Macro and Custom menu features allow you to complete your applications. As you are going through the examples, consider how you can apply these features to the applications you have developed.

With the exception of the Write module, you have focused on creating databases and reports—the heart of an application. But by adding macros and Custom menus, you can make the application really useful and easy to use. The macro feature acts like a keystroke tape recorder; whatever you record, you can play back. Custom menus allow you to group similar tasks together and either supplement the Q&A menus or replace them entirely.

The examples in the chapter will provide a main menu for all your applications and a completed submenu for the Names application. The chapter also includes macros for a variety of tasks: adding data, searching for data, printing the Names report, and updating the direct mail codes. In the Design section, you will add a menu to the Main Application menu and add a macro to the new submenu.

Macros are a powerful feature that can greatly enhance your productivity. Creating a macro is easy. All you have to do is invoke the macro recorder, type your keystrokes, and save the macro with a name. Macros do not have to be used with Custom menus. Whenever you create a macro, it is automatically placed on a special Macro menu. Thus, to replay the macro, you need only press Alt-F2 and select the desired macro. Macros can be used for printing reports, updating data, deleting data, printing letters and labels, etc. In short, any task you can do manually in Q&A can be done automatically by using a recorded macro.

Custom menus are a new feature added to Version 4.0. With Custom menus, you can create your own custom applications and completely eliminate the standard Q&A menus. This feature can help reduce the learning curve by presenting only the features your users must see in order to do their jobs. As their skill level increases, you can give them access to the standard Q&A menus and features.

Macros and Custom menus are stored in a macro file called QAMACRO.ASC and can be edited with a word processor. This macro file can be encrypted so that no one can modify it. Taken together, these features offer the possibility of creating complete custom applications tailored to your specific needs.

Application Explained

You can run macros independently of Custom menus. Each time you create a macro, it is added to the Macro Names menu shown in Figure 10.1. To invoke this menu, press Alt-F2 from anywhere in the program and the menu will appear. To run the macro, move the cursor to the desired selection and press Enter.

I have created a macro to launch the main Application menu; it is Alt-M. This menu is a Custom menu and is shown in Figure 10.2. It has entries on it for the Names, Inventory/Invoicing, Sales Management, and Personnel applications. These menus work the same way the Q&A menus work. You press the first letter of the entry, or you press Enter on the entry. The entries on the main Application menu can launch macros or other submenus. On this menu, the Names application has a submenu. If you press **N**, you can invoke the submenu. It is shown in Figure 10.3.

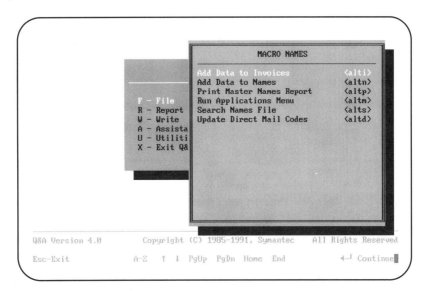

Figure 10.1   Macro Names menu.

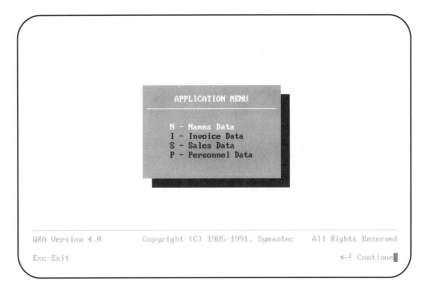

Figure 10.2   Custom Application menu.

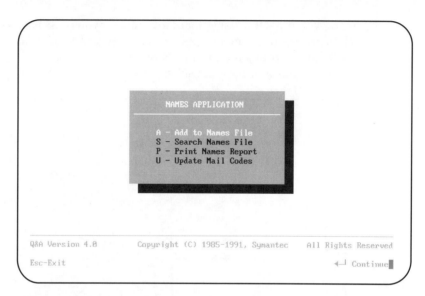

NAMES APPLICATION

A - Add to Names File
S - Search Names File
P - Print Names Report
U - Update Mail Codes

Q&A Version 4.0   Copyright (C) 1985-1991, Symantec   All Rights Reserved

Esc-Exit   ◄─┘ Continue

Figure 10.3   Submenu of Application menu.

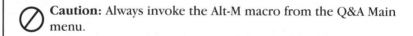

Caution: Always invoke the Alt-M macro from the Q&A Main menu.

Guided Modifications

The first part of this section will focus on understanding and developing macros. The second part will concentrate on the Custom menus.

Developing Macros

Chapter 2 explained in detail how to develop a macro. If you did not read that chapter, you should read it now so that you fully understand how to develop a macro. This discussion merely reviews what was covered in Chapter 2 and then discusses other aspects of the macro feature.

With Q&A's macro facility, you can record a series of keystrokes and then replay them at any time. You are saved the time and effort of retyping those particular keystrokes. For example, the Phone List macro in Chapter 2 will print a phone list automatically. Performing these tasks manually would be tedious, but with a macro it is a snap.

Recording a Macro

1. Decide what you want to automate.

2. Turn on the macro recording facility by pressing Shift-F2. Press **D** for Define Macro. Designate a macro identifier (a *macro identifier* is any keystroke combination, such as Alt-A).

3. Perform the tasks. Turn off the recording facility by pressing Shift-F2.

4. Give the macro a name and then save it by pressing F10 and Enter.

Every time you create a macro or Custom menu, Q&A stores the information in the file QAMACRO.ASC. The file resides in the QA subdirectory. If you create a macro file larger than 3,000 characters, you will be unable to load the macro. You can also receive a "macro buffer full" error message if you reach this limit while developing a macro. To overcome this limitation, you must increase Q&A's macro buffer size. Do this by starting Q&A with the *-b* switch followed by a number slightly larger than your macro file. For example, starting Q&A with the command **QA -b10000** would allow you to load a macro file having 10,000 characters.

If you are not going to use Custom menus, there are three ways that you can replay a macro. The first is to type the macro identifier you assigned to the macro (for example, Alt-A). The next way is to display a list of all macros and their names by pressing Alt-F2 from anywhere in the program. The last way, and most cumbersome, is to display the Macro menu Shift-F2 and choose **R** for Run Macros.

When you are running a macro, keep in mind where you initially started recording. If you started the recording process in the File menu, and now you want to run the macro from the Program menu, the macro will malfunction. A few more tips to heed when developing a macro are

- Start all procedures from the Q&A Main menu.

- Do not use the arrow keys to make selections. Press the letter of the menu selection.

- For report and file names, always type the full name of the item.

To access the Macro menu, shown in Figure 10.4, press Shift-F2. Notice the seven options in the menu. I will describe each of the options except the last one, which will be explained in the next section.

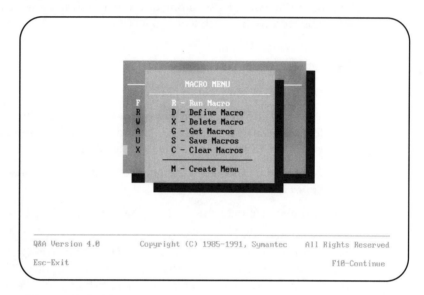

Figure 10.4   Macro menu.

Use the *Run Macro option* when you have already developed a macro and want to run it. You can invoke this menu by pressing **R** for Run, highlighting the macro, and pressing Enter. This will display the same menu as when you press Alt-F2. Each time you create a macro, Q&A adds it to this menu.

To select the *Define Macro option*, press **D** for Define. This option will be thoroughly covered later in the chapter. If you find that a macro is no longer needed, use the *Delete Macro option*. To delete the macro from the Macro file, press **X** for Delete Macro, move to the selection on the Macro Names menu, and press Enter.

At times, you may want to store different types of macros in different files. You might do this if you have two groups of applications that you want to use at the same time. Setting up separate macro files involves three steps: initially creating an ASCII file with the correct name, getting the macro file (explained in step 3 of the next example) by using the Get Macro option, and then saving your macros into the new file.

Creating a New Macro File

1. Press **W** for Write and **T** for Type/Edit.

2. You are at a blank Write screen. Press Ctrl-F8 to save an ASCII file. Press Shift-F4 to clear the path and type `C:\qa\filename.mac`, substituting for `filename.mac` any filename you like. Press Enter. You now have a new macro file in which to save your macros.

3. The *Get Macro option* allows you to get another macro file. Use this option if you edit your current macro file and want the changes to be present in memory. When you are ready to save your macro into the new file, press **G** for Get, type the new macro filename, and press Enter. Your macro is saved into the new file.

Shortcut

You can edit a macro file by using an ASCII editor or the Write module in ASCII mode.

The *Save Macro option* seems to serve no useful purpose. The *Clear Macro option* clears an existing macro file from memory. Press **C** for Clear.

Q&A allows you to change its default settings through a feature called *switches*. Switches are set *outside* the program at the DOS prompt when you are starting the program. The syntax for setting a switch is QA -X, where X is the command. Here are some useful switches:

- QA -AL filename, where AL stands for auto load and filename is the name of the macro file you want to load instead of the default file QAMACRO.ASC.

- QA -AD filename, where AD stands for auto default and filename is the name of the new default macro file. To reset the default macro file, type **QA -AD**.

- QA -Mx, where x is the macro number for a specific macro that you want to load automatically at start-up time. Any macro that you want to load using this switch has to have a macro identifier consisting of the Alt key and a number from 0 to 9 (for example, Alt-1). These are the only macros that can be called with the -M switch. This feature could be used to automatically load a Custom menu.

A new feature added to Version 4.0 is the ability to lock people out of your macro files after the files are created. Once you load a locked macro file, you cannot use the other features of the Macro menu until you load an unlocked macro file. After you are done creating your macros and Custom menus, you can lock the macro file.

Locking a Macro File

1. Press **F** for File, **D** for Design, and **A** for Customize Applications.

2. Type the filename of the macro file and press Enter.

3. Type the filename of the new locked macro file and press Enter. (I recommend that you use a .LOC extension on any locked macro files.)

   In the next example, you will record a macro that prints sales invoices. Then, in the "Custom Menus" section, you will add this macro to a Custom menu.

Practice Recording a Macro to Print Sales Invoices

1. From the Q&A Main menu, press Shift-F2 to display the Macro menu.

2. Press **D** for Define Macro and press Alt-H for the macro identifier. You are now going to record the keystrokes necessary to print sales invoices.

3. Press **F** for File and **P** for Print. Type the filename **INVOICE** and press Enter. Press **P** for Print Records and select Sales Invoice. Type **Y** for Make Temporary Changes.

Any changes you make will not be saved in the Report spec.

4. You are now at the Retrieve spec. This is where you tell Q&A which records you want to print. Press the Down Arrow ten times until you are at the DATE field. Press Alt-F2 twice to cause the macro to pause on playback.

   There already is a default Retrieve spec of BAL & INT 0 in this report (so that only outstanding invoices are printed). The pause feature will cause the macro to stop at this point on playback so that you can enter a date. This can be used if you don't want to send invoices to everyone. Whenever you want a macro to pause at some specific spot during playback, press Alt-F2 twice at that spot. You can use this concept with all macros.

5. Press F10 to progress to the Field spec. Here you tell Q&A which fields you want to print. Press Alt-F2 twice to cause the macro to pause here on playback.

6. Press F10 to progress to the Print Options screen. Press Alt-F2 twice to cause the macro to pause here on playback.

7. Press F10 to print the report.

8. Press Esc twice to return to the Main menu.

9. Press Shift-F2 to bring up the Macro Options screen, shown in Figure 10.5. Type **Print Sales Invoices** and press Enter.

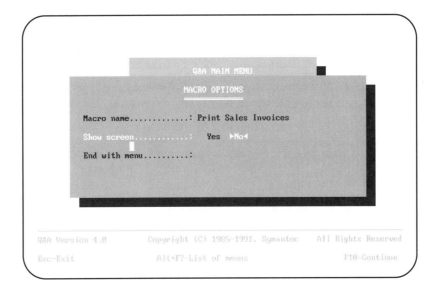

Figure 10.5   Macro Options.

The next option, Show Screen, gives you the option of suppressing all the unnecessary screens. Change it to No. The last option allows you to call another menu after this macro is done playing if you are using Custom menus. If you are using Custom menus, and you want to return to the menu that you came from, leave this option blank.

10. Press F10 and Enter to save the macro into the macro file QAMACRO.ASC.

You have now recorded a macro that will print your sales invoices anytime you want. Now replay the macro to make sure that it runs properly.

Practice Replaying a Macro

1. From the Q&A Main menu, press Alt-F2 to display the Macro Names menu. It should have the new macro on it. Move the cursor down to the new macro and press Enter.

2. The macro should move to the DATE field and pause at the Retrieve Spec screen. At the bottom of the screen, it should display the message: `Enter text. Press ↵ to resume macro playback.` This is your signal that you can enter variable text.

> ⊘ **Caution:** DO NOT use the Enter key to move between fields. Pressing Enter is Q&A's signal to restart the macro. Move between fields with the arrow and Tab keys only.

3. Move back up to the BATCH # field and type the number **1** and press Enter. This tells Q&A to print only one invoice.

4. The macro will pause at the Field spec. Press Enter to restart the macro.

5. Next it will pause at the Print Options screen. Press Enter to print the report.

6. If your macro did not perform correctly, rerecord it. If it worked properly, move on to the next section.

You now have the skills necessary to create complex macros. Remember, any task that you can do manually in Q&A can be done automatically with a recorded macro. In this last section you will integrate this macro into a Custom menu.

Custom Menus

With the Custom menu feature, you can create applications specific to your organization. You have the option of eliminating the Q&A menus entirely or just replacing selective menus. When you replace a Q&A menu with a Custom menu, it comes up in place of the original Q&A menu. In the example you are about to go through, the Main Application menu is designed to let you get back to the Q&A menus by pressing Esc. However, before you begin developing a menu, run an existing Custom menu.

Practice Running an Existing Custom Menu

1. Press Alt-M at the Q&A Main Application menu, shown in Figure 10.6. Press **N** for Names. You will see the Names Application menu.

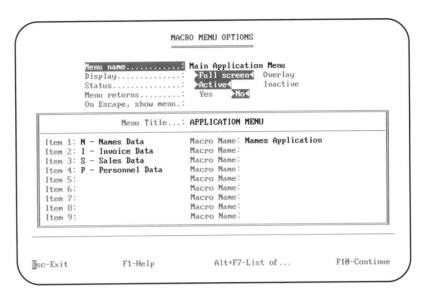

Figure 10.6   Macro menu options for Main Application menu.

2. Press **A** for Add Data to Names. You will be taken to the Names file in Add mode.

3. Press Esc once to return to the Names Application menu. Press Esc again to return to the Main Applications menu. Press Esc a third time to arrive back at the Q&A Main menu.

As you can see from the preceding brief example, Custom menus work just like regular Q&A menus. What took you to the Names file was a simple macro—just like the one you developed.

Next we will decipher the existing menus. Press Shift-F2 to bring up the Macro menu and press **M** for Create menu. Choose the Main Application menu and press Enter. You are now at the Menu Options screen, as shown in Figure 10.6. This is where you define all the options that control your Custom menus.

The first option, *Menu name*, is where you name the menu; this is the name that will appear when you bring up the list of menus. This is also where you can replace an existing Q&A menu. Press Alt-F7 to see all the Q&A menus that you can replace (these can be seen in Figure 10.7). If you use one of these names, the next time you invoke the menu with this name from the Q&A menus, your Custom menu will appear. To completely limit a user's access to the Q&A menus, put the Q&A Main menu title on this line in your main Custom menu.

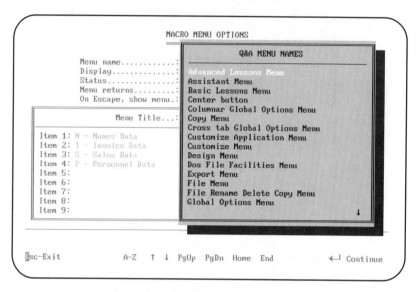

Figure 10.7   Replace Q&A menus.

The *Display* option controls whether you want the menu to appear full screen or as an overlay on the previous screen. As a rule, set the Main menu to Full Screen and all subsequent menus to Overlays. In this way, you always know where you are. The *Status* option lets you create a menu and keep it inactive until you are ready to use it. If the *Menu returns* option is set to Yes, and a macro on this menu performs a specific Q&A action, such as opening a file in Add mode, you are returned to this menu when you are done with that action.

The *On Escape, show menu* option allows you to specify which menu you want to go to when you press Esc from this menu. Normally it is the previous menu. If it is the Main menu, leave the option blank. You then can return to the Q&A menus or place another name here and return to the Custom menu when you press Esc.

The next portion of the screen is where you add your menu choices. The text you type on the left side of the screen in the Item field is the text that will be displayed on your menu. As you will notice, I used the Q&A convention of setting off the first letter with a dash. The right side of the screen contains the macros you want to run or other submenus. You will notice that this menu contains only one submenu for the Names Application. If you press Alt-F7 while you are on a macro field, a menu will pop up, showing you the only options you can place in that field. Figure 10.8 displays these options. When you are done viewing these options, press F10 and Enter to save any changes. If you press Esc, any changes will be lost.

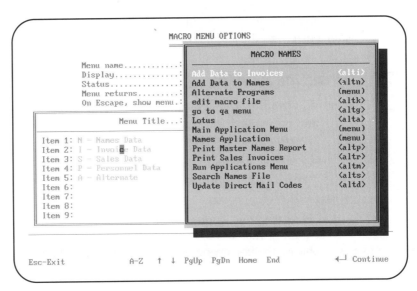

Figure 10.8   Available macros displayed.

You should still be at the Macro menu. Press **M** and select the Names Application menu, shown in Figure 10.9. You will see that the Display is set to Overlay, Menu returns is Yes, and all Items on the menu are macros. Press Esc two times to return to the Q&A Main menu.

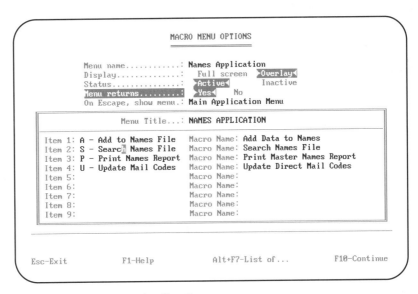

Figure 10.9   Names Application menu.

In this final exercise, you are going to add a submenu to the Main menu and a macro to the submenu.

Practice Adding a Submenu and a Macro

1. Press Shift-F2 to invoke the Macro menu. Press **M** for Create Menu and press Enter for New Menu. At the menu Name field, type **Invoice Application** and press Enter.

2. Set the Display option to Overlay, set Status to Active, and set the Menu returns option to Yes. At the On Escape, show menu option, press Alt-F7.

3. Select the Main Application menu and press Enter. Move to Item 1, type **A - Add Data Invoices**, and press Enter. Press Alt-F7, choose the corresponding macro, and press Enter. Type **P - Print Invoices** and press Enter. Press Alt-F7 and choose the corresponding macro. Press F10 and Enter to save the menu.

4. Press **M** again and choose the Main Application menu. Move down to the Item 2 macro field and press Alt-F7. Choose Invoice Application and press Enter. Press F10 and Enter to save the menu.

5. Press Esc and press Alt-M to launch the Custom menu and test your new options. If it works, you are through with this chapter. If it doesn't, go back and fix it.

Summary

You have just completed using two features that can really improve your applications. The first feature, a *macro*, acts like a tape recorder to record any keystrokes you type. Anything you can do manually in Q&A, you can record a macro to do automatically for you. To invoke the Macro menu, press Shift-F2. To run a macro, press Alt-F2 and select it from the menu, or press the macro identifier.

All your macros and menus are contained in the file QAMACRO.ASC and can be edited in the Write module. If your macro file exceeds 3,000 bytes, you will not be able to record any more macros. To remedy this problem, start Q&A each time with the *-b* switch and a number. The macros you create can be accessed from Custom menus.

Custom menus, the second feature, can replace Q&A menus or can be used in conjunction with them. If you do decide to replace any Q&A menu, do so with caution because you may lock yourself out of certain important Q&A features. They are created from the same menu as the macros are. Press Shift-F2 and **M** for Create menus. Once you are at the Macro Menu Options screen, you can configure the menus in many different ways. To launch a Custom menu, create a macro that calls only the Main menu.

Installation

This appendix will tell you how to install Q&A, set up your printer, and customize Q&A to your exact specifications.

Overview

Before you can use Q&A, you have to install it and configure it. The installation procedure you use will depend on whether you have a hard drive and whether the system will be used on one computer, known as a *single-user system*, or on a *local area network* (LAN), known as a multiuser system. The installation procedures will be divided into two sections: single-user and local area network (LAN).

If you are installing Q&A on a network and want more than one person to be able to access it at a time, you will have to purchase the Q&A Network Pack. Each Network Pack allows four users to access the program and the databases simultaneously.

After the LAN installation section, you will find procedures for configuring your printer, choosing the correct monitor driver, and customizing Q&A to your exact specifications. The final section will tell you how to make it easier to start Q&A on a daily basis.

If you are using Q&A and do not have a hard drive, I highly recommend that you install one. The cost is nominal, and to use the system effectively you must have one. In fact, all the exercises in this book assume that you are using a computer with hard drive.

System Requirements

Q&A runs on any IBM or compatible hardware: XT, AT/286, 386, or 486 models. *A 286- or 386-based computer is highly recommended.* Q&A uses approximately 1.5 megabytes of hard disk space for program files. The amount of hard disk space for data storage depends on how many documents and databases you develop and how much data is stored in those database files. The size of your data files is limited only by disk space. The program requires *640K of random access memory* (RAM). Your computer must be running PC DOS or MS-DOS 2.0 or higher for single users, and MS-DOS 3.1 or higher for local area networks. Q&A runs on any fully compatible IBM PC DOS or MS-DOS network, including 3Com, Novell, IBM Token Ring, Lantastic, 10net, and PC Appleshare.

Procedure Summary

The following list summarizes the steps involved in installing Q&A, setting up your printer, and customizing Q&A to fit your needs. In the upcoming sections, you will find specific instructions for the various steps.

Summary of Procedures

1. Check to make sure that your system meets the minimum requirements mentioned previously and that your hardware is set up and operating correctly.

2. Install Q&A.

3. Install Q&A Network Pack.

4. Configure your printer.

5. Set your data path.

6. Set the Q&A monitor switches.

7. Finish the network installation.

8. Start Q&A.

What to Do

Installing Q&A

1. Turn on your computer. If necessary, change to the hard drive (normally it is C or D). Type **c:** and press Enter.

2. Change to the root directory, make a directory for Q&A called QA, and then change to the QA directory. Type **cd** and press Enter. Type **md\qa** and press Enter. Type **cd\qa** and press Enter.

3. Create separate subdirectories for your word processing and database files. Type **md word** and press Enter. Type **md file** and press Enter.

4. Change to the A drive. Type **a:** and press Enter.

5. Put the Install disk in the A drive and begin to install Q&A on your hard disk. Type **install** and press Enter.

6. A message appears on the screen: Welcome to the Q&A 4.0 Installation. At this point, you can press Ctrl-Q to exit to DOS or Esc to cancel. You press Enter to continue.

7. Q&A asks you to highlight the *source* drive selection (the drive FROM which Q&A is being installed). This is drive A. Highlight A: and press Enter.

8. Q&A now asks for the *destination* drive selection (the drive TO which Q&A is being installed). This is drive C. Highlight C: and press Enter.

9. The Install program searches for other copies of Q&A. If it finds another copy of Q&A, it displays the subdirectory name and lets you create another directory. If it finds none, the Install program asks for the *destination* drive selection. In the middle of the screen is a prompt window that says: Enter Pathname: C:\QA. If you are going to copy Q&A into a subdirectory named QA in drive C— which you are—then you can simply press Enter. If you created a Q&A subdirectory with a different name, then backspace over the QA prompt and type the correct subdirectory name and press Enter.

10. The Install program asks if this will be a Complete Installation or a Selective Installation. Highlight C - Complete Installation and press Enter.

11. A message box at the bottom of the screen says: Q&A FILES BEING INSTALLED. Another message box in the middle of the screen shows the progression of the Q&A files being installed on the hard disk. When the files from the first disk have been installed, a prompt asks you to put in the second disk. The Install program will ask for each disk in order.

12. When the installation is complete, a message box appears at the top of the screen stating: Installation of Program Files Successfully Completed - All files of the specified type were installed successfully. Press Enter to move on.

13. At the top of the screen, you will see another message box stating: Hit ⌐ to install fonts, or Esc to Cancel. At the bottom of the screen, you will see the message: INSTALL SELECT FONT FILES - Font description files are required if your printer has fonts and you are planning on using fonts with Q&A. Press Enter at this point.

14. A window displaying all the Printer files appears. Scroll up and down through the choices and highlight the printer you use. Press the Spacebar to tag the printer. A checkmark appears next to your choice. You can choose several printers if you need to. After selecting a printer or several printers, press Enter. A prompt for the pathname appears. The pathname for the fonts is the same as that for the program files (it is the same path you gave at step 9). Press Enter.

15. The Install program will ask you to put disk 6 in drive A. Put the disk in drive A and press Enter. The correct printer file is then installed into the QA subdirectory. The Install program displays a message box stating that the installation of the file was successful. Press Enter.

16. A message box appears at the top of the screen stating: Hit ⌐ to install tutorial files, or Esc to Cancel. At the bottom of the screen a message box states: INSTALL SELECT TUTORIAL FILES - The tutorial files are required if you plan on using the tutorial included with Q&A. Press Esc to cancel at this point. You are not going to install the tutorial files.

17. The next message box now appears at the top of the screen stating: `Hit ⏎ to install ready-to-use files, or Esc to Cancel.` At the bottom of the screen is a message stating: `INSTALL SELECT READY-TO-USE FILES - The ready-to-use files are data-base templates that are ready to use for a variety of applications.` You are going to install these files. Press Enter.

18. You will see a window displaying all the ready-to-use files. Press F5 to tag all the files. A checkmark appears next to every file. After selecting the files, press Enter. A prompt for the pathname appears. The pathname for the ready-to-use files is the FILE subdirectory (which you created in step 3). Type **file**. (The prompt is: `Enter Pathname: C:\QA\`, so typing `file` makes it C:\QA\FILE.)

19. The Install program asks you to put disk 7 in drive A. Put the disk in drive A and press Enter. All the ready-to-use files are installed into the QA\FILE subdirectory. The Install program displays a message box stating that the Install of the files was successful. Press Enter.

20. Another message box appears at the top of the screen stating: `Hit ⏎ to install utilities, or Esc to Cancel.` At the bottom of the screen is the message: `INSTALL SELECT UTILITY FILES - The utility files are miscellaneous files that can be used in addition to Q&A, and will enhance Q&A's func-tionality.` You are going to install these files. Press Enter.

21. A window displaying all the utility files appears. Press F5 to tag all the files. A checkmark appears next to every file. After selecting the files, press Enter. A prompt for the pathname appears. The path-name for the utility files is C:\QA, the same as that for the program files and font files (it is the same path you gave at steps 9 and 14).

22. The Install program asks you to put disk 7 in drive A. Put the disk in drive A and press Enter. All the utility files are installed into the QA subdirectory. The Install program displays a message box stating that the Install of the files was successful. Press Enter.

23. At the bottom of the screen, you will see a message: `INSTALLATION SUCCESSFUL - All files of the specified type were installed successfully.` The installation for all the Q&A files is complete at this point.

24. The last step is to have Install adjust your CONFIG.SYS file. A message box appears at the top of the screen stating: Hit ↵ to modify your CONFIG.SYS, or Esc to Cancel. Press Enter to have Install correctly adjust your CONFIG.SYS file. If no changes are required, Q&A displays a message box at the top of the screen stating: No Changes Required and a message box at the bottom of the screen stating: NO MODIFICATION REQUIRED - Your config.sys file does not require modification. If changes are necessary, the changes are made and the installation is complete.

25. A message box appears stating that Install was successful. Press Enter to return to DOS. You are now back at the C:\QA prompt.

Beginner's Tip

A CONFIG.SYS file is stored in your root directory and is automatically read each time the computer is started. This file can contain commands that tell the computer how many memory buffers to use, how many files can be open at once, and which device drivers to load.

Q&A is now installed for a single user and will have a directory structure like that shown in Figure A.1.

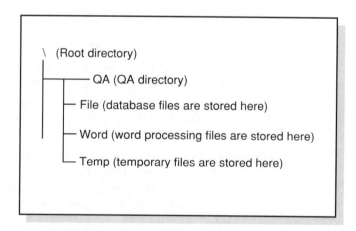

Figure A.1   Directory structure.

Installing the Network Pack

To make your system multiuser, you must purchase the Q&A Network Pack. For additional installation instructions, see Symantec's "Network Pack Administrator's Guide."

Before you install the Network Pack, you must make sure that everyone who will be using Q&A has full rights to the QA subdirectory. *Rights* is a networking term signifying that a person is allowed to utilize programs in a particular directory.

> **Note:** Setting up network rights is beyond the scope of this book. Please refer to your network operating system manuals.

Installing the Network Pack

1. Insert the Network Pack diskette into the A: drive. Type **A:** and press Enter. Type **Adduser**.

2. The system will ask you to enter the drive and path where Q&A is located. On a Novell LAN, this is normally F. However, it could be mapped to a different letter. Find out before proceeding. Type **F:\qa** and press Enter.

3. Repeat this process for each Network Pack. Each Network Pack adds four additional users to your system.

    Q&A is now installed for multiple users.

Configure Your Printer

Q&A allows you to have a total of five printers configured to any combination of parallel and serial ports. The printer configuration procedure consists of choosing a printer, a port, a manufacturer, a model number, and several options. The following instructions explain how to install one parallel printer and one serial printer.

Advanced Tip: If you have more than one printer, or if you have a laserjet printer, and you want both portrait and landscape modes, you can set up multiple printers and select the appropriate one for each report.

Installing a Parallel Printer

1. To install a *parallel printer*, type **U** for Utilities and **P** for Printer.

2. Choose a printer letter (normally printer A) by pressing Enter.

3. Move to the correct printer port (normally this is LPT1) and press Enter.

4. Move to the correct manufacturer and press Enter. Move to the correct model and press Enter.

5. Press Enter to confirm the selection. If you have another printer, press Yes and repeat the process. Otherwise, press No. Figure A.2 shows the Printer Selection screen.

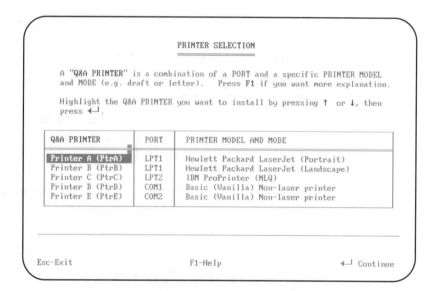

```
                              PRINTER SELECTION
                              ════════════════

        A "Q&A PRINTER" is a combination of a PORT and a specific PRINTER MODEL
        and MODE (e.g. draft or letter).  Press F1 if you want more explanation.

        Highlight the Q&A PRINTER you want to install by pressing ↑ or ↓, then
        press ←┘.

        ┌─────────────────┬──────┬──────────────────────────────────────────┐
        │ Q&A PRINTER     │ PORT │ PRINTER MODEL AND MODE                     │
        ├─────────────────┼──────┼──────────────────────────────────────────┤
        │ Printer A (PtrA)│ LPT1 │ Hewlett Packard LaserJet (Portrait)       │
        │ Printer B (PtrB)│ LPT1 │ Hewlett Packard LaserJet (Landscape)      │
        │ Printer C (PtrC)│ LPT2 │ IBM ProPrinter (NLQ)                      │
        │ Printer D (PtrD)│ COM1 │ Basic (Vanilla) Non-laser printer         │
        │ Printer E (PtrE)│ COM2 │ Basic (Vanilla) Non-laser printer         │
        └─────────────────┴──────┴──────────────────────────────────────────┘


        Esc-Exit                    F1-Help                      ←┘ Continue
```

Figure A.2   Printer Selection screen.

Installing a Serial Printer

1. To install a serial printer, type **U** for Utilities and **P** for Printer.

2. Choose a printer letter (normally printer A) by pressing Enter.

3. Move to the correct printer port and press Enter (normally COM1).

4. Move to the correct manufacturer and press Enter. Move to the correct model and press Enter.

5. Press Enter to confirm the selection. If you have another printer, press Yes and repeat the process. Otherwise, press No. Figure A.3 shows the final Printer Configuration screen.

Advanced Tip: After selecting the model number, you have the option of pressing F8 for more printer options. If you are installing a parallel printer, these options cover printer timeout, length of timeout, and several other features. If you are installing a serial printer, you will have the option of configuring the baud rate, data bit, stop bit, and parity.

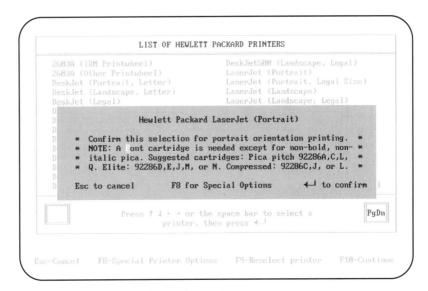

Figure A.3   Final Printer Configuration screen.

Configure the Data Path

Before you can start creating files, you need to tell Q&A where to store them. In the installation portion, you created two subdirectories: WORD and FILE. You now need to tell Q&A to place the database files in the subdirectory FILE and the word processing documents in the subdirectory WORD.

Configuring the Data Path

1. Press **U** for Utilities and **S** for Set Global Defaults.

2. Move to the document files path. Type **word** and press Enter.

3. Move to the database files path. Press Enter, F10, and Esc. Figure A.4 shows the Set Global Options screen.

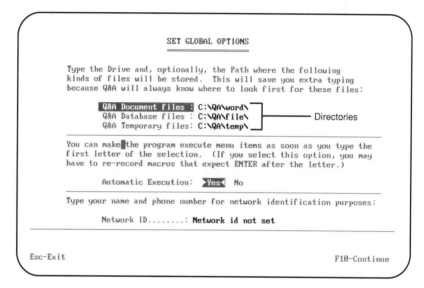

Figure A.4   Set Global Options screen.

Set Monitor Switches

If you have trouble loading Q&A, or if Q&A doesn't look right on the screen, you may need to type a special "switch" when you load Q&A. A *switch* is a command that instructs Q&A to change how it displays itself on your screen. Whether you need to load a switch is based on how your computer is configured. If Q&A looks fine when you start it, there is no need to change anything. Once you set a switch, Q&A remembers it and keeps it in effect until another switch is set.

All switches are activated while starting Q&A at the DOS prompt C:>.

410

Setting Monitor Switches

1. If your system's monitor is *color*, type **QA -SCC** and press Enter.

2. If your system's monitor is *monochrome*, type **QA -SMC -A** and press Enter. If that doesn't work, type **QA -SMM** and press Enter.

3. If you are using a composite monitor, type **QA -A** and press Enter.

Use the preceding switches with these appropriate display monitors:

Display	Switch
NEC Multispeed	**QA -st**
ATT 6300 mono monitor	**QA -smc**
Any PS/2 with mono display	**QA -smc -a**
Toshiba 1100, 3100	**QA -smc**
Zenith laptops	**QA -a**
COMPAQ with color monitor	**QA -scc**
LCD display computers	**QA -a** or **QA -st**

Finish Network Installation

These installation instructions focus on the Novell operating system. If you have a different network, consult your Q&A documentation for the specifics on how to configure Q&A for your LAN.

Q&A gives you the option of configuring each user's system to meet individual preferences. These settings can include choice of printers, page defaults, personal spelling dictionaries, editing options, and the like. Q&A stores all this information in personal configuration files. If Q&A did not store these personal settings in each user's individual subdirectory, every time a user changed his or her personal settings, the previous user's settings would be overwritten.

The following instructions will explain how to designate a personal path for each user. This *personal path* is where the user's individual configuration files will be stored. Once the personal paths have been designated, you will need to start Q&A as if you were the user and do some minimum configuration.

Advanced Tip: These configuration files have a .CFG extension.

Personal Paths

You have two options for invoking a personal path for each user: individually or batch mode. *Individually* requires that the user type the complete path each time he or she starts Q&A. *Batch mode* means that a batch file invokes the personal path for the user. I recommend the latter method.

Setting a Personal Path

1. To set a personal path *individually*, the user must switch to the QA subdirectory and type **QA** and his or her path each time the user wants to use Q&A. The user types **cd\qa** (or the mapped drive) **QA -P<drivename:pathname>** and presses Enter. For example, **QA -PC:\data** would store the user's configuration files on his or her own (local) hard drive in the DATA subdirectory. The -P switch is the command that tells Q&A to use the drive and path that follow it.

2. To set a personal path with a *batch file*, use a text editor to create a batch file, QA1.BAT, similar to this one:

```
F:
cd\qa
QA %1 %2 -PC:\
```

On the C: drive, the user would type **QA1** followed by the subdirectory. If the user does not have a local hard drive, substitute the C with the drive letter mapped to the user's personal subdirectory.

Setting the Network ID and Data Path

1. Using the individual or batch file method, start Q&A for each user by using the person's personal path.

2. Type **U** for Utilities and **S** for Set Global Defaults.

3. Move to the data path and type the subdirectory name where the user's files are being stored.

4. Then move down to the Network ID and type the user's name and, optionally, phone number. Press F10 and Esc. Figure A.5 shows a sample network identification.

```
                        SET GLOBAL OPTIONS


      Type the Drive and, optionally, the Path where the following
      kinds of files will be stored.  This will save you extra typing
      because Q&A will always know where to look first for these files:


           Q&A Document files : C:\QA\word\
           Q&A Database files : C:\QA\file\
           Q&A Temporary files: C:\QA\temp\

      You can make the program execute menu items as soon as you type the
      first letter of the selection.  (If you select this option, you may
      have to re-record macros that expect ENTER after the letter.)

           Automatic Execution:  >Yes<  No

      Type your name and phone number for network identification purposes:

           Network ID........: John 555-4567─────────── Network ID


      Esc-Exit                                            F10-Continue
```

Figure A.5   Sample network identification.

Your system is now configured for each user and ready to use.

413

IN
BUSINESS

What's New in 4.0

This chapter explains the major new features added to Version 4.0.

Overview

Version 4.0 contains significant improvements over Version 3.0. This appendix will explain the major improvements by category and, where needed, provide brief examples of how and where to use them.

The File Module

Posting

Q&A has always allowed you to send information from a source database into a target database (this process is known as a *lookup*). However, a problem arises when you make changes to several records in the source database and want to update all the records in the target database.

In Version 3.0, you had to go into each record manually and "re-look up" the data. Now you can use the posting feature and automatically update all the records in the target database at once. For example, after you enter the number of products sold into an invoice form, you can post all the product totals to the corresponding inventory files.

Editable Table View

You can display several records in columnar format on the screen and move to any field in any displayed record and edit it. In Version 3.0, you were limited to viewing only five fields of a particular record and were unable to edit any of them. For example, with Version 4.0 if you have five address changes to make, you can retrieve the five records on the screen and then quickly move to each record and make the desired changes.

Field Editor

There used to be a limit of 255 characters for entering data or programming statements into a field. Now when you press F6 in Add, Search, Program, or Report modes, you get the *long value field editor*. This editor allows you to have up to 32,000 characters per field in a pop-up window. For example, suppose that your database has a REMARKS field and that some records will require a page of remarks and others only a few lines. You can have a small on-screen field that expands as the remarks do, thus saving screen and file space.

Query Programming

When you are searching for data (Retrieve specs), you can use programming statements to improve the flexibility and power of your searches. For example, when you are selecting customers for a sales report, you can request the records of all customers who bought 100 widgets in 1990 but did not buy any in 1991.

Delete Duplicate Records

If your data entry operator enters several duplicate records, Version 4.0 allows you to search and delete the extra records.

Auto Program Recalc

Most of the database forms you develop in Q&A will contain programming statements that are calculated while you are in the form. In Version 3.0, using the Mass Update feature to change several similar records at once meant that you had to go into each record and manually recalculate it.

In the new version, you can have all your programming statements recalculated while you are mass-updating records. For example, suppose you want to raise the prices of several of your products and change the financial totals associated with the value of your inventory. To do this, you do a mass update and then a program recalc. Version 4 automatically increases all the prices and recalculates the financial totals.

Detailed File Description

This new feature for file descriptions lets you attach a 72-character description to your database and word processing files.

Saved Specs

When you are searching or sorting for information, you issue a Retrieve spec or a Sort spec. In the past, these specs were always lost after each request was completed. Now you can save them and use them for future requests.

Case Formatting

Fields in database forms can now be programmed to automatically assign text as lowercase, uppercase, or title format (in title format, the first character in each word is capitalized).

The Write Module

Page Preview/WYSIWYG

In Version 4.0, you can display your documents in "What You See Is What You Get" (WYSIWYG) format. This allows you to see the exact format of your text before printing it.

Document Recovery

Document recovery has long been a standard feature of the File module. Now you can recover damaged word-processing files from the Write module with the new Write-Recover utility. This utility is very easy to use. Simply select Recover File from the Write menu, type the filename, and press F10. Your file is recovered.

Built-in Thesaurus

Version 4.0 offers a thesaurus. While you are typing a document, you can easily look up a synonym for a word or add your own word to the thesaurus.

Scalable Fonts

Version 4.0 supports Hewlett-Packard's LaserJet III scalable font technology. This means that you can assign pitch size to fonts.

Document Import/Export

Importing from, or exporting to, the most popular word processors is now supported. These include WordPerfect, Microsoft Word, MultiMate, and WordStar.

Mail Merge Programming Statements

In Version 4.0, you can use programming statements while doing a mail merge. For example, you can use the `@sum` function to perform calculations on data that has been looked up with `xlookup`. Suppose you are sending a letter informing your sales people how much commission they have earned in each of the last three months but the database does not contain the total of these three months. With this feature, as you are printing the letter, the three-month totals can be summed and placed in the letter.

Merge Documents with Multiple Databases

Rather than being limited to merging a document with a single database, in Version 4.0 you can merge a document with several databases. For example, you want to send a letter to several clients asking for a larger retainer. The letter must include the amount of the client's last retainer and how much business the client has done with you in the past year. The retainer information resides in one database and the sales history resides in another. With this new feature, you can send a letter that extracts the relevant data from the two databases and merges it into one letter.

Text Enhancements

Text enhancements can be assigned to documents, mailing labels, columnar reports, cross-tab reports, and form prints. These enhancements can include bold, underline, and italics, as well as assigning different fonts to text.

Avery Label Support

Version 4.0 supports any Avery label format.

Reports

Cross-Tab Reports

Q&A has added 60-row by 60-column cross-tabular reporting. The data in this type of report can be calculated by using a wide variety of financial formulas. For example, each quarter you could cross-tabulate how many sales each rep made for each month of each product type.

Report Enhancements

Several report enhancements have been added to Version 4.0. These include printing a record on one page or across several pages, printing double-spaced reports, using programming logic on derived columns, indenting multiline text values, and assigning standard deviation and variance calculations to columns.

Utilities

Database/Spreadsheet Import and Export

The types of databases and spreadsheets that can be imported and exported now include dBASE IV, Paradox, Professional File, and graphics from Lotus 1-2-3.

SQL Access

If you need to access an ORACLE or Gupta SQL database, you can with Version 4.0.

Additional Printer Support

Version 4.0 simplifies the overall installation of printers and increases the total number of printers supported. This support includes cut sheet feeders and box drawing without box characters.

Virtual Memory Management

If your computer has extended or expanded memory, Q&A now lets you take advantage of it.

Diagnostic Window Support

This window informs you of the location of databases, documents, and other Q&A files. Further, it indicates which Q&A switches have been loaded, the amount of memory used, and which ports and drives are available.

Mouse Support with Easy-to-Use Menu Support

The menu system is easier to use now, and you can use a mouse to navigate through it.

The Intelligent Assistant

Query Guide

The Intelligent Assistant has been improved in Version 4.0 to include a Query Guide. The Query Guide lets you ask questions of your database and then receive the results in the format you choose. With the Query Guide, you can receive 100-percent-accurate responses to your questions and speed up the time it takes to access the data.

Applications Programming Tools

Run Macros from a List

As you develop macros, you no longer have to remember which keys you assigned to which macro. Simply call up the macro list window and choose the macro you want to execute.

Custom Application Menus

As a VAR or in-house systems developer, you can create your own menus for the programs you develop. These menus can replace the Q&A menus and can include custom macros to perform desired tasks.

Macro Encoder

After you develop a custom program, you can encode it to keep users from making modifications to it. This encoder locks both the macros and the menus.

Custom Database Lock

In addition to the macro encoder just described, Version 4.0 offers a custom database lock feature. You can lock out a user from all redesigning, customizing, and programming of a database.

Program Editor

Version 4.0's Program Editor is a 32K pop-up window that allows you to write more complex programming statements.

Field Template

You can now assign custom templates to fields. The templates can be used for Social Security numbers, phone numbers, inventory numbers, etc.

Read Only Fields

Read only fields are fields that only display data and cannot be altered. This is particularly useful for calculated fields or where information is looked up from another database for informational purposes only.

Required Fields

Q&A now supports true required fields. In the past if you pressed the Enter key twice, you could skip a required field, but not anymore.

Field-Level Security

Field restrictions now include hidden, read only, and read/write fields. You can assign eight different field restrictions to each field, with an unlimited number of users assigned to each group. Each user is given a password that determines how much data the user can see. Thus, each user's view of the form is dependent on which of the eight groups he or she is assigned to. For example, suppose you have three people in the personnel department responsible for maintaining the personnel database. You can give the manager full rights to all data, give the second-in-command the rights to see everything except salaries, and give the data entry clerk rights to just name and address information.

Concurrent Custom Help

You no longer have to clear the help screen before entering data. The help screen can remain on the screen as you fill in a database form.

Programming Enhancements

Several new database enhancements have been added to Version 4.0. The @select function provides IF, THEN, ELSE programming logic to a field. The @mod function returns the remainder from a divisor. The @clear function will let you clear a field. With @replace, you can replace the value in one field with the value from another field. The gosub-return function lets you add subroutines to your programming statements. Lastly, there is a function to identify a field based on the results from another field or expression.

Print Program Spec

Once you have programmed a database, you can print all the programming specifications for each field. This is particularly useful for documenting the application and/or debugging it.

Field Navigation

Version 4.0 allows programming logic to be separated from field navigation. This means that the cursor can move from field to field as needed and that the programming statements will not execute until necessary.

Network Support

Automatic Record Locking

If a group of users wants to simultaneously share the same database, they can.

Instant Screen Update

The screen is now instantly updated. For example, suppose that five users have a record on the screen and one user makes a change. The screens of the other four users will simultaneously be updated.

Password Protection

Database security has been expanded to include five levels of access rights.

Interoperability

Q&A for the Macintosh

When the Q&A Macintosh version is released, applications written for the IBM will run on the Macintosh. Thus, users on a network that use IBM and Macintosh computers can share the same database.

I N D E X

D

L

M

N

O

Q

R

T

U

V

Sams—Covering The Latest In Computer And Technical Topics!

Audio

udio Production Techniques for Video	$29.95
udio Systems Design and Installation	$59.95
udio Technology Fundamentals	$24.95
ompact Disc Troubleshooting and Repair	$24.95
andbook for Sound Engineers:	
The New Audio Cyclopedia	$79.95
troduction to Professional Recording Techniques	$29.95
lodern Recording Techniques, 3rd Ed.	$29.95
rinciples of Digital Audio, 2nd Ed.	$29.95
ound Recording Handbook	$49.95
ound System Engineering, 2nd Ed.	$49.95

Electricity/Electronics

asic AC Circuits	$29.95
lectricity 1, Revised 2nd Ed.	$14.95
lectricity 1-7, Revised 2nd Ed.	$49.95
lectricity 2, Revised 2nd Ed.	$14.95
lectricity 3, Revised 2nd Ed.	$14.95
lectricity 4, Revised 2nd Ed.	$14.95
lectricity 5, Revised 2nd Ed.	$14.95
lectricity 6, Revised 2nd Ed.	$14.95
lectricity 7, Revised 2nd Ed.	$14.95
lectronics 1-7, Revised 2nd Ed.	$49.95

Electronics Technical

ctive-Filter Cookbook	$19.95
amcorder Survival Guide	$ 9.95
MOS Cookbook, 2nd Ed.	$24.95
esign of OP-AMP Circuits with Experiments	$19.95
esign of Phase-Locked Loop Circuits	
with Experiments	$19.95
lectrical Test Equipment	$19.95
lectrical Wiring	$19.95
ow to Read Schematics, 4th Ed.	$19.95
Op-Amp Cookbook, 3rd Ed.	$24.95
Timer Cookbook, 2nd Ed.	$19.95
User's Casebook	$19.95
adio Handbook, 23rd Ed.	$39.95
adio Operator's License Q&A Manual, 11th Ed.	$24.95
F Circuit Design	$24.95
ransformers and Motors	$24.95
TL Cookbook	$19.95
ndergrounding Electric Lines	$14.95
nderstanding Telephone Electronics, 2nd Ed.	$19.95
CR Troubleshooting & Repair Guide	$19.95
ideo Scrambling & Descrambling	
for Satellite & Cable TV	$19.95

Games

eyond the Nintendo Masters	$ 9.95
lastering Nintendo Video Games II	$ 9.95
ricks of the Nintendo Masters	$ 9.95
ideoGames & Computer Entertainment	
Complete Guide to Nintendo Video Games	$ 9.50
Vinner's Guide to Nintendo Game Boy	$ 9.95
Vinner's Guide to Sega Genesis	$ 9.95

Hardware/Technical

ard Disk Power with the Jamsa Disk Utilities	$39.95
M PC Advanced Troubleshooting & Repair	$24.95
M Personal Computer	
Troubleshooting & Repair	$24.95
M Personal Computer Upgrade Guide	$24.95
licrocomputer Troubleshooting & Repair	$24.95
nderstanding Communications Systems, 2nd Ed.	$19.95
nderstanding Data Communications, 2nd Ed.	$19.95
nderstanding FAX and Electronic Mail	$19.95
nderstanding Fiber Optics	$19.95

IBM: Business

est Book of Microsoft Works for the PC, 2nd Ed.	$24.95
est Book of PFS: First Choice	$24.95
est Book of Professional Write and File	$22.95
irst Book of Fastback Plus	$16.95
irst Book of Norton Utilities	$16.95
irst Book of Personal Computing	$16.95
irst Book of PROCOMM PLUS	$16.95

IBM: Database

Best Book of Paradox 3	$27.95
dBASE III Plus Programmer's Reference Guide	$24.95
dBASE IV Programmer's Reference Guide	$24.95
First Book of Paradox 3	$16.95
Mastering ORACLE	
Featuring ORACLE's SQL Standard	$24.95

IBM: Graphics/Desktop Publishing

Best Book of Autodesk Animator	$29.95
Best Book of Harvard Graphics	$24.95
First Book of DrawPerfect	$16.95
First Book of Harvard Graphics	$16.95
First Book of PC Paintbrush	$16.95
First Book of PFS: First Publisher	$16.95

IBM: Spreadsheets/Financial

Best Book of Lotus 1-2-3 Release 3.1	$27.95
Best Book of Lotus 1-2-3, Release 2.2, 3rd Ed.	$26.95
Best Book of Peachtree Complete III	$24.95
First Book of Lotus 1-2-3, Release 2.2	$16.95
First Book of Lotus 1-2-3/G	$16.95
First Book of Microsoft Excel for the PC	$16.95
Lotus 1-2-3: Step-by-Step	$24.95

IBM: Word Processing

Best Book of Microsoft Word 5	$24.95
Best Book of Microsoft Word for Windows	$24.95
Best Book of WordPerfect 5.1	$26.95
Best Book of WordPerfect Version 5.0	$24.95
First Book of PC Write	$16.95
First Book of WordPerfect 5.1	$16.95
WordPerfect 5.1: Step-by-Step	$24.95

Macintosh/Apple

Best Book of AppleWorks	$24.95
Best Book of MacWrite II	$24.95
Best Book of Microsoft Word for the Macintosh	$24.95
Macintosh Printer Secrets	$34.95
Macintosh Repair & Upgrade Secrets	$34.95
Macintosh Revealed, Expanding the Toolbox,	
Vol. 4	$29.95
Macintosh Revealed, Mastering the Toolbox,	
Vol. 3	$29.95
Macintosh Revealed, Programming with the Toolbox,	
Vol. 2, 2nd Ed.	$29.95
Macintosh Revealed, Unlocking the Toolbox,	
Vol. 1, 2nd Ed.	$29.95
Using ORACLE with HyperCard	$24.95

Operating Systems/Networking

Best Book of DESQview	$24.95
Best Book of DOS	$24.95
Best Book of Microsoft Windows 3	$24.95
Business Guide to Local Area Networks	$24.95
Exploring the UNIX System, 2nd Ed.	$29.95
First Book of DeskMate	$16.95
First Book of Microsoft QuickPascal	$16.95
First Book of MS-DOS	$16.95
First Book of UNIX	$16.95
Interfacing to the IBM Personal Computer,	
2nd Ed.	$24.95
Mastering NetWare	$29.95
The Waite Group's Discovering MS-DOS	$19.95
The Waite Group's Inside XENIX	$29.95
The Waite Group's MS-DOS Bible, 3rd Ed.	$24.95
The Waite Group's MS-DOS Developer's Guide,	
2nd Ed.	$29.95
The Waite Group's Tricks of the MS-DOS Masters,	
2nd Ed.	$29.95
The Waite Group's Tricks of the UNIX Masters	$29.95
The Waite Group's Understanding MS-DOS,	
2nd Ed.	$19.95
The Waite Group's UNIX Primer Plus, 2nd Ed.	$29.95
The Waite Group's UNIX System V Bible	$29.95
The Waite Group's UNIX System V Primer,	
Revised Ed.	$29.95
Understanding Local Area Networks, 2nd Ed.	$24.95

Understanding NetWare	$24.95
UNIX Applications Programming:	
Mastering the Shell	$29.95
UNIX Networking	$29.95
UNIX Shell Programming, Revised Ed.	$29.95
UNIX System Administration	$29.95
UNIX System Security	$34.95
UNIX Text Processing	$29.95
UNIX: Step-by-Step	$29.95

Professional/Reference

Data Communications, Networks, and Systems	$39.95
Gallium Arsenide Technology, Volume II	$69.95
Handbook of Computer-Communications Standards,	
Vol. 1, 2nd Ed.	$39.95
Handbook of Computer-Communications Standards,	
Vol. 2, 2nd Ed.	$39.95
Handbook of Computer-Communications Standards,	
Vol. 3, 2nd Ed.	$39.95
Handbook of Electronics Tables and Formulas,	
6th Ed.	$24.95
ISDN, DECnet, and SNA Communications	$44.95
Modern Dictionary of Electronics, 6th Ed.	$39.95
Programmable Logic Designer's Guide	$29.95
Reference Data for Engineers: Radio, Electronics,	
Computer, and Communications, 7th Ed.	$99.95
Surface-Mount Technology for PC Board Design	$49.95
World Satellite Almanac, 2nd Ed.	$39.95

Programming

Advanced C: Tips and Techniques	$29.95
C Programmer's Guide to NetBIOS	$29.95
C Programmer's Guide to Serial Communications	$29.95
Commodore 64 Programmer's Reference Guide	$19.95
DOS Batch File Power	$39.95
First Book of GW-BASIC	$16.95
How to Write Macintosh Software, 2nd Ed.	$29.95
Mastering Turbo Assembler	$29.95
Mastering Turbo Debugger	$29.95
Mastering Turbo Pascal 5.5, 3rd Ed.	$29.95
Microsoft QuickBASIC Programmer's Reference	$29.95
Programming in ANSI C	$29.95
Programming in C, Revised Ed.	$29.95
QuickC Programming	$29.95
The Waite Group's BASIC Programming	
Primer, 2nd Ed.	$24.95
The Waite Group's C Programming	
Using Turbo C++	$29.95
The Waite Group's C++ Programming	$24.95
The Waite Group's C: Step-by-Step	$29.95
The Waite Group's GW-BASIC Primer Plus	$24.95
The Waite Group's Microsoft C Bible, 2nd Ed.	$29.95
The Waite Group's Microsoft C Programming	
for the PC, 2nd Ed.	$29.95
The Waite Group's Microsoft Macro	
Assembler Bible	$29.95
The Waite Group's New C Primer Plus	$29.95
The Waite Group's QuickC Bible	$29.95
The Waite Group's Turbo Assembler Bible	$29.95
The Waite Group's Turbo C Bible	$29.95
The Waite Group's Turbo C Programming	
for the PC, Revised Ed.	$29.95
The Waite Group's TWG Turbo C++Bible	$29.95
X Window System Programming	$29.95

For More Information, Call Toll Free

1-800-257-5755

All prices are subject to change without notice.
Non-U.S. prices may be higher. Printed in the U.S.A.

Sams' Series Puts You "In Business"

The *In Business* books have been specially designed to help business users increase their productivity and efficiency. Each book comes with a companion disk that contains templates for common business tasks, as well as tear-out quick references for common commands. In addition, the books feature Business Shortcuts—boxed notes and tips on how to improve the performance of the software. Regardless of the size of the business or the level of user, these books will teach you how to get the most out of your business applications.

Quattro Pro In Business
Chris Van Buren
400 pages, 7³/8 x 9¹/4, $29.95 USA
0-672-22793-2

Lotus 1-2-3 In Business
Michael Griffin
400 pages, 7³/8 x 9¹/4, $29.95 USA
0-672-22803-3

Q&A In Business
David B. Adams
400 pages, 7³/8 x 9¹/4, $29.95 USA
0-672-22801-7

WordPerfect In Business
Neil Salkind
400 pages, 7³/8 x 9¹/4, $29.95 USA
0-672-22795-9

SAMS

To order books, call 1-800-428-5331.

Sams' First Books Get You Started Fast!

IF YOUR COMPUTER USES 3.5" DISKS

While most personal computers use 5.25" disks to store information, some newer computers use 3.5" disks. If your computer uses 3.5" disks, you can return this form to SAMS to obtain a 3.5" disk to use with this book.

Print the required information on this reply form and mail the form to:

Q&A In Business Disk Exchange
SAMS
11711 N. College Avenue
Carmel, IN 46032

Name: _____

Address: _____

City: _____ State: _____ Zip: _____

Phone: _____

COMMAND REFERENCE CARD

Write Module

Feature	Keystrokes
Calculate	Alt-F9
Check spelling (doc)	Shift-F1
Check spelling (word)	Ctrl-F1
Continue	F10
Copy block	F5
Copy block to file	Ctrl-F5
Define page	Ctrl-F6
Delete to end of line	Ctrl-F4
Delete word (Ctrl-T)	F4
Delete line (Ctrl-Y)	Shift-F4
Delete block	F3
Document statistics	Ctrl-F3
Enhance text	Shift-F6
Export document	Ctrl-F8
Go to page/line	Ctrl-F7
Help	F1
Hyphenate	Alt-F6
List fields	Alt-F7
Make font assignments	Ctrl-F9
Move block to file	Alt-F5
Move block	Shift-F5
Move to beginning of line	Home(1)
Move to top of screen	Home(2)
Move to top of page	Home(3)
Move to top of document	Home(4)
Move to end of line	End(1)

Feature	Keystrokes
Move to bottom of screen	End(2)
Move to bottom of page	End(3)
Move to bottom of document	End(4)
Options menu	F8
Print text block	Ctrl-F2
Print document	F2
Restore text	Shift-F7
Save document	Shift-F8
Scroll screen up	F9
Scroll screen down	Shift-F9
Search & replace	F7
Set temporary margins	F6
Thesaurus	Alt-F1
Use macros	Shift-F2

Cursor Movement Keys in Write

Key	Action
↓	Down one line
←	Left one column
→	Right one column
PgUp	Previous screen
PgDn	Next screen
Ctrl ←	Previous word
Ctrl →	Next word
Ctrl-PgUp	Previous page
Ctrl-PgDn	Next page
Ctrl-Home	Top of doc
Ctrl-End	Bottom of doc

COMMAND REFERENCE CARD

File Module: Add & Search/Update Mode

Feature	Keystrokes
Add records (updating)	Ctrl-F6
Alternate Search mode	Ctrl-F7
Auto-type current date	Ctrl-F5
Auto-type current time	Alt-F5
Calc	F8
Calculate record	F8
Continue	F10
Define Table View (update)	Shift-F6
Delete current record	F3
Delete to end of line	Ctrl-F4
Delete word	F4
Delete line	Shift-F4
Ditto field (adding)	F5
Ditto record (adding)	Shift-F5
Edit field value	F6
Exit	Esc
Expand field	F6
Go to Customize specs	Shift-F9
Go to first record	Ctrl-Home
Go to last record	Ctrl-End
Help	F1
List of restricted values	Alt-F7
List Retrieve specs (updating)	Alt-F8
Macros	Shift-F2
Move to beginning of field	Home(1)

Feature	Keystrokes
Move to top of page	Home(2)
Move to top of form	Home(3)
Move to end of field	End(1)
Move to bottom of page	End(2)
Move to bottom of form	End(3)
Print current record	F2
Print to end of stack	Ctrl-F2
Reset @NUMBER	Ctrl-F8
Save record and exit	Shift-F10
Save and get previous record	F9
Save and get next record	F10
Save Retrieve specs	Shift-F8
Search for records	F7
Set Calc mode	Shift-F8
Sort data (updating)	F8
Table View (updating)	Alt-F6
Undo editing (updating)	Shift-F7

Cursor Movements in File

Key	Action
↑	Up a field
↓	Down a field
←	Left one character
→	Right one character
Shift-Tab	Previous field
Tab or Enter	Next field
Ctrl ←	Previous word
Ctrl →	Next word
PgUp	Previous page
PgDn	Next page